RETIRING RIGHT

2002 EDITION

PLANNING FOR A SUCCESSFUL RETIREMENT

LAWRENCE J. KAPLAN

SQUAREONE

FINANCE GUIDES

The publisher hereby grants the right to photocopy any forms presented in this book for personal use. The forms in this book cannot, however, be sold or used in any commercial endeavor without the written consent of the publisher.

Cover Designer: Phaedra Mastrocola
In-House Editor: Joanne Abrams
Typesetter: Gary A. Rosenberg

Square One Publishers
Garden City Park, NY 11040
(516) 535–2010
www.squareonepublishers.com

Library of Congress Cataloging-in-Publication Data
Kaplan, Lawrence J. (Lawrence Jay), 1915–
    Retiring right: planning for a successful retirement / by Lawrence J. Kaplan
        p. cm.
Includes bibliographical references and index.
    ISBN 0-7570-0042-8
    1. Retirement—United States—Planning. 2. Retirement income—United States—Planning. I. Title.
    HQ1063.2.U6 K37 2001
    646.7'9—dc21
                                                    00-010597

Printed in the United States of America

10   9   8   7   6   5   4   3   2   1

Contents

Part 3 DAY-TO-DAY FINANCIAL CONSIDERATIONS

Part 4 INSURANCE

Part 5 FINAL FACTS

APPENDICES

ACKNOWLEDGMENTS

Many people have assisted me in collecting material for *Retiring Right*, and I am indebted to all of them. I particularly wish to thank those with whom I have been in close contact, who have steered me in the right direction, and who have helped me check facts and figures in order to maintain accuracy.

I extend my deepest gratitude to the following people: Dr. Jane Ross Moore, Professor Emerita, Graduate Center, The City University of New York; Robert L. Schneps, Estate Planning Attorney; Holly Wallace and Glenn Patti, Investment Advisors; John Clark, Public Affairs Officer, Social Security Administration; Kevin McKeen, Media Relations, Internal Revenue Service; Ellen B. Griffith, Office of Public Affairs, Centers for Medicare and Medicaid Services, U.S. Department of Health and Human Services; Maria Diacogiannis, Information Specialist, Centers for Medicare and Medicaid Services, U.S. Department of Health and Human Services; Loretta Burridge, Coordinator, Empire Medicare Services; Suzanne Levin, Director, Client Services, Medicare Rights Center; Ross Devine, U.S. Office of Personnel Management; J. Anthony Pineiro, Economist, Bureau of Labor Statistics, U.S. Department of Labor; David McCarthy, Pension and Welfare Administration, U.S. Department of Labor; Louise Brown and John Thompson, Public Affairs, Pension Benefit Guaranty Corporation; Elizabeth Gaskin, Information Services, Bureau of the Census, U.S. Department of Commerce; Thomas D. Musco, Director of Research and Planning, Health Insurance Association of America; Claire Mather Sheahan, Press Officer, and Camellia Amadio, Long-Term Care Marketing, Teachers Insurance and Annuity Association–College Retirement Equities Fund; Carolyn L. Ayres, Theresa A. Cahill, Lisa R. Crandall, Anne May, Ann Marie Moore, and Regina M. Sylvestri, Reference Librarians, Manhasset Public Library; Rudy Shur, my publisher, for his encouragement and his unfailing sense of humor; Joanne Abrams, my editor at Square One Publishers, for her dedication and her meticulous attention to detail; and Robert Love of Square One, for his cheerfulness and support.

Finally, I thank my wife, Jeanne, for her support, encouragement, and input throughout the development of this project and always.

PREFACE

Today, with modern science and technology, it is possible for Americans to live longer, healthier lives. The good news is that at retirement, the average person can now expect to live another twenty to thirty years. The bad news is that for those extra years, you will need additional money. Those extra years also mean that inflation, taxes, and health care will have more time to erode your resources. Your goal in retirement planning, therefore, should be to make certain that your assets last at least as long as you do. This is a complex task, and few are armed for it.

To plan properly requires knowledge of financial planning, the very heart of successful retirement. In addition, successful planning involves some knowledge of pensions and Social Security, of life and health insurance, of basic legal considerations, and of housing options. Finally, we all need to know how to plan realistically to make it easier to cope with life's inevitable losses.

Over the years, while serving as an officer of a welfare fund, I have had the opportunity to observe many individuals approaching retirement. In most cases, they are unaware of the basic considerations relating to retirement until the reality is upon them. These people seldom recognize that thinking and planning ahead can make the difference between a successful retirement and one marred by faulty decisions. This is true even for those who consider themselves knowledgeable in the field.

Many books currently on the market attempt to supply necessary information, but a review of these works indicates that many of them fail to grapple with the central issues. In some, the coverage is cursory; in others, encyclopedic. Some completely omit important components of a practical retirement plan or are out of date. To overcome these weaknesses, I have sought to cover the major areas simply and succinctly in order to provide you with a clear understanding of the issues, and to make all of the information I present up-to-date, easy to understand, and easy to find.

Various chapters in *Retiring Right* delve into specific retirement concerns: the roles of work and leisure in retirement; budgeting; and sources of income such as Social Security, pensions, savings, investments, life insurance, and annuities. Medical concerns—Medicare, Medicaid, and health insurance—as well as housing options and legal affairs—property ownership, second and late marriages, and choosing and using a lawyer—are also explained. Rounding out the coverage are chapters on estate planning, care facilities, and funeral arrangements. Most important, *Retiring Right* offers you, the reader, the opportunity to personalize the material through self-study. Each chapter provides Self-Study sections and worksheets that enable you to develop an individual retirement program. Such an interaction between book and reader is also provided in the Inventory of Personal and Financial Data. Opportunities to further develop an effective retirement plan are provided by the Resources and Suggested Readings sections. In

addition, the Glossary offers definitions of technical words and terms.

This 2001 edition of *Retiring Right* reflects the most current information on every aspect of retirement planning. You will learn about great new investment vehicles such as Roth IRAs. And you will learn about new laws—such as the 2000 federal law that lifted restrictions on the earnings of Social Security beneficiaries—that offer good news for seniors.

Thinking and planning ahead can make a significant difference in your future. To enjoy the good life after retirement, it is essential that you plan for it now. What follows will help you achieve that goal.

INTRODUCTION

Why plan for retirement? If you are under 55, you probably have not given much thought to retirement. You see getting old as something that happens to other people. You tell yourself that you will plan for retirement when the time comes—that there is no need to think about it now. Wrong!

If you want the so-called golden years of your life to be truly golden, you must prepare for them now. The sooner you get started and the more you investigate and understand your situation, the better your retirement will be. Planning for your retirement will enable you to reach the following goals:

❏ **Eliminate fear and uncertainty, and achieve a sense of security.** Many people approach retirement with fear and trepidation. This is quite natural because most people fear the unknown. Thinking about the future and planning for it will allow you to reach the retirement stage of your life with knowledge and preparation. The unknown will become known, and the fear and uncertainty of retirement will be replaced with a sense of security.

❏ **Prepare for the unexpected.** As you move along in life, problems will constantly present themselves. Without a plan that looks into the future, you will tackle each crisis in a purely haphazard manner. If you plan ahead, however, you will not be thrown by an unexpected problem such as an illness in the family or a downturn in the economy that affects your savings or investments. You will be better able to cope with the difficulty and make the necessary adjustments.

❏ **Gain flexibility.** By starting your planning early, you will have enough time to prepare for the things that you want to do when you retire. You will have time to prepare for a second career, if you want one, or to learn a new hobby or sport. If you change your mind about your choice, you will have enough time to modify your plan and try something else.

❏ **Make the right decisions.** If you plan for retirement, you will not have to make hasty, ill-considered decisions. For example, housing plays a large role in shaping retirement. By investigating numerous housing locations and living arrangements during your pre-retirement years, you will be able to make an informed decision regarding your retirement housing.

We all approach retirement with different needs, interests, and attitudes. All of us, however, have the same goal: a successful retirement. That means a sound financial plan, psychological and social stability, and stimulating and satisfying activities that provide a sense of accomplishment and a feeling of usefulness. The purpose of this book is to help you develop a total, individualized retirement plan that will generate maximum satisfaction, security, and fulfillment.

Look Who's Turning Sixty-Five!

Every year, millions of Americans reach that magic age of retirement, sixty-five. Among these potential retirees are a few people we all know—people whose names, faces, and achievements have been part of our lives for many years. The following list—which includes *both* actresses who portrayed *MASH's* "Hot Lips" Houlihan, as well as a number of other names that may surprise you—lets you know about some of the famous folks who will be celebrating their sixty-fifth birthday in the year 2002.

Max Baer, Jr. December 5, 1937	**Glenda Jackson** March 9, 1937
Shirley Bassey January 8, 1937	**Waylon Jennings** June 15, 1937
Ned Beatty July 6, 1937	**Sally Kellerman** June 2, 1937
Warren Beatty March 30, 1937	**Mary Tyler Moore** December 29, 1937
Bill Cosby July 11, 1937	**Jack Nicholson** April 22, 1937
Tom Courteney February 25, 1937	**Margaret O'Brien** January 15, 1937
William Devane September 15, 1937	**Suzanne Pleshette** January 31, 1937
Elinor Donahue April 19, 1937	**General Colin Powell** April 5, 1937
Peter Duchin July 28, 1937	**Robert Redford** August 18, 1937
Chad Everett June 10, 1937	**Vanessa Redgrave** January 30, 1937
Don Everly February 1, 1937	**Tommy Smothers** February 2, 1937
Robert Guillaume November 30, 1937	**Loretta Swit** November 4, 1937
Merle Haggard April 6, 1937	**Frankie Valli** May 3, 1937
Dustin Hoffman August 8, 1937	**Billy Dee Williams** April 6, 1937
Anthony Hopkins December 31, 1937	**Nancy Wilson** February 20, 1937

FIRST FACTS ABOUT RETIREMENT *and* PLANNING

What is retirement? Retirement can be defined as a withdrawal from one's office, service, or business that brings with it a lifestyle that is less structured and offers more free time. If we assume that the life cycle consists of four stages—childhood, the teen years, the mature years, and the retirement years—then the retirement years are the culmination of the mature years, which are also the working years. At this stage of the life cycle, an individual can reach the highest level of development, and harvest and enjoy the fruits of a lifetime of labor. Or this period can plunge a person into boredom, restlessness, depression, or even despair. Remember that with increasing longevity, some people may spend as many or even more years in retirement than they spent working.

WHO ARE THE RETIREES?

Our youth-oriented society generates many misconceptions about the 65-and-older population, which is usually retired. These myths are so pervasive that many older people accept them as fact. Popular myths include the following: Most older people live in old-age homes, nursing homes, or mental hospitals. As a group, older people are lonely, socially isolated, bored, and no longer able to enjoy life. If older people have jobs, the jobs are unproductive. Older people cannot learn new things. And, in terms of economic status, they are the most poverty-stricken group in the country. Are these allegations true? Not at all, as you will see by the following description of Americans aged 65 and over.

Numbers

In 2000, the 65-and-older population was estimated to be nearly 35 million—2 million greater than it had been in 1994. As the population born during the post-World War II baby boom continues to age and to join the ranks of the elderly, the 65-and-older group will continue to grow. In fact, it is estimated to increase to approximately 90 million by 2040.

Life Expectancy

Babies born in the year 1900 could not anticipate very long lives—only 46 years for men and 48 years for women, for an average of 47 years. Americans are now living far longer. As of 1998,

3

the age expectancy was nearly 74 years for men and 80 years for women, for an average of about 77 years. In other words, babies born now can anticipate life spans that are more than 30 years longer than those of their great-grandparents.

Income

The majority of people 65 or older have incomes well above the official poverty level, which a recent Department of Health and Human Services report estimated at about $10,850 for a couple. One report showed that only 10.5 percent of people 65 or older are classified as poor or living below the poverty line. The percentage would probably be even lower if noncash benefits for the poor, such as food stamps, Medicare, and Medicaid, were counted as income. Nevertheless, there are elderly Americans living below the poverty level, struggling to feed and house themselves.

The majority of the elderly are living comfortably. Social Security benefits are indexed to keep pace with inflation and are for the most part tax-free. At the same time, the children of most older people are grown and on their own, mortgages generally are paid off, and work-related expenses no longer are straining the budget.

Employment

The United States Bureau of Labor Statistics (BLS) reports that the civilian labor force was 141 million in 2000. The long-term trend among men in their mid-50s and early 60s has been to retire early, before the age when they are eligible to receive full retirement benefits. Although female workers in their late 50s have been increasingly likely to remain in the labor force, BLS projects that, in general, labor force participation rates for older workers will continue to decline, but at a slower pace.

As for the myth that elderly workers are unproductive, studies of the labor force reveal that the elderly perform as well as or better than younger workers, even though a decline in perception and reaction speed has been noted. While it may take an elderly employee a little longer to learn something new, older workers can learn new things as well as younger workers can.

Housing

Housing surveys show that the elderly live in homes that are older than those occupied by the rest of the population. However, this generally is because they purchased their homes thirty or forty years before retiring. The overwhelming majority of the elderly live in safe, standard housing. At the same time, though, many elderly below the poverty line do not live in proper housing. Some live in shabby hotels, in broken-down tenements, or, worse yet, on the streets. A significant percentage of the homeless in America are over 65. It has been estimated that 30 to 40 percent of the elderly living in nursing homes are there because they cannot care for themselves and have nowhere else to go. The Census Bureau reports that less than 5 percent of the elderly live in old-age or nursing homes.

Physical Health

The health of 80 percent of the 65-and-older group is excellent, good, or fair. Among the healthy elderly, a significant decline in activities and interests occurs only among those who are 85 or older, a population that in 1998 numbered slightly over 4 million, or about 12 percent of the over-65 population. The overwhelming majority of elderly people are well and living normal lives. However, as retired people know, health care becomes a much more important cost item after age 65. Health care for the elderly is estimated to cost three to four times what it costs younger Americans.

Mental Health

Although as much as a third of the elderly experience stress or have an occasional bout of depression, the proportion is not substantially different from that of the younger population. It is significant to note that not more than 10 percent of the elderly suffer from senility. Perhaps another small percentage suffers from defective memory, but about 80 to 85 percent of the elderly enjoy good to excellent mental health.

Social Activity

While almost a third of the elderly live alone, the majority have friends and relatives, and actively participate in various functions sponsored by religious congregations or other voluntary organizations. They are neither socially isolated nor lonely. Studies show that most older people prefer some degree of separation from their children, even if their family ties are close. The elderly are generally happy, have high morale, and enjoy life. The most comfortable among them probably spent time planning for their retirement.

MAJOR CATEGORIES OF RETIREMENT PLANNING

Retirement planning involves the projection of individual needs and goals into the future in an effort to adequately and properly prepare for the retirement years. It can be divided into six major categories.

1. **The retirement lifestyle.** This category deals with work options and challenges at or after retirement, such as second careers, full- or part-time work, volunteer work, and job hunting. It also covers the entire area of leisure planning.

2. **Housing.** This area requires an assessment of housing needs—deciding whether to stay where you are or to move elsewhere; considering whether to buy or to rent; evaluating condominiums, cooperatives, mobile homes, and other housing alternatives; and taking into account all the financial aspects of the housing decision.

3. **Legal affairs.** Some of the legal concerns of retirement planning involve the various forms of property ownership, a late or second marriage, bankruptcy, setting up a new business, and choosing and using a lawyer.

4. **Financial planning.** Financial planning is concerned with income and expenses during the retirement years. The major sources of retirement income include Social Security, pensions, savings, investments, life insurance, and annuities, which usually form the basis of the retirement budget. Useful activities in planning a budget are calculating net worth, using credit, coping with inflation, applying tax benefits for older citizens, and using tax shelters.

5. **Physical and mental health.** This category entails the maintenance of good health. An important related aspect is interpreting Medicare—how it works and what you need to supplement it. You should also be familiar with other forms of health insurance, such as health maintenance organizations and Blue Cross-Blue Shield. Mental or psychological health includes the adjustments that need to be made as part of the transition from work to retirement. It can also involve the treatment of alcoholism, drug abuse, and mental illness.

6. **Estate planning.** This area of planning involves designing a program for the effective management or disposition of assets at death at the least possible tax cost. Estate-planning tools include wills and trusts.

STEPS IN THE PLANNING PROCESS

The four steps involved in the retirement planning process are presented below.

1. **Analyze the present.** Analyze your present situation by assembling all the relevant facts and information for each of the major categories of retirement planning. This will give you a starting point from which you can project into the future.

2. **Expand your research efforts.** Broaden your sources of information. Talk to retirees you know to learn about the problems they faced when making the transition to retirement. Talk to counselors who are trained to offer guidance and assistance. Visit your local library, which may have an extensive collection of senior citizen books and articles.

3. **Set retirement goals.** Write down some of the goals you would like to achieve in retirement. (The Self-Study sheet on page 11 will help you record your retirement goals.)

4. **Update your plan periodically.** Review your plan from time to time and update it as the need arises. Obviously, if your present situation changes, you must make adjustments that reflect the changes.

A TIMETABLE FOR RETIREMENT PLANNING

When should you start to plan for your retirement? Actually, you took your first steps in the retirement planning process when you got your first full-time job—you began making contributions to Social Security, and, hopefully, you joined your employer's pension plan. Thus, full-time employment set into motion the accumulation of your nest egg. But during this early period of employment, most people are immersed in job and family responsibilities, and retirement is just too far in the future to be seriously considered.

So a realistic time to start the retirement planning process is *at least ten years before your estimated retirement date.* Ten years of lead time will enable you to make corrections and adjustments in the major planning areas. In your financial plan, for example, you can check your annual net-worth analysis against your financial goals. If you find that your income is inadequate, you have enough time to change jobs, to earn more money in a second job, to save more, or to change your investment portfolio. These options are generally not available to individuals already in their 60s. In addition, by thinking ahead and planning ahead, you may be able to avoid the trauma of *retirement shock,* a psychological condition that results from a total lack of preparedness for retirement.

But all is not lost if you do not start ten years in advance. You can start five years, or even one year, in advance and still benefit. In fact, the guidelines here will be helpful to you even if you are already retired. But remember, the earlier you start, the more flexibility you will have.

MAKING THE RETIREMENT DECISION

Unless you are forced to retire, you will probably reach a time in your working life when you must decide whether to retire or to remain on the job. Aside from health concerns, the most important factor affecting the decision will most likely be economic, revolving around the question, "Will my retirement income be sufficient to enable my spouse and me to live reasonably well?" A significant related question is, "Will my retirement income be adequate five years from now? Ten years from now?" (For tips on making the retirement decision, see the inset on page 8.)

Because they are concerned with inflation and general economic uncertainties, some older Americans postpone retirement. Others retire and then return to work. Yet a recent Congressional study indicates that 65 is no longer the standard retirement age. The median age at which workers start drawing pensions is 62, with almost 60 percent receiving pensions before age 65.

Reasons for Retiring

There are many incentives to retire. The anticipation of a reasonably sufficient retirement income is the strongest incentive. Until the mid-1970s, this fact was reflected in the official statistics on the number of people working. Between the early 1950s and mid-1970s, half the work force retired by age 65. Inflation during that period was not a problem, and the economy was enjoying continued prosperity. Related to the preceding are three additional factors that may prompt retirement.

The first factor is that the Social Security program encourages older workers to retire by providing a full pension at age 65, or a pension with actuarially reduced benefits at age 62, 63, or 64. Early retirement between the ages of 62 and 64 began for women in 1956 and for men in 1961. The number of people opting for early retirement increased significantly when these changes in the Social Security law were approved. (It should be noted that between the years 2000 and 2022, the retirement age for full Social Security benefits will gradually be raised from 65 to 67. See Chapter 7 for further details.)

A second factor encouraging retirement is the knowledge that Social Security benefits will increase as the cost of living increases. Known as the *cost-of-living adjustment (COLA)*, this periodic adjustment in benefits enables Social Security income to keep up with inflation.

A third factor that encourages older workers to leave the job market is the growth of private pensions. Over the last thirty or forty years, private businesses have initiated a variety of retirement benefit programs for their employees. Most beneficiaries find that these private pensions, supplemented by Social Security, provide a comfortable retirement income.

A variety of other reasons for retirement are worth noting:

❑ Some retirements are prompted by poor health or by unsatisfactory working conditions.

❑ Some people are encouraged to retire by their employers because of their age, even though federal law no longer mandates retirement at age 70.

❑ Some people retire in order to realize and expand their talents more fully; to engage in new interests or develop new or existing skills; to pursue new knowledge; or to begin a second career.

❑ Some people want to have leisure time to develop closer relationships with their children, other family members, or friends.

Reasons for Continuing to Work

For a long time, 65 was considered to be the appropriate retirement age. Then, in 1967, federal law established 70 as a mandatory retirement age. The government later changed its policy, and under the Federal Age Discrimination in Employment Act Amendments of 1986, mandatory retirement at any age was eliminated. The thinking behind the most recent law was that individual ability to do a job—not age—should be the basis for continued employment, and most people agree.

How Do You Know When It's Time to Retire?

Most people assume that retirement can and should begin when they reach age 65 and their Social Security checks start streaming in. Especially if they expect to receive a pension as well as Social Security benefits, in some vague way, they believe that they will have adequate income to live comfortably throughout their retirement years.

The fact is, however, that many people discover too late that they simply don't have the income they need to enjoy a secure and rewarding retirement. Retirement plans must be based on real numbers. Fortunately, everyone has the ability to assess their financial situation and to determine when the time is right to retire. That's why *Retiring Right* was written—to help you zero in on the numbers that count, assess them realistically, and devise a plan that is right for you.

How can you determine when you can retire? The following is an overview of the steps you can take to insure that you retire right.

1. Determine your pre-retirement income and expenses. Your first step is to look at your yearly pre-retirement income. In other words, how much income are you making *right now?* Unless your finances are very complex, it should not be too difficult to arrive at this figure.

Now realistically determine how much you are spending each year. Remember to include all of your costs, from groceries, to rent and mortgage payments, to utilities, to clothing, to health care, to taxes. Worksheet 10.3, found on page 166, will help insure that no expenses are forgotten.

Now write down the two figures you have just determined—your current income and your current expenses. Keep the figures on hand, as they will help you complete the next step.

2. Estimate your postretirement income and expenses. Once you have determined your present income and expenditures, you'll want to look ahead to your retirement years. How much income can you expect to receive during each year of retirement, and how much money can you expect to spend?

To estimate your future income, of course, you will have to examine your future Social Security benefits, your potential pension income and annuities, your savings and investments, and all other possible sources of income. To estimate your future expenditures, you will probably want to take a good look at your present expenses. However, be aware that even here, you will have to make adjustments. For instance, while work-related expenses such as transportation may stop, other expenses—those related to health care, for instance—may increase. If all this seems like an overwhelming task, don't panic. Worksheets 10.4 and 10.5, found on pages 168 and 169, will help you come up with realistic numbers regarding both the money you will receive and the money you will spend.

Some financial planners feel that it isn't necessary to estimate future expenses on an item-by-item basis. Instead, they provide simple guidelines that, they feel, determine the percentage of your current yearly income that will be needed after retirement. Specifically, they state that if you make under $50,000, you will need 100 percent of your annual pre-retirement income during your retirement; if you make $50,000 to $100,000, you will need 80 to 90 percent; and if you make $100,000 or more, you will need 70 to 80 percent. It is certainly true that as your income rises, more of the money you earn can be considered surplus income. However, it is important to recognize that each person is unique, and has his or her own needs, spending patterns, and standards of living. In addition, due to the widely varying costs of everything from housing to health care in different regions of the country, an income that can support a more-than-comfortable lifestyle in one area may barely enable you to make ends meet in another area. So although the rule of thumb just discussed may be helpful, it is nevertheless important to realistically assess not only your projected income but also your projected expenses, and to come up with figures that accurately reflect your particular situation.

3. Compare your postretirement income with your postretirement expenses, and make any necessary adjustments. Now you know how much income you will receive annually during your retirement years, and you know what your expenses are likely to be. If you're fortunate, you'll find that your income will more than keep up with your expenses. If this is the case, congratulations! You should be able to enjoy a financially secure retirement.

Of course, you may find that your projected income fails to meet your expenditures. Does this mean that you simply can't retire? Of course not! But it does mean that you may have to rethink your retirement plans. Depending on your lifestyle and on the degree of any shortfall, you will be able to choose from a variety of options, all of which are covered in

Retiring Right. You may, for instance, choose a part-time job—possibly a job that always appealed to you, but that you never had the time to explore. Or you may opt for different, more affordable housing. Many retirees, for instance, find that by moving abroad, they can enjoy a lavish lifestyle at a fraction of their present cost of living. Still another possibility is to take a life insurance policy that is no longer needed, and convert it into an annuity that provides a constant flow of income. The possibilities may surprise you, and may end up giving you a new and exciting perspective on retirement.

4. Plan exciting retirement activities. If you have determined how and if your future expenses will be covered by your future income, you have taken an important step in determining when you can retire. But retiring right means more than being able to meet your expenses. It is absolutely vital that you consider how you are going to spend all those hours that you previously spent working, and that you begin laying the groundwork for the years ahead. You will want to fill your time with pursuits that you find rewarding and fulfilling. *Retiring Right* will help you here, too, by making you aware of all the many great activities—from volunteer work to hobbies to jobs—that can make your golden years happy, productive, and meaningful.

Most people look forward to their years of retirement—years when they can escape the demands of their jobs, and fully enjoy what life has to offer. By exploring every important retirement issue, from housing, to investments, to recreational activities, to budgeting, to health care, and more, this book will help you chart your course to years of happy retirement.

The 1979 amendment to the Social Security law also offered encouragement for retiring at a later age. Under this amendment, potential retirees can receive an increase in benefits for each year beyond age 65 that they continue to work and postpone retirement.

The threat of inflation is another reason for continuing to work. Many older workers think that their dreams of retirement are unaffordable. They worry about their economic future. Even though Social Security's cost-of-living clause offsets the impact of inflation, most private pensions are not raised automatically as prices rise.

A final reason for remaining at work is that many jobs which used to be strenuous and physically draining are easier to perform with the aid of newly developed machines. Similarly, boring and repetitive types of work are being eliminated by automated robots on assembly lines. These changes are encouraging older workers to stay on the job.

Whether you choose to continue working or you decide to retire in the near future, your later years will be happier and less stressful if you clarify your goals, and construct a plan that will allow you to realize them. The remainder of this book will guide you in making the decision that is right for you, and in formulating and implementing a truly realistic retirement plan.

Who Can You Turn To?

As you approach retirement, a variety of professionals are available to help you assess your financial situation, enhance your nest egg, identify and resolve possible problems, and make any arrangements necessary for a safe and secure future. The following are just a few of the people and institutions that you can turn to for advice, guidance, or practical help.

Financial Planner. A financial planner can take stock of your existing resources and establish an individualized plan designed to prepare you for your retirement years. (To learn more about financial planners, see the inset on page 100.)

Certified Public Accountant. In addition to preparing your yearly income tax return, a savvy CPA can guide you in making money-saving decisions about a variety of tax-related issues.

Stockbroker. Although the stock market has its ups and downs, in the long-term, stocks offer the best return of any investment. A good stockbroker can help you select stocks that will allow you to meet your goals, and can also aid you in purchasing other investments, from certificates of deposit to bonds.

Bank. Most banks now offer a broad range of investment products, from money market accounts to mutual funds. Many banks even offer individually managed investment portfolios.

Human Resources Department. A knowledgeable staff member in your company's Human Resources Department can explain exactly what you will receive from the company pension plan, and offer other information related to retirement planning.

Elder-Care Lawyer. Experienced in meeting the objectives of the older client, elder-care lawyers can provide assistance with estate planning, housing, and a range of other retirement issues. (For more information on elder-care lawyers, see the inset on page 81.)

Self-study

RECORD YOUR RETIREMENT GOALS

Record your preliminary retirement goals. Of course, all of these will begin as approximations and be subject to change as you progress in the retirement planning process. (This list omits the financial, estate planning, and legal areas. Self-study sections are found in chapters dealing with those topics.)

PHYSICAL AND MENTAL HEALTH

1. **Physical.** What is your plan for a program of physical activity—a sport, an exercise program, or another physical activity (such as walking, dancing, or gardening)?

_____

_____

_____

_____

2. **Social.** How do you plan to make new friends—through political, cultural, or social activities; volunteer work; senior centers?

_____

_____

_____

_____

3. **Religious.** What is your plan, if any, for becoming active or more active in religious activities?

_____

_____

_____

_____

RETIREMENT LIFESTYLE

1. **Housing.** What is your retirement housing plan—stay where you are or relocate; be an owner or a renter; live in a single-family home, a two-family home, a multi-family home, a condominium, or a cooperative; reside in a retirement village?

_____

_____

2. **Leisure.** What is your leisure plan—engage in hobbies, travel, do volunteer work?

_____

_____

_____

3. **Employment.** What is your employment plan after retirement—no work at all, full-time or part-time work, same type of work or a different occupation? What training or retraining, if any, is required?

_____

_____

4. **Educational.** What is your plan for continuing your education—take individual courses of interest; participate in a structured program leading to an undergraduate, graduate, or professional degree?

_____

_____

5. **Cultural.** What is your plan for developing a greater interest and involvement in the arts and letters—attending theater productions, listening to concerts, visiting the library, viewing museum exhibits?

_____

_____

6. **Artistic.** If you have artistic or musical talent, how do you propose to develop these abilities?

_____

_____

LIFESTYLES

WORKING *in* RETIREMENT

At some point in your life, perhaps when you are in your 50s or 60s, you will retire from your job and begin a new lifestyle. You may retire by choice—because you have had enough of the work routine—or by the force of circumstances—because of ill health, because your firm goes out of business or changes management, or because your job is no longer necessary. Whatever the reason, you will leave the labor force and become a retiree. Suddenly, you will have at least 50 extra hours a week to spend however you choose. Some people enjoy the additional leisure time and find retirement to be the most rewarding period of their lives. Others are unable to cope with all the free time, and quickly become bored and restless.

THE ROLE OF WORK IN YOUR LIFE

Research evidence indicates that if retirees had a choice, most would opt for some kind of work, because work contributes something to life that cannot easily be replaced. Some of the satisfactions offered by work include:

❏ A feeling of self-worth stemming from the contribution you are making.

❏ A sense of fulfillment because you enjoy your work and others appreciate and recognize your ability.

❏ A sense of belonging provided by the social contacts and friendships you make at work.

❏ A structure to your life that gives order to your day and makes time pass quickly.

The need for such satisfactions and goals do not disappear at retirement. Whether you are actively employed or retired, these needs remain the same because they are basic human needs. You can satisfy these needs at or after retirement through the following four options:

1. Working full-time at the same job or in a new career.

2. Working part-time for the same employer or for a different employer.

3. Doing volunteer work in the community.

4. Establishing and operating a small business.

A discussion of each of these options follows. In addition, Self-Study 1.1 will help you examine your work options and assess your readiness to find employment.

Option 1—Continue Full-Time Work

If you wish to work beyond age 65 or 70 as a full-time paid employee, you might want to approach your employer to discuss the possibility. With your lifetime experience in your job, you may very well qualify to serve as a consultant on a full-time basis, acting as a company troubleshooter whenever problems arise; as a trainer for younger staff members, who often need guidance and advice; or as an ombudsman who handles the gripes of individual employees. A recent Social Security Administration poll revealed that 80 percent of white-collar workers, who generally do office or professional work, and 60 percent of blue-collar workers, who generally do manual labor, get new jobs in their fields after they retire.

If you remain at the same company beyond your retirement date, several work arrangements are possible. The following five are the most common:

1. **Job reassignment.** Request a transfer to another position with a different set of job specifications. However, if the job is less demanding, you may be asked to accept less money.

2. **Job redesign.** You can have your job specifications, or job description, changed to eliminate functions that cause you physical or mental stress.

3. **Compressed work week.** Work fewer days by doing your week's work in, for example, four 10-hour shifts instead of five 8-hour shifts.

4. **Flexible location.** You can spend part of your week working on the company's premises, and the other part working at home.

5. **Flextime.** You can arrange a flexible work schedule to fit a new set of job specifications. For instance, you can come in earlier and leave earlier, or start later and leave later.

Arrangements such as these can yield benefits for both your employer and you. Or, you may instead decide to work full-time at a new career. This can be a job that you have always wanted to do but for one reason or another could not undertake. Retirement gives you the opportunity to make a fresh start. You may wish to enter a field that requires more traveling, or less. You may want to work with your hands after having spent your first career at a desk. You may enjoy cooking professionally or spending your time at a college or university, teaching in your area of expertise. Retirement is the time to take advantage of these options while continuing to earn income.

Option 2—Shift to Part-Time Work

Most people who are retired would like to have a not-too-demanding part-time job that provides some income and keeps them in the mainstream. For many people, part-time work—employment of fewer than 35 hours a week—offers a chance to retire from the work force gradually. Some people feel that temporary positions in their own fields are preferable to jobs that are regular but outside their fields. If such thinking is part of your retirement plan, you should approach the quest with the same care and lead time you used when seeking a new full-time job while still in the labor market. Some occupations have better part-time prospects than others do. A retired lawyer can continue in his or her profession by serving a reduced number of established clients. A teacher can become an adjunct at a college, or can become a tutor. An office or factory worker can fill in for people who are ill or on vacation.

Businesses are now hiring more part-timers because this arrangement fits their needs, too. Fast-food restaurants, for example, hire many workers only for peak hours. In some places, the demand for computer specialists is so great that companies are offering part-time positions to attract skilled workers, even though they might prefer full-time employees. And, of course, many companies hire part-time workers because the practice saves money. Part-time and temporary workers do not receive the costly fringe benefits of full-time workers. The company does not have to make pension contributions; offer participation in a profit-sharing plan; or pay for Blue Cross, Blue Shield, or any other type of health insurance. This is a significant advantage for employers.

Part-time workers are continuing to grow in number, and currently total about 20 percent of the nonfarm work force. About a third of Americans over age 65 have part-time jobs. In industry, a new concept known as *phased retirement* has been developed, and appears to be adding more part-time workers to the labor force. *Job sharing,* too, permits many more people to enjoy part-time employment.

Phased Retirement

Phased retirement helps older employees retire gradually by reducing their present work time without reducing their ultimate pension benefits. In this program, as you reduce your work time, you also reduce your take-home pay, which helps you adjust to living on less money. In addition to helping you make a financial adjustment, phased retirement increases your free time, thus enabling you to slowly increase your leisure-time activities. For the employer, this program has the positive financial advantage of gradual salary reductions. At the same time, the company derives the benefit of utilizing a veteran employee's job knowledge to train new workers, and of keeping job functions operative. Variations of the phased retirement program include:

❑ Varied part-time schedules such as mornings

only, afternoons only, alternating mornings and afternoons, or reduced daily hours.

❑ Alternation of regular daily work hours and extended vacation time, such as two months work followed by a one-month vacation.

Job Sharing

In job sharing, two workers divide the hours and responsibilities of a single full-time job. For example, one person may work from 8:30 AM to 1:00 PM, and the other person may work from 11:30 AM to 4:00 PM. For many people, this is the perfect answer. Some job-sharing arrangements are family affairs in which neither party wants to work full-time. For example, a mother and a daughter may operate a small business. One works on Mondays and Wednesdays; the other, on Tuesdays and Thursdays; and both, on Fridays—one in the morning and one in the afternoon.

If any of these variations of reduced work hours is of interest to you, discuss it with your company management or with your union.

Option 3—Do Volunteer Work

If you wish to participate in a volunteer activity after you retire, retirement planning gives you the opportunity to try out various volunteer jobs in your spare time. By sampling several different organizations and several types of volunteer work, you will be better able to choose the activity and group that will provide the greatest fulfillment. If you make your choice sufficiently in advance of your actual retirement, you will also have the opportunity to gain a great deal of experience, possibly even enough to qualify for a volunteer executive position after you retire.

A variety of groups and organizations utilize volunteers on the local level. They include:

❑ **Hospitals.** Hospitals generally rely heavily

on the work of volunteers. All types of jobs are available, but basically, you must be capable of working closely with people who need help on the road to recovery. A smile and a helping hand brighten the day for the sick or infirm. If you are interested, contact your nearest hospital.

❑ **Cultural institutions.** Many cultural institutions, such as museums and public television stations, offer opportunities for volunteers. Typical jobs include guiding tours, raising funds, and stuffing envelopes.

❑ **Schools.** School volunteers assist teachers in the classroom or tutor students in basic skills. Contact your local school.

❑ **Community service organizations.** Churches and synagogues offer a variety of volunteer jobs. In addition, charitable organizations, neighborhood groups, and YMCAs, YWCAs, and YMHAs are always seeking the assistance of volunteers.

Option 4—Own a Business

You may be interested in starting your own business after you retire. Such a venture will offer you the opportunity to be your own boss, to be financially independent, and to work in a field that you enjoy. The idea is enticing to many people who are contemplating work options after retirement. Many small businesses succeed and generate high incomes for their entrepreneurs. However, most do not survive for very long. According to the Small Business Administration (SBA), which studies mortality rates of small businesses, about 20 percent close in the first year, 20 percent in the second, and another 10 percent in the third year.

The reasons for small-business failure are varied. They include poor location, poor management, insufficient capital, ineffective purchasing, and unsuccessful marketing. Each of these areas should be thoroughly studied prior to starting a small business. Some of the knowledge required in these areas can be learned by working for a few years in the type of business you are thinking of running, or by supplementing your personal experience with formal education or training. The probability of failure is high for the inexperienced and untrained. However, there are many resources available, including free ones such as the Small Business Administration. (See the Resources section.)

You might also consult various books, such as *The Complete Small-Business Sourcebook: Information, Services, and Experts Every Small and Home-Based Business Needs* by Carl Hausman and Wilbur Cross. This handy reference work recommends useful books, websites, and trade associations for the entrepreneur.

JOB HUNTING

Job hunting is a difficult and frustrating experience for most people. The rejections appear to pile up all too quickly. But in the back of your mind, you know that your goal is the single acceptance that is out there somewhere. And by using certain tools and techniques, you can maximize your chance of success.

Job-Hunting Methods

The methods used in job hunting include the following:

❑ **Visit personnel departments.** Experts estimate that about 27 percent of job-seekers are hired directly by the personnel officers of companies through whose doors they walk. The *personnel officer* is the company staffer in charge of hiring and firing employees. So choose a company for which you would like to work and visit the personnel department. If a vacancy exists and if you meet the requirements, you may have a job. It is always wise to draw up a plan of company visits and to know precisely what type of work you are seeking.

❏ **Read classified help-wanted advertisements.** Read the employment ads in the classified sections of all your local publications, and check off the ones that describe jobs for which you may be particularly well qualified. Answering an ad may require a personal visit, a letter, or a phone call.

❏ **Use Internet job listings.** Several Internet sites are devoted to helping employers find qualified workers, and workers find appropriate employment. Monster.com, for instance, allows you to search for jobs by location (e.g., Long Island, New York) and category (e.g., real estate). Simply use the search engine of your choice to look for "job listings," and scan the listings for up-to-the-minute information on job openings.

❏ **Visit employment agencies.** Two kinds of employment agencies are available—state employment services, which are tax-supported agencies, and private employment agencies, which charge either the employer or the employee a fee for filling or finding a job. Since private agencies generally specialize in certain fields or types of jobs, be sure to select an agency in your area of expertise. In your job hunt, apply at both public and private agencies.

❏ **Network for job leads.** When you are in the job market, networking may prove helpful. Networking involves talking to personnel officers as well as to friends and relatives. In the course of a conversation, a job lead may be offered. Follow up on all these leads, leaving no stone unturned.

The Resumé

One of the most important tools in job hunting is the resumé. While you cannot rely on a resumé alone to get the job you want, you can use it to open the door.

Essentially, a resumé is a summary of your work experience, your education, and your training. If properly prepared, it can indicate that you do, indeed, have something positive to offer a potential employer. It should be easy to read, well organized, and preferably no longer than one page. Self-Study 1.2 will guide you in composing an appropriate resumé. The following information should be included:

❏ Name, address, telephone number, and any other contact information, such as an e-mail address or fax number.

❏ Job objective.

❏ Relevant work history.

❏ Relevant education and special training.

❏ Relevant awards and activities.

❏ A note stating that references will be supplied upon request.

If you mail your resumé to a prospective employer, be sure to enclose a cover letter along with it. Here are a few points that should be included:

❏ Identify the position for which you are applying, and indicate how you learned about the firm and the position.

❏ Indicate why you are applying for this particular position.

❏ Describe your main qualifications.

❏ Refer the reader to the enclosed resumé.

❏ Request the next step in the employment process—a personal interview and an answer to your letter.

❏ Be sure to sign the letter.

The Interview

When you are called in for an interview, you have an opportunity to sell yourself and your specialized experience and training to a prospective employer. The two key elements during interviews are personal appearance and attitude. Be prepared to answer a variety of questions about your work experience, your education, and your beliefs and personality. Highlight the special benefits of mature workers. Remember that you cannot be denied a job because of age. Prepare in advance the answers to possible questions, turning weak points into strengths that may benefit the employer. Self-Study 1.3 was designed to help you prepare for job interviews.

The Thank-You Letter

After an interview, send a thank-you letter as a follow-up. Later, you can write additional letters or telephone periodically to determine if any jobs have opened up. You have made a contact, and if you continue to display an interest in working for that particular employer, you may eventually land a job.

Where Are the Jobs?

The job market changes almost daily. Because of this, mature individuals re-entering the job market in the twenty-first century may require some retraining or upgrading of skills to help them find employment on their own terms. For example, while experienced typists and stenographers are still in demand, experienced typists and stenographers with computer skills will find it far easier to locate a position. Fortunately, mature individuals can learn how to operate a computer without learning how a computer functions.

With the 65-and-over group expanding more rapidly than the population as a whole, the need for retirement counselors and pension-planning consultants is growing. The health-care field will also be offering enormous opportunities over the next decade since more and more people will be needed to provide health care for the aged. In addition, the health-insurance field is expanding because younger Americans are becoming increasingly concerned about their health and are purchasing more insurance than ever before.

The field of retail sales has always offered opportunities to older individuals. Salesperson and clerk positions in retail stores account for millions of jobs, with hundreds of thousands becoming available each year. A growing company may suddenly need to increase its staff, causing a whole network of positions to open.

Retirees who are looking for part-time work will find the greatest number of jobs in the service industries, including schools, libraries, restaurants, cafeterias, and day-care centers. Many part-time jobs are also available in businesses that have evening hours.

Throughout the last decade, opportunities grew in financial services such as banks and brokerage houses. In some areas, teachers are in great demand, and special incentives are being offered to applicants. The fact is that job trends change constantly, leading to openings in areas that may be of interest to you.

Work—whether part-time or full-time—can contribute greatly to physical and emotional health, in addition to providing a financial return. Because older workers need the same sense of usefulness and accomplishment that younger workers do, you will find that work is a worthwhile pursuit during your retirement years.

Self-Study 1.1

RATE YOURSELF FOR POSTRETIREMENT WORK

1. What are your long-range plans for work after retirement? Check the appropriate box or boxes.

Work Options After Retirement	Full-time	Part-time
Continue in present job	❏	❏
Seek a new position in pre-retirement field	❏	❏
Seek a position in a new field	❏	❏
Do volunteer work	❏	❏
Start a business	❏	❏
Stop working, enjoy leisure	❏	❏

2. Personnel officers as well as owners and managers of large and small businesses have pinpointed the characteristics of employees that they feel are the most important to the success of their enterprises. How would you rate yourself on each of the following characteristics? Check the appropriate boxes. If most of your ratings are above average, your employability index is high. Your first step is to find a vacancy.

Characteristic	Above Average	Average	Below Average
Appearance	❏	❏	❏
Work habits (punctuality, absenteeism)	❏	❏	❏
Writing, spelling, and mathematical skills	❏	❏	❏
Ability to accept supervision	❏	❏	❏
Attitude (minimum irritability or anger)	❏	❏	❏
Pride in work	❏	❏	❏
Thoroughness	❏	❏	❏
Ability to complete assignments	❏	❏	❏

Characteristic	Above Average	Average	Below Average
Knowledge and skill	❏	❏	❏
Personality	❏	❏	❏
Productivity	❏	❏	❏
Company loyalty	❏	❏	❏
Motivation	❏	❏	❏
Enthusiasm	❏	❏	❏
Flexibility	❏	❏	❏

3. The following are characteristics of people who have successfully run their own small businesses. How do you rate? Check the appropriate boxes.

❏ Willingness to work long hours

❏ High energy level

❏ High initiative

❏ Ability to persevere

❏ High sincerity level

❏ Good leadership skills

❏ Ability to organize

❏ Industriousness

❏ Pleasant attitude

❏ Ability to make good decisions

❏ Willingness to take responsibility

❏ Emotional strength to cushion possible failure

❏ Financial reserves to keep you afloat in case of setbacks

Self-Study 1.2
COMPOSE YOUR RESUMÉ

An attractive, well-organized resumé highlighting your most important qualifications can successfully introduce you to a company or organization for which you would like to work. It also remains after the interview, leaving an impression of you that is independent of the opinions or impressions of the interviewer. To prepare your personal resumé, follow the guidelines below.

SAMPLE RESUMÉ
PERSONAL INFORMATION

Name _____

Address _____

City _____ State _____ Zip _____

Telephone number (_____)_____

Job objective_____

_____

_____

WORK HISTORY
(List current or most recent employment first)

Dates From To	Job title and duties in brief	Name and title of supervisor Employer name and address
____ ____	_____	_____
____ ____	_____	_____
____ ____	_____	_____
____ ____	_____	_____

EDUCATION

Dates				
From	To	Name and address of school	Degree	Major
_____	_____	_____	_____	_____
		(High school)		
_____	_____	_____	_____	_____
		(College)		
_____	_____	_____	_____	_____
		(Graduate school)		

SPECIAL TRAINING

(Company training courses, armed forces schools, adult education courses, home study, correspondence courses)

Dates		
From	To	Type of training, sponsor's name and address
_____	_____	_____
_____	_____	_____
_____	_____	_____

References are available upon request.

Self-study 1.3
Prepare for Job Interviews

A job interview gives you an opportunity to present yourself and your qualifications to a representative of a company or organization for which you want to work. Following are questions that often come up during interviews. To prepare for an interview, you can practice your responses in advance.

WORK

What type of job are you seeking?_____

_____

What did you enjoy doing most in your last job? _____

_____

What did you not enjoy doing?_____

_____

How would your supervisor have described you as a person?_____

_____

For what did he/she criticize you?_____

_____

For what did he/she praise you?_____

_____

EDUCATION

How would you describe your educational accomplishments?_____

_____

How did you come to choose the kind of work you did?_____

_____

Has not having a college degree (or graduate degree) hindered you
in your vocational progress?_____

_____

PERSONAL

How would you describe yourself?_____

_____

_____

_____

How do you spend your leisure time?_____

_____

_____

What are your major strengths?_____

_____

_____

_____

What are your weaknesses?_____

_____

_____

_____

Why do you want to work for us?_____

_____

_____

_____

What salary are you seeking?_____

Are you seeking full-time or part-time employment?_____

Playing *in* Retirement

The proper use of leisure time in retirement is the basic determinant of whether your retirement will be happy and fulfilling or boring and restless. The transition from full-time worker to retiree adds at least 50 additional hours a week with which you can do as you please. You must begin planning early to use this extra time so that your feeling of usefulness to society will continue. In fact, effective time management should be given primary consideration as you approach retirement.

Some people turn to *hobbies* to provide the satisfaction of creativity and recognition that had previously come from work. Library shelves are filled with books that can guide you in selecting one or more for fulfillment in retirement. Many retirees also turn to the world of *education and learning*. Throughout the nation, older adults are studying to achieve never-completed degrees, or are simply pursuing new academic interests and enjoying the excitement and sense of purpose generated by the world of academia. Still others turn to *travel* in retirement. With your extra time, you will need only a little imagination to satisfy the wanderlust. As discussed in Chapter 1, some retirees become involved in

volunteer work to preserve the sense of identity, self-worth, and usefulness that were previously derived from their careers. Carefully selected volunteer work will give you all the job satisfaction you need.

HOBBIES

Hobbies are important to retirees. Those who enjoy a hobby appear to be happier and better adjusted to the retirement lifestyle than those who do not.

During their working years, many people discover various hobbies that help them unwind, relax, and enjoy whatever spare time they manage to find. Others become so absorbed in work and everyday essentials that they have little time for extra activities. Retirement provides an excellent opportunity to continue and expand those hobbies that might have been ongoing for years, or to develop new interests that can become gratifying and fulfilling.

The variety of hobbies available is unlimited. Some are thousands of years old; others are being developed daily. Some are indoors and sedentary; others are outdoors and ambulatory. Some exercise the mind; others exercise the body. For example, collections of almost anything you can name have become popular in the last decade or so. Some people collect buttons, bottles, small banks, butterflies, baseball cards, beads—and that's only the beginning of the alphabet for collectibles. The list is endless. In short, there are as many hobbies as there are people to create them.

Most hobbies are inexpensive, but some require an outlay of cash for clothing and equipment. Golf requires clubs, a golf bag, special shoes, and, of course, fees to play the game. Painting requires brushes, paint, and canvas. Before investing money, it is wise to borrow or rent what you need until you are certain that the hobby is really something you'll enjoy. It might also be helpful to take an adult education course or to read up on the activity before making any commitment, financial or otherwise.

Hobbies can be classified according to four general classes: doing things, collecting things, making things, and studying and learning about things. Self-Study 2.1 offers some ideas for each of these categories.

A few hobbies are of particular interest to many retirees. Over 600,000 people, retirees included, enjoy the useful and interesting hobby of being amateur radio operators. These radio amateurs, or *hams,* send messages on their home radio stations to new friends on the next block or halfway around the world. Messages can be sent by voice (talking) or by Morse code.

The governments of most countries encourage radio amateurs because trained radio operators are needed in emergencies. Hams provide emergency communications during floods, fires, tornadoes, hurricanes, and earthquakes. The Federal Communications Commission (FCC) has often praised hams for their voluntary work in emergencies.

Amateur radio is the only hobby regulated by international treaty. Transmitting channels,

agreed upon by most nations, are sandwiched in among the short-wave radio frequencies assigned to ships, aircraft, international broadcasting stations, armed forces, police, and others. To operate an amateur station in the United States, an amateur must first obtain a license from the FCC. Information about procuring a license can be obtained from the American Radio Relay League (ARRL). (See the Resources section.)

EDUCATION AND LEARNING

Education for seniors is not a new concept; it dates back to medieval times when scholars traveled from city to city to conduct lectures and discussions. Today, opportunities abound for the older student. Many local colleges offer special programs for older adults that enable seniors to audit classes, attend lectures, or even register at modest fees for courses that are part of the regular curriculum. Many high schools offer evening classes for which seniors may enroll. And public libraries frequently sponsor afternoon programs such as book discussions, slide shows, and even museum visits.

The courses and programs offered cover a wide range of topics. You can brush up on your computer skills, study music and art, learn a new craft, or improve your understanding of finance and investing. The course you take may lead to a new and fascinating hobby, or may even help you start a whole new career. Nearby educational institutions and other organizations will be glad to send you course catalogues and event calendars. A few phone calls to local schools and libraries can open up a whole new world.

Of course, while many educational opportunities are close at hand, many seniors choose to combine travel and learning. If this idea appeals to you, look into Elderhostel, which offers academic programs throughout the United States and abroad. (See page 29.)

TRAVEL

In recent years, tourism has become a thriving industry, and much of its success can be attributed to retirees and senior citizens. These are the people who have the time, energy, and curiosity to discover and explore new areas. An important positive feature is that the cost of transportation can vary to suit any income level. You can choose automobile, bus, train, ship, or plane. You can chart your own course by studying maps and travel magazines, or you can consult a travel agent. You can travel alone, with friends, or with family, or you can join a tour group—an option that can remove much of the stress of travel by taking care of reservations and transportation. You can explore your own state, or you can travel across the country. You can even branch out to other continents and different cultures by visiting places as distant as the Mideast, the Far East, Africa, and Australia.

For those who wish to combine travel and education, Elderhostel, a nonprofit organization, offers inexpensive, short-term academic programs hosted by educational institutions in the United States, Canada, and over eighty other countries. In 2000, about 200,000 people enrolled in Elderhostel programs.

Elderhostel participants live on college and university campuses, in conference centers, or in other facilities, and enjoy the cultural and recreational resources of the area. For as little as $450 plus travel costs, a participant can enjoy a one-week stay on a college campus in the United States during the academic year or during the summer. The fee includes a dorm room, cafeteria meals, three college-credit courses, and extra-curricular activities. The program requires no homework and no prior knowledge of the subject, and involves no grades. For more information, contact Elderhostel. (See the Resources section.)

VOLUNTEER WORK

Volunteer work can bring you a whole new slant on life during your retirement years. Perhaps you were one of those people who went to work every day, just waiting for pay day. Now you have an opportunity to become one of the scores of people who are "paid" by the smiles, thanks, and comfort of those they help.

Volunteers visit the elderly and shut-ins, help school children learn their lessons, teach adults to read, distribute magazines in hospitals, serve as guides in museums, and do office work for fund-raising organizations. Contact your local school, hospital, library, or museum for information about volunteer programs at those institutions, or call your favorite philanthropic or civic organization and offer your assistance. You can also call Volunteers of America or Literacy Volunteers of America for information about programs in your area. (See the Resources section.)

CONSIDERATIONS WHEN PLANNING LEISURE TIME ACTIVITIES

Keep the following factors in mind as you plan your leisure time. Also consult Self-Study 2.2 for further help.

❑ **Variety.** Try to develop a reasonable mix of activities. Variety will keep you interested *and* interesting. Select some pastimes that involve physical activity, some that are intellectual, and some that are creative. And don't forget to take the issue of physical ability into account.

❑ **Interaction.** Choose some activities that will enable you to enjoy social contact with other people. Socialization and communication are basic to sound psychological adjustment. At the same time, each person needs private time for reading, listening to music, watching television, or contemplation.

❑ **Overextension.** In the early enthusiasm of re-tirement, many individuals tend to overextend themselves, trying to do too much. Develop your involvement in your leisure activities slow-ly, adding or subtracting time as your interest increases or diminishes. Do not take on more than you can handle, and keep your leisure plan flexible.

❑ **Fulfillment.** There is much to be said for lightening the burdens of others. To maintain your feeling of self-worth, choose one activity that gives you the opportunity to spend time helping others who may be less fortunate than you—in other words, a volunteer activity. Enor-mous satisfaction can be derived by contributing to the welfare of people in need: spending time

with them, meeting simple needs, and engaging in conversation.

❑ **Pre-retirement experimentation.** Try out a few new activities before you retire. See how well you enjoy the activity before making a com-mitment.

So many people look forward to their retire-ment years—and then experience boredom and even depression simply because they have not found rewarding activities with which to fill their days. Fortunately, this does not have to be the case. Through planning and creativity, your retirement years can be marked not only by free-dom from work, but also by satisfying activities that make life enjoyable each and every day.

Starting a Reading Group

If you love books and long to share your passion for reading with other people—and possibly make some new friends in the process—a reading group may be just the activity you're looking for. How do these groups work? First, either the group or the group leader chooses a book that will be read by all members. Then, a time is set for a meeting at which members can exchange ideas and insights about the topic, the author, the writing style, and other aspects of the work.

If you are interested in joining an existing reading group, pay a visit to your local library, which may either host a group or know of one. If you can't locate a reading group to your liking, consider starting one of your own. Before you take the plunge, though, read through the follow-ing tips, which can help insure success.

❑ Consider where you want to hold your group meetings. In your home? In a restaurant? The right environment will help everyone feel more comfortable.

❑ After assigning a book, be sure to set a firm deadline for the next meeting. Monthly gather-ings usually give members adequate time to read the assigned works.

❑ To keep things interesting, try to select a mix of books: classics and modern works, fiction and nonfiction. To minimize costs, choose older books rather than bestsellers so that pa-

perback and library copies can be used. Also contact local bookstores to see if they offer reading group discounts.

❑ Determine if the publisher of the assigned work has printed a reading group guide. (Check the publisher's website.) These guides provide author interviews, biographies, and questions designed to spark discussion.

❑ If you need help in making your group work, consult one of the books available on the topic. One good choice is *The Reading Group Handbook* by Rachel W. Jacobsohn.

Self-study 2.1
NEW DIRECTIONS OF ACTIVITY

Review the following examples of hobbies and check those that may interest you.

Doing Things

This group of hobbies is probably the most common.

❏ Amateur radio operation   ❏ Photography

❏ Card games   ❏ Playing a musical instrument

❏ Chess and checkers   ❏ Raising pets

❏ Computer activities   ❏ Sports (ping-pong, tennis, swimming,
   (games, bulletin boards)   softball)

❏ Dancing   ❏ Storytelling

❏ Gardening   ❏ Yachting

❏ Hunting   ❏ Other

Collecting Things

The desire to own things is one of man's strongest instincts.

❏ Antiques   ❏ Matchbooks

❏ Art   ❏ Rare books

❏ Butterflies   ❏ Shells

❏ Buttons   ❏ Stamps

❏ Coins   ❏ Other

Making Things

Many people prefer to make things rather than to collect them.

❑ Bookbinding	❑ Sculpting
❑ Building model train layouts	❑ Sewing
❑ Building furniture	❑ Weaving
❑ Knitting	❑ Writing stories, poems, essays
❑ Building model ships, planes, and cars	❑ Other

Learning

Some people make a hobby of studying a particular subject or of investigating many different fields.

❑ American sign language	❑ Literature
❑ Computer operation and programming	❑ Managing and investing money
❑ Continuing education	❑ Meditation
❑ Culinary arts	❑ Personal development
❑ Drama	❑ Philosophy
❑ Foreign language(s)	❑ Public speaking
❑ Home repair	❑ Voice and diction
❑ Interior decorating	❑ Other

Self-Study 2.2
YOUR PLAN FOR LEISURE ACTIVITIES

1. To develop a retirement plan for leisure, you must first determine the number of hours a week to be considered. Counting time at work and the time consumed getting to and from work, how many additional free hours per week will you have after you retire?

2. Which of your present activities would you like to continue after you retire? How much of your additional free time would you like to devote to each?

	HOURS PER WEEK FOR EACH ACTIVITY	
Present activities	**Now**	**After retirement**

3. What new activities would you like to pursue after retirement? Are you taking classes or receiving training for these activities?

New activities	**Current preparation for these activities**

4. Courses and classes in any subject might open new horizons for you.

List schools and colleges in your area that offer classes in various academic areas.	

List subject matter areas in which you have an interest.

_____   _____

_____   _____

_____   _____

_____   _____

_____

5. Seniors, in particular, enjoy meeting new people and making friends with others who have similar interests at places such as religious groups, community groups, libraries, senior centers.

List groups and senior clubs in your area that encourage new members to join.

_____   _____

_____   _____

_____   _____

_____   _____

6. Often, individuals seek others to join them in making new contacts.

List friends who may be willing to join you in broadening your circle of acquaintances.

_____   _____

_____   _____

_____   _____

_____   _____

3

RETIREMENT HOUSING

Food, clothing, and shelter are the basic ingredients of any budget. The retirement budget, detailed on page 160, distributes expenses of these three elements as 22 percent, 5 percent, and 30 percent, respectively, for a total of 57 percent. Shelter, the largest budgetary component, can take many forms.

Certainly, once you have decided to retire, the most difficult decision you will have to make is *where* to live after retirement. Over 90 percent of retirees choose to remain in the area in which they have been living, either in their own home or in a rented apartment. The rest move to a new location; a few move hundreds of miles away. Among the considerations in choosing a new residence are the type of ownership, size of residence, degree of privacy, and types of conveniences desired. These are urgent issues that require thorough research and study, because the housing decision is at the very heart of any financial retirement plan. This chapter provides information that can help you make important decisions regarding your housing during retirement.

YOUR HOUSING REQUIREMENTS

Before deciding on the type of retirement housing you desire and need, you should first review the specific characteristics you are seeking.

❑ **Size.** How many bedrooms do you need? If you have children or other family members who visit you periodically and stay for one or more days, you may require a second or third bedroom. Extra bedrooms generally require extra bathrooms. Also, do you periodically entertain family or friends in a formal setting, and therefore need a dining room?

❑ **Layout.** Should you seek a home that is all on one floor, thus avoiding the need for walking up and down stairs? Do you or your spouse have any ailments that require your living on one level? Generally, a single-level home is more desirable for retirees who are 65 or older.

❑ **Extras.** Do you favor a large kitchen with a great deal of counter space, or would you settle for a smaller kitchen? Is a garage or fireplace essential to your lifestyle?

❑ **Climate.** Northern states generally have very cold winters and heavy snows. People approaching retirement often dream of escaping such areas for regions of the Sunbelt such as Florida, southern California, or the southwestern states. But it is important to keep in mind that southern Florida and states bordering the Gulf Coast have very hot summers with extremely high humidity. To avoid exchanging one problematic climate for another, try living for a while in the state of your dreams before making your housing decision.

Self-Study 3.1 was designed to help you assess your housing needs.

YOUR SOCIAL NEEDS

The dwelling in which you are now living has given you community roots that developed over many years. Your home or apartment may be close to your children and grandchildren, as well as to your relatives, friends, and neighbors. Sickness or bereavement can highlight the importance of these associations. Moving more than 25 miles away from your present home will result in some loss of these close relationships, and moving even farther away can sever them completely. These personal associations represent a significant component of your housing requirements, and will have to be redeveloped if you choose to move to a new area. Some other requirements that affect housing decisions include those discussed below.

❑ **Professional services.** Over the years, you have probably developed associations with a family physician, a family dentist, an attorney, an accountant, a stock broker, and/or a banker. If you move, new relationships will have to be made with one or more of these professionals. This may be of particular concern if you have a physical ailment that requires a particular type of medical treatment.

❑ **Recreational facilities.** A neighborhood religious institution may provide recreational activities in addition to religious services. Such a center of activities may host lectures, concerts, and sports activities. Local libraries offer many intellectual activities. Are such facilities available in the new community? Do you participate in civic, social, or political groups in your present community?

SHOULD YOU MOVE OR STAY IN YOUR PRESENT HOUSING?

At the point of retirement, chances are that your children are on their own, and that the house or apartment that provided for everyone's needs is now too big. You and your spouse are probably overburdened with maintenance chores. On the other hand, you may like the community, have many friends, enjoy your neighbors, and be accustomed to the comforts that your dwelling provides. Take a close look at both your reasons for remaining in your present housing and your reasons for wanting to move.

Reasons for Staying in Your Present Housing

If you are a homeowner or renter, you may have the following reasons for remaining where you are:

❑ You enjoy the space and have room for visits from children, grandchildren, and friends who can stay overnight.

❑ You get along well with your neighbors and are involved in community activities.

❑ The neighborhood is still very nice since many of your friends and neighbors remain.

❏ Shopping and medical facilities are conveniently located.

❏ Your home or apartment is exactly the way you want it. The furniture fits in just right, and you can avoid the trauma of a move.

❏ The happy events you enjoyed in your home make for pleasant memories.

A homeowner has additional considerations:

❏ You have probably paid off the mortgage and can afford to maintain your home on your anticipated fixed income.

❏ If you ever need money, you can borrow against the equity in your home.

Reasons for Moving

If you are a homeowner or renter, you may have the following reasons for wanting to move:

❏ Your house or apartment is too big and is hard to keep clean.

❏ The neighborhood is changing, and many of your friends and neighbors have moved.

❏ Your children have moved to distant states and visit infrequently.

❏ You live far from shopping and medical facilities.

A homeowner has additional considerations:

❏ Maintenance is a problem. Cutting the grass and snow removal are becoming harder, and hired help is expensive.

❏ Taxes, the cost of utilities, and the cost of repairs keep rising every year. These and other expenses may become more than you can afford.

❏ Stairs are becoming a problem.

❏ If you sell, according to the Taxpayer Relief Act of 1997, you can enjoy a tax-free profit of $250,000 for individuals or $500,000 for couples, as long as you have lived in your home for at least two of the last five years. This tax break is available to you regardless of your age. Details can be found in the IRS publication *Older American's Tax Guide,* Publication Number 554. Order a copy by calling the IRS toll-free, or download it from the IRS website. (See the Resources section.)

SHOULD YOU OWN OR RENT?

If you decide to move elsewhere, you must next choose between owning and renting. Living in a mortgage-free home is cheaper than paying rent in most parts of the country. Against this, you have to consider the gain of the interest or dividends you would earn if you sold your home and invested the proceeds.

The Advantages of Owning

The advantages of owning your own home are the following:

❏ You are not subject to the terms of a lease, and are free to do as you wish.

❏ Home ownership is a sound investment.

❏ You enjoy pride in ownership.

❏ Your living situation is more permanent.

❏ Interest paid on your mortgage loan is tax-deductible.

❏ Property taxes paid are tax-deductible.

The Disadvantages of Owning

The disadvantages of owning your own home are the following:

❏ You have the responsibility for maintenance.

❏ Capital that is tied up in your home can earn a greater return elsewhere.

❏ Owning a home is a long-term commitment.

❏ You always face the potential deterioration of your neighborhood.

The Advantages of Renting

Among the advantages of renting are the following:

❏ The landlord or owner is responsible for maintenance.

❏ Exterior chores, such as cutting the grass and snow removal, are handled by paid staff or by the landlord himself.

❏ You know the monthly rent, and know whether you can handle it without too much difficulty.

❏ You have the freedom to travel or to move—if not bound by a long-term lease.

The Disadvantages of Renting

The disadvantages of renting are the following:

❏ You build up no equity.

❏ There is no possibility of long-term capital gain.

❏ A lease limits your freedom of action.

❏ Your lease may not be renewed.

❏ Rents can be raised to meet inflationary pressures.

❏ There is always the possibility that your structure may be converted into a cooperative or a condominium.

IF YOU STAY IN YOUR PRESENT HOME

If you are a homeowner, it probably makes sense to stay in your present dwelling during your retirement years, as your home is an important part of your life and reflects your style of living. But even if you have decided to remain where you are, you should evaluate your home in terms of future needs and, if necessary, prepare it for this time of your life. Does your home provide the facilities you will need to do all that you plan to do during your retirement? For example, does it provide individual space for you and your spouse in which to relax or study and to pursue separate hobbies and interests? Some useful changes may include the following:

❏ **Remodeling.** You may wish to add a bathroom on the main floor to eliminate the need for using stairs. Or you may wish to make a major room addition, such as an extra bedroom or den that may be used as a study or hobby room. Such changes can be expensive, but moving costs and refurnishing costs are also high. Money can be saved by replacing a bed with a sofa-sleeper, thus converting a spare bedroom into a study or some other type of room.

❏ **Safety improvements.** Older individuals are particularly prone to disabling accidents in the home. Many of these accidents can be avoided if proper precautions are taken. For example, you can add nonslip surfaces to walkways, driveways, and bathrooms; provide handgrips in bathrooms and bathtubs; install adequate lighting in hallways and stairwells; and add nonskid rubber underliners to rugs and carpets.

❏ **Convenience improvements.** Some renovations can eliminate many maintenance burdens. By making these improvements before you retire, you will provide yourself with more time to do the things that you prefer, save money when your income is fixed and/or limited, and free yourself from tasks that you may not be physically able to perform. For example, aluminum or vinyl siding on your exterior walls will eliminate the need for periodic painting; paneling some interior walls will save on painting; tiling or other floor coverings will make for easier care; rearrangement of utilities in the kitchen and laundry room will save steps; and adding a deck or patio can cut down or eliminate the need for lawn mowing.

❏ **Creating an additional source of income.** Adding a small kitchen and bathroom to a basement or spare room in your home can produce a rental unit that provides a source of income. Rental income can at least pay for monthly maintenance costs and help meet mortgage payments. A renter may offer companionship, or perhaps serve as a house sitter when you're away. Such a change in your home will require approval of your local zoning authority. (In some locales, adding a "kitchen" that does not have a stove removes the two-family label that necessitates zoning approval.)

There are a number of ways in which you can finance any renovations or changes you make in your home. Chief among these is tapping your home equity. Self-Study 3.2 can help you as you plan your home improvements.

TAPPING YOUR HOME EQUITY

Many retired homeowners find themselves in a cash bind each month. The value of their homes has grown, but inflation has reduced the buying power of their pensions. To compound the problem, many retirees cannot sell their houses because affordable alternative housing is not available. A number of options can provide such individuals with a monthly income from property.

A Home Equity Loan

You can tap the equity in your home by signing up for a *home equity loan* that, when approved by your bank, enables you to borrow money as you need it by writing a check or using a credit card. Such a loan should be used only for special needs, such as home improvements, tuition costs, or medical bills—not for buying an auto or paying for a vacation. Failure to make payments on a home equity loan can result in the loss of your home, the collateral that enabled you to make the loan.

If you do decide to apply for a home equity loan, consider the following tips:

❏ **Compare loan offers.** Obtain at least three equity loan offers, and carefully compare the details of each before choosing a lender. You can find many offers on the Internet. Just choose a search engine and type in "'home equity loan."

❏ **Evaluate the list of charges.** The interest charge is the largest, but lenders usually include a number of other charges, such as an application fee, points, and closing costs. Some lenders levy an up-front processing fee of up to $2,000. Ask each potential lender for a list of all charges.

❏ **Make sure that the interest is tied to an accepted index.** In an adjustable rate loan, be sure that interest rate adjustments over time are pegged to one of the accepted common indexes, such as one-year, three-year, or five-year United States Treasury issues. Avoid lenders who peg interest rates to their own internal prime rates.

❏ **Require fixed contract terms.** Contract terms regarding issues other than interest should be fixed and unchangeable. Be sure that the lender does not have the power to change the contract at his own discretion.

❏ **Look for an interest rate cap.** Interest levels on adjustable rate loans can rise to over 15 percent. Seek a home equity loan contract that specifies an interest cap or maximum. Also be sure that there is no "'floor'"—a limit of how low the interest rate can drop.

❏ **Consider a fixed rate loan.** While many lenders favor adjustable rate loans, others offer fixed-rate loans, which means that the interest rate cannot rise or fall over the term of the loan. Depending on fluctuations in interest rates, the fixed rate loan may be more cost-effective over the long run.

❏ **Be sure the loan can be amortized.** Avoid a home equity loan on which you are required to repay interest only, with no amortization (liquidation) of the principal. Under these terms, after a certain period, a large lump sum, or balloon payment, is required. In some cases, a balloon payment can be advantageous. This kind of mortgage permits older people to buy an apartment and make relatively low-interest payments during their lifetime. The heirs then pay the large lump sum after the sale of the apartment. However, many people prefer loans that can be repaid on a regular periodic—usually monthly—basis.

❏ **Check the affordability of loan payments.** Be sure you can afford to repay the monthly interest and amortization specified in the contract. The monthly repayment for all your outstanding loans should not exceed 35 percent of your gross income.

❏ **Seek professional review of the contract.** Before signing a home equity loan contract, have it checked by your accountant or tax attorney. While interest payments on home equity loans may be fully tax-deductible, you should consult a professional before signing on the dotted line.

❏ **Limit withdrawals.** Withdraw from your line of credit only what you need for major, neces-sary expenditures, such as home improvements, college tuition, and medical bills. Avoid using your loan for buying food, clothing, or vacations.

A Reverse Mortgage

The concept of the *reverse mortgage* was approved by the Federal Home Loan Bank Board in December 1978. To understand how a reverse mortgage works, consider the following scenario.

Assume that the market value of a home is $150,000, and that the retirees who own it—a couple in their 70s—need additional income. They approach a savings and loan bank and present their case. The bank then offers to lend them up to 80 percent of the home's current value, or up to $120,000. The bank will then use the money to purchase an annuity that, for this couple, will pay about $14,000 a year. The bank subtracts the interest charge from this amount, and pays the remainder to the couple in monthly checks. These checks will continue to be paid as long as either of the retirees lives. After both have passed away, the home will be sold. Out of the proceeds, the loan from the bank will be repaid and the balance will go to the estate of the deceased.

Sale Leaseback

Under the *sale leaseback* arrangement, the homeowner sells his or her house in exchange for lifetime tenancy and a guaranteed monthly income. An investor buys the home at a discount that can range from 20 percent to 35 percent under the market value. For instance, a 73-year-old man might sell his $150,000 house for $112,500, a 25-percent or $37,500 discount. The investor pays the homeowner a cash-down payment of 10 percent of the purchase price—in this case, $11,250. The homeowner and the investor reach an agreement as to a reasonable rent to be paid by the homeowner—for example, $550 a month. The investor pays all taxes, insurance, and maintenance costs, as well as regular monthly payments to the homeowner—for example, $875 a month—over a period of 10 or 15 years. The investor must also purchase a lifetime annuity to take over when his liability ends, that is, when he has completed his payments for the home.

The homeowner is taken care of by the down payment of $11,250; by the investor's continuing $875 monthly payments; and, ultimately, by the lifelong annuity payments. Moreover, this retiree has a monthly net income of $325 ($875 minus $550). The retiree can continue to live in the home for life at the established rent. The benefits to the investor are notable, too. He has purchased a home at a 25-percent discount; he has a regular monthly rental income; and he will probably realize a significant capital gain after the seller has passed away or decided to move.

A Charitable Remainder Trust

In this case, the property is donated to a worthwhile institution in exchange for a lifetime annuity and the privilege of remaining in the home for life. (For further details, see page 282.)

IF YOU DECIDE TO MOVE

If you decide to move from your present home, it makes good sense to analyze and evaluate the advantages and disadvantages of the alternative types of housing available. You should also compare housing costs and the suitability of the new location before you sever your ties with your present location. (Self-Study 3.3 will help you compare the cost of your present housing with that of other housing options.)

Buying or selling a home or leasing an apartment or a house have both legal and eco-nomic implications. Be sure to consult a lawyer before signing any documents relating to any of these major transactions. An accountant and/or investment adviser should be consulted prior to undertaking any negotiations involving a large sum of money.

Selling Your Present Home

You can sell your home through a licensed real estate agent, or you can sell it on your own. At some stage, you will need a lawyer for the closing, particularly if you are working with an agent. If you decide to sell your house on your own, you will need a lawyer at the outset. As a seller, you have certain legal obligations and financial liabilities. No standard printed sales contract fits every situation. Every property sale is unique and requires a contract that is drawn to suit the particular situation.

If you select a real estate agent to sell your house, you can offer an *exclusive listing*—an agreement that gives one real estate agent the right to sell the property for a specified period of time, but does not restrict the right of the owner to sell the property on his or her own without payment of a commission. An agent can also have an *exclusive right-to-sell listing*—a written agreement that gives a real estate agent the exclusive right to sell, and entitles him or her to a commission regardless of who sells the property during the period of the agreement. Or you can use the brokers' *central listing service*. Also called a *multiple listing service,* this service advises the realtors in your area that your house is on the market, but awards a percentage of the commission to the listing realtor regardless of who makes the actual sale.

Selling property involves a number of legal documents, agreements, and tax liabilities. A qualified lawyer can help you avoid mistakes and realize the maximum return.

Economic Considerations

The market is not always advantageous for selling or for buying. The ups and downs of the economy bring with it inflation on one hand and recession and unemployment on the other. For instance, the record-high mortgage rates that were offered from 1979 to 1983 made buying and selling difficult. Yet the real estate industry did make adjustments. In some of the new types of mortgages, interest rates rise and fall with changes in the money market.

Tax Implications

As explained earlier in the chapter, anyone, regardless of age, can enjoy a tax-free profit of $250,000 to $500,000 on the sale of a house or condominium. (See page 43 for further details.)

There are also tax implications when you move to another state. Some retirees choose to relocate to Sunbelt states, such as Arizona, Florida, Nevada, or Texas, to enjoy warm winter temperatures and possibly lower taxes. If you are considering a move to one of these states or to any other state, you should be aware of the tax implications. If you do not plan carefully, you may find that you owe taxes in two states at the same time. This involves the concept of *domicile*, which refers to the state in which you have established permanent (legal) residence and intend to remain.

Most state laws specify the number of days you must live in the state in order to be a legal resident. In New York and New Jersey, for example, you are considered a legal resident if you maintain residence in the state and spend more than 183 days a year there. As a resident, you are responsible for paying the state's taxes, including the personal income tax. If your new state has a personal income tax, you must file a tax return there even though you may be eligible for a credit from one of the two states.

Any out-of-state real estate and personal property you own, such as a home, jewelry, or works of art, are generally subject to estate and/or inheritance taxes in the state in which the property is located. If you maintain residences in two states, then your estate must pay estate and/or inheritance taxes in both states because you are a legal resident in both.

If you plan to relocate, the following tips may prove helpful:

❑ **File a declaration of nondomicile.** To make sure your former state knows you are relocating, file a declaration of nondomicile with your last state income tax return. If such a form is not available in your former state, attach a statement announcing your move when you file your next tax return.

❑ **Establish domicile in your new state.** To become a legal resident in your new state, file a statement of domicile with the clerk of the circuit court in your new county. You should also change your auto registration, driver's license, bank accounts, and voter registration. It is important also to draw up a new will, not only to conform with the community property rules of some states, but also to declare that you are a legal resident of the new state.

❑ **Sell your old home.** If you are certain that you will remain in the new state and do not wish to maintain two homes, it would be wise to sell your old home, thus confirming your decision to establish a legal residence in your new state.

❑ **Maintain careful records if you retain two homes.** If you retain your old home and establish domicile in another state, you must keep careful records showing that you do not spend more days in your old home than specified by your former state's laws on legal residency. If you become subject to an income tax audit, the burden of proof as to where you legally reside will be yours.

❏ **Roll over capital gains within two years.** If you sell your principal residence in your former state, you have two years to roll over any capital gains into a new primary home, or you must pay income taxes on the capital gain.

❏ **Profit from the $250,00-to-$500,00 exclusion from federal tax.** As previously explained, upon the sale of a house or condominium, a single person can enjoy a tax-free profit of $250,000, and a couple, $500,000.

Buying a Smaller Home

Prior to their retirement, many people buy a relatively small home that they use for their vacations. Sometimes, such a second home is in a quieter, more rural area. While working, the people pay off the mortgage, and at the time of retirement, the smaller home is available as a primary residence. The people like the smaller home; are familiar with the area; and, over the years, have developed good relationships with their neighbors. When they retire, they can rent their old house rather than sell it, and use the rental income to supplement their pension and Social Security income; or they can sell the larger residence and invest the profits.

This may be ideal for some people, but others—although they may have chosen a secluded area for their vacation spot—want to live closer to the central city with more people around and with urban cultural and recreational activities readily available.

In any case, if your present home is too large, a smaller home offers many advantages:

❏ A smaller home costs less than your present home.

❏ Surplus capital from the sale of your larger house can be invested.

❏ A bank will grant a mortgage loan if you need one.

❏ Cleaning chores are reduced.

❏ Lawn cutting and snow shoveling are reduced.

❏ You retain the privacy and comfort of owning your own home.

❏ Home ownership is a good investment.

❏ You can choose your ideal location.

The disadvantages of a smaller house are the following:

❏ Your home still requires cleaning and upkeep.

❏ Your home still requires exterior and interior maintenance.

❏ The house ties up a portion of your investment capital.

❏ Appreciation in value may be less rapid than you anticipated.

❏ Living quarters may be more cramped than you had expected.

Legal Considerations

Buying a home or condominium involves several transactions, each of which requires an agreement in writing. If your interests are not properly protected, you may suffer significant financial loss and frustration.

First, an offer to buy is usually made in writing and includes a deposit or binder. This sales agreement indicates under what conditions the deposit will be returned if the purchase is not consummated; the purchase price; a legal description of the property; and fees and taxes to be paid.

Second, the purchase may involve a mortgage in which the inclusion or omission of a few significant clauses can cost you a large sum of money before you pay it off. For example, is the interest rate fixed or is it flexible to reflect the changing cost of mortgage funds? Is there a penalty for prepayment? These and other contract terms involve thousands of dollars.

Third, taking title to your home is more than the mere transfer of ownership. The type of property ownership, as detailed in Chapter 5, could have a significant impact on estate planning. This stage of the transaction also requires a *title search*—that is, checking conditions that may affect your ownership, as well as other legal details, such as title insurance.

Finally, a purchaser of property may also be party to an escrow agreement, which sets forth the conditions that must be fulfilled before any money, held by a third party, can be paid. It is important that the interests of the buyer be protected.

Renting an Apartment

Renting an apartment is another alternative. By living in a rented apartment, you can enjoy a relatively carefree lifestyle. This is especially desirable for people who enjoy traveling and do not wish to be burdened with the responsibilities of home maintenance.

The federal government sponsors subsidized or public housing projects for older people. Rents in these developments are set on a sliding scale based on income. People 62 or older and handicapped people can qualify for a federal rent subsidy in nonprofit housing projects built under this program.

People planning to retire whose incomes are moderate, but too high for public housing, should consider rental housing for people over 62 sponsored by nonprofit groups and financed with low-interest government mortgages.

The advantages of apartment renting are the following:

❏ Monthly rent is fixed for the duration of the lease.

❏ Maintenance costs are included in the rent.

❏ Lawn care and snow removal services are provided.

❏ You can enjoy the freedom to move or to travel.

❏ Renting requires a minimal financial investment, permitting more favorable investments of your capital.

❏ The trouble and expense of selling are eliminated.

❏ Renting may include recreational facilities at no additional cost.

The disadvantages of apartment renting are the following:

❏ Renting generally provides less space than owning.

❏ The landlord has the right to evict a tenant under certain conditions.

❏ The landlord may choose not to renew a lease if he wishes to convert to cooperatives or condominiums.

❏ The tenant builds up no equity and merely collects rent receipts.

❏ The tenant enjoys no income tax savings.

❏ A portion of the rent includes vacancy costs and landlord profit.

❏ The lease usually restricts tenant activities, such as ownership of pets.

❏ The monthly rent may include extra charges for garage space or air conditioning units.

Legal Considerations

Many leases are written in archaic legalese, and say things in two or three ways. However, the average person can read a lease and understand it. If you do not understand something, ask the landlord or property manager to explain it. If you still have doubts, by all means, ask a lawyer to go over the lease with you. The fee will be small.

Although most leases are written contracts, the simplest kind of lease is an oral agreement. You rent by the month, and either you or the landlord can terminate the contract by giving thirty days' notice. To be safe, put your notification in writing.

For any lease, whether oral or written, you should check the following points:

❏ **Term of the lease.** Leases usually run for a year or more.

❏ **Expiration clause.** You may be able to remain on a month-to-month basis. Or the lease can be automatically renewed for another term.

❏ **Move-out notice.** This clause specifies the number of days you must give as notice before moving out. The landlord may be subject to a similar requirement.

❏ **Legal notice of rent increase, change in lease terms, or eviction.** Do not waive your right requiring legal notification of rent increase, change in lease terms, or eviction.

❏ **Children and/or pets.** Lease terms state whether you may have children and/or pets in the unit.

Other clauses in a lease that may restrict you include such points as the following: a cost-escalator clause by which the rent can be increased as maintenance costs and taxes rise; a clause specifying the penalty for late rent payment; rules regarding the subletting of your quarters and/or the maintenance of appliances; and a schedule of repainting. Make sure that the lease you sign contains provisions you can accept.

Buying a Condominium

"Condominium" was a strange-sounding word twenty years ago, but today, the concept has spread into every aspect of real estate. What is a condominium? A *condominium* is a legal plan of ownership in which you buy and own your house or apartment, and have joint ownership of any common facilities, such as grounds, hallways, elevators, and recreational areas. For use of the facilities, you pay a monthly maintenance fee. You can purchase this home by making a down payment and borrowing the rest of the cost from a lending institution in the form of a mortgage.

Increasingly, people are choosing to live in condominiums rather than in one-family detached homes or rentals. American Community Bankers estimated that there were about 85,000 condos in the United States in 1970. Today, there are approximately 5,300,000 condos in the United States. About 24 percent of these are headed by individuals of age 65 or older.

One of the most significant attractions for the individual or couple contemplating the purchase of a condominium is the cost-saving potential. The large-scale construction of condominium complexes with shared roofs, walls, and heating facilities reduces unit costs. Condominium units, therefore, sell for 10 to 12 percent less than equivalent single-family homes. For this reason, condominiums account for about 25 percent of all homes purchased, up from only 11 percent in 1979.

Owning a condominium has both advantages and disadvantages. The advantages of condominium living are the following:

❑ It is usually a safe investment against inflation.

❑ Monthly mortgage payments will build up equity.

❑ Condominium ownership provides income tax savings, as mortgage interest and real estate taxes are income tax deductions.

❑ You enjoy the freedom to change your property as you wish.

❑ Exterior property maintenance is provided.

❑ Monthly costs are not related to a landlord's overhead and profit.

❑ Policies are set by the owners' association, in which you have a vote.

The disadvantages of condominium living are the following:

❑ Buying a condominium requires a significant down payment, with the potential loss of income from more favorable investment alternatives.

❑ The collective judgment of the owners may not yield the wisest operating decisions.

❑ The monthly maintenance fee may be increased to keep pace with inflation and/or poor management.

❑ The time and costs involved in selling are the same as those associated with home ownership.

❑ The structure or complex may be overcrowded, with a consequent loss of privacy.

❑ The different lifestyles and interests of your immediate neighbors may be displeasing.

Legal Considerations

As with the purchase of a house, your interests should be properly protected to avoid financial loss and frustration. The transactions involved in buying a condominium are the same as those for buying a house. Please see page 42 for specific information.

Buying a Cooperative

A *cooperative*, or *co-op*, is a legal plan of ownership in which you buy shares not in the living space itself, but in the corporation that owns the land and the entire structure or complex. You cannot get a mortgage, but may get a loan to purchase the shares. This obviously differs from a condominium. If you leave the cooperative, you sell your shares, either to the corporation or directly to the new shareholder, as required by the bylaws. The corporation is composed of the inhabitants of the building, who together share the responsibility of overall management. The amount of your monthly maintenance fee depends on the size of your dwelling, which may be an apartment, a row house, or an individual home.

The bylaws of a cooperative may give the board of directors the authority to approve or disapprove the buyer of a particular share or dwelling unit. Cooperatives exist almost exclusively in urban areas.

The advantages of cooperative living are the following:

❑ Co-ops are usually located in the best areas of cities.

❑ Co-op membership motivates pride of ownership.

❑ Shareholders have a vote in setting management policies.

❑ Co-ops offer an opportunity for capital gain.

The disadvantages of cooperative living are the following:

❏ Some co-ops are overcrowded, resulting in loss of privacy.

❏ The bylaws of some co-ops, set by members of the association, do not allow children or pets.

❏ Decisions on interior and exterior painting are controlled by the board of directors, resulting in loss of control by a co-op shareholder.

❏ Inept management can result in rising monthly maintenance costs.

Buying a Mobile Home

A *mobile home* is a factory-manufactured housing unit that is transported on wheels from the factory where it was built to a more-or-less permanent site. There, the wheels are removed and the unit is set upon a permanent foundation of concrete blocks or poured concrete.

Mobile homes are reasonably priced. On a per-square-foot basis, the highest-quality mobile home costs about half the price of a traditional home. This includes only the cost of the house. After buying the house, you have to locate a mobile home park where a vacancy exists, and then either buy or rent a site. A mobile home park contains dozens of units that share a certain look-alike appearance.

A mobile home offers a unique opportunity for a retired couple to own a low-cost housing unit and settle in a community with other retired people who have chosen a similar lifestyle. Residents often have access to a recreation building that contains a swimming pool, sauna, gymnasium, music room, club room, and auditorium.

The advantages of a mobile home are the following:

❏ The cost of a mobile home on a per-square-foot basis is half or less than half of the cost of a traditional home. (This excludes the land, which is a costly component if purchased.)

❏ A mobile home is frequently taxed as personal property—which is a low tax—whereas a regular home is taxed as real property.

❏ Mobile home parks generally offer outstanding social and recreational opportunities.

❏ Occupants are usually of similar age and financial position.

❏ Maintenance costs are low.

❏ Occupants have the opportunity to live in resort areas without making a large investment.

The disadvantages of a mobile home are the following:

❏ The opportunity for appreciation in land value is less in a mobile home park, where the land is usually rented.

❏ As a mobile home becomes older, the costs of repair and maintenance increase.

❏ The value of the mobile home itself tends to fluctuate. Some homes have depreciated in value.

❏ While monthly rents in a mobile home park are cheaper than renting a traditional home, rents do go up, and often quite rapidly.

❏ After a few years, some owners no longer enjoy the lifestyle, but find it too costly to make a change.

❏ It is costly to move a mobile home.

❏ Mortgage institutions may not be willing to offer a loan for the purchase of a used mobile home.

OTHER HOUSING ARRANGEMENTS

Individuals who are seeking to lighten the chores of daily living should consider two housing options not previously discussed. They can ask someone to live with them, or they can move in with others.

Asking Someone to Live With You

How times have changed! When America had a rural economy, it was very common to find three generations of a family living together under one roof. Each member of the family had specific chores to perform to keep the farm functioning. The farm house was spacious, and as parents became older, the chores they performed changed, but living space was always available for them.

Today, in our urbanized economy and with the mobility that characterizes our society, many young couples buy a house, live in it for a while, find jobs in other places, sell the house, and buy another. If generations lived together, it would restrict both mobility and easy turnover of housing. Older parents, for the most part, are on their own. The children grow up and make their own lives, leaving an empty nest.

In some cases, however, a satisfying living arrangement can be achieved by an older person asking a friend or relative to live with him or her to provide companionship and/or assistance with day-to-day chores. If you choose this option, a formal agreement in writing that sets forth specific financial arrangements should be considered. The agreement should be prepared by a lawyer. In appreciation, you may wish to leave such an individual or individuals some portion of your estate. If a bequest is to be made, it should be included in your will.

In many cases, the individual involved may be a son or a daughter, making it seem inappropriate to discuss financial arrangements. Such a situation, however, may create many subsequent problems when an estate is divided up among survivors. For example, the offspring who as-

sumed the responsibilities associated with living with an elderly parent may feel that he or she is entitled to a larger share of the estate. If you ask someone to live with you, you should address the issue of the disposition of individual and/or joint assets in case of death.

Living With Others

Still another arrangement involves an older person moving in with his or her children or with other younger relatives. Often, this is done for companionship. In other cases, the older person may have health or financial problems that make the new arrangement advantageous. Both generations can benefit from such a relationship.

In other cases, several unrelated older adults may decide to share a household, thus pooling their financial resources. In this arrangement, each adult may have his or her own bedroom, but share the kitchen and other common areas. Each individual should carefully evaluate whether this option is best, since it may not be a suitable arrangement for everyone. You may wish to move in together on a trial basis before making a final decision.

The advantages of moving in with others are the following:

❑ All parties in the relationship enjoy companionship.

❑ Living with others offers a degree of security.

❑ The arrangement is less expensive than owning a home or renting an apartment alone.

❑ House maintenance chores are shared.

❑ You are free to take periodic vacations without having to close the house.

❑ It is convenient and reassuring to have someone nearby in case of illness.

The disadvantages of moving in with others are the following:

❏ You give up your personal privacy.

❏ Living with another individual or family may bring differences to the forefront.

❏ The feeling of independence is lost in such a relationship.

❏ A disruption in lifestyle may occur because of a feeling of responsibility for another individual.

Other Options

As people age, they often seek housing options that will not only reduce the responsibilities of home maintenance, but also provide them with assistance in the tasks of daily living. To meet these needs, a variety of residences and communities geared specifically for retirees have been designed. These options are discussed in Chapter 4.

OF SPECIAL INTEREST TO WOMEN

When couples plan for retirement, it is important that they sit down together and decide on the type of housing that would best suit their needs. That's a good starting point. But then, women must project beyond the immediate decision. Remember that about 50 percent of all women 65 or older in the United States are widows, and, in general, about 85 percent of women die as singles.

If the husband dies and the widow lives in the family home alone, the housing issue arises again. With both children and husband gone, the house may simply seem too large and too expensive to maintain. Fortunately, under the terms of the Taxpayer Relief Act of 1997, profits from the sale of a principal residence are not subject to taxation unless they exceed $250,000

for an individual, provided that the widow has lived in the house for at least two of the last five years. A divorced woman is entitled to the same exemption.

RETIREMENT HAVENS ABROAD

Although individuals at all income levels *think* about retiring to a country outside of the United States, they may not consider it seriously. However, individuals with limited incomes may be surprised to discover that some retirement havens abroad offer gracious living in beautiful surroundings even for those on a meager budget. And retirees with higher incomes can live regally in some of these retirement Edens. The decision to start a new life in another part of the world should not be made hastily, but should be based on careful research and planning. Self-Study 3.4 lists the wide range of factors you should consider when making this decision.

Of course, no place in the world is perfect in every respect. But some locations offer natural beauty, a climate that is comfortable year-round, and, most important, a significantly higher level of living than a limited income can buy in the United States. Retirement Edens at bargain prices can be found in many countries, including Costa Rica, Greece, Italy, Mexico, Portugal, and Spain.

A few examples will show you just how affordable the good life can be in certain areas of the world—and how popular these areas have become with American retirees. For instance, retirees have become an ever-growing segment of the population in Mexico, where over 50,000 Americans enjoy an ideal year-round climate. Most American expatriates choose one of three areas: Guadalajara (Las Puentes, Chapalita, Ciudad Buganvilias, and Rancho Alegre); Lake Chapala (the villages of Chapala, Chula Vista, and Ajijic); and San Miguel de Allende, a university town with a high concentration of writers and artisans. In these areas, $800 a month will provide a couple with a two-bedroom house, ample and delicious food, and full-time help. Any money left over can be used for travel and entertainment, including trips back to the United States for visits with family and friends. An annual income of only $15,000 to $20,000 can provide a comfortable life.

About 8,000 more Social Security recipients live in Spain, with a large number of them residing in Costa Del Sol—the Sun Coast—overlooking the blue Mediterranean. The principal towns there include Malaga, Benalmadena, Torremolinos, Fuengirola, and Marbella. In these beautiful areas, a couple can live well for about $2,000 a month, which includes the cost of domestic help.

The Social Security Administration mails 396,482 monthly checks to retirees who live in foreign countries, a fact that demonstrates the large number of Americans who have chosen to spend their retirement years abroad. If this option interests you, contact the embassy of the country in which you're interested, and you will receive a wealth of information.

The advantages of retirement abroad include the following:

❏ You will continue to receive Social Security checks while you live abroad.

❏ In many countries, you can enjoy a fuller lifestyle on a limited budget.

❏ You can experience amenities of life not available to you in the United States because of cost.

❏ Some of the low-cost-of-living countries offer an ideal year-round climate in beautiful surroundings.

❏ You may fulfill a wish to return to your family's roots.

The disadvantages of retirement abroad are the following:

❏ Medicare coverage ends if you live outside the United States.

❏ You may lose contact with your family and friends.

❏ A poor choice of location can prove both expensive and time-consuming to remedy.

❏ You may not have access to the same level of medical competence available in the United States.

If you plan to retire abroad, the tips given below may prove helpful.

❏ Before you make a final decision to move to a foreign retirement haven, take a couple of vacations there, or perhaps spend a winter or summer season as a visitor.

❏ Don't burn your bridges. Try the new living arrangements for a year or two before you abandon your ties to your old neighborhood. You can rent your present home for the time you're away.

❏ Carefully consider the state of your health and your need for specialized medical and/or hospital services.

❏ Carefully evaluate all the features and characteristics of a retirement haven using Self-Study 3.4 as a guide.

❏ If you've made the move and find you've made a mistake, remember that the decision is not irrevocable. Retrace your steps.

The decision regarding housing after retirement is a difficult one for many people. But if you make it with care, taking into consideration both your immediate needs and those that are likely to crop up in the future, you can insure a retirement that is both secure and satisfying.

Self-Study 3.1
PRIORITIZING YOUR HOUSING NEEDS

Check the characteristics of your retirement housing that you consider most important:

Number of bedrooms: _____   Number of bathrooms: _____

❑ Dining room   ❑ Modern appearance
❑ Living room   ❑ Terrace
❑ Den   ❑ Garage
❑ Eat-in kitchen   ❑ Single-level
❑ Fireplace   ❑ Hot climate
❑ Gardens and grounds   ❑ Cold climate

Check nonhousing requirements you consider important:

❑ Near a medical building   ❑ Steam room and sauna
  (doctors and dentists)   ❑ Library
❑ Near a general hospital   ❑ Churches and synagogues
❑ Recreational facilities   ❑ Commuting convenience
❑ Cultural facilities   ❑ Large complex
❑ Swimming pool   ❑ Younger families

Factors you should consider in your decision to move or stay in your present home:

_____   _____

_____   _____

_____   _____

_____   _____

_____   _____

Based on the above, should you move or stay in your present home?

_____

Self-Study 3.2
FINANCIAL DATA FOR MAKING CHANGES IN CURRENT HOUSING

1. If you are planning to stay in your present home at retirement, evaluate the home in terms of future needs. List the changes you would like to make and indicate the estimated cost for each change.

Change	Estimated Cost

2. Have you considered tapping into your home equity?   ❏ Yes   ❏ No

If yes, which option do you favor?

❏ Reverse mortgage

❏ Sale leaseback

❏ Charitable remainder trust

❏ Home equity loan

Make sure you get appropriate advice from your lawyer and/or accountant before deciding on which course of action to take.

Self-Study 3.3
COMPARATIVE HOUSING COSTS—
PRESENT HOUSING VS. RETIREMENT HOUSING

I. Before making a decision on retirement housing, it is wise to compare the costs of your present accommodations with the costs of a prospective new location. To assist you in making this analysis, a comparative housing cost worksheet is provided below. The worksheet is also useful in that it suggests ways of cutting costs in your present home.

	AVERAGE MONTHLY EXPENSES		
	Present housing	Retirement housing	
Cost item		Alternative A	Alternative B
Mortgage payment or rent	$ _____	$ _____	$ _____
Property taxes[1,2]	_____	_____	_____
Insurance on house[1,3]	_____	_____	_____
Fuel[1,4]	_____	_____	_____
Electricity[1]	_____	_____	_____
Gas[1]	_____	_____	_____
Water[1]	_____	_____	_____
Furnace maintenance[5]	_____	_____	_____
Repairs[6]	_____	_____	_____
Services[7]	_____	_____	_____
Painting	_____	_____	_____
Total	_____	_____	_____

[1] Total your annual expenses using your bills or check stubs, and divide the year's total by 12 to get your average monthly cost.

[2] If your county or town grants a property tax reduction for homeowners over 65, use your senior citizen tax rate to compare with retirement housing costs.

[3] Check to determine whether your home insurance premium can be reduced by switching to a different company, taking a policy for a longer period, combining coverages in a homeowner policy, or taking a larger deductible.

[4] Can you reduce fuel costs with more adequate insulation; storm doors and windows; weatherstripping of doors and windows; or a more efficient burner?

[5] Includes repairs, cleaning, and burner insurance.

[6] Includes repairs on roofing, gutters, leaders, plumbing, electrical, and windows.

[7] Includes cost of lawn service (seeding, fertilizing, pest control), lawn cutting, shrubs, lawn and shrubbery supplies, tools, and snow removal.

2. In addition to comparing alternative costs for retirement housing, you must also consider two related factors: furnishings and security.

Furnishings: Will your present furniture and furnishings fit into your retirement home?

❏ Yes   ❏ No

If no, estimate the cost for new furniture, new draperies, and carpeting in your retirement housing, using the following worksheet:

	Retirement housing	
Furnishings	**Alternative A**	**Alternative B**
Furniture	_____	_____
Draperies	_____	_____
Carpeting	_____	_____
Total	_____	_____

Security: The issue of personal security and safety must be taken into account in planning for retirement housing. Will the alternatives you are considering offer you the security you want, both in your housing unit and in the public areas outside your unit?   ❏ Yes   ❏ No

3. If you are planning to sell your home, list the names, addresses, and telephone numbers of three real estate firms in your community who can serve as your agent:

_____

_____

_____

4. List the locations you are considering for retirement housing and evaluate each in terms of advantages and disadvantages.

Location	Advantages	Disadvantages
_____	_____	_____
_____	_____	_____
_____	_____	_____
_____	_____	_____

5. To arrange for your retirement housing, will you be involved in buying or selling a home, leasing an apartment or a house, or entering a care facility?   ❏ Yes   ❏ No

If yes, discuss your plans with your lawyer.

Self-Study 3.4
EVALUATING A RETIREMENT HAVEN ABROAD

Economic Considerations

1. What is the cost of living as compared with the United States?
2. What are the tax consequences of living in this foreign country?
3. Does the haven offer economic freedom to invest, buy and sell property, or set up a business?
4. What are the job opportunities in that country if you should decide to re-enter the labor force?
5. What types of housing are available and what are their costs?

Physical Aspects

6. What is the climate?
7. Do sanitation and water quality present problems?
8. Is the potential location accessible to an international airport?
9. What is the quantity and quality of roads, trains, and buses? Telephone and mail services?

Political Structure

10. Is the government stable, or is it subject to revolutionary upheavals?
11. What will be your legal status as a long-term resident?
12. Is your potential location subject to crime and violence?
13. As a foreign resident, can you enjoy personal and property safety?
14. Do the people there enjoy the freedoms of speech, press, religion, and assembly?

Amenities

15. What is the quantity and quality of the following facilities?
    ❑ Educational: schools and colleges ❑ Cultural and religious: museums, libraries, and houses of worship ❑ Entertainment: theaters and movies ❑ Recreational: sports stadium, television, radio, and nightclubs ❑ Shopping: specialty stores and department stores
16. What are the food and travel facilities like in this country, including restaurants, bars, and hotels?
17. Is there any language barrier?
18. Is the native population friendly?

Health Facilities

19. What is the level of medical, hospital, and dental services in terms of quality and cost? *Please note that Medicare benefits are not payable outside the United States.*
20. Are health facilities accessible to your potential location?
21. Are medical insurance policies available, and what are their costs?

Six Top Retirement Spots

While most people choose to spend their retirement years in the area they've known for years, some retirees search for a new location—perhaps one that offers a richer cultural atmosphere or more beautiful surroundings. With this in mind, in 2001, the editors of CNN and *Money Magazine* examined cities across America, comparing housing costs, tax rates, access to recreational facilities, and a variety of other features. They then pinpointed six American cities that are true standouts as retirement havens. Below, you'll find a thumbnail sketch of each of the winners.

Escondido, California. Like the other areas highlighted here, Escondido offers both natural beauty and cultural attractions. Residents can enjoy the serenity of mountains, deserts, and surf; explore the California Center for the Arts; or browse shops in the downtown area. And the cost of housing is low for Southern California. A three-bedroom home, for instance, is available for under $350,000.

Eugene, Oregon. Located two hours from Portland and an hour from the Pacific Ocean, Eugene, Oregon is surrounded by natural beauty—forests; wilderness inhabited by elk and other wildlife; and twenty-one state parks. And the city is as exhilarating as its surroundings, with a wealth of cultural amenities, including the Hult Center for the Performing Arts and the University of Oregon. As a bonus, housing costs are low in Eugene, with three-bedroom homes beginning under $250,000.

Hanover, New Hampshire. Boasting the cultural advantages of a college town, Hanover seems designed for the individual who wants an active retirement in a tranquil setting. Residents can take courses at the Institute for Lifelong Education at Dartmouth, hike the Appalachian Trail, or simply enjoy the charms of a tight-knit New England community. Although homes begin at $350,000, the town's offerings make it a great value.

Oxford, Mississippi. Combining the relaxed pace of the South with the amenities of a college town, Oxford has much to offer its residents. Retirees can take free courses at the University of Mississippi; stroll the beautifully restored downtown area; or enjoy Oxford's many recreational facilities, as well as the nearby 147,000-acre Holly Springs National Forest. Plus, housing costs are low, with three-bedroom homes available for under $200,000.

Seabrook and Edisto, South Carolina. Two islands off the coast of Charleston, South Carolina, Seabrook and Edisto offer both the warmth of Southern charm and the beauty of the sea. A gated community, Seabrook provides the amenities of a resort, while Edisto features simpler pleasures, such as local produce stands. Both are close to Charleston, a city with abundant cultural facilities. Predictably, housing costs are higher on Seabrook ($350,000 for a three-bedroom home) than on Edisto ($275,000 for a comparable residence).

Tucson, Arizona. Tucson may best be known for its stunning surroundings, which include the Sonoran Desert, the Santa Catalina Mountains, and the Saguaro National Park, which all offer abundant recreational facilities. But cultural resources also abound in the form of the Tucson Symphony, the Arizona Theater Company, and the Tucson Museum of Art. To top it off, housing costs are low; a three-bedroom house begins at $200,000.

RETIREMENT COMMUNITIES *and* CARE FACILITIES

When people reach age 60 or so, it is not uncommon for them to think about reducing home maintenance responsibilities. When the leaves pile up on the lawn and the snow piles up in the driveway, a retirement community is an attractive alternative.

Later, when retirees reach their 70s and 80s, independent living can become even more difficult. Often, an assisted living facility or, ultimately, a nursing home is able to provide the services that may be required at this time.

In response to the need for good retirement housing, a fourth type of retirement facility has evolved in recent years. The continuing care retirement community combines features of standard retirement communities, assisted living facilities, and nursing homes. Thus, retirees can enjoy the community when they are healthy and active, and can remain in the same community even if skilled nursing services become necessary.

RETIREMENT COMMUNITIES

A retirement community can provide secure and enjoyable accommodations for individuals who are capable of meeting their own basic needs. These communities give particular attention to the social and recreational requirements of the residents, rather than emphasizing medical needs. They also relieve the anxiety and frustration that may have previously existed by providing housekeeping services, including meals, and some medical assistance as required.

The types of retirement community housing available include single-family detached homes, duplexes, town houses, and high-rise buildings. Units can range in size from one to three bedrooms, and may be purchased or rented. Some retirement villages are sponsored by nonprofit organizations, such as churches, unions, fraternal societies, veterans' organizations, civic associations, and teachers' organizations. Others are sponsored by business corporations as investments.

Types of Services Offered

While retirement communities vary in terms of the services they offer, all communities provide security guards to give the residents peace of mind, and all provide a dining facility, a bed linen service, and a housekeeping service. Most communities include access to a shopping center, and many include medical facilities, as well. In addition, recreational facilities such as a golf course, swimming pool, library, club room, and auditorium may be available, and a variety of activities are planned by staff members to keep seniors busy and involved.

Costs

A retirement community usually charges a one-time entrance fee, sometimes referred to as a community fee, that ranges from $2,500 to $4,000. This fee is based on the size of the apartment, and varies from state to state due to differences in the cost of living.

In addition to the entrance fee, retirement communities charge a monthly fee that, for a single occupant, ranges from $3,000 to $4,000 for a one-bedroom unit, and from $4,000 to $5,000 for a two-bedroom unit. A second occupant adds another $500 to $600 a month to the fee. The monthly fee typically covers the services described above.

The Advantages and Disadvantages of a Retirement Community

A retirement community has many appealing features for the healthy and active retiree. The advantages of a retirement community include the following:

❑ It is a self-contained community that meets all your needs.

❑ Recreational and social facilities are usually excellent.

❑ Planned activities for the residents keep active seniors busy.

❑ Security guards protect entrances and grounds.

❑ Medical services may be available.

The disadvantages of a retirement community include the following:

❑ The initial entrance cost is high.

❑ The monthly maintenance fee is often high, and keeps rising.

❑ The lifestyle requires close living with neighbors.

❑ Social contacts limited to a small group may become confining.

❑ Because the location is usually isolated, you may miss the action of a big city.

❑ Some communities do not offer medical care.

ASSISTED LIVING FACILITIES

While new retirement communities may start out with a 60-plus population, the residents soon grow older, and when they reach the 70-to-80-plus bracket, their needs often change.

Assisted living facilities have been designed for people who are not completely able to live independently, and who may require some help with the *activities of daily living (ADLs)*—getting dressed and undressed, bathing, using the toilet, getting into or out of a bed or chair, and walking. In addition, these individuals may require reminders to take prescribed medication. However, they do not need the services of a nursing home. The American Seniors Housing Association in Fairfax, Virginia, reports that about 7,000 professionally run assisted living facilities operate nationwide, for a total of about 520,000 separate units.

Types of Services Offered

An assisted living facility offers rented rooms or

apartments in a structure where meals may be served in a dining room, and where housekeeping and personal services are available. The Marriott and Hyatt hotel chains are constructing this type of facility nationwide to operate like resort hotels. The assisted living facility provides a program of social and recreational activities, as well as security and medical services. A significant advantage of such a facility is the opportunity for its residents to enjoy social contact.

Costs

The one-time entrance fee for a typical assisted living facility is equal to one month's rent at that facility. For a single-occupant room or apartment, this monthly rental fee can range from $2,500 to $4,000. A second occupant adds another $500 to $600 a month.

In addition to the entrance fee and the monthly rent, the facility may charge a supplemental fee based on the services rendered that month. Depending on whether the assistance provided is considered minimum, moderate, or complete, this supplemental fee can range from $2,500 to $4,500 a month.

Advantages and Disadvantages of an Assisted Living Facility

An assisted living facility is an excellent solution for the person who requires some daily assistance, but does not need the level of care provided in a nursing home. The advantages of an assisted living facility include the following:

❑ Assistance is provided with the activities of daily living, such as dressing and bathing.

❑ Meal services are usually provided.

❑ Social and recreational activities keep active seniors involved.

❑ Security is provided.

The disadvantages of an assisted living facility include the following:

❑ Monthly rental fees are high.

❑ Because medical facilities are limited, as your health needs change, you may have to move to another type of facility.

❑ Social contacts are limited to a small group, and may become boring.

NURSING HOMES

When it is no longer possible for an individual to handle the activities of daily living, such as getting dressed and undressed and bathing, a nursing home is a possible solution. According to a 1999 Brown University study, one in two women and one in three men who reach advanced years will spend some time in a nursing home.

In nursing homes, registered nurses are on duty, and the patients are in hospital beds or wheelchairs. Some of the people who go to nursing homes are partially paralyzed as a result of strokes; some have no bowel or bladder control; and some require special care, such as medication or the changing of dressings. Their primary need is personal maintenance. Physical, occupational, and other therapies are provided to help restore the patient's health. Services are provided on a round-the-clock basis.

Anyone who has ever given the subject any thought probably has a preconceived notion about nursing homes. The stereotype, usually negative, pictures a place to locate the elderly when the family can no longer respond to the individual's needs, and the individual is unable to care for him- or herself. Surprisingly, a nursing home is not what most people envision. Such a facility is actually meant for people of all ages who are convalescents. Some of these people will recover completely and quickly, and some will need long-term care. Residents who require care for an acute illness or surgery are transferred to medical hospitals.

Types of Services Offered

Nursing homes provide a variety of services to patients requiring care, whether they are elderly or not. These include nursing care, personal care, and residential service.

❏ **Nursing care** requires the professional skill of a registered nurse or a licensed practical nurse. The nurse follows the instructions of the attending physician, and may be called upon to administer medications and injections. Additionally, the nursing home provides physical therapy, occupational therapy, dental services, dietary consultation, and X-ray services for post-hospital care of stroke, heart, or orthopedic cases. A pharmaceutical dispensary is usually available.

❏ **Personal care** provides a patient with help getting in and out of bed, bathing, dressing, eating, and walking. Attention is also given to special diets that are prescribed by the physician.

❏ **Residential service** means that a nursing home offers a secure environment in which the patient is comfortable, as well as a program that meets the individual's social and recreational needs. In some cases, religious services are also offered.

Costs

With all the services offered by a nursing home, costs are high. Nationwide, the average cost is about $50,000 a year, but costs vary widely. In New York City, for instance, a nursing home costs $250 or more a day—close to $100,000 a year.

Medicare covers one hundred days in a nursing facility, and pays all costs for all covered services for the first twenty days. As of 2002, individuals pay $101.50 in coinsurance each day for the twenty-first through the hundredth day of continuous confinement. After a hundred days, individuals must pay all the costs of their care. Medicaid coverage for skilled nursing facilities varies from state to state, and is only for the indigent. (For information on other types of available insurance coverage, see Chapter 17.)

Rights of Patients in Nursing Homes

The Omnibus Budget Reconciliation Act of 1987, signed into law by President Ronald Reagan on December 22, 1987, imposed dozens of rules for nursing homes that protect the rights of patients. The law also provides rules for home health agencies and guarantees home-care patients many of the same rights as nursing home residents, such as the right to be informed in advance of any treatment, the right to help plan their own care, and the right to voice grievances. Some of the most important requirements are the following:

❏ **Quality.** Nursing homes must maintain or enhance "the quality of life of each resident."

❏ **Evaluation.** At least once a year, nursing homes must conduct a comprehensive assessment of each patient's ability to perform such everyday activities as bathing, dressing, eating, and walking. Results of such assessments must then be used to prepare a written plan of care, which describes how the person's medical, psychological, and social needs will be met.

❏ **Screening.** A nursing home must not admit any patient who is mentally challenged unless a state agency first certifies that the person requires the type of care provided in a nursing home. The state agency must also determine whether the person needs "active treatment" for either mental illness or retardation.

❏ **Nurses.** A nursing home must have licensed nurses on duty around the clock, and must have a registered nurse on duty for at least eight hours a day, seven days a week. State officials may grant an exemption if the nursing home can show that it was unable to recruit the necessary personnel, and that the exemption will not endanger the health or safety of patients.

❏ **Training.** Every nurse's aide must receive at least seventy-five hours of training in nursing skills and residents' rights. Nursing homes are responsible for making sure that nurses' aides are competent to perform the tasks they are assigned.

❏ **Registry.** Each state must maintain a registry of people who have completed the training course for nurses' aides. If an aide is accused of neglecting or abusing patients or stealing their property, the state must investigate. If the charge is verified, the finding will be recorded in the registry. Nursing homes must check the registry before hiring nurse's aides.

❏ **Staff.** Any nursing home with more than 120 beds must have at least one full-time social worker with at least a bachelor's degree in social work or sufficient years of service to qualify for being "grandfathered" into the profession.

❏ **Transfers.** Nursing homes must ordinarily give thirty days' notice before discharging or transferring a patient. The patient may challenge such decisions by filing an appeal under procedures established by each state.

❏ **Access.** Residents of nursing homes must be granted the right to see family or officials if they so desire. Nursing homes must permit "immediate access" to any resident by relatives and by federal and state officials, including a specially designated ombudsman. Every state appoints an ombudsman to investigate complaints about

long-term care facilities. Patients, their relatives, and their lawyers may file complaints. To obtain an ombudsman, call your local senior citizens' hotline.

❏ **Penalties.** If a nursing home fails to meet federal standards, the government may deny payment under Medicare and Medicaid, and may appoint new managers to operate the facility. Payment must be withheld if the home is found to be substandard in three consecutive annual surveys.

The law protects more than 1.5 million people in 17,176 nursing homes that participate in Medicaid or Medicare. In addition, the law protects 2 million people who receive care in the home each year from 18,500 home health agencies and hospices paid by Medicare or Medicaid. The costs of compliance are shared by nursing homes, federal and state governments, and some patients. The overall purpose of the law is to help residents of nursing homes attain the highest level of physical, mental, psychological, and social well-being.

Advantages and Disadvantages of a Nursing Home

A nursing home can be an excellent choice, but it is important to realize that it has certain advantages and certain drawbacks. The advantages of a nursing home include the following:

❏ It provides housing as well as facilities for personal and medical care.

❏ An individual or a couple that requires personal and medical services can choose a nursing home most suitable to their needs.

❏ Many of these facilities are subsidized by the government.

The disadvantages of a nursing home include the following:

❏ Costs in a nursing home are high.

❏ It is difficult to locate the best possible facility.

CONTINUING CARE RETIREMENT COMMUNITIES

Another housing option for retirees—and one that has been attracting wide attention in recent years—is the *continuing care retirement community* (CCRC). Also known as life care communities, CCRCs combine elements of the three housing facilities discussed so far—retirement communities, assisted living facilities, and nursing homes. Many residents start out by living independently in an apartment or small house. Some of them maintain their own cars, and some even continue working. Then, as they age and require more help with the activities of daily living, the CCRC provides assisted living and, ultimately, skilled nursing care.

Many people prefer CCRCs over the other housing alternatives because when you join the CCRC, you move only once. Then, if and when assisted living care or skilled nursing care becomes necessary, the transition is easier because you remain in the same community. If a couple moves into a CCRC, and one spouse enters an assisted living facility or a nursing home, the other can continue to live independently and remain close enough for daily visits.

Types of Services Offered

Continuing care retirement communities offer a range of services to their members, including health care, personal care, and groundskeeping, to name just a few. Of course, these services vary from community to community. The following

list of services covered by the monthly fees of one CCRC provides an idea of what is generally offered.

❏ One meal per day served in a dining room or casual café.

❏ Housekeeping, including weekly light cleaning and bed linen service.

❏ Full home maintenance, inside and out.

❏ Lawn and landscaping services, and snow and leaf removal.

❏ Nursing care and assisted living care on the grounds of the community.

❏ Transportation in the form of scheduled routine trips to shopping areas, and to libraries, museums, and other cultural centers.

❏ Security personnel on a round-the-clock basis.

❏ Emergency response on a round-the-clock basis.

❏ Parking for both members and guests.

❏ Repair and replacement of provided appliances.

❏ Access to all recreational and community facilities, activities, and programs.

Costs

CCRC financial contracts vary, but essentially can be Extensive, Modified, or Fee-for-Service Agreements. Since the monthly fees charged by a CCRC vary according to the services provided, it is important to understand the three types of agreements that may be offered.

The *Extensive Agreement* includes housing and residential services, and also provides for prepayment of health-care expenses, similar to an insurance arrangement. Sometimes referred to as a *life care agreement,* it offers most health-related services for one predetermined monthly fee.

The *Modified Agreement* includes housing, residential services, and a specified amount of long-term health care as part of the monthly fee. Any additional health care is available on a fee-for-service basis.

The *Fee-for-Service Agreement* includes housing and residential services, but not long-term health care, in its monthly fees. While residents receive priority admission to the nursing care facility, the full daily rate for care is charged according to the services rendered.

The entrance fee or cost of admission into a CCRC is high, ranging from $150,000 to $900,000. The wide range can be attributed to differences in labor costs, the size of housing unit chosen, and geographical location, as well as the quality of the care provided. The entrance fee includes a residential component and a life care component.

In some CCRCs, 50 to 90 percent of the residential component of the entrance fee is refunded upon death or withdrawal from the facility.

Depending on whether the unit is a one-bedroom, two-bedroom, or three-bedroom residence—and, of course, on the services provided—the monthly fee for single occupancy ranges from $1,500 to $4,500. A second person would mean an additional $750 to $1,000 per month.

The residential component of the entrance fee and a portion of the monthly fees cover the costs of living in the community; use of the individual residence; property taxes; availability and use of common facilities; scheduled local transportation; and residential services, such as utilities, housekeeping and linens, a meal plan, and maintenance of all buildings and grounds.

The life care component of the entrance fee and a portion of the monthly fees also cover a comprehensive package of health-care services, including therapies, assisted living care, and long-term care for life. Residents are expected to maintain medical and surgical insurance—typically, Medicare Parts A and B and a Medigap plan—at their own expense.

Advantages and Disadvantages of a CCRC

For many retirees, a CCRC is a wonderful housing option. But, like any other type of facility, it has its advantages and disadvantages. The advantages of a CCRC include the following:

❏ It provides housing, recreational facilities, housekeeping and maintenance services, and health-care facilities all in one community.

❏ If and when your health-care needs change, you will not have to move off the grounds of the community.

❏ Security guards protect the entrances and grounds.

❏ In some cases, a portion of the entrance fee is refundable upon death or withdrawal from the facility.

The disadvantages of a CCRC include the following:

❏ Both the initial entrance fee and the monthly maintenance fee are high. In some communities, the monthly fee alone amounts to $54,000 a year for a single-occupancy residence.

❏ Certain contracts include only limited health-care services in the monthly fee. All other health care is provided on a fee-for-service basis.

❏ The lifestyle requires close living with neighbors.

❏ Social contacts may become confining.

The Home Health Care Option

This chapter explores various care facilities where you can reside, either temporarily or permanently, so that you can receive the help you need with daily tasks and, if necessary, with medical care. But even if you require long-term health care, you may wish to consider another option—home health care.

Many people find that home health care allows them to lead healthier, happier, more independent lives. The benefits of home care include the comfort of familiar surroundings and the support of family and friends. In some cases, home care can help you avoid a stay in a hospital or nursing home. And if you must temporarily receive care in a hospital or other facility, home care may allow you to return home sooner. Home health care can also cost significantly less than many other forms of care.

A variety of services can be provided in the home. Some visiting nurse agencies, for instance, offer private-duty skilled nursing, which may be performed by a registered nurse or a licensed practical nurse; home health aides, who can assist you with personal care such as bathing and shaving; homemakers, who can help with meal preparation, light housekeeping, laundry, and even shopping; and companions and sitters, who offer company and security. A good agency can evaluate your special needs, identify the options available, and arrange for the appropriate services. If special supplies are needed—hospital beds, bedside commodes, or seat-lift chairs, for instance—many agencies can help you rent or purchase these, as well.

It is helpful to become familiar with the major types of home care providers. Most of the services fall into one of the following categories:

❑ **Home health agencies.** These agencies provide services through physicians, nurses, therapists, social workers, and homemakers. The term "home health agency" indicates that a home care provider is Medicare certified, and has met federal minimum requirements for patient care and management. Therefore, these agencies can provide Medicare and Medicaid home health services.

❑ **Homemaker and home care aide agencies.** These agencies provide homemakers and companions who support individuals through meal preparation, bathing, dressing, and housekeeping. Some states require these agencies to be licensed and meet minimum standards.

❑ **Staffing and private-duty agencies.** These are generally nursing agencies that provide individuals with nursing, homemaker, and companion services. Most states do not require these agencies to be licensed.

❑ **Independent providers.** This category includes nurses, therapists, aides, homemakers, and companions who are privately employed by the individuals who need such services. Aides, homemakers, and companions are not required to be licensed or to meet government standards, except in cases where they receive state funding. Patients must pay the providers directly.

❑ **Pharmaceutical and infusion therapy companies.** These companies specialize in the delivery of drugs, equipment, and professional services to individuals who receive intravenous or nutritional therapies through specially placed tubes. Pharmacists prepare the solutions and arrange for delivery, while nurses teach self-administration in patients' homes. Some of these agencies are certified by Medicare, and some states require these organizations to be licensed.

❏ **Hospices.** Hospice care involves a team of skilled professionals and volunteers who provide comprehensive medical, psychological, and spiritual care for the terminally ill and their families. Most hospice agencies are Medicare certified and licensed according to state requirements.

Currently, there are more than 18,500 home health agencies and hospices in the United States, and there are a variety of ways in which you can find home health services in your area. Referral is one means of locating a good agency. Speak to friends in your area, and see if they can offer a recommendation. Another option is to contact local houses of worship, many of which will be glad to put you in touch with reputable home care services. If you or your loved one is now receiving hospital care,

the hospital social worker will be able to tell you what help is available, will determine if the fees will be paid by Medicare or Medicaid, and may even be able to make the necessary arrangements. (For general information on Medicare and Medicaid coverage for home care, see Chapter 16.) You can also check your local Yellow Pages by looking under "Home Health Services," "Nurses," and "Senior Citizens Service Organizations." These listings will not only direct you to nurses and nurses aides, but will also guide you to Meals on Wheels. Finally, if you have access to the Internet, you can find a number of services by performing a search for "Home Health Care." One helpful Internet service is provided by the National Association for Home Care. This trade association can guide you to member home care providers in your area. (See the Resources section for contact information.)

It may take some time to find a home care service that provides the assistance that you need at a price you can afford. But once you find the individual or agency that meets your requirements, you, like many others, may find that you can receive all the medical attention and practical assistance that you require in the comfort of your own home.

CHOOSING A RETIREMENT COMMUNITY OR FACILITY

The first step in choosing a retirement community or facility is locating the type of retirement housing you need in your area of choice. Fortunately, a number of resources can guide you to the kind of facility you need in the region you have chosen.

If you are looking for a nursing home, you

can obtain some guidance by referring to the *Directory of Nursing Homes,* which is available in libraries. This comprehensive national listing of nursing facilities includes detailed information about more than 16,000 nursing homes in the United States. The nursing facilities are arranged alphabetically, first by state, and then by city. Each entry includes the name, address, and telephone number of the facility. The administrator, medical director, director of nursing, and number and type of staff—part-time, full-time, and consulting—may also be listed. An index sorted by facility name is included for easy access to information.

A number of other resources can guide you to not just nursing homes, but also other types of senior housing facilities. All of the following resources are listed in the Resources section under "Retirement Communities and Care Facilities."

The Retirement Living Information Center was established to assist seniors in finding housing that matches their needs. You can contact the center by mail or phone, or you can visit its website, which provides a handy guide that allows you to find the type of facility you are looking for in the state of your choice. When using the website, you first enter the desired location, and then indicate the type of facility for which you are looking, whether a retirement community for independent living, assisted living community, nursing care facility, continuing care retirement community, or Alzheimer's care facility. Once a "match" is found, you are provided with a detailed description of the facility and its features, as well as contact information.

New Life-Styles provides a service that is similar to that of the Retirement Living Information Center. Accessible online and by telephone, New Life-Styles asks you to specify the type of care you desire, as well as your first, second, and third choices regarding location. It then matches you with suitable housing facilities. The New Life-Styles' website also offers a step-by-step guide to determining the type of senior housing facility or care option that will meet your needs, desires, and resources.

The American Association of Homes and Services for the Aging has a membership of over 5,000 not-for-profit retirement communities, assisted living facilities, nursing homes, and continuing care retirement communities. In addition to helping you locate an appropriate facility, this association—which can be contacted by mail, by phone, or online—provides helpful tips for assessing any facility or community that is of interest to you.

Once you have located one or several facilities in your area, you must appraise each one to make sure that it meets your personal needs and criteria. The first step is to prepare a list of the facilities under consideration, and arrange to visit each of the facilities on the list. Ask for a tour of the premises as well as an opportunity to speak to the administrator. When you visit the facility, be sure to bring a list of the questions that you would like answered. Self-Study 4.1 provides a checklist for evaluating nursing homes. When evaluating other types of facilities, consider the following questions:

❏ Is the monthly fee fixed, and if so, how long will it remain so?

❏ What services are covered by the monthly fee?

❏ What kinds of facilities are available for shopping, recreation, and medical care?

❏ Are there rules regarding pets, visitors, and home maintenance?

❏ In the case of an assisted living facility, does the state in which the facility is located require the facility to be licensed, and, if so, does the facility have such a license?

As you receive answers to your questions, you will be able to narrow your list to those facilities that are most suitable, and, ultimately, make an informed selection. Most important, you must take the time to *personally inspect* each facility or community to make sure that the housing you choose will meet your specific needs.

LEGAL CONSIDERATIONS

Before you sign the contract for any type of facility, it is essential that you understand clearly what services you will receive, what costs will be involved, and what rules and regulations, if any, you will be expected to follow. Self-Study 4.2 lists the details that should be incorporated in your contract.

Even if you have carefully read your contract and feel that you have a firm grasp of your rights and responsibilities, it is vital that you consult a lawyer before signing on the dotted line. Because many of these contracts run as many as twenty or thirty pages in length, and because the terms of the contract can have such a great impact on your retirement years, professional assistance in interpreting the details and avoiding possible problems is well worth the fee involved. An elder-care lawyer, who specializes in elder-care issues such as senior housing and health care, will be your best bet. (For information on locating an appropriate lawyer, see "Choosing a Lawyer" in Chapter 5.)

The right retirement community or care facility can provide all of the assistance that you need, whether you merely require others to perform housekeeping tasks or you must have daily medical attention. By taking the time to research your options and find the best and most appropriate facility available, you will insure that all of your needs—medical, social, recreational, and more—are met throughout your retirement years.

A Spotlight on CCRCs

Combining the elements of a retirement community, assisted living facility, and nursing home, continuing care retirement communities (CCRCs) provide a unique combination of features. What can you expect from a good CCRC? Perhaps the best way to answer this question is to look at a CCRC that was voted "One of America's 20 Best"—Kendal at Hanover.

Although located in Hanover, New Hampshire, Kendal is affiliated with the Kendal Corporation of Kennett Square, Pennsylvania, a not-for-profit organization founded on a tradition of Quaker values.

Five types of residences are available at Kendal: studio, one-bedroom, one-bedroom plus den, two-bedroom, and two-bedroom plus den. Each residence includes a full kitchen and a weekly housekeeping service.

The majority of people at Kendal live independent, active lives. For them, Kendal provides feature films, music recitals, a 7,000-volume library, a swimming pool, an art studio, a wood shop, a computer lab, and more.

Some Kendal residents, of course, do require help with the tasks of daily living. Residents in the assisted-living program receive aid with activities such as bathing and taking medications. Those residents who require more care stay in Kendal's health center, where they receive individualized care in the form of on-site physical therapy, dentistry, and other services designed to promote wellness.

One of the beauties of Kendal is that as a resident's health status changes, he can remain in the community that has become his home. And even when one spouse is living independently and the other is a resident of the health center, couples can visit with each other and share in Kendal's activities and services.

Self-Study 4.1
HOW TO EVALUATE A NURSING FACILITY

If the occasion should arise that you need a skilled nursing care facility, use the following checklist to compare the facilities that are available. The importance of personal inspection cannot be overemphasized.

EVALUATION OF A NURSING FACILITY		
Item	Yes	No
1. Is the facility tidy?	❏	❏
2. Does it have a clean smell?	❏	❏
3. Are the food menus acceptable?	❏	❏
4. Does it have cheerful day rooms?	❏	❏
5. Do the patients appear well-cared-for?	❏	❏
6. Is the building fireproof?	❏	❏
7. Are handrails and other safety aids in evidence?	❏	❏
8. Are the physical and occupational programs satisfactory?	❏	❏
9. Is your own physician on ready-call?	❏	❏
10. Are house physicians on ready-call?	❏	❏
11. Is the nursing staff adequate?	❏	❏
12. Have you studied the facility's operating certificate to confirm the services offered?	❏	❏
13. Have you seen the Department of Health inspection report?	❏	❏
14. Is the general atmosphere of the facility pleasant?	❏	❏
15. Have you spoken to a few patients?	❏	❏

Self-Study 4.2

CHECKLIST FOR A FACILITY CONTRACT

Before signing any contract, it is imperative to review the terms of the contract carefully. This is particularly true of a contract for a care facility, whether it is a retirement community, assisted living facility, nursing home, or continuing care retirement community. Because some of these contracts run twenty to thirty pages in length, you would be wise to consult a lawyer before signing. This, of course, would involve a fee, but remember that the lawyer's input can provide valuable protection.

Following are some of the items that should be carefully spelled out in your facility contract.

❏ **A description of your living quarters.**
The contract should specify the space, location, furnishings, and utility charges.

❏ **Food.**
The contract should state the number of meals served daily, how dietary needs will be met, and the financial arrangements for meals.

❏ **Transportation.**
The contract should include the cost for bus or shuttle services to the library, bank, doctors' offices, and movies or theater.

❏ **Medical care.**
The agreement should detail the availability of doctors, the availability of therapeutic and nursing care, and the location of the nearest hospital.

❏ **Other services.**
The agreement should specify any services that will be provided beyond food, transportation, and medical care, and should state their costs.

❏ **Surcharges.**
The agreement should specify additional fees charged for recreational and educational activities.

❏ **Taxes.**
The agreement should specify any state and local taxes involved.

❏ **Membership rights, rules, and regulations.**
The contract should specify the rights you have as a patient in the facility. These rights may include your ability to have input in decisions regarding your daily care; the items of furniture and other personal possessions that you can keep in your living quarters; and the right to sell or bequeath your

property. The contract should also specify rules and regulations, such as any limitations that may be imposed on visiting privileges or television viewing.

❏ **Fee escalation.**

The contract should detail the procedures through which fees may be escalated to reflect increased costs.

❏ **Refund policy.**

The contract should spell out the conditions under which money will be refunded in the event of death or withdrawal from the facility.

5

LEGAL AFFAIRS

Although you may consider yourself a free and independent spirit, you belong to a society that is directed by law. In fact, law regulates an extraordinary number of your activities. From the filing of birth, marriage, and death certificates to enrollment in school at a set age, from the payment of taxes to the signing of documents to purchase an automobile, from the possession of a passport while traveling in a foreign country to the meeting of certain health requirements, you are affected by laws every day. And every day, new laws are being considered for future implementation. Your life would not be the same without laws. Indeed, civilized society could not exist without them.

In this chapter, the law will be reviewed in relation to retirement planning. Legal questions that may affect you as a retiree involve property ownership, premarital planning, age discrimination, paid companions, new business setup, personal bankruptcy, and contracts. A lawyer can play an essential role in many of these areas, and in quite a few other areas as well. For example, laws regarding Social Security and pensions are complex and frequently require legal interpretation. Likewise, protection of your savings and

investments may on occasion call for legal intervention. In estate planning, a lawyer is important in helping you draw up a will to assure that your bequests are executed according to your wishes. (Please note that further information on wills is supplied in Chapter 18.) Clearly, the law plays just as important a role in retirement planning as it does in every other aspect of your life.

FORMS OF PROPERTY OWNERSHIP

The word *property* is a general term for things that people own. The two basic types of property are real property and personal property. *Real property*, also known as *real estate*, is land and the buildings on it. *Personal property* can be tangible or intangible. *Tangible personal property* consists of items that you can touch, such as a car, boat, clothing, or stamp collections. *Intangible personal property* consists of things such as a right or an interest that is protected by law. Examples are an invention, a musical composition, a stock certificate, or a savings account.

Items of both real and personal property can be owned or possessed to control or enjoy their private use. Items can also be possessed without being owned. For example, the tenant in an apartment or the driver of a rented car possesses the item without owning it. Conversely, items can be owned without being possessed. The owner of an apartment building is not in possession of the rented apartments. The car rental agency owns the cars, but is not in possession of them once they have been rented.

Property can be owned by an individual or a group. When one individual owns a piece of property, he or she has sole ownership. When two or more people own the same piece of property at the same time, they have concurrent ownership, which is also called plural ownership.

Sole Ownership

The basic form of property ownership is sole ownership. In *sole ownership,* one person owns and controls a piece of property and has the right to leave it to whichever heirs he or she chooses. An owner of property is said to have *title*—that is, evidence of his or her right to possess or enjoy property to the exclusion of all others and to dispose of the property. Title to any type of property—real or personal—exists once the property is owned by someone. A seashell, for example, belongs to no one while it is lying on the beach, but once you pick it up for your collection, you have greater rights to it than anyone else does. Disposing of property is accomplished by transferring the title.

In many situations, even those involving married couples, sole ownership may be the wisest choice. For example, the husband can be the sole owner of a couple's securities and automobile, and the wife can be the sole owner of the couple's real estate. In this way, each can pass $1,000,000 to their heirs, tax-free. The assignment of ownership to a husband and wife is a complicated matter, and is treated differently in the various states. In forty-one states, the *separate-property system* is followed. Under this system, each spouse has sole ownership of property acquired after marriage in his or her name, but all real estate is owned jointly. The remaining nine states follow the *community-property system,* under which property acquired after marriage is owned equally by both partners. (For a discussion of community property, see page 74.)

Concurrent Ownership

Concurrent ownership exists when two or more people have ownership rights to the same piece of property at the same time. The types of concurrent ownership are joint tenancy with right of survivorship, tenancy in common, tenancy by the entirety, and community property. Each type is treated differently upon the death of an owner.

Joint Tenancy With Right of Survivorship

Joint tenancy with right of survivorship (JTWROS) is a traditional way for husbands and wives to hold property. Each owns 50 percent of the property, and when one of the owners dies, the property goes to the surviving owner free from the claims of the heirs or creditors of the deceased owner.

If there are three joint tenants, each owns a third of the property. When one of the three owners dies, the surviving co-owners each own half of the property. When a second of the original three co-owners dies, the remaining one becomes the recipient and owner of all the property.

Since property held as JTWROS passes to the surviving owners, it bypasses the directives of a person's will, thus eliminating probate proceedings. This is one of the principal reasons many people opt for this type of ownership. Nevertheless, it is wise to indicate in the will to whom the property should pass, just in case both owners die simultaneously in an accident or within a short time of each other. Designating an ultimate beneficiary in a will is a prudent clarification of the owners' wishes.

Bank accounts are usually opened as JTWROS. If you are considering this type of ownership, it is important that both you and your spouse or other partner understand that either owner of the account can withdraw all the funds at any time.

All in all, there are many advantages to JTWROS. Among them are the following:

❑ **A sense of togetherness.** JTWROS indicates that the marriage is a joint relationship in which the two individuals involved share everything. It provides a feeling of unity, harmony, and security.

❑ **Protection for a wife.** If a wife has no wealth of her own, JTWROS offers her protection, because neither owner can sell the property or borrow against it without permission from the other.

❑ **Automatic transfer to the survivors.** When one owner dies, the property automatically passes to the survivors outside of the will and without probate.

❑ **Protection from claims after death.** In many states, certain jointly owned property is not subject to claims made by creditors or to damage-injury claims made against the deceased owner.

❑ **Avoidance of publicity.** Prompt transfer of ownership can be completed without the publicity that might accompany the probate of a will.

❑ **Reduction of estate administration costs.** Since ownership of JTWROS property passes automatically to the survivors, administration expenses of probate are not applicable to that part of the estate.

❑ **Tax consideration.** If the joint tenants are spouses, at the death of one, half of the value of the property is included in the estate of the deceased for federal estate tax purposes.

Among the disadvantages of joint tenancy with right of survivorship are:

❑ **Loss of the right to dispose of the property at death.** A person who places property in joint ownership usually gives up the right to dispose of it using a will. This applies even though the person states in the will that the property is to go to someone other than the co-owner.

❑ **Need for complete agreement.** Decisions concerning how jointly held property is to be used, managed, and invested must be made harmoniously. Such unanimity may be difficult to achieve, especially in cases of separation, divorce, or intrafamily dispute.

❑ **Need to protect children of first marriage.** If you have children from a first marriage, marry a second time, place your property in JTWROS, and die before your second spouse, your second spouse will inherit all your property. This individual may not be concerned with the welfare of your children from the first marriage.

❑ **Loss of control.** In most cases, joint tenancy reduces a person's legal control over property. If you have a joint bank account and become ill, the other joint tenant can withdraw sums of money from the account without your knowledge or consent. If your marriage is bad, you may find one day that your spouse has withdrawn all your money and left town.

❑ **Freezing of a joint bank account.** A joint bank account may be frozen in some states when one spouse dies so that the state can make sure all required taxes and claims have been settled. It may take some time for the funds to be released. Each spouse, therefore, should have some money in an individual account.

Tenancy in Common

Tenancy in common is a form of joint ownership with no right of survivorship and no automatic transfer at death. If two people co-own property, each can own 50 percent or any other percentage of the total. If four people invest in property as tenants in common, one can own 35 percent; another, 25 percent; and the last two, 20 percent each. The portion owned by each partner can be sold, given away, used as collateral, or passed on by a will.

In most cases, a deceased tenant in common's share of property is passed on by means of a will. If a co-owner dies without a will, his or her share of the property is disposed of according to applicable state laws. Ownership under tenancy in common is convenient for two or more friends or relatives who wish to co-own a piece of property, but also want to preserve their freedom to dispose of their individual shares as they like.

To inherit property held under tenancy in common, a survivor must depend upon a will.

Tenancy by the Entirety

Tenancy by the entirety is a form of joint ownership in which a husband and wife own property—usually real estate—jointly because each spouse in his or her own right owns the *entire* property. Under this arrangement, the property passes to the surviving spouse in the same way it does under JTWROS. Tenancy by the entirety is usually applicable only to real property, and the owners must be husband and wife. Some states do not recognize this type of holding.

Community Property

In certain states, the laws provide that property

acquired after marriage is community property. *Community property* is property that is owned equally—50 percent each—by both spouses no matter who contributes the money to pay for its purchase or upkeep. Nine states have community property laws—Arizona, California, Idaho, Louisiana, Nevada, New Mexico, Texas, Washington, and Wisconsin. The remaining states determine property rights according to *common law,* which is law based on court decisions and customs rather than on written codes. Common law states follow one of two rules concerning property acquired after marriage. The first rule is that property acquired after marriage is owned solely by the husband even if the wife contributed money toward the purchase. The other rule is that each spouse owns the property derived from his or her earnings.

In both common law and community property states, property owned by either spouse before marriage is the sole property of the original owner. Furthermore, the income or capital gain produced by premarital property is separate property. In addition, in community property states only, property acquired after marriage by gift or inheritance is excluded from community property rules.

Community property does not carry the right of survivorship. When one spouse dies, the other does not automatically assume full ownership of the property. The deceased partner's half is disposed of by will or, if there is no will, by the state's intestacy laws. Only the deceased partner's half of the property is included as part of the estate for tax purposes. If, however, the property is willed to the spouse, then it qualifies for the unlimited marital deduction. Community property laws usually permit couples to set up other types of ownership, either separate or joint, but the laws in each of the nine community property states differ. If you move from a common law state to a community property state, or vice versa, be sure to have your will checked.

WHICH TYPE OF OWNERSHIP IS BEST?

An estate attorney is the best adviser concerning the way various types of property should be held. Some forms of property should be in your own name because this gives you maximum flexibility in handling the property. You can sell the property, use it as collateral, give it away, or pass it on to your heirs through your will. The following are examples of property for which individual ownership is suggested:

❏ **Life insurance.** A life insurance policy can be written in the name of the insured or in the name of the insured's spouse, with the same beneficiaries. Many people put their policy in their spouse's name to keep the proceeds of the policy out of their estate if they should die, but this is no longer necessary because of the unlimited marital deduction. In addition, the proceeds of a life insurance policy pass to beneficiaries outside of the will, avoiding probate.

❏ **Stocks and bonds.** Individual ownership makes sense for stocks and bonds. Since only one signature is needed, sole ownership allows flexibility in the purchase and sale of these instruments. The couple can agree privately to split ownership, with each holding about 50 percent.

❏ **Car.** Individual ownership is suggested for a car. In case of a lawsuit for damages, only the assets of the owner are threatened. With joint ownership, the assets of both owners are vulnerable.

Some forms of property that would benefit from joint ownership are the following:

❏ **House.** Joint ownership with the right of survivorship is the usual method of ownership of a house. Home ownership is considered a joint effort. Furthermore, when one spouse passes away, the surviving spouse and children are guaranteed a roof over their heads. A jointly owned house passes to the survivors outside the will. However, when an estate exceeds $1,000,000, ownership of a house should be changed to tenancy in common in order to save on estate taxes.

❏ **Savings and checking accounts.** Joint accounts are convenient because both spouses have access to them. In some states, however, savings and/or checking accounts can be frozen by the bank when one of the account holders dies. Occasionally, an alert survivor who is aware of this possibility withdraws the money immediately. Instead of counting on speed, however, it is better for each spouse to maintain an individual account of a few thousand dollars so that each has readily available cash if the joint accounts are frozen.

❏ **Safe deposit box.** Most couples keep a safe deposit box in joint ownership so that they can enjoy equal access. When one spouse dies, the surviving spouse should empty the box immediately because the bank may seal it until the tax authorities can inventory its contents and collect whatever taxes are due. To avoid the problem of a sealed box, a married couple can store the husband's will and valuables in a box rented in the wife's name, and her will and valuables in a box rented in his name. It is also possible to name a deputy—an adult child, relative, or friend—who has access to the box.

ASPECTS OF RETIREMENT WITH LEGAL IMPLICATIONS

Situations may arise during the retirement years that require legal assistance. In the case of a second marriage or late first marriage, a legal agreement should be made to protect the property rights of one or both partners or their children. Legal guidance may also be helpful if you ask someone to care for you or to handle your financial affairs during an illness. This also applies if you are asked to provide the care. Knowledge of the law is additionally invaluable when you run into problems associated with age discrimination, bankruptcy, new business setup, or contracts.

Late or Second Marriage

If you marry late in life, either for the first time or for a second or third time, you should be aware of potential legal problems, especially in relation to property. Take the case of a second marriage in which each spouse has children from a first marriage. On the death of one spouse, the second spouse inherits all the property. The surviving spouse can then draw up a will leaving all the property to his or her children, with nothing going to the children of the deceased.

A lawyer should be consulted to determine whether a *premarital agreement*—also called a *prenuptial* or *antenuptial agreement*—would help to protect the property rights of children, if any, from a previous marriage. The lawyer can help you draw up such an agreement, which is entered into *before* marriage. This is a contract between a man and a woman in which the property rights and interests of either the prospective husband or wife or both are determined, or in which property is guaranteed to one or both, or to their children. Such an agreement is helpful not only in the event of the death of either spouse, but also in the event that the marriage is dissolved.

A premarital agreement can be supplemented by a *trust agreement*. By leaving all of his or her assets in a trust, the first spouse to die can

guarantee that the surviving spouse will enjoy an income from the trust for life, but that upon the surviving spouse's death, part of the remainder will go to the first spouse's children. Or the arrangements can be that all of the remainder of the trust fund will go to the first spouse's children, or that any part of it will go to anyone else desired. This type of agreement provides you with control of the ultimate distribution of your assets. A lawyer can advise you and your future spouse of potential financial and/or legal problems that may arise if valid agreements are not made before marriage. (See Chapter 20 for more information about trusts.)

If a marriage terminates in divorce, it is essential for you to consult an attorney to avoid the many pitfalls that may occur. Know your legal rights to insure fair handling of all the major financial transactions involved. The attorney you select should be an independent and not involved in any of your husband's or wife's business affairs so that you have total commitment. Again, a good premarital agreement can set forth the details of property distribution in the event of divorce.

If your spouse dies, advise your attorney immediately so that probate proceedings and the filing of the will can be initiated. Be aware that the legal and professional fees you pay are deductible if your miscellaneous deductions exceed 2 percent of your adjusted gross income (AGI).

Individuals who live together unmarried should be aware that in the event of death, all property of the deceased will go to the family of the deceased, and not to the live-in partner, unless a will spells out the desired distribution of property. Hire an attorney to draw up a written cohabitation agreement to spell out specifics in case the relationship ends due to death or a decision to separate.

Someone to Care for You

At retirement, most people are in good health and fully capable of handling all sorts of activities, such as managing an investment portfolio, depositing monthly Social Security and pension checks, paying bills, taking care of household chores, and walking the dog. Suddenly, however, you may suffer a mild stroke or other health problem, necessitating time in the hospital followed by several months of recuperation at home or in a nursing facility. Who will take care of your myriad daily activities? You can plan ahead so that everything will be handled the way you want until you are once again able to take over.

Informally, you can arrange with your spouse or a relative or friend who knows your economic affairs to step in if such a crisis should arise. Or you can make more formal arrangements, granting power of attorney to a person of integrity so that he or she can take care of your affairs while you are incapacitated.

A *power of attorney* is a legal document by which the principal (you, the signer) designates an agent (such as your lawyer, a relative, or a friend) to act for you in financial transactions. The laws of all states permit you to give someone a power of attorney. However, in the case of an ordinary power of attorney, if you become *incompetent*—unable to manage personal affairs such as handling mail, making bank transactions, and paying bills—the power may automatically be revoked. State law provides that a power of attorney may contain appropriate language so that even if you become incompetent, the designated holder of the power can continue to act in your behalf. A power of attorney that contains this language is known as a *durable power of attorney*. (See page 255 for a full discussion.) The holder of the power can deposit and withdraw money from your bank accounts, buy and sell property and securities on your behalf, and negotiate contracts for you.

Your lawyer should prepare the power of attorney. Do not buy a printed form and fill it in yourself. A properly executed power of attorney protects not only you, but also your agent and those with whom he or she deals.

Caring for Someone Else

Many people have an elderly parent or other relative who is unable to handle his or her affairs because of illness or senility. If this is your situation, it may become necessary for you to petition a court to appoint you or another relative as the person's *conservator*. For a conservator to be appointed, the *ward* must first be proven incompetent.

The functions of a conservator include responsibility for all the ward's monies as well as real and personal property; maintenance of an accurate record of income and expenditures; and meeting of housing, medical, food, and clothing needs. To have an individual declared incompetent requires the services of an attorney, since so many legal responsibilities are involved.

Age Discrimination

Almost all Americans are covered by the Federal Age Discrimination in Employment Act (ADEA) of 1968, as amended in 1978. The ADEA makes it illegal for employers to practice *age discrimination*—that is, to refuse to hire, promote, or reward an individual because of age if that person is above 40. The act applies to private employers of twenty or more people in industries that affect commerce. Most federal, state, and local government employees are covered, as are employment agencies serving covered employers and labor unions representing twenty-five or more members or functioning as hiring halls.

As amended in 1986, the ADEA also prohibits mandatory retirement at any age for employees protected by the law. And in general, the act prohibits discrimination in job retention, promotions, compensation, and other terms and conditions of employment. People who believe that their rights have been violated under the act can file a charge with the Equal Employment Opportunity Commission.

The federal ADEA and its amendments do not preempt state age discrimination laws if the state laws are more liberal. Therefore, employers located in states that have age discrimination laws are subject to both the federal and state laws, and must generally comply with the more liberal provisions of each. For example, if a state law does not permit the tenured employee exemption, then the state law applies.

The Age Discrimination Act (ADA) of 1975 is different from the ADEA. The ADA's prohibition against age discrimination affects Americans of every age, and forbids most age discrimination in programs and activities receiving federal financial assistance. The ADA's effects are widespread, as many institutions receive federal money in some form. Complaints under the ADA can be filed with any or all agencies that provide money for the program or activity in question. All complaints within the jurisdiction of the act are referred to the Federal Mediation and Conciliation Service, which then tries to reach a solution satisfactory to both parties.

Bankruptcy

Occasionally, individuals become mired in debt. Whatever the reason for this unfortunate situation, these people may have no alternative but to declare *bankruptcy*—that is, to declare in a bankruptcy court that they cannot pay their accumulated debts. Legally, bankruptcy is a constitutionally guaranteed right of Americans.

Under federal bankruptcy law as revised in 1978, bankruptcy can take one of two forms for an individual. These are straight bankruptcy (Chapter 7 of the Bankruptcy Act) and the wage earner's plan (Chapter 13 of the Bankruptcy Act). Under *straight bankruptcy*, the court appoints a trustee to list all your debts, to determine whether it is possible for you to repay the debts, and, if it is not possible, to sell your assets to repay as many of the debts as possible. You and your spouse are allowed to retain specified equity in a home as well as other specified items such as a car, furniture, appliances, clothing, jewelry, and tools used for a livelihood. Once the process of straight bankruptcy has been completed, your debts are considered wiped out and you are judged free and clear. However, you cannot declare bankruptcy again for six years.

Under the *wage earner's plan*, you are permitted to keep your property, but you must set up a monthly budget plan, approved by the court, to pay off your creditors within a three-year period. The budget indicates how much you can afford to pay your creditors after paying your living expenses. Your payback may be ten cents or more on the dollar, depending on your income and essential living expenses. While you are in the process of repaying part or all of your debts, your creditors may not contact you about your financial obligations. After the plan is completed, whatever debts you had are considered eliminated. However, some debts—including taxes, fines, alimony, and child support—cannot be erased.

In some states, if you file for bankruptcy, your private pension accounts, including IRAs and Keoghs, may be subject to creditors' claims if you have access to the money, even with a penalty. Under the rules of bankruptcy, payments from stock-bonus, pension, profit-sharing, annuity, and similar plans are exempt only to the extent that they are necessary to support the account owner and his or her dependents.

Even though you can file for bankruptcy on your own, if you are considering bankruptcy, it is a good idea to contact a lawyer for advice and guidance. The law is complex, and a lawyer can help you protect your property and advise you whether to file under Chapter 7 or Chapter 13.

Setting Up a New Business

Some retirees set up a small business to keep themselves occupied, to enjoy personal satisfaction, and/or to earn extra money. Free advice and guidance on small business is available from the federal government's Small Business Administration. (See the Resources section.)

If you decide to set up a business, you can structure it as an individual proprietorship, a partnership, or a corporation. In both an *individual proprietorship,* a business structure in which one person owns and manages the enterprise, and a *partnership,* a business structure in which two or more individuals own and manage the enterprise, you have *unlimited liability.* This means that you are responsible to the full extent of your assets, both personal and business, for any debts incurred by the business. In a *corporation,* a business structure in which the enterprise is treated as a natural person and allowed to conduct business as such, you have *limited liability.* This means that you are liable only for the money you invest, and not for any of your personal assets. Limited liability is, in fact, the principal feature of the corporate structure. To set up a corporation, you must have a lawyer draw up incorporation papers and other documents. For a partnership, the lawyer must draw up a detailed partnership agreement that covers all aspects of the business relationship, and includes a suitable escape clause in case the partnership is dissolved.

Some points to check before starting a small business are the following:

❏ **Taxes.** You will need a tax number for filing reports, a sales tax number for purchasing materials, and special records for state income and sales taxes as well as for local taxes. Also, you must pay Social Security taxes for yourself and your employees.

❏ **Insurance.** You will have to purchase fire and liability insurance as well as workmen's compensation if you hire anyone.

❏ **Licenses and permits.** You may need a special license or permit to operate your business.

No matter what type of business you choose to start or how many employees you plan to hire, if any, it is essential that you retain a lawyer who is knowledgeable in the field of business law and is familiar with the regulations of your city and state.

Signing a Contract

You may wish to spend part of your retirement income to join a social club, to register in an exercise program, or to buy hobby equipment. These purchases may involve a contract requiring you to pay a large sum of money, either in advance or on an installment plan. You must remember that a *contract* is a binding legal agreement. Before you sign it, be sure you understand what it says. You have the right to read the contract carefully first and check it with your lawyer.

A widely used type of contract is the *conditional sales agreement.* If you sign such an agreement, you are committing yourself to pay an agreed amount per month for a given number of months. Under this agreement, the buyer takes possession of the purchased item—whether it is an automobile, home appliance, or furniture— but title, or ownership, remains with the seller until the final installment has been paid. Failure to meet the payments gives the legal owner, or seller, the right to repossess the item, resell it, and sue you for any deficiency plus whatever costs were incurred in the course of the court procedure.

Sometimes, a *chattel mortgage* is used. In this case, the buyer acquires title to the purchased item but pledges it as security for the balance due. Again, failure to make the payments gives the lender, usually a bank or finance company, the right to foreclose the loan, repossess the item, and sue for the remaining balance plus court costs.

Some Tips on Contracts

Because contracts closely touch your everyday life, it is important for you to be aware of their major pitfalls and know how to avoid them. The following basic tips can save you time and money.

❏ **Watch for blank spaces.** Do not sign a contract that has blank spaces in it. Be sure that every space is filled in to your satisfaction.

❏ **Retain the right to change a printed form.** You have the right to change a printed form so that the agreement meets the terms you are willing to accept.

❏ **Reject oral promises.** Every provision agreed upon must be written into the contract in order to be enforceable. Do not accept oral promises.

❏ **Check with your lawyer.** Most important, before you sign a contract, show it to your lawyer. Failure to do so can be costly and time-consuming.

CHOOSING AND USING A LAWYER

A lawyer is a highly trained professional who is qualified to assist you in handling your financial resources, property, housing arrangements, estate planning, and a variety of family affairs. Laws today are much too complex to be correctly interpreted and applied by the layman. Many individuals practicing do-it-yourself law have found that they multiplied both their problems and the legal fees that had to be paid to resolve the problems. And when you pass age 50, the opportunities for correcting expensive errors are fewer. Therefore, if you do not already have a lawyer, it is essential that you choose one who can give you a legal checkup in the various areas of retirement planning—financial planning; estate planning; buying or selling a home; civil or criminal court actions; starting a business; and tax consequences of charitable contributions, bequests, medical expenses, and trusts.

Choosing a Lawyer

One way to select a lawyer is to find a satisfied client. You may be able to get a lead by talking to family and friends, or to your financial adviser. Be sure that the lawyer you choose handles your particular problem, since lawyers in larger cities generally specialize in certain branches of the law.

If you live in a rural area or small town, contact your local bank for the names of a few reliable attorneys. In larger towns or cities, call your local bar association, most of which sponsor a lawyer referral service. Other agencies that may be of help include the American Association of Retired Persons (AARP) and your local Social Security office.

Most local libraries have a copy of the *Martindale-Hubbell Law Directory*, which covers every state and is updated annually. This directory lists lawyers and law firms alphabetically, providing the academic background of each lawyer and his or her current address.

If you have access to the Internet, you can

take advantage of a free service called Attorney Locate. (See the Resources section.) This service allows you to search for an attorney based on location and practice area—elder law, contract law, age discrimination, and so on. Once you find a lawyer who practices in your geographical area and has the appropriate expertise, the site will provide you with a professional profile of that attorney, along with contact information.

Another Internet service that may be of help is that provided by the National Academy of Elder Law Attorneys (NAELA). (See the Resources section.) The membership of the NAELA is comprised of attorneys in the private or public sec-

What Is an Elder-Care Lawyer?

Many business experts now recommend that seniors in search of legal counsel contact an elder-care lawyer, rather than an attorney who specializes in other areas of the law. They urge older people to have a good elder-care lawyer perform a line-by-line review of contracts with assisted-living facilities and other types of senior housing. And they feel that the expertise of such specialists is invaluable to seniors involved in financial and estate planning.

What is an elder-care lawyer? *Elder-care lawyers*, sometimes called *elder law attorneys*, focus on the legal needs of the elderly, and work with a variety of legal tools—as well as a network of social workers, psychologists, and other elder-care professionals, as necessary—to meet the goals and objectives of the older client. Elder-care law encompasses many different fields of law, including, but not limited to, the following:

❑ Estate planning, including the use of wills, trusts, and other planning documents

❑ Probate

❑ Housing issues, including discrimination

❑ Long-term care placements in nursing homes and other care facilities

❑ Nursing home issues, including questions of patients' rights

❑ Medicaid and Medicare claims and appeals

❑ Supplemental and long-term health insurance issues

❑ Age discrimination

❑ Retirement issues, including pension benefits, public and private retirement benefits, and survivors' benefits

❑ Social Security and disability claims and appeals

❑ Disability planning, including the use of durable powers of attorney, living trusts, living wills, and other means of delegating decision-making to another in the case of incapacity

It is important to understand that most elder-care lawyers do not specialize in every one of the areas covered by elder-care law. Therefore, when contacting an attorney, it is essential to ask if he or she regularly handles matters in your area of concern. Only a lawyer with the appropriate experience will be qualified to understand the issues that are of concern to you, to avoid potential complications, and to provide appropriate counsel.

tors who deal with issues that affect the elderly. (See the inset "What Is an Elder-Care Lawyer?" on page 81.) You can contact the NAELA by mail or phone, or you can visit their website and locate a member of the NAELA by entering criteria such as desired location and desired area of expertise. A good elder-care attorney has the training and experience needed to provide sound counsel and assistance in estate planning, retirement planning, disability planning, and many other areas of the law that affect seniors.

Once you have found an appropriate attorney, for a small fee, you can arrange an interview to discuss your legal concerns. Be sure to organize and bring all the information pertinent to your situation to the interview. As you confer about your situation, you can get to know the attorney and determine if you can work comfortably with him or her. (See Self-Study 5.1, which will help you evaluate the qualifications that you consider essential in a lawyer.) If for any reason you are dissatisfied, you can look for someone else.

Legal Fees

Legal fees vary according to where you live and the complexity of your case. Ordinarily, a lawyer charges on the basis of the amount of time he spends serving you. This includes time spent talking to you in his office and on the telephone, looking up the law, preparing legal documents, writing letters, and negotiating with others on your behalf.

Sometimes a lawyer sets a flat fee for certain types of work, such as closing on real estate, drawing a will, and probating an estate. Many county and state bar associations have set up schedules of minimum fees for most common types of legal work. However, at your first contact with a lawyer, you should ask how much the charge will be in your particular case, and what method of payment is requested. Payment possibilities include payment in advance; a deposit, with the balance to come at the conclusion of the work; and periodic payments. Financial arrangements made in advance usually avoid disagreement and confusion later on. If you believe that a particular lawyer's fee is too high, you are free to contact another lawyer whose charge may be more modest.

For certain kinds of legal work, a lawyer's fee is subject to approval by a court or by a state or federal agency. For example, lawyers' fees are controlled in cases involving guardianships and the estates of deceased persons, and in proceedings concerning certain types of retirement benefits, such as Social Security.

KNOW YOUR RIGHTS

Many new rights and protections have been extended to older Americans by recent federal laws, as well as by state and local laws. If you believe that any of your rights have been violated, these laws spell out the ways in which you can obtain redress. Many laws permit you to file a suit against the party that you believe injured you. However, filing a suit can be expensive and time-consuming, and does not guarantee that you will win your case.

Several factors should be considered before filing a lawsuit. They include:

❏ **Violation of a law.** You and your lawyer must consider whether a law has been violated. Even though you may not like something or think that it is unfair, it does not mean that a law has been violated. Your lawyer must carefully check the law's provisions.

❏ **Payment of legal expenses.** In many cases, the court requires the losing side to pay all legal expenses. This means that if you lose, you must pay both your own and your opponent's legal fees. You must decide whether the initiation of a lawsuit is worth this possible high cost.

❑ **Proving your case.** In a lawsuit, you are required to prove to the satisfaction of the court that you have been harmed. While you may be certain that you have been injured, you and your lawyer must determine if you are able to prove it.

❑ **Time and aggravation.** You must carefully weigh whether the time, costs, and aggravation of a lawsuit are worth any potential compensation. Always bear in mind that you may *lose*.

The initiation of a lawsuit should be made with great care and in consultation with your lawyer.

This chapter has demonstrated how law affects so many aspects of the retirement years. A basic understanding of the law in relation to the different areas of your life—your property, your business, your will, and more—will enable you to make realistic retirement plans and avoid a variety of potentially devastating pitfalls and problems.

Self-Study 5.1
EVALUATING A LAWYER

1. Which of the following qualifications do you consider essential in a lawyer?

Qualification	Essential	Not Essential
Communicative	❑	❑
Compassionate	❑	❑
Competent	❑	❑
Discreet	❑	❑
Forceful	❑	❑
Honest	❑	❑
Independent	❑	❑
Knowledgeable in field	❑	❑
Reasonably priced	❑	❑
Respected	❑	❑
Up-to-date	❑	❑

2. To what extent does your current lawyer meet these standards?

_____

_____

_____

_____

_____

LONG-TERM FUNDING
for RETIREMENT

6

SAVINGS *and* INVESTMENTS

More than most countries, the United States is a land of consumers. The rate of savings in the United States is the lowest of any industrialized nation. Currently, of every dollar of after-tax income, the average American spends almost 98 cents and saves only 2 cents—actually, a bit under 2 percent. By contrast, the savings rate in Japan and Germany is well above 10 percent.

On the brighter side, the *savings rate*, defined as a percentage of disposable income that is not spent, has always been an inadequate measure of how well people plan for the future. The rate is based only on income, and does not include capital gains from equity in a home, or the growth of the value of stocks, mutual funds, and other assets. In reality, the average American accumulates a small personal nest egg for retirement by making monthly payments on a mortgage and by purchasing ordinary life insurance. Monthly mortgage payments build up equity in a family home, *equity* being the net investment in a home and representing ownership. *Insurance premiums*, which are installment payments toward the purchase of a life insurance policy, increase the cash value of the life insurance. And many individuals and families do try to save.

These savings are usually deposited in a savings bank, savings and loan association, or commercial bank. Other Americans build up their capital through investments in stocks, government securities, and real estate.

Some people make investments throughout their working lives, and acquire a general picture of the intricacies of the subject. Others are unable to save and invest, and thus are novices in the field when they try to do so. However, many public pension systems permit the lump-sum distribution of excess reserves or the rollover of tax-deferred annuity funds at the point of retirement, and many private pension plans also allow lump-sum distribution at this time. If your pension fund allows this, you will need to make some investment decisions. It is therefore essential that you understand savings and investment alternatives in terms of both safety and yield.

SAVINGS ACCOUNTS

Banks and savings and loan associations offer a variety of savings accounts. Some of the more popular ones are the passbook savings account, the savings account with check-writing privileges, the money market deposit account (MMDA), and the certificate of deposit (CD).

Passbook Savings Account

Passbook savings accounts are offered by savings banks, savings and loan associations, and commercial banks. The money in these accounts is *liquid*—available for withdrawal whenever the need for cash arises. However, the accounts pay a relatively low interest rate, recently under 2 percent. These rates can rise or fall. *Interest* is the fee that banks pay to depositors for use of their money. Although, for many years, passbook savings accounts did not involve a minimum balance, most accounts now do require a minimum daily balance to avoid monthly service fees. The savings are safe, since up to $100,000 per account is insured by the United States Federal Deposit Insurance Corporation (FDIC).

Savings Account With Check-Writing Privileges

A new era in banking services began in 1981, when commercial banks, savings and loan associations, mutual savings banks, and credit unions were authorized to offer savings accounts with check-writing privileges. The balance requirements and interest rates of these accounts vary from bank to bank. For instance, a bank may offer an interest-bearing checking account that allows unlimited check writing, but requires a minimum daily balance of $2,500. If the amount in the account falls below the minimum balance, the bank may then impose a monthly maintenance fee and also charge a fee for each check written. All of these accounts—regardless of the rules and regulations—enjoy protection of the FDIC for amounts of up to $100,000.

Money Market Deposit Account

Money market deposit accounts (MMDA) pay a higher interest rate than passbook savings accounts do, but also require that a higher minimum balance be maintained. If the balance in an MMDA falls below the bank's specified minimum, the lower passbook savings account interest rate is paid. MMDA accounts are offered by savings banks, savings and loan associations, and commercial banks, which use the account balances for investment in money market instruments (see page 96). The savings are insured by the FDIC up to $100,000 per account, and the money in the account is liquid, meaning that it is available for withdrawal whenever the need for cash arises. Some MMDA accounts offer check-writing privileges. If your savings are in a passbook savings account, you might want to transfer your funds into a higher-yielding MMDA. Check the interest rates at several banks.

Certificate of Deposit

A *certificate of deposit* (CD) is a type of savings account in which a specified sum of money is deposited for a set period of time. CDs are also instruments of the money market (see page 96). They were instituted to induce savers to keep their money in banks instead of shifting it to money market mutual funds. Certificates of Deposit are safe, and they yield competitive returns.

Since the deregulation of banking in 1983, each bank has been able to set its own interest rates, terms, and minimum deposit requirements for CDs. Most banks currently accept $500 minimum deposits, and many accept deposits as low as $100. The interest rates paid are competitive. In addition, your entire investment in CDs, as in any savings account, is insured up to $100,000 by the FDIC.

CDs of $100,000 or more feature *negotiable interest rates;* that is, the rate of interest paid is negotiated between the investor and the institution. Individuals or institutions purchasing these CDs usually shop around for the highest interest rates available.

Since all bank interest is fully taxable, the interest earned on a CD is also fully taxable. In addition, if you withdraw any of the principal before maturity for any reason, you must pay a penalty. The minimum loss is thirty-one days' interest on accounts that are due in one year or less. If you have not earned sufficient interest to pay the penalty, you will have the penalty deducted from your principal.

THE EMERGENCY SAVINGS FUND

All retirees should have an emergency savings fund as a cushion in case of an unforeseeable crisis such as an accident or serious illness. Emergency reserves are important because they give you protection against the unexpected. The amount set aside in an emergency fund should equal the retirement cost of living for a period of three to six months. For example, a retired couple whose living expenses are $2,000 a month should have between $6,000 and $12,000 in an emergency savings fund. An emergency fund is necessary even though Social Security and pension incomes are certain, and will continue. Self-Study 6.1 was designed to help you calculate the status of your emergency savings fund.

At least $5,000 of your emergency savings fund should be kept in a money market deposit account, which not only offers safety and a competitive yield, but also allows you to tap into the money quickly. The balance should be deposited in a mutual fund, which allows you to immediately redeem your investment by phone at any time. (See page 99 for information on mutual funds.)

STOCKS

The term *stock* actually refers to two types of investment instruments. One is known as common stock, and the other is called preferred stock. Both types are discussed in the following sections.

Common Stocks

Common stocks are the most popular form of investment throughout the United States. About 79 million individual American investors now own common stocks, which they hold either individually or through their interests in pension funds as well as a variety of other intermediaries, such as insurance companies.

When you buy shares of common stocks, you become a part owner of the enterprise that issued the stock and can expect to participate in the profits of the firm, if there are any. *Common stocks* can be defined as shares in a corporation that give their owners the right to control the enterprise and to share in the profits. The amount of the dividend paid to common stockholders out of the profits and the time of the payment are within the discretion of the board of directors of the corporation.

Traditionally, common stocks have been considered a means of protection against inflation, as they rise in value as prices increase. However, average stock prices are erratic. In some periods, stock prices decline while consumer prices rise. But studies have shown that in the *long term,* which is ten or more years, investments in stocks yield a return that is at least twice as high as the return yielded by other types of securities, such as corporate bonds and Treasury bills. That is why every portfolio should contain a significant amount of stocks and/or stock mutual funds to achieve maximum gains.

Preferred Stocks

Preferred stocks are shares in a corporation that entitle their owners to receive fixed and stated dividends before any earnings are distributed to the common stockholders. However, the fixed return is not guaranteed. The company's board of directors has the authority to pay or not pay the preferred stockholders' dividends, depending on the amount of profits earned during the year. If the company does not pay dividends to the preferred stockholders, it cannot pay dividends to the common stockholders either.

Preferred stock is "preferred" not only because of its payment of dividends, but also because of its payment to stockholders if and when the corporation is dissolved. When an enterprise is folded, the claims of the preferred shareholders have precedence over those of the common stockholders. However, the claims of bondholders come first.

Preferred stocks are not necessarily better than other types of investments.

BONDS

Bonds are written promises to repay a loan on a specified date, called the *date of maturity*, while paying the bondholder a specified amount of interest at regular intervals—usually twice a year. On the date of maturity, the borrower, either a company or a governmental unit, returns the investor's capital. Referred to as *fixed income assets*, bonds are usually issued in units of $1,000 or more and bear a fixed interest rate, known as the *coupon rate*. The *interest* is the fee that the company pays the bondholder for the use of his or her money.

The value of the bond fluctuates in the bond market in an inverse manner with interest rates, so that when interest rates are high, bond prices are low, and when interest rates are low, bond prices are high. Maturity dates extend from ten to thirty or more years.

When you buy a bond, you will know exactly how much you will receive when interest is paid. If you hold the bond until the date of maturity, you will get back your initial investment in full. If you sell your bond before maturity, depending upon the bond's market price at the time of the sale, you may earn a *capital gain*, making money on the sale, or take a *capital loss*, losing money.

Several types of bonds are available, including government bonds, zero coupon bonds, and corporate bonds.

Government Bonds

A large variety of government bonds is available for sale to investors. Included are United States Savings bonds; United States Treasury bonds; United States agency securities, such as those issued by the Government National Mortgage Association, the Federal National Mortgage Association, and the Federal Home Loan Mortgage Corporation; and municipal bonds, which are issued by states, counties, and municipalities, as well as their various agencies.

States may not tax the interest earned on United States government bonds, according to a Supreme Court decision of 1819. In *McCulloch v. Maryland*, Chief Justice John Marshall said that a state or local tax on a federal instrumentality is invalid. However, United States government bonds are not exempt from federal income tax. On the other hand, the federal government may not tax the interest earned on a municipal bond, which is an instrumentality of a state, county, or local government, because of the general constitutional principle of mutual independence of the federal and state governments. These latter bonds are also tax-exempt in the states and municipalities in which they are issued. However, you are liable for taxes on the interest you earn on bonds issued by states other than the one in which you live. For example, if you live in New York and receive interest on a bond issued by the State of Colorado, you must report the income in your New York State tax return. But if you live in New York and own a bond issued by the State of New York, you will not have to pay federal, state, or city taxes on the interest.

United States Savings Bonds

United States Savings bonds are securities sold by the federal government that offer fixed income with minimum risk. The United States government offers three types of savings bonds—Series I savings bonds, Series EE savings bonds, and Series HH savings bonds.

SERIES I SAVINGS BONDS

Introduced by the United States Treasury in September 1998, the *Series I* savings bond is a savings/investment vehicle with many positive features. Most important, it goes a long way toward guaranteeing that inflation will not eat away its value.

The I bonds can be bought in eight denominations—ranging from $50 to $10,000—that grow with inflation-indexed earnings for up to thirty years, the life of the bond. These bonds are purchased at face value, and the maximum purchase that anyone can make in one year is $30,000. The bonds are backed by the full faith and credit of the United States government.

I bonds usually increase in value every month, and interest is compounded semiannually. The bonds are liquid, and can be turned into cash at any time after six months. However, if you cash in the bonds within the first five years, you will forfeit three months of earnings.

Holders of I bonds, like holders of most other savings bonds, do not owe tax until the bonds mature or are cashed in. At that time, only federal taxes are due; the bonds are exempt from state and local income taxes.

I bonds can be purchased at most savings banks, through brokerage firms, and from any Federal Reserve bank. (See the inset on page 93.) If you purchase them through a brokerage firm, though, you will pay a commission.

SERIES EE SAVINGS BONDS

An alternative to the I bond is the *Series EE* savings bond, an accrual type savings/investment security. The purchase price of an EE bond is 50 percent of its face amount. For example, a $100 bond costs $50. Bonds are available in $50, $75, $100, $200, $500, $1,000, $5,000 and $10,000 denominations. Interest is added to the redemption value every month, and is paid to the investor when the bond is redeemed.

The issue date for EE bonds, printed in the upper right-hand corner, is the month and year an authorized issuing agent received the full purchase price of the bond. The issue date determines when a bond begins and stops earning interest. Each May 1 and November 1, the Treasury announces a Series EE savings bond rate that is based on market yields of actively traded United States Treasury notes and bonds. Bonds earn these rates right from the start, and continue to earn interest for seventeen to thirty years from the issue date. The Treasury guarantees that the face value of each bond will be achieved in seventeen years. After the bond reaches face value, it continues to earn interest.

Like the holders of I bonds, EE bondholders do not owe tax until the bonds mature or are cashed in. At that time, only federal taxes are due; the bonds are exempt from state and local income taxes. Also like I bonds, EE bonds can be purchased at most savings banks, through brokerage firms, and from any Federal Reserve bank. (See the inset on page 93.) Many employers sponsor payroll savings plans for EE bonds.

SERIES HH SAVINGS BONDS

Series HH savings bonds are available in denominations of $500, $1,000, and $10,000. At retirement, many individuals exchange the EE bonds they accumulated during their working years for HH bonds so that they can receive current income. In fact, Series HH bonds cannot be purchased directly, but can be obtained only in exchange for E and EE bonds. This exchange can be made only through a Federal Reserve bank.

HH bonds are called *current income bonds* because they pay interest semiannually at a fixed rate. The interest rate earned on HH bonds is exempt from state and local income taxes, but is subject to federal income tax, which must be paid the year the interest is earned. HH bonds are now paying 4 percent per year, and earn interest for a total of twenty years.

For a free guide to United States savings bonds, write for *The Savings Bond Question and Answer Book,* which is available from the Department of the Treasury. You can also find current information about government bonds by visiting the Treasury's website or by calling its toll-free number. (See the Resources section.)

United States Treasury Bonds

United States Treasury bonds are obligations of the United States government with maturities of ten or more years. The older United States Treasury bonds are *bearer bonds;* that is, the owner's name does not appear on the certificate and is not registered on the books of the issuer. But since January 1983, all new Treasury bonds have been issued in *registered* form only, which means that the owner's name is inscribed on the certificate and is recorded on the Treasury's books. Owner-

ship of these bonds may be registered to one person, to two or more persons, or to minors. These bonds are *coupon bonds;* attached to them are postdated interest coupons representing ownership. The owners clip these coupons every six months as they come due, and present them at a bank for deposit or in exchange for cash.

In the early 1980s, Treasury bonds paid 12 to 14 percent interest. Issues since then have been paying lower rates. The return on United States Treasury bonds is about one percentage point less than the return on triple-A corporate bonds. This is to be expected because corporate bonds involve a somewhat greater risk than United States Treasury bonds do, and the interest on corporate bonds is fully taxable.

United States Treasury bonds are issued in denominations of $1,000, $5,000, $10,000, $100,000, and $1,000,000. Currently, only thirty-year bonds are being issued. Interest rates are set by auction three times a year—in February, August, and November.

For detailed information on purchasing a United States Treasury bond, contact one of the Federal Reserve bank's twelve regional offices. (See the inset on page 93.) The Federal Reserve bank also sells United States Treasury bills and United States Treasury notes, described on pages 97 and 98, as well as the newer inflation-indexed securities, described on page 99.

United States Treasury bonds are a good choice for the investor seeking maximum safety of capital and a steady, high rate of interest. When interest rates begin to fall, the astute investor seeks to lock in a high rate of interest by buying for the long term. You must carefully follow interest rate movements to determine the ideal time to buy United States Treasury bonds. You can find this information in the financial pages of your daily newspaper or by contacting the nearest branch of the Federal Reserve bank.

Federal Reserve Banks

United States Treasury bonds, bills, notes, and inflation-indexed securities can all be purchased from one of the twelve regional offices of the Federal Reserve bank listed below. For many years, you could visit these offices in person to buy your securities. Now, however, you must initially purchase Treasury securities by mail to establish your account. Once your account has been established, further securities can be purchased through the mail; via the telephone; or online through the Bureau of the Public Debt, which is the bureau that issues, services, and redeems Treasury securities. (See the Resources section.)

NORTHEAST
600 Atlantic Avenue
Boston, MA 02106
(617) 973–3000
Website: http://www.bos.frb.org

33 Liberty Street
New York, NY 10045-0001
(212) 720–5000
Website: http://www.ny.frb.org

Ten Independence Mall
Philadelphia, PA 19106-1574
(215) 574–6000
Website: http://www.phil.frb.org

MIDWEST
PO BO 6387
Cleveland, OH 44101-1387
(888) 333–2538
Website: http://www.clev.frb.org

230 South LaSalle Street
PO Box 834
Chicago, IL 60604
(312) 322–5111
Website: http://www.frbchi.org

411 Locust Street
PO Box 442
St. Louis, MO 63166
(314) 444–8444
Website: http://www.stls.frb.org

90 Hennepin Avenue
PO Box 291
Minneapolis, MN 55480-0291
(612) 204–5000
Website: http://www.woodrow.mpls.frb.fed.us

925 Grand Boulevard
Kansas City, MO 64198-0001
(816) 881–2683
Website: http://www.frbkc.org

SOUTHEAST
701 East Byrd Street
PO Box 27622
Richmond, VA 23261-7622
(804) 697–8000
Website: http://www.rich.frb.org

104 Marietta Street, NW
Atlanta, GA 30303-2713
(404) 521–8500
Website: http://www.frbatlanta.org

SOUTHWEST
2200 North Pearl Street
Dallas, TX 75265
(214) 922–6000
Website: http://www.dallasfed.org

WEST
101 Market Street
San Francisco, CA 94105
(415) 974–2000
Website: http://www.frbsf.org

United States Agency Securities

Some of the United States government agencies that raise funds through public offerings include the Government National Mortgage Association, the Federal National Mortgage Association, and the Federal Home Loan Mortgage Corporation. The bonds sold by these agencies are referred to in the investment world by the nicknames *Ginnie Mae, Fannie Mae,* and *Freddie Mac.* Ginnie Maes are backed by government-insured Federal Housing Administration (FHA) and Veterans' Administration (VA) mortgages, which add a safety feature for the individual investor. Fannie Maes and Freddie Macs are backed by conventional (uninsured) mortgages, and are favored by institutional investors, not individual investors. All of these bonds can be purchased only through a commercial bank or a stock brokerage firm, requiring payment of a commission. They cannot be purchased directly from the government agency that issues them.

The government agencies that issue the bonds buy the mortgages from financial institutions, which actually make the loans. The agencies then package a number of similar mortgages into pools amounting to millions of dollars. The agency securities backed by these mortgages are sold to investors, who receive a return that reflects the interest paid by the individual homeowners. Agency bonds are called *pass-through securities* because the homeowner's payments of interest and principal are *passed through* to the investors, who have bought shares in one or more of the mortgage pools. Holders of the bonds receive interest payments by check. The interest is subject to federal income tax, but is exempt from state and local income taxes.

GINNIE MAES

The Government National Mortgage Association (GNMA) is a branch of the United States Department of Housing and Urban Development. It is the leading issuer of pass-through securities, with over $447.6 billion worth outstanding, representing more than 333,000 separate pools of mortgages. The Ginnie Mae offers the highest interest rate of any government security, and is generally sold in maturities of thirty years and minimum denominations of $25,000. Many mutual funds hold only Ginnie Maes. (See page 99 for a description of mutual funds.) A *unit investment trust* is a mutual fund that sells units of ownership. The advantage of buying into a Ginnie Mae mutual fund or unit investment trust is that the monthly principal and/or interest can be reinvested when the fund or trust is instructed to do so.

Most government securities pay interest semiannually. Ginnie Maes, on the other hand, make payments monthly, which most retirees prefer. However, you must realize that the monthly check includes principal as well as interest. If you spend the whole check, you will discover later that your principal has diminished. It is important that you spend only the interest each month, setting aside the principal for further investment. The principal is paid back because many homeowners try to repay their mortgages quickly or to refinance existing mortgages at lower rates.

FANNIE MAES AND FREDDIE MACS

Fannie Maes and Freddie Macs, both government-sponsored, are siblings of Ginnie Maes. Like the GNMA, the Federal National Mortgage Association (Fannie Mae) and Federal Home Loan Mortgage Corporation (Freddie Mac) pool mortgages. These are conventional home mortgages, and are, therefore, a little less safe than the Ginnie Mae pools, which are composed of guaranteed home mortgages.

Through Fannie Mae and Freddie Mac

bonds, investors receive principal and interest payments from homeowners' payments. Freddie Mac investors are guaranteed interest and principal payments every month, even when homeowners skip payments. Fannie Mae investors are guaranteed only interest; the principal may come later. As a result, the interest paid on Fannie Mae bonds is a fraction higher than the interest paid on Freddie Mac bonds.

Fannie Mae and Freddie Mac certificates are bought through brokerage firms, not from the government. The bonds are available in $10,000 and $5,000 increments. You can purchase them by buying into a mutual fund, which generally has a lower entry fee.

Municipal Bonds

Municipal bonds are issued by a state, county, or city and are called *municipals* for short. These bonds offer tax advantages that make them attractive to people in higher income tax brackets. For example, a New York City resident who owns a New York City or New York State bond pays no taxes to the federal, New York State, or New York City governments on the interest earned. The decision to buy or not buy a municipal depends upon the stated interest rate, or coupon rate, and the investor's tax bracket. In addition, municipals, like taxable bonds, must be considered in terms of their safety. If a municipality is about to go bankrupt, a bond issued by it is not a sound investment. It is important to ascertain the bond rating of the municipal. Choose *high-grade bonds*, which are bonds that are rated triple-A. The risk-return relationship pertains to municipals just as it does to stocks— the higher the risk, the higher the interest return. If there is an element of risk involved, the state or city will give you a higher rate to make the offering more attractive.

There are two principal varieties of munici-

pal bonds. *General obligation bonds* pledge the faith and credit of the government that issues them, meaning that the taxing authority of the issuer will insure the payment of interest and principal. The repayment of *revenue bonds* is tied to a particular source of revenue, such as a bridge, tunnel, or airport, or to a specific tax, such as a sales tax. Always check the bond rating before buying.

Since July 1, 1983, issuers of municipal bonds have been required to maintain records that show who owns the bonds and who receives interest payments. This is intended to discourage tax evasion. These recorded municipals are also called *registered bonds*. Before July 1983, issuers kept no records of ownership and paid interest on bearer bonds to whomever submitted an interest coupon.

Zero Coupon Bonds

A popular investment vehicle is the zero coupon bond. As the name implies, *zero coupon bonds*, called *zeros* for short, have no coupons. Zeros can be purchased at a fraction of their ultimate redemption value, perhaps at a quarter or a half of their *par value*—that is, their face value. The bond increases in value at a compound interest rate until maturity.

Zeros are issued by the United States Treasury and other federal agencies, as well as by municipalities and corporations. If you own a federal zero coupon bond, each year, you must pay federal income tax, but not state or city tax, on the interest that accrues, even though you will not receive any interest until the bond matures. Buying a home-state municipal zero coupon bond eliminates the tax problem.

Many large brokerage firms package these securities and sell them to investors through investment trusts. Some examples of United States government zero coupon bonds are Treasury

Investment Growth Receipts (TIGRs), Certificates of Accrual on Treasury Securities (CATS), and Separate Trading of Interest and Principal of Securities (STRIPS). Some of these issues are traded on the New York Stock Exchange and, therefore, can be bought or sold prior to maturity.

Although most zero coupon bonds have a face value of $1,000, some zeros can be purchased for as little as $100 to $200. Brokerage firms charge a commission that ranges from 2 to 5 percent of the purchase price. The main difference between zeros and other bonds is that zeros do not pay interest until maturity. Zero coupon bonds are attractive to small investors because the purchase cost is less than that of conventional bonds.

Zeros are recommended for long-term retirement planning if the maturity date coincides with the retirement date. They should not be purchased after retirement, however, since most retirees seek a regular monthly flow of income.

Corporate Bonds

Corporations issue a wide variety of bonds. For example, *mortgage bonds* are secured by a mortgage on a specific piece of property, which is usually of a durable nature such as land, buildings, or machinery. *General mortgage bonds* are secured by a blanket mortgage on a company's property. *Debenture bonds* are not backed by any specific piece of property but by the general credit of the corporation. *Convertibles* give their holders the right, at a particular time and under certain stated terms, to change the bonds into stock.

Corporate bonds are bought and sold for the public by brokers and securities dealers. You do not need to keep a bond until it matures—you can sell a bond you hold or buy one previously held by someone else. In the process of trading, you may earn a capital gain or incur a loss.

Bond-Rating Services

An investor must be able to assess the financial soundness of a bond before buying it. A bond with a higher degree of risk may pay a higher interest yield to compensate the investor for assuming the higher risk. Individual investors do not have the expertise to rate bonds. They rely on independent bond-rating services. The two largest are *Moody's Investors Service* and *Standard & Poor's Corporation*. The best quality bond with the smallest degree of risk is rated Aaa by Moody's and AAA by Standard & Poor's. These bonds are known as triple-A bonds. The scale used by Moody's continues Aa1, Aa2, Aa3, A1, A2, A3, Baa1, Baa2, and Baa3. The last three ratings designate medium grades, which are still investment grades. Below-investment-grade ratings are Ba1, Ba2, Ba3, B1, B2, B3, Caa, Ca, and C. If you are interested in buying a bond, tell your broker that you want an issue rated Aa1, Aa2, Aa3, or, preferably, Aaa.

MONEY MARKET INSTRUMENTS

Money market is the collective name for transactions involving the borrowing or lending of money for a short term by the government, banks, large corporations, securities dealers, or individual investors. In investment circles, *short term* is considered to be one year or less. When individuals or businesses have more cash on hand than they currently need, they often find the money market an attractive place to temporarily invest the funds to earn interest. At the same time, the government or a business may require funds for a short term, and be willing to pay interest for the use of the money.

Some of the short-term instruments traded in the money market include United States Treasury bills, United States Treasury notes, certificates of deposit, commercial paper, banker's acceptances, and repurchase agreements. Most of these money market instruments can be purchased by individuals through the banking system, but many require a minimum purchase amount ranging from $10,000 to $25,000. Much less is required to purchase a small portion of a portfolio of money market instruments through a money market mutual fund (see page 100).

The short-term credit instruments traded in the money market have two very important characteristics—a very high degree of safety, and a high degree of liquidity. Short-term investments are responsive to current market conditions, such as interest rate changes.

Certificates of deposit were discussed earlier in the chapter. Other money market instruments are discussed below.

United States Treasury Bills

The United States government sells securities that are of the highest quality. In today's uncertain investment market, the ultimate safe haven for short-term funds is the United States Treasury bill. *Treasury bills,* or *T-bills,* are short-term securities that mature in three, six, or twelve months, and are backed by the full faith and credit of the United States government. Since August 1998, the minimum investment has been $1,000.

T-bills pay a yield that is not subject to state or local income taxes, only to federal income taxes. These taxes are payable in the year the T-bill matures, not in the year in which you receive the income or discount. T-bills are almost as liquid as cash, since they may be sold at any time without interest penalty.

T-bills are unique in that you receive your interest as soon as the Federal Reserve bank receives your money. Investments such as certificates of deposit, savings accounts, and most bonds pay interest only after the institutions that

issued them have had the use of your money. The reason that interest on T-bills is paid so promptly is that you buy the bills at a discount from their face value. For example, you send the Treasury $1,000, the minimum amount required to buy a T-bill. If the actual cost of a ninety-one-day (three-month) bill is $964, within a few days, the Federal Reserve bank sends you a check for $36. About a month before the T-bill matures, the Federal Reserve bank sends you a form that gives you the options of getting back your full $1,000 investment, or of rolling it over into a new bill and again getting a discount. You pay no commission or redemption fee.

Since you receive the discount well in advance of the maturity of the bill, the true yield on an annual basis works out to be higher than the discount. The difference can be a percentage point or more.

There are several ways in which you can buy Treasury bills. You can buy a T-bill through your bank or broker, paying a fee, or you can buy it from any Federal Reserve bank branch. (See the inset on page 93.) To buy a T-bill, you must fill out an application known as a *tender,* or bid, which requires only your name, address, Social Security number, signature, date, whether you want to reinvest at maturity at whatever rate is then prevailing, and whether you are submitting a competitive or noncompetitive bid. A purchaser spending under $1,000,000 buys on a *noncompetitive* basis. This means that the buyer will receive a price or discount equal to the average bid of all the big-money bidders.

To buy a T-bill, you need to send a cashier's check or certified personal check payable to the Federal Reserve bank along with the completed tender. You will then receive a receipt as evidence of ownership. Engraved certificates are no longer given, which is an advantage since they can be stolen or counterfeited.

Interest rates for three- and six-month T-bills

are set by the Treasury at auctions held weekly, every Monday. Auctions for twelve-month T-bills are held by the Treasury on a monthly basis, every third Thursday. If you buy by mail, the envelope containing your application and check must be postmarked no later than midnight of the day preceding the auction. If it is late, your application and check will be automatically held until the next week's auction.

The decision to buy short-term or relatively long-term bills depends on your individual situation and your guess concerning the future course of interest rates. In a period of declining rates, you would be prudent to nail down current higher yields by buying longer-term bills. But in periods of uncertainty, many investors stick to short-term bills.

United States Treasury Notes

The United States government borrows billions of dollars each year by selling Treasury notes. *Treasury notes,* or *T-notes,* are IOUs backed by the full faith and credit of the United States government. They have maturities of two years, five years, or ten years. Since August 1998, the minimum investment has been $1,000. Like the interest on T-bills, the interest on T-notes is not subject to state or local income tax, but is taxed by the federal government.

Interest rates on Treasury notes are set by auction. The auction for two-year notes is held monthly on the third or fourth Tuesday. The auction for five-year and ten-year notes is held quarterly, in February, May, August, and November.

You can buy a T-note through your bank or broker, paying a fee, or you can buy it from any Federal Reserve bank branch. (See the inset on page 93.) A Treasury note can be paid for by a cashier's check or certified personal check payable to the Federal Reserve. After you have sent in a completed application form and your payment, you will receive a receipt as evidence of ownership. The interest earned is automatically sent to you by the United States Treasury every six months from the issue date.

Treasury notes can be considered a money market instrument even though they run longer than one year. This is because they can be traded when they are close to maturity.

Commercial Paper

Corporations pay investors for the short-term use of cash. A corporate IOU is issued to raise funds for a limited period of time, usually thirty days or less. The certificates, called *commercial paper,* are generally issued in denominations of $100,000 or more. The investor receives no collateral for this loan, but the interest paid is above that of T-bills. Be sure to check the ratings of commercial paper. The highest ratings are F-1 (Fitch Investors Service), Prime-1 (Moody's), and A-1 (Standard & Poor's). Commercial paper is sold directly by issuers and by dealers, brokers, and investment bankers. It is not for amateur investors.

Banker's Acceptances

Import and export transactions involve a loan known as a *banker's acceptance.* In these transactions, a seller draws a *draft,* a document for transferring money, payable by the buyer within a stipulated period of time. The bank financing the transaction accepts the draft, guaranteeing payment at maturity and thereby making the draft salable in the open market. The money market fund can buy the acceptance at a discount and be paid the full amount at maturity.

Repurchase Agreements

In a *repurchase agreement,* or *repo,* a bank that is anxious to borrow money for a short period of time sells United States Treasury bills to a money market mutual fund with the promise that it will buy them back the next day, or within an agreed-upon period of time. The bank must buy back the T-bills at a higher price or at a specified interest rate. Repos actually are loans that use United States Treasury securities as the collateral.

INFLATION-INDEXED SECURITIES

In January 1997, the United States Treasury introduced a new type of security, known as *Treasury inflation-indexed securities*. As the name suggests, these securities are designed to help protect investors against one of the risks of owning securities—inflation. Like interest on all U.S. Treasury securities, the semiannual interest payments on inflation-indexed securities are exempt from state and local income taxes, but are taxable by the federal government in the year in which you receive the interest. In addition, these securities are backed by the full faith and credit of the government.

Inflation-indexed securities are issued with maturities that range from two to thirty years. Like most conventional Treasury notes and bonds, they are sold in minimum denominations and multiples of $1,000. The interest rates are set by auction, which is held quarterly, in January, April, July, and October. What makes these securities different from others is that the principal is indexed to the Consumer Price Index, and is continually adjusted for inflation. At maturity, the Treasury will redeem your securities at their inflation-adjusted principal or at the par amount, whichever is greater. The interest is also protected from inflation, as the fixed semiannual rate is applied to the principal, which is continually being inflation-adjusted.

Inflation-indexed securities are ideal for anyone who is saving for longer-term goals such as retirement, and is concerned that continued increases in the cost of living may erode the purchasing power of their investments. Through inflation-indexed securities, you can benefit from an inflation-adjusted stream of interest payments and principal repayment at maturity.

You can buy a T-note through your bank or broker, paying a fee, or you can buy it from any Federal Reserve bank branch. (See the inset on page 93.)

MUTUAL FUNDS

A *mutual fund*, which currently is a popular investment, is a company that collects the funds of hundreds of thousands of small investors through the sale of stock, and then uses the collected funds for investment purposes. The investment philosophy of a specific fund and the types of investments it makes are spelled out in its prospectus. About 8,000 mutual funds currently operate in the United States, with assets of $6.4 trillion.

Mutual funds can be classified according to their investment objectives. Some common types of mutual funds are the following:

❏ **Growth funds.** Also known as *equity mutual funds* and *stock mutual funds*, growth funds are the most popular form of mutual fund. They invest primarily in common stocks and seek capital appreciation.

❏ **Aggressive growth funds.** These funds take more risk to earn higher returns.

❏ **Income funds.** These mutual funds invest in quality bonds to maintain a high level of income for their shareholders, making income funds attractive to retired investors. Income funds specialize in particular types of bonds, including corporate bonds, United States government bonds, Ginnie Maes, and municipal bonds.

Do You Need a Financial Planner?

As you plan for your retirement, you may decide to manage your finances on your own. This is a good choice if your financial affairs are relatively simple and/or you have the time and temperament necessary to create and implement a solid financial strategy. But a growing number of people have discovered that a professional financial planner can be a wonderful asset as they work towards retirement. Just what can a financial planner do for you? The primary goal is to take stock of your existing resources and then draw up a comprehensive plan that can help you meet your short- and long-term goals in the best way possible. Such a plan may involve a budget, a savings strategy, and specific types of investments. You can then implement the plan on your own, or your adviser can help you select qualified professionals who will assist you with investments.

If you choose to seek out a professional to guide your financial decisions, it is important to find a capable and experienced person who respects your ideas for handling money. Begin by asking for referrals from family members and friends, your accountant, your lawyer, and your banker. Then check with industry associations such as the Financial Planning Association, the National Association of Personal Financial Advisors, and the Society of Financial Service Professionals. These organizations will send you lists of financial planners in your area. (See the Resources section.)

Some planners are actually salespeople who wish to sell specific investments for which they earn a commission. Avoid such planners, and look for advisers who charge a straight fee for services. Also avoid planners whose training is in tax preparation and accounting, but who are not well versed in other areas of finance.

When you have gathered the names of several planners, set up an interview with each one to see who would best meet your needs. Start by checking the credentials of the adviser. Your best bet is to look for a financial planner with one or more of the following credentials:

❑ **Certified Financial Planner (CFP).** This designation indicates that the person had at least

---

❑ **Growth and income funds.** These funds invest in both stocks and bonds to provide capital growth as well as regular, fixed income. Sometimes referred to as *balanced funds*, they combine the objectives of growth funds and income funds.

❑ **Long-term growth funds.** These funds take less risk and seek long-term growth.

❑ **Money market funds.** These mutual funds invest in instruments of the money market such as United States Treasury bills and commercial paper. Money market mutual funds are popular today, but only for storage of money, not for income or capital growth.

❑ **International and global funds.** These funds invest in corporations and businesses located anywhere in the world, such as Europe in general or specific countries, like France or Canada, for example. Their objective is growth.

three years of work experience in the financial planning field, has completed an approved course of study, and has passed a rigorous exam on financial planning offered by the Certified Financial Planner Board of Standards.

❏ **Chartered Financial Consultants (ChFC).** This designation is given to people who have completed a specific course of study and passed examinations on personal finance offered by The American College in Bryn Mawr, Pennsylvania.

❏ **Certified Public Accountant (CPA) certified as Personal Finance Specialist (PFS).** A CPA designation alone indicates only that the individual has passed examinations on tax preparation and accounting. The PFS designation, however, is awarded by the American Institute of CPAs to those who meet specific requirements in the area of personal financial planning.

❏ **Registered Financial Consultant (RFC).** The RFC designation shows that the consultant has met strict requirements of education, experience, and integrity in the financial services industry.

Once you have established the planner's credentials, move on to the subject of experience. You'll want to know if he or she has advised clients with financial situations similar to your own. You'll also want to assess the adviser's investment philosophy to see whether it is compatible with yours, and you'll want to make sure that the adviser pays attention to what you have to say—that he or she truly understands your personal goals. Of course, you must also make sure that the compensation required by the adviser is in line with what you are willing to pay. Finally, you'll want to ask for the names of long-term clients whom you can contact for further information.

Once you have chosen a financial adviser and have devised a satisfactory financial plan, be sure to meet with your adviser at least once a year to review your financial situation and make any necessary adjustments in your strategy. As you work with your planner year after year, remember that this person is working for *you,* and that the financial plan you have developed is *yours.* You have the right to make decisions, to know where your funds are, and to withdraw your money for any reason. You also have the right to switch to another planner if your relationship with your present one proves to be unsatisfactory in any way.

❏ **Sector funds.** These funds invest in particular areas of the economy, such as energy, chemicals, or nonprecious metals.

❏ **Specialized funds.** Some of these mutual funds invest solely in new businesses. Others invest in gold, gold bullion, or Eurodollars, which are American dollars deposited in foreign banks. Some seek maximum capital gains by investing in highly speculative items such as *call options,* which are the right to buy stock at certain prices within certain time limits; *put options,* which are the right to sell stock at certain prices within certain time limits; or *futures contracts,* which are contracts to buy or sell commodities at a certain price on a certain future date. Many of these funds are extremely risky and are not recommended for retiree investment.

In addition to their investment objectives, mutual funds can be classified according to whether they are closed- or open-end funds, and whether they are load or no-load funds. A *closed-end company* is a mutual fund that has issued a fixed number of shares of stock, which are traded at the prevailing market prices listed on one or more of the major stock exchanges. It issues new shares infrequently. In contrast, an *open-end company* continuously sells new shares of stock and purchases shares from people desiring redemption. It buys and sells its shares at a fixed price, and uses whatever funds it has for its investments.

A *load fund* is a mutual fund that charges a commission, or *load*, on the shares you buy or sell. The load ranges from 7.5 percent to 8.5 percent, which is the maximum allowed by the United States Securities and Exchange Commission (SEC). A *no-load fund* charges no sales fee, has no sales force, and waits for investors to come to it to purchase shares. Both load and no-load funds charge a management fee, which amounts to 3 percent or less of the interest earned on the money you have invested in the fund.

There are many advantages to investing in a mutual fund. Among them are the following:

❏ **Small investment.** Only a small investment is required by mutual funds. In fact, some accept initial investments of as little as $50, with subsequent investments as low as $25. Check the individual fund.

❏ **Professional management.** Your money is managed by full-time, professional money managers whose education and experience qualify them to handle money prudently.

❏ **Low management fee.** The usual management fee is small, ranging from 1 to 3 percent.

❏ **No sales commission.** About half of all mutual funds do not charge a sales commission, or load. Your full investment works for you from the outset.

❏ **Diversification.** Mutual funds offer a much larger measure of diversity than most investors can afford to achieve on their own. This reduces risk.

❏ **Liquidity.** Redemption of your money often requires no more than a telephone call to the headquarters of your fund. You can receive your money quickly.

❏ **Flexibility.** Some of the larger mutual fund companies that have a variety of mutual funds under the same overall administration allow you to transfer freely among the funds.

HOMES AND OTHER REAL ESTATE

Home ownership has always been a sound investment in terms of capital gains. The deductions you enjoy on your income taxes include the interest you pay on your mortgage loan as well as the payments you make on your property taxes. And if you sell your home, you can enjoy a tax-free profit of up to $500,000. (See Chapter 3 for further details.)

In addition to their homes, many older people and retirees have moderate investments in other real estate and in mortgages that earn extra retirement income.

Real Estate Investment Trust

Buying stock in a *Real Estate Investment Trust (REIT)* is considered an ideal way to participate in real estate investment if you do not want to buy property or make a mortgage loan on your own. Professionally managed, REITs make investments in big commercial properties and shopping centers. Individual investors are able to pull out at any time by selling their shares.

GOLD, SILVER, AND COLLECTIBLES

During the past several years, many investors

have been putting their money into tangibles such as gold and silver and a variety of *collectibles,* including diamonds and other precious stones, art, antique furniture, stamps, coins, rare books, antique cars, and Tiffany glass. Many investors turn to gold to counteract high rates of inflation, to diversify an investment portfolio, or to have an insurance policy against the day when all paper assets may be worthless. Some investors buy gold coins or gold bars. Others invest in gold commodity futures, gold-mining stocks, or shares in gold mutual funds, which probably invest in a combination of bullion, coins, and mining stocks. Silver prices have been precisely following the movement of gold prices. People invest in collectibles in the hope that their items will increase in value, yielding a profit.

INVESTMENT TIPS

The interest or dividend return that you can earn on an investment is directly related to the amount of risk you assume. An axiom of investing is that the greater the risk you take, the greater the return you can expect. Very high-risk investments will yield very high returns *if* you select winners. But risk always involves the element of potential loss, and if you select a loser, you may lose most or all of what you have invested.

Each individual has a specific level of risk tolerance. To determine your own risk quotient, see Self-Study 6.2. As an investor, it is your responsibility to stay in the risk zone that leaves you comfortable with your selection. High-risk investments should not be undertaken by people who are concerned about the safety of their principal. Such investments should be undertaken only by wealthy individuals who have a high risk quotient and will not suffer too much in the event of significant losses.

The investment pyramid in Figure 6.1 shows the levels of risk. The foundation of the pyramid represents the minimum-risk investments in which most of a retiree's portfolio should be stored. The items in this group are the financial instruments that are worry-free, can be easily converted into cash, and pay market interest rates—money market deposit accounts, money market mutual funds, certificates of deposit, United States Treasury bills and notes, and any of the other forms of investment that are listed for Level 4. A much smaller portion should go into moderate-risk investments, such as blue chip common and preferred stocks, real estate, and certain stock and bond mutual funds. *Blue chip stock* is stock in a company known nationally for the quality and wide acceptance of its product or services, and for its ability to earn large profits and to pay dividends regularly. Again, the investor's risk tolerance must be considered. Average small investors should not risk capital in very high- or high-risk investments, which are the forms of investment included in Levels 1 and 2 of the investment pyramid. None of a retiree's money should be put into these investments.

If you are a prospective retiree, you must begin to think about maximizing your retirement income and keeping your taxes as low as possible. In addition, you want to have the feeling of security that comes from knowing that your monthly income is certain and uninterrupted. Therefore, you should take a conservative approach, seeking investments that offer safety, liquidity, and good yields with minimum risk. (See Figure 6.1.) Before deciding on an optimum portfolio mix, first analyze your current portfolio using Self-Study 6.3. Then, keeping your risk quotient in mind, you can begin to make adjustments to your portfolio.

Table 6.1 on page 105 presents a suggested investment strategy for the average small

Figure 6.1. The Investment Pyramid.

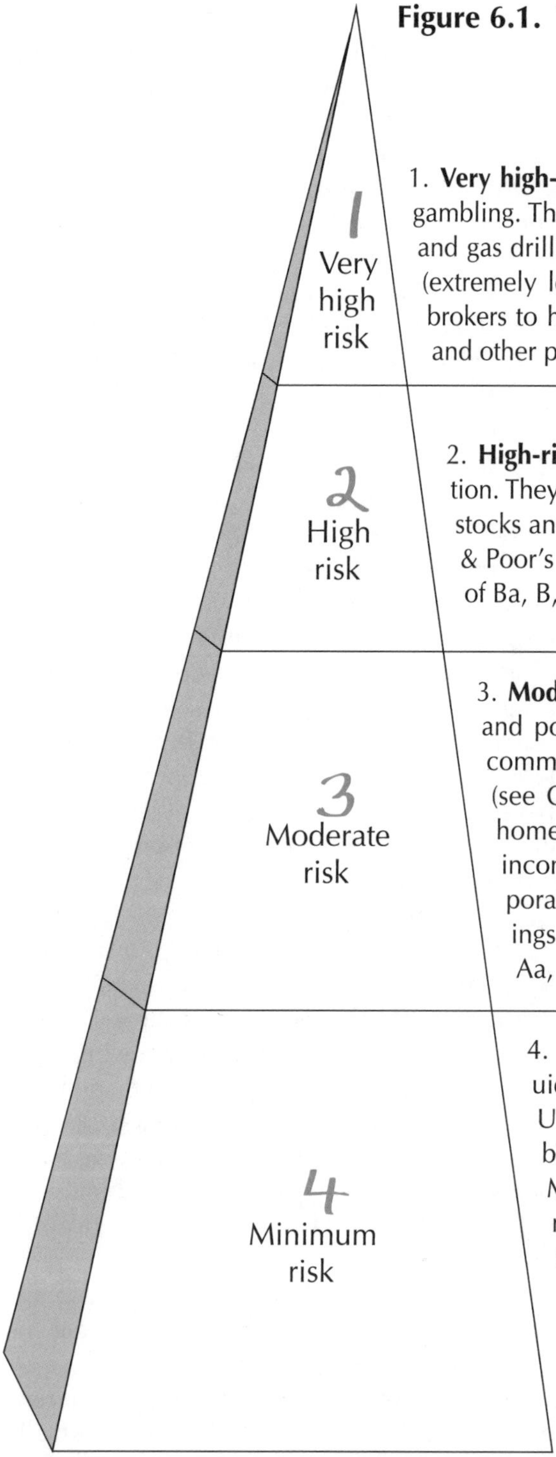

1. **Very high-risk investments.** These are a sophisticated form of gambling. They include futures contracts, options, collectibles, oil and gas drilling ventures, raw land, foreign stocks, *penny stocks* (extremely low priced stocks), *margin accounts* (accounts with brokers to help pay for the purchase of stock), and gold, silver, and other precious metals.

1 Very high risk

2. **High-risk investments.** These contain elements of speculation. They include common stocks of low quality, new issues of stocks and bonds, and speculative grade bonds with Standard & Poor's ratings of BB, B, CCC, CC, or D, or Moody's ratings of Ba, B, Caa, Ca, or C.

2 High risk

3. **Moderate-risk investments.** These offer regular income and potential long-term growth. They include blue chip common stocks and preferred stocks, variable annuities (see Chapter 9), investment real estate other than your home, stock and bond mutual funds whose goals are income and long-term growth, and investment grade corporate and municipal bonds with Standard & Poor's ratings of AAA, AA, A, or BBB, or Moody's ratings of Aaa, Aa, A, or Baa.

3 Moderate risk

4. **Minimum-risk investments.** These offer safety, liquidity, and good yield. They include Series I and EE United States savings bonds, United States Treasury bills and notes, federal agency bonds such as Ginnie Maes and Fannie Maes, individual tax-exempt municipal bonds rated triple-A, money market mutual funds, tax-exempt bond mutual funds, and bank offerings such as certificates of deposit and money market accounts. They also include other safe items such as equity, or net investment, in your own home; fixed annuities (see Chapter 9); and cash value of life insurance.

4 Minimum risk

TABLE 6.1

	Portfolio Composition		
Goals and Investments	**More Than 5 Years to Retirement**	**Within 5 Years of Retirement**	**Retired**
Safety of Principal Money market mutual funds United States Treasury bills Certificates of deposit U.S. savings bonds	20%	25%	30%
Income United States Treasury bonds Corporate bonds Municipal bonds Bond mutual funds Ginnie Maes	30%	35%	45%
Growth Common stocks Stock mutual funds Real Estate	50%	40%	25%
Total	100%	100%	100%

ASSET ALLOCATION FOR MODERATE RISK INVESTORS

investor who is able to tolerate moderate risk. The percentage distributions can be modified to suit your individual needs or risk quotient. If you are planning for retirement, you should put more of your assets into minimum-risk investments than you would if you were still working. The mix of investments should also depend on how close you are to your actual retirement.

CONSUMPTION OF SAVINGS

The savings and investments you accumulated while working are significant sources of retirement income. If, after retirement, you withdraw a portion of your capital every month for living expenses, how long will your nest egg last? The answer depends on the interest rate the money is earning and the amount you withdraw monthly.

Table 6.2 on page 106 shows the number of years a sum of money can last when it is earning various interest rates, and various percentages are being withdrawn annually. Regardless of the amount of capital you consume, if the interest rate paid by the savings institution equals the percent of principal you withdraw, the fund will last indefinitely. If you have $10,000 invested, earning 8 percent interest, and you withdraw just 8 percent a year, your capital will last indefinitely because you are withdrawing only the

TABLE 6.2

Interest Rate Paid	Percentage of Principal Withdrawn Annually										
	5%	6%	7%	8%	9%	10%	11%	12%	13%	14%	15%
5%		37	26	20	16	14	12	11	10	9	8
6%		∞	34	24	19	16	13	12	10	9	9
7%			∞	31	22	18	15	13	11	10	9
8%				∞	29	21	17	14	12	11	10
9%					∞	27	20	16	13	12	10
10%						∞	26	19	15	13	11
11%							∞	24	18	14	12
12%								∞	23	17	14
13%									∞	22	16
14%										∞	21
15%											∞

NUMBER OF YEARS MONEY CAN LAST AT VARIOUS INTEREST RATES AND PERCENTAGES OF PRINCIPAL WITHDRAWN ANNUALLY*

Source: Reprinted with permission of American Community Bankers.

*Assumptions made in this table are the following:

1. Withdrawals are made at the end of each month.

2. There are no penalties for premature withdrawal.

3. Interest is compounded daily, which provides the highest return possible under current banking regulations. Compounding is the process of earning interest on the interest already earned on an investment.

∞ Indefinitely (the symbol means "infinity").

interest that you are earning. On the other hand, if you have $10,000 invested, earning 8 percent interest, and you withdraw 12 percent a year, your $10,000 will last only about 14 years.

In short, your savings will last as long as you live if you withdraw only the interest earned.

Savings and investments are at the core of a solid retirement plan. If you choose savings and investment vehicles that are well suited to both your level of risk tolerance and the amount of capital you will consume during your retirement years, you can feel confident that these years will be ones of safety and security.

Self-Study 6.1

CALCULATE THE STATUS
OF YOUR EMERGENCY SAVINGS FUND

Your financial retirement plan should include an emergency savings fund equal to three to six months of your annual cost of living. Calculate the status of your emergency savings fund and set a goal for achieving the required amount as follows:

Emergency savings for a single retiree or a couple:

Yearly cost of living in _____ $_____

Emergency savings fund should be $_____

Actual savings are $_____

Surplus or shortage is $_____

If your savings are short, divide the shortage by the amount of money you can afford to save each week to determine the number of weeks you need to reach your goal. For example:

$$\frac{\$3,000 \text{ shortage}}{\text{Can save } \$30 \text{ a week}} \quad = \quad 100 \text{ weeks, or about 2 years.}$$

Self-Study 6.2

CALCULATE YOUR RISK QUOTIENT

Now that you know the types of investments that are available, as well as the level of risk associated with each, you can calculate your *risk quotient* (RQ). This exercise will enable you to determine the level of risk that you are economically and psychologically suited to undertake.

To determine your RQ, circle the response for each item that most closely describes you and enter the score in the final column. Then, add all the individual scores for a total score, which will give you your RQ and an approximate indication of your most suitable portfolio mix.

If your RQ is between 31 and 80, you can be classified as a moderate risk investor. See page 105 for a suggested portfolio mix. If your score is 81 or higher, you can handle a larger percentage of high risk investments. And if your score is 30 or less, you would do best with minimum risk investments, remembering that some proportion of your portfolio should be in growth type investments, which in the long run outperform other types of investments.

Item						Score
Your age	21–30 4	31–40 5	41–50 7	51–60 5	Over 60 1	
Total family income	$10,000–20,000 1	$20,001–30,000 2	$30,001–50,000 4	$50,001–75,000 6	Over $75,000 8	
Total savings	$2,000–5,000 1	$5,001–15,000 3	$15,001–40,000 5	$40,001–75,000 8	Over $75,000 10	
Value of Your home (Equity)	$20,000–60,000 1	$60,001–100,000 2	$100,001–150,000 3	$150,001–200,000 4	Over $200,000 5	
Life insurance coverage	$10,000–20,000 1	$20,001–50,000 2	$50,001–100,000 3	$100,001–200,000 4	Over $200,000 5	
Number of dependents	Only yourself 10	1 additional 6	2–3 additional 4	4–5 additional 2	More than 5 1	
Investment income used for living costs	Never 10	Seldom 8	Occasionally 5	Often 3	Always 1	
Employment and income security	Very stable 10		Fairly stable 5		Unstable 1	
Major medical or disability income	Have both 10		Have one 4		Have neither 1	
Your attitude toward taking risk	Enjoy risk-taking 10		Take occasional risks 5		Avoid risk 1	
Investment principal earmarked for major goals	Yes: for education and retirement 1		No: but need for overall security 4		Could afford to lose my principal 15	
					Total	

Source: Reprinted with permission of R. & R. Newkirk, P.O. Box 1727, Indianapolis, Indiana.

Self-Study 6.3
ANALYSIS OF YOUR PORTFOLIO

Before deciding on an optimum portfolio mix, you should first analyze your current portfolio. Using the format on the following page, enter the current dollar value of each of your assets. Then, compute the percentage of your portfolio in each type of investment. This will enable you to determine whether the proportions conform with your needs or desires.

Current Value and Percentage Distribution of Your Assets as of _____

Assets	Current dollar value	Percent of total
Safety of Principal		
Savings accounts		
Certificates of Deposit		
U.S. Savings Bonds: Series I and EE		
U.S. Treasury paper: Bills and Notes		
Money Market Mutual Funds		
Total		

Income		
U.S. Treasury Bonds		
Corporate Bonds		
Corporate Bond Mutual Funds		
Municipal Bonds		
Ginnie Maes (GNMA)		
Ginnie Mae Mutual Funds		
Total		

Assets	Current dollar value	Percent of total
Growth		
Common Stocks		
Common Stock Mutual Funds		
Preferred stocks/mutual funds		
Equity in your home(s)*		
Real Estate Investment Trusts		
Other real estate		
Total		

Other Investments		
Other Investments		
Gold, silver, collectibles		
Itemize:		
Total		
Grand Total		100%

* Estimated market value of your home(s) minus mortgage balance.

7

SOCIAL SECURITY

The philosophy of the American government for its first 150 years of existence was that responsibility for the care of the poor and the aged was a private matter, one that belonged to the family. State and local communities did help on occasion, but only in cases of dire need. When the Social Security Act was signed into law by President Franklin D. Roosevelt in August 1935, responsibility for the aged was transferred from the individual family to society. This was a giant step forward for the United States, taken long after the industrial nations of Europe had adopted some form of retirement benefits for their citizens.

Today, our Social Security program is an integral part of the American economic system. It is a federal program that provides comprehensive benefits for you and your family—a package of benefits that would otherwise be unaffordable. Payments for benefits are derived by taxing the earnings of working people. This package includes retirement, disability, and survivors' benefits. Supplemental Security Income, a fourth program, is payable to the blind, disabled, and people age 65 or older whose principal sources of income are insufficient to provide

a minimum standard of living. Medicare, a fifth program, provides hospitalization and medical expense benefits to those 65 or older. (For a detailed discussion of Medicare, see Chapter 16.)

Under the Old Age (Retirement), Survivors, and Disability Insurance program (OASDI), the Social Security system provides the following benefits:

❑ Monthly benefits to retirees and their spouses.

❑ Monthly benefits for the survivors of deceased workers.

❑ Monthly benefits for disabled workers and their dependents.

❑ A lump-sum death benefit payment for certain insured workers.

The Health Insurance portion of the system, known as Medicare, includes both hospital insurance benefits (Part A) and medical insurance benefits that pay for doctors' bills (Part B). The medical benefits program is a voluntary supplementary program that is partially financed by each person who enrolls. The monthly premium covers about a quarter of the cost, with the rest funded by general tax revenues of the federal government.

A notable change affecting the Social Security Administration came from the Social Security Independence and Program Improvement Act of 1994. According to this act, on March 31, 1995, the Social Security Administration was removed from the United States Department of Health and Human Services and became an independent agency. An immediate benefit was greater visibility and accountability. Independence insulates the agency from politics and enables it to help the public understand that Social Security will be a healthy program for generations to come.

THE SOCIAL SECURITY SYSTEM

Many people see the Social Security system as complex and confusing. The following explanations may help clarify some details and therefore make the system easier to understand. Also refer to Table 7.1, which provides a handy summary of essential Social Security facts.

Social Security Financing

Social Security and Medicare Part A are financed by matching contributions from employees and employers, currently 7.65 percent of a person's wages. Of this amount, 6.2 percent of earnings up to maximum wages of $84,900 goes into two separate trust funds—5.6 percent goes into the Old Age and Survivors Insurance (OASI) Trust Fund, and 0.6 percent into the Disability Insurance (DI) Trust Fund. To view this another way, 85 cents of each Social Security tax dollar goes to the OASI Trust Fund, and 15 cents goes to the DI Trust Fund.

At the present time, the federal government borrows Social Security surpluses to balance its own annual budget. The spending of these surplus funds by the government hides the true size of the federal deficit, which is attributable to other spending programs, not to the payment of Social Security benefits. In exchange for these monies, the government issues United States Treasury bonds that the Social Security trust funds hold as reserves.

Currently, more than 45.2 million men, women, and children are receiving benefits from Social Security. Benefits are being paid to approximately:

❑ 29.5 million retirees and their spouses

❑ 7.5 million widows and widowers

❑ 5 million disabled workers and their spouses

❑ 3 million children of retired, deceased, or disabled workers

More than 150 million workers in the United States are now contributing to the Social Security system through earnings deductions, and therefore are building the *earned right* to future retirement benefits for themselves and their dependents; disability benefits to protect them and their dependents in the event of severe, long-term disability; and, when they die, survivors' benefits for their spouses and dependent children and/or dependent parents.

Social Security Payroll Deductions

As explained earlier, the benefits paid by Social Security are derived by taxing the earnings of working people. In addition, for every dollar you pay, your employer contributes an equal amount. If you are self-employed, you pay twice what individual employees pay because you do not have an employer to match your contribution. On your paycheck, the abbreviation "FICA," which stands for Federal Insurance Contributions Act,

TABLE 7.1

SOCIAL SECURITY FACT SHEET		
Year	**2002**	**2001**
Maximum taxable wages	**$84,900**	**$80,400**
Withholding tax:		
Employee	7.65% [a]	7.65%
Employer	7.65% [a]	7.65%
Self-employed	15.30% [b]	15.30%
Maximum earnings while receiving benefits:		
Ages 62–64	$11,280/year [c] ($940/month)	$10,680/year ($890/month)
Age 65 or higher	No limit [d]	No limit
Cost-of-living adjustment (COLA)	2.6%	3.5%
Quarters of coverage required if you reach age 62 in year shown	40	40
Maximum benefit starting at age 65	$1,660/month	$1,536/month
Average benefit: retired workers	$874/month	$852/month
Quarter of coverage (Earnings)	$870	$830
Lump-sum death benefit	$255	$255

[a] The tax remains at 7.65%. 6.2 % goes for OASDI (Old Age, Survivors, and Disability Insurance) on wages up to $84,900 and 1.45 percent on *all wages* earned in 2002 for HI (Hospital Insurance) which is a tax that pays for Medicare, Part A (Hospitalization costs).

[b] Of the 15.30 percent, 12.4 percent goes for OASDI on wages up to $84,900, and 2.9 percent goes for HI on *all wages* for 2002.

[c] Beneficiaries earning over this amount will lose $1 of their benefits for each $2 in earnings above the limit.

[d] The senior Citizens' Freedom to Work Act of 2000, signed into law by President Clinton on April 7, 2000, eliminated the Retirement Earnings Test for Ages 65–69, effective January 2000. Age 70 or higher had no limit on earnings.

identifies your Social Security payroll deductions. Social Security taxes are collected by the Internal Revenue Service, which transmits them to the United States Treasury.

The amount of money collected by the Social Security system depends on two factors— the *tax rate* and the *maximum taxable amount*, which, as the term implies, is the maximum amount of earnings that can be taxed. Table 7.2 presents the tax rates and maximum taxable amounts for the years 1990 through 2002.

When Congress decides to increase the Social Security tax rate or maximum taxable amount, it simply amends the Federal Insurance Contributions Act (FICA) for employees and employers, and the Self-Employment Contributions Act for the self-employed. Although increases in the tax rates and taxable amounts mean that workers in the higher income brackets pay more into Social Security, higher paid workers also are

able to count on greater benefits when they retire. This is because benefit amounts are based upon earnings credited for Social Security.

The Soundness of the Social Security Program

Until 1983, the Social Security program operated as a *pay-as-you-go system*, with each year's income used to pay for that year's beneficiaries. Since 1983, as a result of amendments to the Social Security Act, the program has been operating under a *partial reserve* method of funding, and accumulates reserves for the future. The system's current income is greater than its current expenditures, and, as mentioned earlier, the surpluses that are accumulating in the form of United States Treasury bonds actually help finance the federal deficit.

Currently, the Social Security system is so

TABLE 7.2

	SOCIAL SECURITY TAX RATES AND MAXIMUM TAXABLE AMOUNTS SINCE 1990			
Year	Employee Tax Rate	Employer Tax Rate	Self-Employed Tax Rate	Maximum Taxable Amount
1990	7.65%	7.65%	15.30%	$51,300
1991	7.65	7.65	15.30	53,400
1992	7.65	7.65	15.30	55,500
1993	7.65	7.65	15.30	57,600
1994	7.65	7.65	15.30	60,600
1995	7.65	7.65	15.30	61,200
1996	7.65	7.65	15.30	62,700
1997	7.65	7.65	15.30	65,400
1998	7.65	7.65	15.30	68,400
1999	7.65	7.65	15.30	72,600
2000	7.65	7.65	15.30	76,200
2001	7.65	7.65	15.30	80,400
2002	7.65	7.65	15.30	84,900

well funded that annual surpluses will continue for many years. In 1995, there was a $70 billion surplus; by 2001, the surplus had grown to over a trillion dollars. The income interest alone in 2000 was $53.5 billion—an effective interest rate yield of 6.9 percent. At the current rate of growth, the fund is expected to reach more than *$6 trillion* by 2020.

According to the 2001 Social Security Trustees Report, Social Security will be able to pay full benefits until 2038. Many plans are being suggested to insure benefit payments beyond that year. Relatively minor changes could guarantee 100 percent of benefits paid until 2075 and beyond. Baby boomers can be reassured that, with a few minor adjustments, Social Security will be financially sound for many years to come.

Tax and Legal Status of Benefits

Not everyone who receives Social Security benefits is required to pay taxes on the payments received. When adjusted gross income (AGI) is less than $25,000 for a single beneficiary and $32,000 for a married couple, the benefits are exempt from taxation. However, those whose incomes exceed these thresholds are obliged to pay tax on some part of their benefits. Note that income from all sources is counted, including tax-exempt municipal bond interest and half of your Social Security benefit.

Social Security beneficiaries with an AGI of $25,000 to $34,000 for singles and $32,000 to $44,000 for couples are subject to tax for 50 percent of their benefits. Beneficiaries with an AGI above $34,000 for singles and $44,000 for couples are subject to tax for 85 percent of benefits. This does not mean that you pay 85 percent of your benefit. These taxes are paid according to your regular income tax bracket rate. The instructions included in your annual income tax forms provide a worksheet to help you figure out how much of your benefit is subject to taxation.

Since its inception, Social Security benefits were not subject to garnishment or attachment, except for delinquent federal taxes, child support, or alimony payments. But due to the 1996 Debt Collection Improvement Act, the government can now withhold up to 15 percent of benefits due beneficiaries who have defaulted on veterans mortgage, small business, disaster, and student loans. However, the first $750 of monthly Social Security payments are exempt from seizure, and no benefits are withheld from people with disabilities or those on Supplemental Security Income.

UNDERSTANDING HOW RETIREMENT BENEFITS ARE CALCULATED

Several factors determine your eligibility for retirement benefits, and establish what the actual dollar amount of your benefit will be. You should have a basic understanding of how you can qualify for Social Security; how your monthly benefit is computed; and how the income you receive from Social Security is affected by your age at retirement and increases in the cost of living.

Qualifications for Retirement Benefits

To qualify for retirement benefits, you must satisfy three requirements:

1. You must have reached *retirement age*. Retirement age is currently set at 65. However, at any point from age 62 on, you can retire and receive a monthly benefit for life.

2. You must be *fully insured*, having worked the required number of *quarters of coverage (QCs)* for your age. A quarter is one-fourth of a year, or three months. The four quarters in the year are January 1–March 31, April 1–June 30, July 1–September 30, and October 1–December 31.

In addition, during each quarter of coverage, you must have earned a certain minimum amount—an amount that is adjusted annually to keep pace with inflation. For instance, in 2002, you must earn a minimum of $870 within a specified quarter to earn one QC. If you have ten years of work credit, or forty QCs, you are fully insured and will never need additional QCs regardless of your age. For any type of benefit, you must have a minimum of six QCs, but the benefit will be scaled down. "Fully insured" does not mean that you will get the highest monthly benefit. It merely means that you have enough QCs to be eligible to receive benefits when you retire, or for your survivors to receive benefits when you die.

3. You must file an application, since benefits are not paid automatically when you retire.

Determining Your Social Security Retirement Benefit

Social Security benefits are based on earnings averaged over your lifetime. Your actual earnings are first adjusted, or "indexed," to account for wage increases due to inflation. The Social Security Administration then calculates your average monthly indexed earnings during the thirty-five years in which your income was the greatest. They then apply a formula to these earnings to arrive at your basic benefit, which is called the *primary insurance amount* (PIA). This is the amount you will receive at your full retirement at age 65 or older.

These days, it is very easy to get an official estimate of your Social Security benefit. In 1999, the Social Security Administration began annually mailing out Social Security statements—a record of earnings and estimates of benefits—to workers age 25 and older, so you may already have an estimate on hand. If you did not receive this statement, phone the Social Security Administration and ask for a Request for Earnings and Benefit Estimate Statement (Form SSA-7004). When you receive the form, fill it out and mail it as directed. In response, you will receive an official record of earnings and benefit estimates. You can also download the form from the Social Security website. Or you can calculate your benefit using the programs available on the website. (See the Resources section for all contact information.)

It is important to understand, though, that the benefit you actually receive from Social Security may be higher or lower than your calculated basic benefit. The factors that can raise or lower your retirement benefit include cost-of-living adjustments, early retirement, continuing to work after retirement, and late retirement. These factors are explored in the following discussions.

Cost-of-Living Adjustments (COLAs)

When most people retire, one of their main concerns is protecting their retirement income against inflation. Fortunately, some protection is built into the Social Security payment system in that the payments are raised each year on a scale that is tied to the increase in the cost of living. The United States Congress approved these automatic increases in Social Security benefits, called *cost-of-living adjustments (COLAs)*, starting in 1975. Using the United States Consumer Price Index as the guideline, Social Security makes the adjustment once a year.

Table 7.3 shows the cost-of-living adjustments for 1990 to 2001. Originally, the adjustment was made effective July 1, and the dollar increase was included in the July benefit check. The Social Security Amendments of 1983, however, postponed the payment of the cost-of-living increase for six months, moving it from July 1983 to January 1984. Since then, January has been the permanent month for COLA increases.

TABLE 7.3

COST-OF-LIVING ADJUSTMENTS, 1990–2001	
Date of Payment	Percentage of Increase in Benefits
December 1990	5.4
December 1991	3.7
December 1992	3.0
December 1993	2.6
December 1994	2.8
December 1995	2.6
December 1996	2.9
December 1997	2.1
December 1998	1.3
December 1999	2.4
December 2000	3.5
December 2001	2.6

It is comforting for benefit recipients and potential retirees to know that benefit payments will continue to rise as living costs increase.

Retiring at 62 Versus 65

The earliest age at which you can receive Social Security benefits is 62. If you take an early retirement, you will lose five-ninths of 1 percent of your primary insurance amount for each month that you receive your benefits before age 65. If, for instance, you retire at age 62, you will have to settle for only 80 percent of your full benefits. This reduction is permanent; your benefit will not increase to your full PIA at normal retirement age. Furthermore, your benefits will be reduced because your Social Security contributions will have been less. If, however, you retire at age 65, you will get 100 percent of your full benefits.

The principal advantage of retiring at 62 on a reduced benefit is the collection of several thousand dollars during the three years prior to age 65. If you defer retirement until 65, it will take you several years to reach the break-even point, that point at which you will have made up the amount you would have received between the ages of 62 and 65. Table 7.4 on page 118 illustrates this concept. Whether it is better for you to retire at age 62 or wait until age 65 depends on how long you will live, which is something that most people cannot predict.

Effects on Benefits of Continuing to Work

For many years, Social Security beneficiaries between ages 65 and 69 had their benefits reduced by $1 for every $3 earned over an annual limit of $17,000. But on April 7, 2000, President Bill Clinton signed into law a measure that eliminated the earnings limit. The new law, retroactive to January 1, 2000, allows people in this age group to earn whatever they can without experiencing a reduction of benefits.

It should be noted that the new law does not change the rules governing individuals who take early retirement at age 62 and continue to work. Workers ages 62 to 64 as of 2001 will continue to lose $1 for every $2 earned over $10,680 a year. Also, the new law does not change the status of workers who as of 2001 are at least 70 years old. These beneficiaries may continue to earn whatever they can without any reduction in benefits.

At income tax time, those Social Security beneficiaries whose earnings exceed any remaining limits must submit a report to the Social Security Administration indicating their previous year's earnings. Filing an income tax return does not take the place of filing this report with the Social Security Administration. A substantial penalty is levied when such earnings are not reported.

TABLE 7.4

	How Long It Takes to Reach the Break-Even Point				
	80% of Primary Insurance Amount		100% of Primary Insurance Amount		
	Amount Received		Amount Received		
Age	Annual	Cumulative	Annual	Cumulative	
62	$8,000	$8,000	0	0	
63	8,000	16,000	0	0	
64	8,000	24,000	0	0	
65	8,000	32,000	$10,000	$10,000	
66	8,000	40,000	10,000	20,000	
67	8,000	48,000	10,000	30,000	
68	8,000	56,000	10,000	40,000	
69	8,000	64,000	10,000	50,000	
70	8,000	72,000	10,000	60,000	
71	8,000	80,000	10,000	70,000	
72	8,000	88,000	10,000	80,000	
73	8,000	96,000	10,000	90,000	
74	8,000	104,000	10,000	100,000	
75	8,000	112,000	10,000	110,000	
76	8,000	120,000	10,000	120,000	
Total	**$120,000**		**$120,000**		

The Delayed Retirement Credit

If you take a *late retirement*—that is, you work between the ages of 65 and 70—and do not collect any Social Security benefits before retiring, your retirement benefits will be increased by a specified percentage. If you are age 65 in 2002 to 2003, the increase will be 6.5 percent of your PIA. If you work all five years—ages 65 through 70—you will receive 32.5 percent, or 6.5 percent for each of the five years. This benefit, known as the *delayed retirement credit*, increases every two years, and will be 8 percent a year for people born in 1943 or later. In other words, for each year beyond your full retirement age that you delay receiving Social Security benefits, you will receive an additional two-thirds percent per month. See Table 7.5 for more information.

Raising the Retirement Age

Between the years 2000 and 2022, the retirement age for full benefits will be raised gradually, in two-month increments, from 65 to 67. This change, under the Social Security Amendments of 1983, will be made for two reasons—to insure

TABLE 7.5

DELAYED RETIREMENT CREDIT		
Year of Birth	**Year You Reach 65**	**Monthly %**
Prior to 1916	Prior to 1982	1.0
1917–24	1982–89	3.0
1925–26	1990–91	3.5
1927–28	1992–93	4.0
1929–30	1994–95	4.5
1931–32	1996–97	5.0
1933–34	1998–99	5.5
1935–36	2000–01	6.0
1937–38	2002–03	6.5
1939–40	2004–05	7.0
1941–42	2006–07	7.5
1943 or later	2008 or later	8.0

TABLE 7.6

TIMETABLE FOR RAISING THE RETIREMENT AGE FROM 65 TO 67	
Year of Birth	**Age Necessary for Full Benefits**
1937 or earlier	65 years
1938	65 years, 2 months
1939	65 years, 4 months
1940	65 years, 6 months
1941	65 years, 8 months
1942	65 years, 10 months
1943–1954	66 years
1955	66 years, 2 months
1956	66 years, 4 months
1957	66 years, 6 months
1958	66 years, 8 months
1959	66 years, 10 months
1960 and after	67 years

the long-term financial solvency of the Social Security trust funds, and to adjust the retirement age to the increased life expectancy over the years. It will still be possible to retire at age 62, but the benefits will gradually be reduced. For instance, someone who retired at age 62 in 1999 now receives 80 percent of his or her PIA; in 2005, a 62-year-old retiree will receive 75 percent; in 2022, 70 percent. Table 7.6 presents the timetable for raising the retirement age from 65 to 67.

BENEFITS FOR FAMILY MEMBERS

So far, this chapter has focused on the Social Security benefits that you, as a retired worker, will receive based upon your earnings. But other family members—a spouse, a child, or even a parent—may also benefit from the credits you earned during your years of employment. Similarly, at your retirement, you may receive benefits based on the earnings of another member of your family. The following information applies to benefits paid to family members *during your lifetime.* For information on survivors' benefits, which are paid to family members after a worker's death, see page 120.

Benefits for a Spouse

If a spouse has never worked at paid employment and, therefore, is not entitled to his or her own Social Security benefits, then at age 62, the spouse receives 37.5 percent of the worker's PIA. At age 65, the spouse receives 50 percent of the worker's PIA. If a spouse has worked a little and is entitled to retirement benefits equaling less than 50 percent of the worker's PIA, the spouse still receives 50 percent. If a spouse has worked enough to be entitled to a benefit greater than 50 percent of the worker's PIA, the spouse collects benefits based on his or her own earnings. In other words, if a husband and wife both worked and paid Social Security taxes, each is entitled to his or her own benefits.

Benefits for a Divorced Spouse

A divorced man or woman who has not remarried can receive benefits on his or her former spouse's record if they were married for at least ten years. Benefits are the same as they would be if the couple had remained married. This means that the ex-spouses must both be of retirement age, 62 or older. A divorced man or woman who has reached retirement age may claim benefits on his or her own record until the former spouse retires, and can then file for the spousal benefit if it is higher.

Benefits for Children

Each dependent child or grandchild is entitled to receive 50 percent of the retired worker's PIA. A *dependent child* is a person under 18 years of age, a full-time elementary or secondary school student up to age 19, or an older child with a disability that began before age 22. A *dependent grandchild* is a child under the age of 18 both of whose parents are disabled or deceased.

Benefits for Parents

At 62 years of age, a dependent parent—one who is receiving at least 50 percent of support from his or her offspring—is entitled to receive 82.5 percent of his or her retired child's PIA. If both parents are dependent, each can get 75 percent of the child's PIA.

SURVIVORS' BENEFITS

When a worker dies, certain members of that person's family may be eligible for benefits on the worker's Social Security record if he or she earned enough credits while working. These family members include:

❏ A widow or widower, age 60 or older.

❏ A widow or widower, age 50 or older and disabled.

❏ A widow or widower of any age if he or she is caring for a dependent child who is receiving Social Security benefits.

❏ Children who are unmarried and under age 18; of age 19, but full-time students in elementary or secondary school; or of any age with a disability that began before age 22.

❏ Parents, if they were dependent on their offspring for at least half of their support.

The amount payable to survivors is a percentage of the deceased worker's basic Social Security benefit, the primary insurance amount, usually in a range of 75 to 100 percent for each beneficiary. However, there is a limit to the amount of money that will be paid each month to a family. The limit varies, but is generally equal to about 150 to 180 percent of the worker's benefit rate. If the sum of the benefits payable to the surviving family members is greater than this limit, the benefits to the family are reduced proportionately.

Even if a worker is not fully insured when he or she dies, the family may still be eligible for benefits. The worker may be *currently insured*, which means that he or she earned six quarters of coverage (QCs), or six units of Social Security credit, in the three years before death. If the worker had enough credits, a special one-time payment of $255 is also made after his or her death. This benefit, called a *lump-sum death benefit*, is paid only to the widow or widower, or to minor children—children of age 18 or under, or children of age 19 who are still enrolled full-time in a secondary school.

Benefits for Widows and Widowers

A widow or widower can begin collecting Social Security benefits at age 60. If a widow or widower is 60, he or she gets 71.5 percent of the deceased spouse's PIA; at 61, 77.2 percent; at 62, 82.9 percent; at 63, 88.6 percent; at 64, 94.3 percent; and at age 65, 100 percent. At age 62, the widow or widower must decide whether to continue collecting as a survivor or to take his or her own entitled benefits. Of course, the survivor takes the larger of the two. A disabled widow can begin collecting Social Security benefits at any age.

Benefits for Divorced Widows and Widowers

When a worker is divorced and then dies, even if he or she has remarried, an ex-spouse may be eligible for benefits on the worker's record. To qualify, the ex-spouse must:

❏ Be at least 60 years old, or 50 if disabled, and have been married to the worker for at least ten years.

❏ Be any age if caring for a child who is eligible for benefits on the worker's record.

❏ Not be eligible for an equal or higher benefit on his or her own record.

❏ Not be currently married, unless the remarriage occurred after age 60, or age 50 for disabled widows. In cases of remarriage after the age of 60, the ex-spouse is eligible for widows' or widowers' benefits on the worker's record, or for a dependent's benefit on the record of his or her new spouse, whichever is higher.

It is important to note that when an ex-spouse receives benefits on a worker's account, it does not affect the amount of any benefits payable to the worker's other survivors.

Benefits for Children

Unmarried children under age 18—or up to age 19 if they are full-time students in an elementary or secondary school—are entitled to benefits. Also, any child who was disabled before age 22 and remains disabled can receive benefits. Under certain circumstances, benefits can also be paid to the stepchildren and grandchildren of the deceased worker.

Benefits for Parents

Parents of age 62 or older are eligible for survivors' benefits if they were dependent on their offspring for at least half of their support.

FILING FOR RETIREMENT BENEFITS

If you are ready to retire, you should apply for retirement benefits approximately three months before your actual retirement date. You must file your application at your local Social Security office. To get the address of your nearest Social Security office, call Social Security's toll-free phone number, visit the Social Security website (see the Resources section), or contact any social welfare agency in your community. Your benefits will become effective as of the month you reach retirement age. Social Security benefits are retroactive only for the twelve months before the date of filing. Therefore, a delay for any reason, even a disabling illness, may cause loss of benefits.

The following is a list of records you must present when filing for retirement benefits. These records should be certified documents bearing the official seal of the agency from which you obtained them. Photocopies are not acceptable. Your representative will return the documents to you after making a copy for Social Security's records. Documents in foreign languages are acceptable.

When Will Your Social Security Checks Arrive?

Many new Social Security recipients want to know at what time in the month they will receive their benefit checks. Since May 1997, new recipients have received their checks on either the second, third, or fourth Wednesday of each month, depending on either their birthday or the birthday of the person on whose work record their benefits are based. For instance, if you receive benefits as a retired or disabled worker, your benefit payment day will be determined by your own date of birth. If you receive benefits as a spouse, your benefit payment day will be determined by your spouse's date of birth.

Social Security beneficiaries who began receiving benefits prior to May 1997 have continued to receive their benefits on the third day of the month. Supplementary Security Income (SSI) checks are delivered on the first of the month.

The new benefit payment days were added to spread the workload throughout the month. By the year 2020, about 76 million people will be receiving monthly benefit checks. The revised payment schedule will permit Social Security to continue to provide service for all beneficiaries. The following table presents the payment schedule.

Payment Schedule for Social Security Benefit Checks

Date of Birth Falls Between:	Benefits Paid On:
First and tenth day of the month	Second Wednesday
Eleventh and twentieth day of the month	Third Wednesday
Twenty-first and thirty-first day of the month	Fourth Wednesday

❏ **Social Security card or record of Social Security number.**

❏ **Proof of age.** Most people submit their birth certificates or baptismal certificates made before the fifth birthday.

❏ **Form W-2.** Form W-2 should show your earnings for the year prior to the year in which you apply for Social Security retirement benefits. For example, if you apply for benefits in 2002, you should bring your Form W-2 for 2001. If you are self-employed, bring a copy of your last federal income tax return.

❏ **Proof of marriage.** Your marriage certificate is required if you are applying for benefits as a spouse. A divorced spouse needs proof of the divorce in addition to proof of the marriage.

The following records are needed when filing for benefits for children:

❏ **Social Security card or record of Social Security number.**

❏ **Proof of age.**

❏ **Proof of adoption,** if applicable.

❑ **Marriage certificate** of natural parent and stepparent, if applying for stepchild's benefits.

DISABILITY BENEFITS

The disability benefits program, an important component of Social Security, is not directly related to retirement planning because it applies to young and middle-aged workers. These individuals receive benefits because at some point in their working lives, they were struck by a disabling accident or condition that prevented a normal work life. According to Social Security rules, these individuals officially become retirees when they reach age 65. Social Security's coverage of disability benefits is equivalent to a $220,000 disability insurance policy—a policy with a premium that the average worker could never afford. Many experts feel that as protection against immobilizing illness or injury, disability insurance is probably the most important form of Social Security coverage. In short, knowledge of disability benefits is necessary and useful.

Disability benefits were added to the Social Security Act in 1956, and in subsequent years, Congress substantially liberalized the provisions of the law. Today, through the Social Security system, the United States government provides a noncancellable disability policy to almost all its employed citizens.

With disability insurance, you and your family are assured of a monthly income for the length of time you are disabled. Social Security computes these benefits as if you had retired in the year the disability began. The program provides major protection against financial disaster.

Qualifications for a Disability Benefit

An individual is considered to be under a *disability* if the following conditions prevail:

❑ He or she is unable to do any substantial gainful work anywhere in the national economy because of a physical or mental impairment.

❑ The physical or mental condition is expected to last, or has lasted, for at least twelve months, or is expected to result in death.

If you are disabled and cannot engage in either your usual work or any other work, you, your spouse, and your dependent children are eligible for disability benefits at any age. To qualify for a disability benefit, you must have earned twenty quarters of coverage sometime during the ten years before you become disabled. If you become disabled before age 31, you only need to have earned six to ten QCs, depending on your age, between the time you were 21 and the time you become disabled.

To collect benefits, you must file an application and include proof of disability. You must also be willing to accept vocational rehabilitation, if required.

Disability Benefit Amounts

The amount of your monthly disability payment is the same amount you would receive if you were retiring. The disability insurance benefit is, therefore, equal to your average covered monthly earnings over a period of years determined by your date of birth. It is calculated the same way in which retirement benefits are calculated. If you start to receive disability benefits before age 65, your PIA is not reduced.

For disabled widows, disabled surviving divorced wives, and disabled widowers between ages 50 and 62, reduced benefits ranging from 50 percent to 82.9 percent of the deceased spouse's full benefit may be paid if the survivors' disability prevents any substantial gainful work. Widows and widowers are found disabled if they satisfy the requirements of an impairment listed in the "Listing of Impairments" in *Disability Evaluation Under Social Security*, available in any Social Security office.

The maximum family benefits for disabled workers are 85 percent of the worker's average indexed monthly earnings before becoming disabled, or 150 percent of the worker's disability benefits, whichever is less. Maximum family benefits are the total benefits that all the members of one family may receive based upon one worker's earnings.

No benefits are paid for the first five months of disability, which is the required waiting period. The first payment, therefore, is for the sixth full month of disability.

SUPPLEMENTAL SECURITY INCOME

Supplemental Security Income (SSI) became effective January 1, 1974, to insure a basic level of cash income to the aged, blind, and disabled under conditions that promote self-respect and dignity. The program is designed for people in financial need, and provides eligible individuals with monthly payments from the federal government. Even though the Social Security Administration runs the program, SSI is not the same as Social Security. There are two main differences. First, although SSI is administered by the Social Security Administration, it is financed by general funds from the United States Treasury rather than contributions of workers, employers, and self-employed people. Second, while SSI limits the value of the assets and income you are permitted to have and still be eligible for payments, Social Security imposes no limits on the amount of money or property you can have and still receive Social Security payments. However, you can receive both Social Security and SSI if you satisfy the eligibility requirements of each.

SSI checks are payable the first of every month, and cover the benefit for that month. For example, an SSI check dated February 1 is for the month of February. This is different from Social Security checks, which cover the benefit for the prior month. For example, a Social Security check dated February 3 is for the month of January.

Qualifications for SSI Payments

If you apply for Supplemental Security Income, you will be asked five questions. The first question will concern your income, which must be under the allowable limit. Monthly income includes any money received from Social Security, the Veterans' Administration, workers' compensation, pensions, annuities, gifts, and anything similar, as well as earnings. Noncash items such as food, clothing, and shelter are also considered income.

Second, you will be asked if you are 65 or older, blind, or disabled. Third, have you resided for a minimum of thirty consecutive days in one of the fifty states, the District of Columbia, or an American possession? Fourth, are you a citizen of the United States or a legally admitted alien seeking permanent residence in the United States?

The amount of income you can receive each month and still be eligible for SSI varies from state to state. If you don't work, as a general rule of thumb, you may be able to receive SSI if your monthly income is less than $532 for one person, or $789 for a couple. If you do work, you can receive more income each month without losing your SSI. If all of your income is in the form of earnings, you may be able to benefit from SSI if you make less than $1,109 a month for one person, or $1,623 a month for a couple.

The final question concerns the dollar value of your assets. Your assets are the things that you own, such as property, savings accounts, stocks, bonds, jewelry, and other valuables. Assets that are basic necessities of life are not, however, counted. A home that is a primary residence, for example, does not count as an asset, and the government does not ask for a lien on it. A car is not counted at all if it is used to travel to work or to receive regular treatment for a specific medical problem.

At this time, a single person can have assets worth up to $2,000 and still be eligible for Supplemental Security Income. A couple can have assets worth up to $3,000 and still be eligible. Up to $1,500 may be set aside for burial expenses and does not count as an asset.

SSI Payment Amounts

The maximum monthly SSI payment varies according to whether the recipient is an individual or a couple, and whether the recipient is living alone or with others. In 2002, federal SSI payments for an individual living alone are $545 a month; for a couple, they are $817 a month. States supplement this amount, and the SSI check varies from state to state because each state contributes a different amount to the basic benefit provided by the federal government. In addition, the monthly check is reduced if the recipient has other income. Furthermore, special payment rates have been established for individuals who are blind, physically disabled, or mentally disabled. Call your local Social Security office for information about specific SSI payment amounts.

IMPORTANT TIPS

To insure that you and your family receive all the Social Security benefits to which you are entitled, it is important to take the six basic steps described in the remainder of this chapter.

1. Check Your Earnings Record Annually

To protect your investment in Social Security, be sure to check your Social Security earnings and quarters of coverage in your personal account every year to verify that the government's records are correct. As explained earlier in the chapter, you may already have this information on hand, but if not, you can easily obtain it from the Social Security Administration. (See page 116.) Once you have an official statement of earnings, compare the annual figures shown against your W-2 Forms or other earnings records to make sure that they are accurate.

It is important to verify your Social Security records every year because the law sets a time limit for making corrections easily. That time limit currently is three years, three months, and fifteen days after the year in which the wages were paid or the self-employment income was earned. Mistakes can be corrected after this time limit, but it is more difficult to do. The importance of accurate Social Security records increases as you get closer to retirement.

2. Check Your Estimated Benefits

The Social Security statement that provides your record of earnings will also provide an estimate of future benefits. If you do not understand Social Security's calculation of your benefits, visit or write your local Social Security office to have an experienced representative answer your questions.

3. Decide on Your Retirement Date

If you retire at age 65, you will receive 100 percent of your primary insurance amount. If you retire at 62, you will receive only 80 percent of this amount. (Note that this will gradually change as the retirement age is raised. See page 118.) However, retiring at age 62 is financially beneficial compared with retiring at age 65. (See Table 7.4 on page 118.) It takes 14 years for a person who waits until 65 to retire to catch up with a similarly covered person who begins to receive benefits at age 62. Some individuals, for a variety of reasons, prefer to work until age 70 or beyond. For those who delay retirement beyond age 65, present law provides a delayed retirement credit. (See Table 7.5 on page 119.)

4. Gather the Required Documents

The documents you will need to apply for Social Security benefits are listed on pages 122 to 123. You will need similar documents when applying for benefits for children.

5. Apply for Benefits

Under Social Security law, you will not receive benefits automatically. You must apply for them, and should do so during the three months before the month in which you will reach retirement age. Your benefits will become effective as of the month you reach age 62.

6. Inform Your Family Members

Inform your spouse and children of the Social Security benefits for which they may be eligible under various conditions. Furthermore, make sure that your family members know where all relevant documents are located.

Your Social Security benefits can be an important source of income during your retirement years. Your efforts to make sure that your account is accurate and to apply properly for your benefits are well worth the time.

PENSIONS

Analysts in income security for older individuals refer to a "three-legged stool." Social Security is the most important source of income for retirees and covers the greatest number of people. It is, therefore, the first leg. The second leg consists of pensions, including private employer pension plans, public plans for government workers, and individual plans for the self-employed or for employed people who wish to supplement the plans provided by their employers. The third leg consists of a variety of income sources such as savings and investments. A good pension is one that, when added to Social Security and third-leg income, will help retirement income to roughly match working income. Individuals and couples who can count on adequate income from these three legs are indeed fortunate, and can look forward to a secure retirement.

While all workers should be aware of what their pension plans will provide during retirement, women should take an especially close look at their plans so that, if necessary, they can arrange for other types of retirement income. Statistics indicate that only 10 to 20 percent of women over 40 receive or expect to receive a pen-

sion. And if they receive a retirement allowance, the amount is between one-third and one-half of that received by their male colleagues. This occurs because women leave and rejoin the work force more frequently than men to take maternity leave or to provide care when family members are in need; change jobs more frequently than men; and usually work in jobs less likely to have employer-provided retirement plans.

Women—and men, as well—can achieve economic security in retirement only if they start planning for it while still working in order to provide for any shortfall of a pension. This requires that they initiate and maintain an active savings program that will accumulate an adequate retirement nest egg. A portion of the funds saved should be prudently invested to achieve growth. Retirement planning is the key. Guidelines are suggested in Chapter 6, "Savings and Investments." A secure and successful retirement depends on the steps you take early in your working years to provide for your future.

TYPES OF PENSION PLANS

A pension plan, subsidized and regulated by the

government, is a benefit of most jobs in the private sector. The federal government regulates *private pension plans* by granting favorable tax treatment to employers whose plans meet certain standards. Approved plans are government-subsidized, with the total subsidy for all plans currently around $93 billion a year. This total represents the amount of taxes the companies would pay if they were not granted this tax exemption. Government-subsidized plans may be group plans, which are generally offered by larger companies, or individual plans, which were designed for smaller businesses.

The plans set up by self-employed people, known as *Keogh plans,* and the plans set up by employed individuals and others who wish to accumulate retirement savings, known as *Individual Retirement Accounts* (IRAs) and *Roth Individual Retirement Accounts* (Roth IRAs), are voluntary plans. Under Keogh plans, IRAs, and Roth IRAs, the individual decides if he or she wants to set up a plan, how much he or she will put in it (within statutory limits), and how the funds should be invested (again, within statutory limits). Because these plans are subsidized by the government, which provides tax advantages for participants, there are penalties for withdrawing funds before retirement age.

About 90 percent of all government employees—including federal, state, and local, both military and nonmilitary—are covered under some form of *public pension plan.* Some government employees are also covered by Social Security.

Another type of pension plan should be mentioned here. Tax-sheltered annuities—including 401(k) plans, 403(b) plans, and 457 plans—were designed to help company and government employees save retirement nest eggs. Because these plans are structured differently from the pension plans mentioned above, they are detailed in Chapter 9.

Around 40 percent of people over 65 will eventually receive some retirement income from private employer pensions. Government plans will pay benefits to an additional 10 percent of people over 65. And a small percentage of people, mostly in the higher income brackets, will get significant retirement income from Keogh plans and the two forms of IRAs. One or more of the plans discussed in this chapter can provide important supplementation to Social Security.

GROUP PRIVATE PENSION PLANS

Currently, about 43 million people—44 percent of all nongovernmental employees in the United States—are covered by a private pension system. But less than a century ago, the situation was very different. The history of private pension plans in industry reveals that they grew slowly and were often controversial. A major expansion of the private plans occurred after World War II, particularly for workers in organized industries. Because of abuses that became prevalent in the 1960s and 1970s, Congress in 1974 passed the Employee Retirement Income Security Act, known as ERISA, to provide some protection for private pension plan members. Other acts and rulings outlawed sex and age discrimination in pension plans. A detailed discussion of these developments follows, as does a description of the basic features of group private pension plans.

Background

Before the Social Security Act of 1935, few employers thought that they were obligated to do more than pay wages for work performed. Their philosophy was simply that they were buying work, and they could not be good businessmen and also be held responsible for what would happen to their workers in retirement. Organized labor tried to establish pension plans tied to unions, but was unsuccessful. In fact, until the mid-1940s, some unions actually opposed the establishment of private pension plans by employers. They thought that such plans would bind the worker to the industry and the employer, rather than the union.

After World War II, there was a major expansion of private pension plans, particularly for workers in organized industries. By 1955, over 14 million workers were covered. The unions in this period supported the establishment of pension plans in industry to supplement the meager retirement allowances—averaging $25 a month—paid by Social Security. Moreover, with wage and price controls in effect during World War II and for a time thereafter, pensions were one of the few things for which unions could fight to improve the living standards of their members. Industry discovered that a good pension plan could attract and hold employees.

In the 1960s and early 1970s, many workers discovered to their dismay that the benefits they had been expecting to receive were not to materialize. The rules were stacked in favor of employers, and minor deviations, such as *breaks in service* (temporary leaves of absence from employment) or job changes, nullified a member's right to a pension. Abuses were so prevalent that in 1974, Congress took action to provide some protection for pension plan members by passing the Employee Retirement Income Security Act (ERISA).

The Employee Retirement Income Security Act of 1974

The pension reform act approved by the federal government in 1974 established rules regarding eligibility for a pension, funding of pension plans, and day-to-day operations of these plans. This act affects thousands of employers and millions of employees. As the name of the law implies, the primary goal of ERISA is to increase the probability that employees who are covered

by a retirement plan during much of their working careers will, in fact, receive benefits upon retirement. ERISA covers nearly all pension and retirement plans created by private employers engaged in interstate commerce. Its provisions do not apply to plans sponsored by governments, charitable organizations, or firms involved exclusively in intrastate commerce. The law regulates plans that are in existence, but does not require firms to initiate retirement plans. Moreover, ERISA does not force companies to pay any minimum amounts to employees other than those specified in the plan.

ERISA was intended to put private pension programs on a secure financial footing and to assure millions of workers that they can depend on receiving retirement payments. It prescribes minimum standards that covered plans must meet. Among the major items addressed by the law are vesting, benefits, financing, funding, survivors' benefits, and disclosure to participants. ERISA also established the *Pension Benefit Guarantee Corporation (PBGC)*, which guarantees benefits to plan members even when a plan's assets are insufficient to fulfill its commitments. Since 1995, PBGC has guaranteed the basic pension benefits of millions of American workers and retirees participating in thousands of plans. The framers of the law also provided for employees of companies that do not have a pension plan. Such individuals can set up their own retirement system in the form of an IRA that offers substantial tax benefits to encourage saving for retirement. A 1981 law expanded the concept of the IRA to permit individuals who are already covered by a private or public pension to set up an account. The Tax Reform Act of 1986 restricts contributions to IRAs.

The Retirement Equity Act of 1984

Proponents of the Retirement Equity Act of 1984

argued that many women were hurt economically by provisions of the ERISA law of 1974, which they said benefited men but not women. The Retirement Equity Act has made it easier for women to participate in private pension plans and to receive retirement benefits—either their husband's or their own.

Under the 1984 legislation, an employee's spouse must give written permission before the employee can choose a retirement plan that will stop pension payments upon his or her death, as opposed to continuing the payments to the surviving spouse. Until passage of this law, employees did not need a spouse's permission to waive the payment of benefits. Usually, payments to an employee are slightly greater if he or she waives payments to a surviving spouse. Another provision of the law is the payment of benefits to the surviving spouse of a worker who dies before the early retirement age of 55, but is fully or partially vested in the pension plan at the time of death. In a divorce case, the newer law authorizes a court to award an individual a portion of the former spouse's pension as part of the divorce settlement if the individual has not remarried.

In an effort to adjust private pension plans for women who enter the work force relatively early but interrupt their careers to have children, the law lowered the age at which workers must be allowed to participate in such plans from 25 to 21. The 1984 law also requires that when eligibility for a retirement pension is calculated, the *years of service* from the time the employee turned 18 must be counted. Under the 1974 law, the age used for that calculation was 22.

The 1984 law also allows employees who have worked fewer than five years to stop working for five years without losing their pension credit. And it bars pension plans from counting a one-year maternity or paternity leave as a break in service.

The 1984 law has provided a more secure retirement for thousands of American women who had been deprived of pension benefits by loopholes that did not recognize their contribution either inside or outside the home. In pension matters of the private sector, this newer law has been a major step toward true economic equity for women.

Sex Discrimination in Employee Pension Plans

In July 1983, the Justices of the United States Supreme Court issued a 5-to-4 decision in the case of *Arizona Governing Committee v. Norris*, which outlawed sex discrimination in pension plans. Until that time, retirement annuities paid men and women different amounts. The payment schedule was based on the fact that, on average, women live nearly eight years longer than men. Therefore, pension plan administrators reasoned, women should get smaller payments since these payments would naturally be spread out over a longer period of time. The Supreme Court ruling required that the future pension checks of women be increased, and that the checks for men be reduced. Because the decision was based on employment-bias law, it affects only company pension plans and not those offered by insurance companies on the open market.

Age Discrimination in Employee Pension Plans

In October 1986, President Reagan signed the Omnibus Budget Reconciliation Act (OBRA), which addresses the issue of employers' continuing retirement plan contributions after normal retirement age. OBRA amended ERISA and the Internal Revenue Code (IRC) to prohibit discrimination on the basis of age in employee pension benefit plans. The OBRA amendments require employers to continue pension plan benefit accruals and contributions after normal retirement age. The amendments also prohibit pension plans from excluding from participation employees hired at or after the plan's normal retirement age if those employees meet other requirements. OBRA is generally effective for plans that began on or after January 1, 1988.

Types of Group Private Pension Plans

Essentially, there are two types of group private pension plans—the *defined contribution plan* and the *defined benefit plan*. These plans have several variations.

The Defined Contribution Plan

In a defined contribution plan, you and your employer, or your employer alone, contributes a fixed amount each year to a retirement fund. In many cases, the administrator of the plan is responsible for investing the money in a variety of ways. In other cases, you have the opportunity to select the types of investments. When you retire, the contributions and earnings that have accumulated over the years are used to purchase an annuity, which provides regular monthly payments for a specified time period, usually your lifetime. The retirement income you receive is determined by the size of the annuity bought with the money credited to your account.

An outstanding example of a defined contribution plan is the Teachers Insurance and Annuity Association-College Retirement Equities Fund (TIAA-CREF). This plan was founded in 1918 to provide retirement benefits for the staff of colleges, universities, independent schools, and certain other nonprofit and tax-exempt educational and research institutions. Today, nearly 11,000 educational institutions have TIAA-CREF

retirement plans. Over 2,100,000 participants are accumulating future retirement income in annuity contracts, and nearly 300,000 participants are receiving annuity income benefits. The TIAA-CREF defined contribution plans for higher education are fully portable, fully and immediately vested systems. They are designed to permit, perhaps even encourage, the transfer of academic talent from one institution to another without concern about forfeiting pension benefits.

The Defined Benefit Plan

In a defined benefit plan, a formula is used to determine your pension, and your employer is required to contribute enough to the pension fund over the years to insure that your retirement allowance equals the amount prescribed by the formula. Usually, the pension is tied both to years of credited service and to salary. The best pension plans base your retirement allowance upon your earnings in your last year or in your final few years of service, when you are likely to earn the most. Least favorable is a plan that gears your pension to the average earnings for all years.

Variations

Both defined contribution and defined benefit plans may require or allow contributions by employees. If a pension plan is financed entirely by the employer, it is referred to as *noncontributory*. In a *contributory pension plan*, the employer and employee share the cost in some prescribed proportion. The majority of corporate pension plans are noncontributory. Some plans are administered solely by a union and are financed by union dues or assessments.

Some pension plans, called *integrated plans*, are tied in with Social Security benefits. In integrated plans, a participant's monthly pension amount is computed according to the pension plan's benefit formula. Then a percentage of the participant's monthly Social Security benefit is subtracted from the monthly pension amount.

Tax Considerations

In a contributory plan, you pay income taxes on the amount you contribute. When you collect your retirement allowance, the amount you contributed over your working life is, therefore, not taxed. However, you must pay income tax on the contributions of your employer and on the interest earned by all contributions.

According to rules developed by the Internal Revenue Service under provisions of the Internal Revenue Code, employer contributions to qualified pension plans—up to certain limits—can be deducted as a current business expense. Another tax advantage is that the investment income of a qualified pension plan is allowed to accumulate untaxed. Qualification standards apply only to private pension plans and not to retirement plans of governmental or charitable organizations because these last organizations are tax-exempt.

Eligibility Requirements

Most pension plans require employees to meet certain eligibility requirements before they can participate. Depending on other characteristics of the plan, ERISA approved four age-service eligibility standards—age 25 and one year of service; age 25 and three years of service; age 30 and one year of service; and no age requirement, but three years of service. The last requirement applies to Keogh plans, which are the plans used by self-employed people for themselves and their employees (see page 138). These eligibility standards constitute the *maximum* restrictions that an employer can apply to a pension plan.

An employer has the right to make an employee a participant sooner, if the employer so desires.

For defined benefit plans, ERISA recognized a special provision of which you should be aware, especially if you are in your 50s and contemplating a job change. The law permits a defined benefit plan to exclude from membership any person who begins work within five years of the plan's normal retirement age.

Credit for Years of Service

The benefits you earn in a pension plan are usually determined by the number of years you work for your employer. You must know exactly how your employer counts a year of service, and how any breaks in that service can affect the benefits you have accumulated. You must check to be sure that you have earned the pension benefits you think you have, and that any breaks in service you may have taken have not jeopardized your benefits. Under most plans, a year of service is defined as at least 1,000 hours of work in a twelve-consecutive-month period. Some plans, however, use other standards for measuring years of service. Your plan may also define a break in service as work of less than 500 hours in a twelve-consecutive-month period.

Some plans give you credit for work performed before you became a plan participant, while others do not. Under some plans, you stop earning pension credits when you reach the plan's normal retirement age, even if you continue to work. Other plans give credit for years of service after retirement age. To avoid losing some or all of your accumulated benefits because of a break in service, read your Summary Plan Description (SPD), a booklet issued by the employer explaining the pension plan's provisions.

In a defined contribution plan, your accrued benefit at any point equals the amount credited to your account. If the plan puts the money into a cash value life insurance policy, the amount for which the policy can be surrendered represents your accrued benefit.

In a defined benefit plan, the accrual process is different because your retirement allowance is not a special sum set aside for you in the pension fund, but a fixed monthly income that will be paid on retirement. For example, according to one arrangement, if the plan requires thirty years of service and you leave the company after twenty years of covered service, you are entitled to two-thirds of your estimated pension. Another arrangement computes benefits as a fixed percentage each year. The law permits a plan to use a flat rate of not less than 3 percent a year so that an employee accrues 100 percent of his or her projected pension after no more than thirty-three and one-third years of covered service. ERISA also allows plans to apply different percentages for early and later years.

Time Required for Vesting

When an employee is *vested* in a pension plan, it means that the employee has the right to receive money from the plan—even if he or she resigns or is fired—based upon the employee's and employer's contributions. Employees' contributions vest immediately, and can be withdrawn when the employee leaves the job. However, the rights of employees to employer contributions are generally subject to limitations, including service-time requirements and amount limits.

The Tax Reform Act of 1986 accelerated the minimum vesting requirements set by ERISA. The 1986 vesting rules became effective in 1989. Three of the more popular vesting plans are the following:

1. **Cliff vesting.** According to the Tax Reform Act of 1986, cliff vesting provides full benefits after five years of employment. Short of five years, employees receive nothing. They are, in other words, pushed off a cliff.

2. **Graded vesting.** As the name indicates, in graded vesting, employees become vested in stages or grades. Companies vest 20 percent after three years, and an additional 20 percent every year thereafter. This means that an employee is fully vested after seven years.

3. **Vesting upon entry.** The Tax Reform Act of 1986 established a vesting upon entry plan. This plan requires a short waiting period, such as two years, after which the employee enters the pension system and is immediately 100-percent vested.

The Tax Reform Act of 1986 is notable for its impact on pension reform. Acceleration in vesting schedules has provided the following benefits:

❏ More workers have become eligible for pensions at retirement.

❏ Working women, who on average change jobs more often than men do, have increased probability of ultimately receiving a pension.

❏ The younger work force has a more secure retirement ahead.

The 1986 law provided another benefit. Until 1986, pension plans covered only about half of the work force. The 1986 law requires private pension plans to cover 70 percent of employees, thus benefiting more low-income employees.

Under current law, if you request a statement of the amount of vested benefits you have earned, you must be given such a statement. If you leave your job, you should receive such a statement automatically.

Types of Benefits

Most pension plans provide retirement benefits and survivors' benefits. Let's look at each of these forms of pension benefits.

Retirement Benefits

The three types of retirement benefits are as follows:

1. **Normal.** Most pension plans have designed their benefit programs for retirement at age 65, which is considered the *normal retirement age.* Of course, federal law has eliminated mandatory retirement at any age, but it does not require an employer to increase pensions for work after 65. Nevertheless, a member of a defined benefit pension plan usually receives a higher retirement allowance for additional time served on the job.

2. **Early.** Many pension plans allow employees to take *early retirement,* which is retirement sometime prior to the plan's normal retirement age. If you retire early, you will receive a monthly retirement allowance, called an *early retirement benefit,* that is smaller than what you would receive if you retired at the usual retirement age. Because the contribution period is shorter, the monthly income at early retirement is reduced by an actuarial formula that takes into account the likelihood that you will receive the pension for more years than you would if you retired at 65. Some firms encourage early retirement by paying more than the actuarial equivalent or by offering other incentives, such as a lump-sum payment.

3. **Disability.** Some plans provide benefits, known as *disability benefits,* if an employee is unable to work because of illness or disability. Pension plans vary in the definition of disability, as well as in the age and service requirements that determine eligibility for these benefits. Each plan specifies the amount of the benefit you will receive if you are disabled.

Survivors' Benefits

Most pension plans that pay monthly benefits are required by law to include a provision for survivors' benefits, called a *joint and survivor annuity.* This provision allows an employee to designate an individual, usually his or her spouse, to receive benefits if the employee dies. It gives the survivor a minimum of 50 percent of the benefit that would have been payable to the retired employee. In order to provide for a survivor, the retired employee must accept a lower pension while alive.

As explained earlier in this chapter, under the Retirement Equity Act of 1984, an employee does not have the right to waive the survivors' option without obtaining the prior written consent of his or her spouse. If this option is not taken, the retiree can receive a higher pension, but the survivor will receive nothing when the retiree dies. The 1984 law also provides that private pension plans must now pay benefits to a surviving spouse if the employee dies after becoming vested—that is, after having worked long enough to earn the right to receive benefits.

Pension plans have a variety of provisions relating to lump-sum *death benefits.* Death benefit provisions usually are related to an employee's age and years of service. Some pension plans have no death benefit. Instead, they pay survivors a lump sum provided by a group life insurance policy.

Insurance for Plan Termination

ERISA provides an important element of protection in the form of pension plan termination insurance. A provision of the ERISA law established the Pension Benefit Guarantee Corporation (PBGC), whose purpose is to guarantee that pension benefits will be paid to all eligible workers even if their employer's plan has insufficient assets to fulfill its commitments to them. Funding for the PBGC is derived from charges levied against company pension plans regulated by ERISA.

The PBGC has the power to seize up to 30 percent of a company's net worth if the company terminates its defined benefit retirement plan. When a company's pension plan is unable to meet its commitments to beneficiaries, the PBGC will pay up to $750 in monthly retirement benefits per person.

The Pension Benefit Guarantee Corporation is similar to savings bank deposit insurance. However, the number of weak pension plans is much larger than the number of weak savings banks. Even considering the agency's ability to seize company assets, potential claims against the PBGC far exceed the millions in reserves that have built up since 1974.

The Funding of Group Private Plans

The law now requires that every company with a qualified pension plan each year contribute to the plan an amount that will cover the obligations for future benefits that build up during that year. A plan so structured is known as a *fully funded pension plan.* Prior to ERISA, many pension plans were unfunded or underfunded. In each of these cases, a company's pension reserves were nonexistent or inadequate to meet future pension benefits. Such pension plans paid benefits directly from the company's operating budget as claims arose. ERISA requires unfunded and underfunded pension plans to build up their reserves for past obligations over a period

of thirty to forty years. The act also requires that pension funds be invested in safe assets. Most trustees of private pension funds invest in blue chip company stocks or in fixed-return bonds rather than more speculative investments.

Unfortunately, a good many employers have grossly and willfully underfunded their defined benefit pension plans. The General Accounting Office, the Congressional Budget Office, and the House Ways and Means Oversight Subcommittee estimate that in 2000, 10,052 defined benefit pension plans were underfunded by $52.3 million.

As previously explained, the federal government insures defined benefit plans through the Pension Benefit Guarantee Corporation, collecting premiums from all employers who offer such plans. Almost 72 percent of the country's defined benefit pension plans are fully funded, covering 93 percent of pension participants. Many corporations with inadequately funded plans are converting their defined benefit plans into defined contribution plans, further endangering the federal system's financial soundness.

The administration in Washington recognizes the issue of underfunded pension plans, and has promised to address the problem. However, pension reform requires cooperative efforts by corporate management, corporate employees, and taxpayers, all of whom must let their congressional representatives know how they feel about this issue.

The Summary Plan Description

The 1974 pension reform act requires employers to provide each employee covered by a pension plan with a summary description of the plan and of any changes in the plan in a form that can be readily understood by the average participant. This requirement is very important. It means that you have a legal right to obtain the operating details of your private pension plan from your company. If you wish to have these details, contact the personnel department and ask for the company's pension booklet, called a *Summary Plan Description* (SPD). A small company may not have such a document. If you belong to a union, you can probably find out about your pension plan by contacting the union representative responsible for this aspect of your company's benefits.

The SPD must provide a variety of information, including how you meet the eligibility requirements for benefits, how you accumulate benefits, how you can lose benefits, whether the plan is covered by plan termination insurance, and how you can file a claim for benefits. If there are significant changes in your plan, you are entitled to an updated SPD. Be sure to read your SPD carefully. It will help you answer the questions presented in Self-Study 8.1 so that you can acquire a full understanding of your pension benefits.

Your plan administrator is also required to provide you with a Summary Annual Report, which is based on a more comprehensive report that your company files annually with the United States Department of Labor. The Summary Annual Report contains information on the financial activities of your plan for that particular year. If you have difficulty obtaining information about your plan, contact the nearest area office of the Labor-Management Services Administration.

Instructions for Applying for Benefits

As mentioned earlier, your Summary Plan Description must explain the procedures for filing a claim for benefits and for appealing a denied claim. The explanation must include such necessary information as whom you should contact, what documents you must provide, and how long you may have to wait for a decision to be made on your claim.

INDIVIDUAL PRIVATE PENSION PLANS

Most individuals do not plan for a secure retirement by saving enough to generate supplemental postretirement income. To help insure a financially sound retirement, the federal government is encouraging individuals to save. The Economic Recovery Tax Act of 1981 tried to stimulate increased personal savings by allowing every employed person to put away money in an *Individual Retirement Account* (IRA) and subtract that contribution from his or her taxable income as long as he or she had earned income and is under the age of $70\frac{1}{2}$. Later, the Taxpayer Relief Act of 1997 created another type of individual retirement account—the *Roth IRA*.

Self-employed individuals have a special option. Known as a *Keogh plan*, it enables those who are self-employed to make large tax-deductible payments to a pension plan fund.

The Individual Retirement Account

Authorized by the federal government, an Individual Retirement Account (IRA), as its name implies, is a personal retirement fund that can be set up by an individual.

Anyone who has earned income or received alimony can open an IRA in the amount of $3,000 or 100 percent of earned income—whichever is less. An additional contribution of $500 can be made by anyone age 50 or older. But not everyone can deduct his or her contribution from taxable income. The deductibility of your IRA contribution depends partly on whether you or your spouse is an active participant in an employer's qualified retirement plan. If neither one of you is a member of such a retirement plan, your entire contribution will be tax-deductible. However, if one or both of you are members in such a plan, a total or partial deduction may still be possible, depending on your adjusted gross income (AGI).

Before 1998, the yearly IRA maximum contribution was tax-deductible for individuals with incomes of up to $25,000, and couples with incomes of up to $40,000. Starting in 1998, the income limits for the deductibility of contributions to traditional IRAs began increasing, and they will continue to increase until 2007. Table 8.1 shows the maximum income limits that will allow for at least a *partial* tax deduction between 2001 and 2007.

TABLE 8.1

MAXIMUM INCOME LIMITS FOR PARTIAL TAX DEDUCTION OF IRA CONTRIBUTION		
Year	Maximum Income for Single Return	Maximum Income for Joint Return
2001	$33,000–$43,000	$53,000–$63,000
2002	$34,000–$44,000	$54,000–$64,000
2003	$40,000–$50,000	$60,000–$70,000
2004	$45,000–$55,000	$65,000–$75,000
2005	$50,000–$60,000	$70,000–$80,000
2006	$50,000–$60,000	$75,000–$85,000
2007	$50,000–$60,000	$80,000–$100,000

Contributions to a traditional IRA can be made only until you reach $70\frac{1}{2}$ years of age. At that age, you must begin making withdrawals from the account. When the money is withdrawn from an IRA, you will have to pay income tax on the withdrawal. However, because the money is generally withdrawn after retirement, the rate of taxation may be relatively low because of diminished annual income. This is one of the advantages of a traditional IRA: The earnings on the invested money are not taxed

until they are withdrawn. The other advantage, of course, is that contributions to an IRA may decrease your income tax for the year the contribution is made.

Most withdrawals from an IRA before age $59\frac{1}{2}$ result in a 10-percent penalty plus payment of the income tax due. But since 1991, it has been permissible to make withdrawals before that age without penalty as long as the money is being withdrawn to cover up to $10,000 of expenses for the purchase of a first home; or to pay for qualified educational expenses, such as tuition, room, and board. The 10-percent penalty is also waived when withdrawal is due to death or permanent disability; when it is used to pay medical bills that exceed 7.5 percent of your adjusted gross income; and when it is used to pay for medical insurance during an extensive period of unemployment. Taxes apply to all funds withdrawn.

The Roth Individual Retirement Account

Like the traditional IRA, the Roth IRA—named for Senator William V. Roth, Jr.—can be set up by an individual as a retirement account. Eligibility for a Roth IRA is determined by your adjusted gross income (AGI).

Married taxpayers filing jointly, with a combined AGI of $150,00 or less, can each contribute up to $3,000 to a Roth IRA as long as the couple's joint earned income is at least $4,000. If a couple's combined AGI is over $150,000 but less than $160,000, they are each able to make reduced contributions. A couple cannot contribute at all if their combined AGI is more than $160,000.

Single individuals with an AGI of $95,000 or less can contribute up to $3,000 a year to a Roth IRA. Single tax filers with incomes between $95,000 and $110,000 are eligible to make reduced contributions. Individuals with AGIs above $110,000 cannot contribute to a Roth IRA.

If an individual contributes to both a traditional and a Roth IRA, the combined contributions are limited to $3,000 a year. For both individuals and couples, the eligibility to contribute to a Roth IRA is not affected by participation in a qualified pension plan. Moreover, in both cases, an added contribution of $500 can be made by individuals age 50 or older.

Unlike a contribution to a traditional IRA, a contribution to a Roth IRA is not tax-deductible the year in which the contribution is made. However, the Roth IRA has other advantages. This pension plan compounds earnings over a long period of time. Then, if you want to withdraw money from the account, contributions can be withdrawn *tax- and penalty-free* at any time, as long as the account is at least five years old and you have attained the age of 59$\frac{1}{2}$, have become disabled, or use the money for a first-time home purchase. If money is withdrawn from an account that is less than five years old or before age 59$\frac{1}{2}$, the withdrawal is subject to income tax and to a 10-percent withdrawal penalty.

The Roth IRA also has special features that make it attractive for older investors. First, unlike a traditional IRA, the Roth IRA does not require distributions to begin at age 70$\frac{1}{2}$. So if you don't have to withdraw money from your retirement account, you can allow your assets to keep accumulating tax-free. In addition, with the Roth IRA, you can make contributions after the age of 70$\frac{1}{2}$ as long as you continue to earn income. Finally, if desired, the money can be allowed to stay in the account and passed on to heirs income tax-free, although subject to estate taxes.

The Keogh Plan

The Keogh plan, named for Congressman Eugene J. Keogh of New York who sponsored the law, is designed for self-employed individuals— professionals such as doctors, dentists, lawyers, and accountants; small business owners; and members of partnerships. The two basic types of Keoghs are the defined benefit plan and the defined contribution plan.

In the first type of plan, the *defined benefit plan,* a set payout is provided after retirement. An actuary calculates the annual deposits you must make to achieve your predetermined retirement allowance. These annual deposits are tax-deductible. In the second type of Keogh, the *defined contribution plan,* you decide by yourself how much of an annual contribution you will make. The plan's investment performance then determines the ultimate payout. Your annual tax-deductible contribution may equal 25 percent of your earned income from self-employment, up to a maximum of $30,000 a year.

If you do part-time or freelance work, you can open a Keogh account on your part-time or freelance earnings, even if you also work full-time for a firm that has a qualified pension, profit-sharing, or other retirement plan. For example, accountants who work for a corporation but prepare tax returns as a sideline may establish a Keogh account and contribute income based on what they earn from their sideline work. A Keogh plan can be established in any financial institution, including a bank, brokerage firm, or insurance company.

Your plan contributions plus accumulated interest will become payable upon your retirement, but not earlier than age 59$\frac{1}{2}$ or later than 70$\frac{1}{2}$. Distribution cannot be made before age 59$\frac{1}{2}$ without penalty, except in cases of disability or death. If you withdraw money from a Keogh plan early, the withdrawal is subject to a 10-percent penalty tax as well as regular income tax. Under the plan, the account holdings may be distributed in a lump sum or in payments spread over a specified period of time. The period cannot exceed, but may be spread over, the individual's life expectancy or the joint life expectancy of the individual and spouse. These periods are determined using actuarial tables.

Should the Keogh account holder die before reaching age 59½, payment is made to a designated beneficiary. If the Keogh holder suffers permanent disability before age 59½, the money is immediately payable to the account holder without penalty.

EMPLOYER-SPONSORED INDIVIDUAL PENSION PLANS

Many small businesses are reluctant to establish retirement plans for their employees because of the legal and administrative costs of setting up and maintaining such plans, and of complying with federal regulations. The *Simplified Employee Pension* (SEP) and *Savings Incentive Match Plan for Employees* (SIMPLE), were designed so that small businesses could provide their employees with retirement nest eggs. Note that although these plans are sponsored by employers, they are considered individual plans because they are set up for each individual in the firm.

The Simplified Employee Pension (SEP)

The Simplified Employee Pension (SEP) was designed for small businesses—businesses with a maximum of twenty-five employees. In a SEP plan, sometimes called a SEP-IRA, an employer establishes and finances an individual retirement account for each eligible employee. The employee makes no contribution. An employer's contribution is limited to $24,000 (indexed for inflation) or 15 percent of an employee's annual salary, whichever is less. Investment earnings grow tax-deferred until withdrawal.

Acceptance of SEPs was extremely slow. To increase their attractiveness, Congress added a salary-reduction feature in the Tax Reform Act of 1986. The modified plan, known as the *Salary Re-*duction Simplified Employee Pension (SARSEP), allowed both the employer and the employee to contribute money. However, new SARSEP plans could not be established after December 31, 1996. The SARSEP plan was replaced by the Savings Incentive Match Plan for Employees.

The Savings Incentive Match Plan for Employees (SIMPLE)

The easiest pension system that a small business can set up is a Savings Incentive Match Plan for Employees, known as a SIMPLE or SIMPLE-IRA. The plan is designed for a business with fewer than 100 employees.

The SIMPLE is a cross between a 401(k) plan, which is discussed in Chapter 9, and an IRA. But the SIMPLE doesn't involve the government's 401(k) rules. In a SIMPLE, an employee decides how much of his or her salary will be diverted to the plan, up to a maximum of $7,000 per year. An added contribution of $500 can be made by individuals age 50 or older. The employer must match the employee's contribution either dollar for dollar, up to 3 percent of salary, or by depositing a flat 2-percent of salary. Employees decide how the money is invested, and investment earnings grow tax-deferred until withdrawal.

PUBLIC PENSION PLANS

Public pension systems—pension plans for employees of the government, rather than private industry—probably began with the British Superannuation Act of 1834. In the United States, New York City established a pension fund in 1857 for policemen. Part of the financing for this early plan came from the proceeds of sales of confiscated and unclaimed property. In 1911, Massachusetts became the first state to establish a retirement system. At about the same time, many cities began to introduce pension systems for their general municipal employees. Both Philadelphia and Pittsburgh set up pension plans in 1915. In 1920, the United States government approved the Retirement Act to set up a pension system for federal civil service employees.

Since then, both the number of public pension plans and their membership have grown rapidly. Currently, about 2,211 public pension plans cover almost all the employees of the federal, state, and local governments—about 13.5 million active members. Almost 5.4 million more members of public pension plans in the United States are currently receiving benefits.

As discussed earlier in the chapter, in 1983, the Supreme Court handed down a decision requiring that benefits of all pension plans, public and private, be gender-neutral. The court ruled that sex-based mortality tables violate Title VII of the 1964 Civil Rights Act, and that the longer life span of women may not be used to justify the payment of lower monthly benefits when they retire.

Each state and city develops its own pension system. The remainder of the chapter examines federal pension plans.

Federal Civil Service Plans

One of the most favorable features of employment by the federal government is its retirement system. Since 1920, employees have been covered under the Civil Service Retirement System (CSRS). In 1986, President Reagan signed into law an act creating the Federal Employees Retirement System (FERS). The need for a new retirement system for federal employees began with Public Law 98-21, which provided that federal employees hired after December 31, 1983, would be covered by Social Security.

A second law, Public Law 98-168, provided for a transition period from January 1, 1984, to January 1, 1986, for employees hired after December 31, 1983. During this period, employees were fully covered under CSRS and Social Security benefits. This transition period was extended to December 31, 1986, with the passage of Public Law 99-335, which established FERS.

FERS became effective January 1, 1987. All employees hired after December 31, 1983, have been automatically covered by FERS. Federal employees hired before December 31, 1986, and not covered by FERS, have the option to transfer into FERS.

Active members of CSRS and FERS number about 2.5 million, and about 2.4 million retired and disabled civilian federal employees draw pensions.

The Federal Employees Retirement System

FERS is a three-tier retirement plan. The three tiers are:

1. Social Security.

2. Basic Benefit Plan.

3. Savings Plan.

You pay full Social Security taxes and a small contribution to the Basic Benefit Plan. In addition, you can make tax-deferred contributions to the Savings Plan, with a portion matched by the government.

The three components of FERS work together to give you a strong financial foundation for your retirement years. FERS has the following advantages over CSRS:

❑ Members can join a tax-deferred savings plan.

❑ The government matches a portion of each member's savings.

❑ Members can choose from among three different types of investment funds.

❏ Individuals who leave the system with at least five years of service qualify for benefits.

❏ Survivors' and disability benefits are available after eighteen months of service.

The Civil Service Retirement System

Members of CSRS were brought under Social Security by the 1983 Social Security Amendments. Employees hired on or after January 1, 1984, have been automatically covered by FERS and Social Security.

Most workers qualify for retirement at age 55 with thirty years' service, including time in the military. (Credit for military service applies to federal employees and varies for state and local employees.) The amount of required service drops to twenty years at age 60, and to five years at age 62.

Pensions are based on average salary in the three consecutive highest-paid years, and can amount to as much as 80 percent of that figure. A recent tabulation revealed that the average retiree draws about $1,900 a month. Pensions are increased once a year to reflect increases in living costs.

Special Groups of Employees

Firefighters, law enforcement officers, and air traffic controllers receive an unreduced FERS benefit at age 50 with twenty years of service, or at any age with twenty-five years of service. Other groups eligible to join FERS and to receive retirement benefits include military reserve technicians and part-time employees. Members of Congress and congressional employees are also eligible for coverage.

Public Pension Reform

Periodically, a proposal is introduced in the United States Congress to establish federal reporting and disclosure requirements and fiduciary standards for public employee pension plans. Known as the *Public Employee Retirement Income Security Act* (PERISA), the proposal would subject federal, state, and local government pension plans to many of the same standards required of private pension plans under the terms of ERISA.

PERISA addresses such problems as unfunded liabilities; rules for operation and administration; disclosure of the status of plans to members, taxpayers, and government decisionmakers; and prevention of fraud and dishonesty by requiring bonding of the trustees who are responsible for investing a plan's assets.

For most people, pensions are an important source of retirement income. It is therefore vital that you fully understand your pension plan, and that, if necessary, you take steps to compensate for any shortfall, thereby insuring a safe and secure retirement.

Self-Study 8.1
YOUR PENSION PLAN

The following questions should help you to better understand your pension plan, whether it is a private or public plan. If you are a member of a private pension plan and do not know the answer to a particular question, contact the individual in your company who handles the pension plan. If the answer is still not clear, contact the nearest office of the United States Department of Labor, Labor-Management Services Administration. If you are a member of a public pension plan, contact your personnel office for answers.

Type of Plan

1. What type is your pension plan?

   ❑ Defined benefit plan

       ❑ Integrated with Social Security

       ❑ Nonintegrated

   ❑ Defined contribution plan

       ❑ Integrated with Social Security

       ❑ Nonintegrated

2. How is your pension plan financed?

   ❑ By employer contributions only

   ❑ By employer and employee contributions

   ❑ By union dues and assessments

3. What is your contribution to your pension plan?

   $_____ per ❑ mo ❑ wk ❑ hr

   _____ percent of your compensation

Credit for Service

4. How is a year of service earned under your pension plan?

   ❑ By working _____ hours in a twelve-consecutive-month period

   ❑ By meeting other requirements. Specify:

   _____

   _____

   _____

5. When does your plan year (twelve-month period for which plan records are kept) end each year?   On _____ (date)

6. Does your pension plan give credit for work performed before becoming a participant in the plan?   ❑ Yes   ❑ No

7. Does your pension plan give credit for work performed
after the plan's normal retirement age?   ❑ Yes   ❑ No

8. As of _____ (date), how many years of service have you earned? _____ years.

9. What are your plan's *break-in-service* rules?

_____

_____

_____

Vesting

10. Which vesting plan applies to you?
❑ Full and immediate vesting   ❑ Cliff vesting   ❑ Other _____

11. How many additional years of service do you need to be fully vested? _____ years.

Benefits

12. Will working beyond the normal retirement age increase your pension?
❑ Yes   ❑ No

13. How is the normal retirement benefit computed?

_____

_____

_____

14. What are the requirements for early retirement? _____ years of age; _____ years of service.

15. Assuming you have met the age requirement, how many more years
of service do you need to be eligible for early retirement benefits? _____ years.

16. How is the early retirement benefit computed?

_____

_____

_____

17. Will your Social Security benefit be deducted from your pension benefit?
    ❏ Yes   ❏ No
    If yes, what percent of your Social Security benefit? _____ percent.

18. How will your retirement benefit be paid?
    ❏ Monthly for life   ❏ Adjusted periodically for cost-of-living increases
    ❏ In a lump sum   ❏ To your survivor in the event of your death

Disability

19. Does your plan provide disability benefits?   ❏ Yes   ❏ No

20. How does your plan define *disability*?

    _____

    _____

    _____

21. What are your plan's eligibility requirements for disability benefits?

    _____ years of age; _____ years of service.

22. Disablement by which of the following conditions would make you ineligible for disability
    retirement benefits?
    ❏ Alcoholism   ❏ Drug addiction   ❏ Other _____
    ❏ Self-inflicted injury   ❏ Mental incompetence

23. Who decides whether your condition meets your plan's definition of disability?
    ❏ Doctor chosen by you   ❏ Doctor chosen by the plan director

24. How is the disability retirement benefit computed?

    _____

    _____

25. Where do you obtain an application for disability retirement?

    _____

    _____

26. To whom must you send it? _____

27. By when? Within _____ months after termination of work.

28. If you are qualified for disability benefits, for how long will your benefit be paid?
    - ❏ For life, if your disability continues
    - ❏ Until you return to your former job
    - ❏ Until retirement age
    - ❏ Until you are able to work

Survivors' Benefits

29. Does your pension plan offer a joint and survivor option or a similar provision for death benefits? ❏ Yes ❏ No

30. Has the joint and survivor option been waived by your spouse? ❏ Yes ❏ No

31. If death occurs before retirement, what will your survivor receive?

_____

_____

_____

_____

32. Electing a joint and survivor option will cause your pension benefit to be reduced by what percent? _____ percent.

33. If death occurs after retirement, what will your survivor receive? $_____ per month
    - ❏ For life
    - ❏ Until Social Security payments begin
    - ❏ For _____ years
    - ❏ Other _____

Funding of Your Pension Plan

34. What is the funding status of your pension plan?
    - ❏ Fully funded
    - ❏ Underfunded but building up its reserves
    - ❏ Underfunded and not building up its reserves

35. Have the auditors of your pension fund certified that its reserves are invested in high quality assets? ❏ Yes ❏ No

Insurance for Plan Termination

36. Are your benefits insured by the Public Benefit
    Guarantee Corporation?   ❏ Yes   ❏ No

Summary Plan Description

37. Has your company or union given you a
    Summary Plan Description?   ❏ Yes   ❏ No

38. Has your company given you a copy of
    the latest Summary Annual Report?   ❏ Yes   ❏ No

Applying for Benefits

39. Will your employer automatically send you
    a pension application?   ❏ Yes   ❏ No

40. Must your application for pension benefits
    be made on a special form?   ❏ Yes   ❏ No

41. Where and when should the application form be obtained?

    From _____ within __._____ months before retirement.

42. Where should your application for pension benefits be sent?

    _____

    _____

    _____

43. What documents must you present when applying for benefits?

    _____

    _____

44. If your application for benefits is denied, what is the appeal procedure?

    An appeal may be made in writing to _____

    _____ within _____ days.

9

ANNUITIES

Annuities play an important role in retirement planning, enabling you to save money and taxes at the same time. At retirement, you can cash in your annuity and withdraw the accumulated value in a lump sum, or you can opt for monthly payments that provide a lifetime income. The lump-sum withdrawal will enable you to invest the money, spend it, or pass it on to your heirs. If you arrange to collect the monthly payments for life—in other words, if you *annuitize*—the money will no longer be yours. However, you will have a guaranteed income throughout your retirement years, eliminating the fear that you will outlive your savings.

HOW ANNUITIES WORK

When making your financial plans for retirement, you should not forget to consider an annuity. To appreciate the benefits of an annuity, imagine that you are planning to retire at age 65 with a $100,000 nest egg. If you keep the money in a bank that pays 3 to 5 percent interest, it will produce an income of between $250 to $417 a month. If you draw on the principal every month in order to raise your level of living, you will run the risk of using up your money before you die.

The annuity was invented to help solve this type of problem. When an individual buys an annuity, he or she exchanges a sum of money for a promise to be paid back an agreed amount at a set schedule. This payout can begin either immediately or at a designated age, and will continue until death. You can look at an annuity as being like a life insurance policy, but one that works in reverse. With life insurance, survivors are paid when the *annuitant*—the buyer of the annuity—dies. With an annuity, you receive payments while you live.

Annuities are usually purchased from insurance companies. In calculating how much to charge for an annuity, an insurance company uses actuarial tables, just as it does to set the premium on a life insurance policy.

Actuarial tables give "average" life expectancies. Some annuitants live longer than others. Those who die sooner receive fewer payments. The unexpended funds are then used to pay those annuitants who live longer. While this may not seem fair to the ones who die early, it insures that everyone will have an equal guarantee of complete income protection for life.

Since women live longer than men, at one time, the monthly payments to women were lower than those for men of the same age. For example, if a 65-year-old man received $9.30 per $1,000 of accumulated value, a woman of the same age received only $8.50. This was referred to as a *sex-distinct rate*. However, in the 1983 Supreme Court case *Arizona v. Norris*, it was ruled that sex-based computations of retirement benefits discriminate against women, and that retirement benefits must be calculated on a gender-neutral basis. Thus, if you are in a qualified plan and you annuitize, the company must use unisex rates. This means that the company must pay the same amount per $1,000 of accumulated value to both men and women. Table 9.1 shows the actual life expectancies for men and women, as well as the gender-neutral figures that, by law, must be used in the computation of retirement benefits.

TABLE 9.1

LIFE EXPECTANCIES OF MEN AND WOMEN AGES 40–85			
	Average Number of Years Remaining		
Age	**Men**	**Women**	**Unisex**
40	36.4	41.1	38.8
45	31.9	36.4	34.4
50	27.6	31.8	29.8
55	23.5	27.4	25.5
60	19.6	23.2	21.5
65	16.0	19.2	17.8
70	12.8	15.5	14.3
75	10.0	12.2	11.3
80	7.5	9.2	8.6
85	5.5	6.7	6.3

Source: National Center for Health Statistics, Hyattsville, MD 20782.

An annuity, therefore, is a guaranteed income plan usually purchased from a life insurance company and paid back to the annuitant during retirement. When you buy an annuity, you are lending the insurance company money that you will get back with interest at a later date. The company, meanwhile, lends out your money at a higher interest rate.

TYPES OF ANNUITY PLANS

Annuities incorporate a variety of distinctive features. The money can be paid to the issuing company in one of three different ways. To purchase a *single premium annuity*, you give the issuing company one single large payment, often using the proceeds from a lump-sum settlement of a pension fund or insurance policy. You buy a *fixed premium annuity* by making a series of fixed, equal payments on a monthly or annual basis. A *variable premium annuity* is purchased with installment payments, the size of which may be changed at your discretion.

Annuities also vary in how the payments are made to the annuitants. With an *immediate pay annuity*, you make the total premium payment and begin receiving a monthly check the next month. This is related to the single premium annuity. If you prefer to have the payments begin at a later date, you can select a *deferred annuity*. In this annuity, you can arrange for the payments to start at an age specified in your annuity contract.

Other arrangements focus on the time span of the payments made to you. A *straight life annuity* guarantees a stipulated monthly income to one person for life. It pays no death benefits to survivors, nor does it have a *cash surrender value*—a cash value, including both savings and interest, that can be returned to the annuitant in a lump sum. A life annuity with a *term certain* also guarantees one person lifetime income, but

stitution selected by the employer, typically an insurance company, mutual fund, or bank. Employee members of 401(k) plans usually are allowed to change their investment choices periodically.

To be legally "tax qualified," 401(k) plans must meet specified requirements. They must be voluntary; they must be nondiscriminatory, meaning that lower-paid workers must be given the same opportunity to join as higher-paid employees; and all employee contributions and earnings on contributions must vest immediately. Employer contributions must vest in accordance with vesting rules specified in applicable current law.

Section 403(b) and Section 457 Plans

Section 403(b) of the Internal Revenue Code is similar in concept to Section 401(k), except that it covers tax-deferred contributions to retirement savings plans by employees of public schools and nonprofit organizations, including hospitals and churches. The 403(b) tax-deferred savings plan actually preceded the 401(k) plan by many years, and served as a model for the development of the Individual Retirement Account (IRA).

Section 457 of the Internal Revenue Code covers tax-deferred savings plans for employees of municipalities and state governments, following the same general principles of Section 403(b).

As of 2002, both the 403(b) plan and the 457 plan permit employees to contribute up to $11,000 a year to a tax-deferred savings plan— the same as the maximum for 401(k) plans. An added contribution of $1,000 can be made by individuals age 50 or older.

Unlike 401(k) plans, 403(b) and 457 plans do not need to be nondiscriminatory to be legally tax qualified. This allows employers to offer the plan to some employees and to exclude others, such as part-time workers.

Handling Tax-Sheltered Money at Retirement

One of the questions individuals must address when they are about to retire concerns the handling of the tax-sheltered money they have saved during their working years. For some, the amount accumulated may be just a few thousand dollars, but for others, it may be as much as $100,000, $200,000, or even more. What are the alternatives available for retiring individuals? The choices are to either withdraw, roll over, or annuitize the funds, or to defer the decision.

Withdrawing Tax-Sheltered Money

All 401(k), 403(b), and 457 plans permit you to withdraw part or all of your money without penalty starting at age $59\frac{1}{2}$. Withdrawals prior to age $59\frac{1}{2}$ are subject to a 10-percent penalty tax as well as regular income tax. These withdrawals are permitted without penalty only if you separate from service, encounter "hardship," or are disabled. If you die before age $59\frac{1}{2}$, your beneficiary can withdraw the money without penalty.

In 1988, the Internal Revenue Service issued final regulations that define "hardship" for the withdrawal of money from a tax-sheltered annuity account. In order for a situation to be deemed a hardship:

1. The participant must have an immediate and heavy financial need.

2. Other resources to meet that need cannot be reasonably available.

Expenditures that meet the requirements of "immediate and heavy financial need" are limited to medical expenses for the employee, spouse, or dependent; purchase of an employee's primary residence; post-secondary education tuition for the next semester or quarter for the employee, spouse, or dependent; and payments needed to prevent eviction or foreclosure.

A 1991 revision permits withdrawals before age 59½ without penalty if you arrange to deplete your account over your life expectancy or the joint life expectancies of you and your spouse.

Since January 1, 1993, the employer who gives you a lump-sum payment from an employee retirement plan has been required to withhold 20 percent of the amount for income taxes. For example, if the lump sum were $100,000, you would receive $80,000 and have $20,000 withheld. For income tax purposes, the lump-sum distribution is included as regular income for the year in which it is received, and any money withheld is included with all other money withheld for taxes that year. You can avoid the 20-percent withholding only by choosing the direct rollover option, which is discussed directly below.

Rollovers and Tax-Sheltered Money

A *rollover* is a tax-free transfer of money from one investment program to another. Beginning in 2002, employees are free to move assets without penalty from one type of retirement plan to another—from a 457 plan to an IRA, for instance. However, if you choose a lump-sum payment instead of a rollover, your employer will withhold 20 percent of your assets to be paid to the government in taxes.

Annuitizing Tax-Sheltered Money

When you *annuitize*, you convert accumulated savings into an annuity, from which you can draw a regular, usually monthly, benefit. Most people seek annuity payments for life, thus insuring that they will not outlive their savings.

Several standard arrangements are offered

for lifetime payout—a one-life, or maximum-life, annuity for one individual; a joint and survivor annuity, to take care of a surviving spouse or other beneficiary when the annuitant dies; and a guaranteed-minimum annuity, to insure payment for five, ten, fifteen, or twenty years for at least a minimum payback on the investment.

Under the one-life annuity, when the annuitant dies, all the remaining money in the account reverts to the fund, unless the annuitant chose a guaranteed period of payment to continue beyond the date of death. This money would go to a beneficiary.

The Internal Revenue Service requires that you begin receiving your tax-sheltered annuity income by April 1 of the calendar year following the year you reach 70½. If you fail to annuitize when required, you are subject to a 50-percent penalty on the minimum amount *not taken*, plus regular income tax on what is taken out.

Deferring Your Decision

You can retire at any age and leave your tax-sheltered annuity account intact. The account will continue to grow because of the compounding of interest over a relatively long period of time.

After retirement, you can make withdrawals from the account and pay income taxes on the withdrawals, or you can choose annuitization, but you must do so no later than April 1 of the year after you turn 70½. Deferral to age 70½ is permitted by Sections 401(k), 403(b), and 457 of the Internal Revenue Code.

Deferring a decision on the accumulation in your tax-sheltered annuity allows you to devote more time to making decisions regarding your basic retirement plan, such as how to allocate your accumulations among fixed and variable funds, and what payout option to choose.

The choices available can be confusing. Be

sure to seek guidance from counselors who are knowledgeable and specially trained to answer such questions.

Is a Tax-Deferred Account for Everyone?

A tax-deferred account is not necessarily for everyone. It depends on age, needs, and financial resources. For example, individuals who anticipate receiving a large inheritance from relatives may find that investment in a tax-deferred program will tend to increase their tax rate after retirement rather than decrease it.

In addition, while the money in a tax-deferred annuity can be withdrawn before age $59\frac{1}{2}$, the penalty charge is significant. Because of this, the money may not be readily available when you need it. In some instances, it is important for you to keep your assets liquid because they will be needed in the near future. For example, a young person may be trying to save money for a down payment on a house or for a potential business opportunity.

Like every good investment, a tax-deferred account has much to offer *if* you can afford it. However, each person's situation must be analyzed on an individual basis in order to develop the best possible retirement program. Bear in mind that some type of savings plan is beneficial as a supplement to Social Security and a private or public pension.

When planning for your retirement, you may find that an annuity is an excellent option—one that allows you to save both money and taxes, and to later supplement your pension and Social Security benefits. And by understanding your own financial needs as well as the different types of annuities available, you will be able to select the plan that will best serve you throughout your retirement years.

Self-Study 9.1

YOUR ANNUITY(IES) INVENTORY

I. Organize your annuity(ies) information in the following format. If you are not certain of the details, contact your insurance agent or the personnel department of your employer in the case of tax-sheltered annuities, Sections 401(k), 403(b), and 457 plans.

ANNUITY 1 INFORMATION

Name of annuity owner

Company name

Company address

Premium amount

Premium due date(s)

Payout plan

Income per month

Beneficiary(ies)

Survivor's rights

Name of agent

Address of agent

Telephone number of agent

Location of policy(ies)

ANNUITY 2 INFORMATION

Name of annuity owner

Company name

Company address

Premium amount

Premium due date(s)

Payout plan

Income per month

Beneficiary(ies)

Survivor's rights

Name of agent

Address of agent

Telephone number of agent

Location of policy(ies)

2. Handling tax-sheltered money at retirement is a matter that should be addressed in your planning. Your choices for the accumulation are to withdraw, roll over, annuitize, or defer the decision. Consider these alternatives; select the choice that seems reasonable at this time and list the reasons for your choice. (You may wish to discuss your decision with a financial planner.)

_____

_____

_____

_____

_____

_____

_____

_____

_____

_____

_____

_____

_____

_____

_____

_____

_____

DAY-*to*-DAY FINANCIAL CONSIDERATIONS

10

BUDGETING

In retirement planning, it is essential to know your financial goals. The first step is to calculate your net worth, which requires that you list your assets and liabilities. By analyzing your financial situation at a given point, you will be able to plan ahead and to decide where you would like to be financially one year from now, five years from now, and on into retirement. The tool for accomplishing this is a budget.

THE IMPORTANCE OF A RETIREMENT BUDGET

A *budget* is essentially a spending plan that helps you manage your money effectively. Most people would benefit from spending their income more wisely, especially during periods of inflation. Whether you have had experience with a budget or not, it is essential that you prepare a budget before you retire. This will enable you to estimate how much money you will need, and to compare your estimate with the income you expect to have.

Many experts claim that retired people require less income than employed people. It is true that many expenses diminish or disappear entirely during retirement. For example, savings accrue due to the absence of job-related expenses such as income taxes, transportation, clothing, and meals away from home. And additional free time often permits retirees to perform tasks that they previously paid others to do, such as yard work. However, other expenses may increase or arise for the first time, such as hobby and recreational expenses and certain medical costs. People planning for retirement should therefore strive to match their working incomes.

Unfortunately, many retirees find that they cannot meet their retirement-income target. Social Security benefits alone are inadequate for a comfortable retirement. Other sources of income—including pensions, savings, investments, cash value of life insurance, and annuities—are therefore necessary to supplement Social Security benefits. By planning financially and budgeting far enough in advance of retirement, you can insure that your retirement income will allow you to live at the level you desire. If necessary, you will have time to develop additional sources of income or to adjust to the idea of living on less by reducing expenditures.

A TYPICAL RETIREMENT EXPENSE BUDGET

Table 10.1 presents a typical retirement budget for a couple by showing the allocation of the money left after the payment of personal income taxes. The indicated percentages may vary by 5 percent either way, since a budget is a very personal matter and must be adjusted for each couple. However, the percentage distribution among the budgeted items can be useful as a benchmark for evaluating your own expenditure pattern, whether your annual retirement income is $20,000, $40,000, or more. The percentages are derived from actual annual budgets of retired couples, and are an approximation.

TABLE 10.1

ANNUAL BUDGET OF AN AVERAGE RETIRED COUPLE	
Budget Item	**Percentage of Income**
Housing	30 percent
Food	22 percent
Recreation and hobbies	20 percent
Medical and dental care	10 percent
Transportation	8 percent
Clothing and personal care	5 percent
Gifts and contributions	5 percent
Total	100 percent

THE BUDGETING PROCESS

The budgeting process can be summarized in the following six steps:

1. **Calculate your net worth.** Before you attempt to develop and implement a budget, you must learn where you currently stand financially. By determining your *assets*, which

are the financial and material possessions you own; your *liabilities*, which are your debts, or the amounts you owe; and your *net worth*, which is your assets minus your liabilities, you will understand your present financial position and be able to plan for your future more intelligently. If it is adequate, your net-worth position can provide a cushion against special needs and emergencies. An adequate net-worth position can also give you a cushion against inflation, which may someday help restore your budget to balance, if necessary. Worksheet 10.1 on page 163 will help you compute your net worth.

Your net worth changes every year in the same way that your income and spending patterns change. Therefore, you should draw up a net-worth statement at least once a year. This practice will allow you to study your current financial situation, determine whether it has improved or worsened since the previous year, and, if necessary, take steps to better your position.

2. **Record your current expenditures.** Before you can draw up a budget, you must learn what your current spending pattern is by keeping a record of your expenditures. You will be surprised by the information you can glean from such an account, particularly if you have never recorded such data before. You may already be using a formal budget, or you may be functioning just from experience. In any case, before you devise a retirement budget, you must analyze how you are currently spending your money.

To determine your spending pattern, keep an exact record of every expenditure you make every day. A pocket-sized notebook can be used to record daily expenditures. No amount expended, no matter how small, should be omitted. You need to keep these records for at least a year before you can use them for any projection. A year is a reasonable yardstick, since month-to-month expenses vary for such items as clothing, insurance, and even entertainment. This data will reveal much about your personal habits, likes, and dislikes. And certainly, such a record will answer the common question, "Where does all my money go?"

Worksheets 10.2 and 10.3, found on pages 164 and 166, respectively, provide a format for keeping track of your expenditures first by the week, and then by the month. For convenience, purchase large worksheet paper from a stationery store. Then, using Worksheet 10.2 as a model, note the weeks across the top of the paper and list the expense items in the first column.

Worksheet 10.3 is a model for a monthly expense record. Again, using a large worksheet purchased in a stationery store, copy the format of Worksheet 10.3, noting the months along the top of the paper and listing all the expense items in the first column. At the end of each month, total the weekly figures for each expense item and transfer the totals to your monthly worksheet. At the end of the year, total the monthly figures for each expense item and note the amounts in the "Total" column. Finally, to calculate the monthly average expenditure for each expense item, divide the totals by twelve and enter the results in the final column.

3. **Estimate your retirement spending pattern.** Once you have completed Worksheet 10.3, you can transfer the year's totals and monthly averages to columns 2 and 3 of Worksheet 10.4 on page 168. This will enable you to estimate your first year's retirement-spending pattern, noting your estimates in columns 4 and 5 of Worksheet 10.4.

As discussed earlier in the chapter, some of your expenses, particularly those that are job-related, will cease or be considerably reduced when you retire. But others, like health insurance costs, may be considerably higher.

4. **Estimate your first year's retirement income.** Worksheet 10.5 on page 169 was designed to help you estimate your income for your first year of retirement, and compare it with your current annual income. For most retirees, the three major sources of income are Social Security, pensions, and interest and dividends from savings and investments. Additional sources of income may include the following:

❏ *Annuities.* Regular monthly income paid to an individual over a specified period of time or for life.

❏ *Rent.* Income derived from the ownership of residential or commercial property.

❏ *Royalty.* A share of the proceeds or profits paid to the owner of a patent, oil or mineral rights, or copyright.

❏ *Veterans' benefit.* Income from a disability or pension benefit paid to a veteran by the United States Department of Veterans Affairs.

❏ *Reverse mortgage.* Regular monthly income derived by borrowing against the equity in a home.

❏ *Workers' compensation.* A disability benefit paid to a worker for a job-related injury or illness.

❏ *Hobby income.* Income derived from the sale of handcrafted articles, or from payment for hobby services rendered.

5. **Reconcile your income and expenses.** Worksheet 10.6 on page 169 is a summary table that you can use to balance your estimated retirement income and expenses. If your income is greater than your expenses, you have a *surplus.* What an ideal situation! However, if your income is smaller than your expenses, you have a *deficit.* If you have a deficit, you will need to make some adjustments. You can increase your income, reduce your expenses, and/or consume some of your available *capital*—that is, money or its equivalent in property or securities. To consume some of your capital, you can sell securities or real estate, or you can withdraw money from your emergency savings fund or money market mutual fund. However, your future income will be reduced, and you will need to make further adjustments in your calculations. Use Worksheet 10.7 on page 170 to record possible solutions for a deficit in your anticipated retirement budget.

6. **Review and adjust budget items.** Use Worksheet 10.8 on page 171 to keep track of your monthly expenditures for each budget item, and to compare your monthly outlays with your monthly projections. Take the projections from column 5 of Worksheet 10.4 on page 168. Use Worksheet 10.9 on page 172 to keep track of your monthly income and to compare it with your estimated income, taken from column 4 of Worksheet 10.5 on page 169.

Every two or three months, take the time to look at your spending pattern and see if you are in line with your averages, or if you are overspending and building up a deficit. A two- or three-month period is adequate for spotting where problems lie. You may find, for example, that your telephone and restaurant bills are greater than you had anticipated. In such a case, to keep your budget in balance, you must reduce your expenditures in the problem categories or, if you cannot do this, you must cut back on other expenses.

In some instances, you may find it necessary to re-examine your priorities. For instance, if you are saving for a vacation and a new refrigerator, you may decide that you cannot save for both at the same time. If your savings schedule is not on target, you can use devices such as automatic payroll deductions, if still employed, or monthly transfers from your checking account to your savings account.

TIPS ON BUDGETING

Try not to become bogged down in nickel-and-dime details. Round your budget entries to the nearest dollar. Remember that a budget is a tool which, if used correctly, can give you a realistic picture of your income and expenditures, and of how you handle your money. Your budget plan should reflect your retirement goals as well as your goals for the current year, and should be flexible enough to allow you to adapt to changing circumstances.

Every household—and especially a retiree's—needs a financial plan that incorporates specific savings programs for achieving stated goals. Your budget is a very personal tool. It should reflect your current income as well as your projected retirement income, and should be based on your own needs and goals. Do not permit the needs and goals of others to influence your budget. A budget will help you to think about and plan for the future. At the same time, it will help you to live within your means. A budget can make your retirement years secure and satisfying.

Good money-management habits can be developed with time and effort. Once you have mastered the techniques, you will find that you can live free of money problems.

Self-study 10.1
PLAN YOUR BUDGET

Use the following worksheets to plan and adjust your retirement budget. For detailed directions, see pages 160 to 162.

WORKSHEET 10.1	NET WORTH STATEMENT	DATE:
Assets		**Amount**
Cash on hand		$
Savings accounts		$
Checking accounts		$
Life insurance (cash value)		$
Investments		$
Stocks		$
Bonds		$
Mutual funds		$
Real estate (market value)		$
Automobiles (blue book values)		$
Furniture		$
Home appliances		$
Other assets:		$
		$
		$
Total assets:		$
Liabilities		**Amount**
Mortgage balance		$
Auto loan balance		$
Credit card balance		$
Other debts		$
Total liabilities:		$
(total assets minus total liabilities) **Net worth:**		$

WORKSHEET 10.2	WEEKLY EXPENSE RECORD			MONTH:_____		
Expense	Week 1	Week 2	Week 3	Week 4	Week 5	Total
Groceries						
Food away from home						
Total food						
Rent/mortgage payment						
Property/local taxes						
Heat, electricity, gas						
Telephone						
Water						
Home insurance						
Home maintenance						
Total housing						
Auto payments						
Gasoline, oil						
Auto insurance						
Auto maintenance						
Public transport, taxis						
Total transportation						
Clothing						
Dry cleaning						
Laundry						
Clothing repair						
Total clothing						

Expense	Week 1	Week 2	Week 3	Week 4	Week 5	Total
Barber, beauty shop						
Toiletries, cosmetics						
Other personal items						
Total personal care						
Medical						
Dental						
Pharmaceutical						
Hospital/health insurance						
Other health-care items						
Total medical care						
Loan/installment payments						
Life insurance						
Recreation, vacation						
Education						
Gifts, dues, contributions						
Other expenses						
Total miscellaneous expenses						
Social Security taxes						
Personal income taxes						
Savings, pensions						
Total expenditures						

WORKSHEET 10.3 — MONTHLY EXPENSE RECORD — YEAR:						
Expense	**January**	**February**	**March**	**April**	**May**	**June**
Groceries						
Food away from home						
Total food						
Rent/mortgage payment						
Property/local taxes						
Heat, electricity, gas						
Telephone						
Water						
Home insurance						
Home maintenance						
Total housing						
Auto payments						
Gasoline, oil						
Auto insurance						
Auto maintenance						
Public transportation, taxis						
Total transportation						
Clothing						
Dry cleaning						
Laundry						
Clothing repair						
Total clothing						
Barber, beauty shop						
Toiletries, cosmetics						
Other personal items						
Total personal care						
Medical						
Dental						
Pharmaceutical						
Hospital/health insurance						
Other health-care items						
Total medical care						
Loan/installment payments						
Life insurance						
Recreation, vacation						
Education						
Gifts, dues, contributions						
Other expenses						
Total misc. expenses						
Social Security taxes						
Personal income taxes						
Savings, pensions						
Total expenditures						

July	August	September	October	November	December	Total	Mo. Average

WORKSHEET 10.4	ESTIMATE OF FIRST YEAR'S RETIREMENT EXPENSES			
	Current spending pattern		**Estimated retirement spending pattern**	
Expense (1)	Monthly average (2)	Year _____ (3)	First Year (4)	Monthly average (5)
Groceries				
Food away from home				
Total food				
Rent/mortgage payment				
Property/local taxes				
Heat, electricity, gas				
Telephone				
Water				
Home insurance				
Home maintenance				
Total housing				
Auto payments				
Gasoline, oil				
Auto insurance				
Auto maintenance				
Public transportation, taxis				
Total transportation				
Clothing				
Dry cleaning				
Laundry				
Clothing repair				
Total clothing				
Barber, beauty shop				
Toiletries, cosmetics				
Other personal items				
Total personal care				
Medical				
Dental				
Pharmaceutical				
Hospital/health insurance				
Other health-care items				
Total medical care				
Loan/installment payments				
Life insurance				
Recreation, vacation				
Education				
Gifts, dues, contributions				
Other expenses				
Total misc. expenses				
Social Security taxes				
Personal income taxes				
Savings, pensions				
Total expenditures				

WORKSHEET 10.5	ESTIMATE OF 1ST YEAR'S RETIREMENT INCOME			
	Current working income		**Income for first year of retirement**	
Income (1)	**Monthly (2)**	**Year _____ (3)**	**Monthly (4)**	**Year _____ (5)**
Husband's wages or salary				
Wife's wages or salary				
Social Security				
Pensions				
Interest				
Annuities				
Rents				
Royalties				
Other income				
Total income				

WORKSHEET 10.6	SURPLUS/DEFICIT IN 1ST YEAR'S RETIREMENT BUDGET	
Income	**Monthly Dollar Amount**	**First Year Dollar Total**
Total income		
Total expenses		
Surplus or deficit		

WORKSHEET 10.7	**ALTERNATIVE SOLUTIONS FOR A DEFICIT**	
Increase income		
Source of Income	**Gross income**	**Costs arising from work**
Full- or part-time employment		
Other		

Reduce expenses		
Item to be reduced	**Means of reducing**	**Amount of reduction**

Consume capital		
Item to be consumed	**Amount available**	**Resulting future reduction in income**

WORKSHEET 10.8	RETIREMENT EXPENSE BUDGET	DATE:_____
Expense	**Projected**	**Actual**
Groceries		
Food away from home		
Total food		
Rent/mortgage payment		
Property/local taxes		
Heat, electricity, gas		
Telephone		
Water		
Home insurance		
Home maintenance		
Total housing		
Auto payments		
Gasoline, oil		
Auto insurance		
Auto maintenance		
Public transportation, taxis		
Total transportation		
Clothing		
Dry cleaning		
Laundry		
Clothing repair		
Total clothing		
Barber, beauty shop		
Toiletries, cosmetics		
Other personal items		
Total personal care		
Medical		
Dental		
Pharmaceutical		
Hospital/health insurance		
Other health-care items		
Total medical care		
Loan/installment payments		
Life insurance		
Recreation, vacation		
Education		
Gifts, dues, contributions		
Other expenses		
Total misc. expenses		
Social Security taxes		
Personal income taxes		
Savings, pensions		
Total expenditures		

WORKSHEET 10.9 — RETIREMENT INCOME & SURPLUS/DEFICIT DATE:_____		
Expense	**Projected**	**Actual**
Take-home pay (if employed)		
Husband		
Wife		
Pension		
Husband		
Wife		
Social Security benefits		
Husband		
Wife		
Annuities		
Royalties		
Interest		
Dividends		
Veterans' benefits		
Rents		
Profit-sharing plans		
Other income		
Total income		
Total income (from line above)		
Total expenses (from Worksheet 10.8)		
Surplus or deficit (Total income minus total expenses)		

CREDIT

In *Hamlet*, Polonius advises his son, "Neither a borrower, nor a lender be." This advice was eminently sound when Shakespeare penned his play, and remains so today. However, there are times when a situation makes it necessary to seek *credit*, which is a type of loan made to an individual, business, or organization by another individual, business, or organization. If you must borrow, you must also remember that credit costs something—you will have to pay back what you borrowed, along with interest and other charges. If you are planning to borrow, you must first find out how much it will cost and then decide whether you can afford it.

THE COST OF CREDIT

Credit costs vary significantly. Under the terms of the Federal Truth in Lending Law, *creditors*, the sellers or lenders who provide credit, must tell you the finance charge and the annual percentage rate (APR) in writing and before you sign an agreement. The *finance charge* is the total dollar amount you must pay when you borrow a specified amount of money. It includes interest costs; service charges; insurance premiums;

and, possibly, appraisal fees. *Interest* is the annual cost of borrowed money. The *annual percentage rate* is the percentage cost of credit on an annual basis. In addition, creditors must tell you the amount financed, the total of all payments, the number of all payments, and the due dates of payments.

All creditors—including banks, stores, car dealers, credit card companies, and finance companies—must provide the above information *before* you sign a credit contract. Particularly important are the finance charge and the APR, as they will enable you to compare credit costs so that you can get the best terms available. Shop around; do not accept the first offer.

Creditors look for the three Cs of credit to evaluate a borrower. The three Cs are:

1. **Capacity.** Can you repay the debt?
2. **Character.** Will you repay the debt?
3. **Collateral.** Is the creditor fully protected if you fail to repay the debt?

Some creditors use *credit-scoring*, a statistical system that helps predict whether a potential borrower is a good credit risk. They rate applicants on a scale and then decide either to make or to deny the loan.

DISCRIMINATION AND CREDIT

The Federal Equal Credit Opportunity Act says that age, sex, marital status, race, color, religion, national origin, or the fact that someone is poor, on welfare, or collecting Social Security may not be a basis for discrimination in any part of a credit transaction. While this law does not guarantee that you will be given credit, it clearly states that a creditor may not use any of the aforementioned grounds as an excuse to refuse you a loan if you qualify. Furthermore, creditors may not lend you money on terms different from those granted to another person with similar income, expenses, credit history, and collateral.

Prior to the implementation of this law, many older people complained that they were denied credit because of age. Many retirees also found that their credit was suddenly cut off or reduced. The Federal Equal Credit Opportunity Act changed this because under the law, a creditor may ask your age, but may not deny you credit because of your age. Creditors may use a credit-scoring system and score your age. But if you are 62 or older, you must be given at least as many points for age as a person under 62.

An older individual applying for a mortgage loan—for instance, a 65- or 70-year-old person seeking a twenty-five or thirty-year mortgage—may have some difficulty, however. In this situation, the law permits creditors to require specific information related to age, including when the applicant plans to retire or how long the applicant will continue to earn his or her current salary. On the other hand, an older individual who is prepared to make a large down payment on a house might qualify for a relatively small mortgage loan, assuming that the house is a sound investment. Remember that a lending institution owns a mortgaged home until the very last monthly payment of principal and interest is made.

It is important to be aware that there are a number of things that a creditor may *not* question you about. Specifically, creditors may not:

❑ ask if you are divorced or widowed.

❑ ask if you are married or applying for a separate, unsecured account.

❑ ask about your spouse unless the two of you are applying for a loan together.

❑ ask if you are receiving child support or alimony unless you will rely on it for your credit.

❑ ask you about the race of the people who live in the neighborhood where you want to improve or purchase a home.

WOMEN AND CREDIT

Married women often get credit under their spouse's names. If a woman divorces her spouse or if her spouse dies, a credit problem may arise. If you don't already have credit in your own name, you should begin the application process immediately. Credit is a necessity for everyone.

The first step is to apply for a credit card or small loan. If you are denied credit, find out what is in your credit file. You can obtain this information from a credit reporting agency. The three major consumer credit reporting agencies are Equifax Credit Information Services, the Trans Union Corporation, and TRW Information Services Division. Look for the addresses and phone numbers of these agencies in your telephone directory under "Credit Reporting Agencies," or ask your creditors for the name of the credit bureaus to which they report. Remember that you have the *right* to review your file and make sure that the information it contains is correct and complete.

If you have never had credit in your own name before, you may have a problem initially because of lack of a credit history. The Equal Credit Opportunity Act and the Consumer Protection Act make it illegal for a lender to deny you credit due to marital status or sex. These laws allow you to rely on the credit history of a spouse or former spouse if you can show that you helped build that history.

If you are still having a problem getting credit, a good first step is to open a department store credit account, the easiest type of credit to obtain. After using the store's credit card for a few months, you will have established some credit history. You can strengthen your financial position by opening a checking and savings account in your name. Your attorney may be helpful in getting you a major credit card.

You can also build a credit history by paying off a consumer loan. Buy a car or other large purchase, and make a large down payment. This will make it easier to apply for credit to pay off the balance. To enhance your credit history, be sure to make regular, prompt payments.

BORROWING AGAINST ASSETS

Assets include anything owned that has exchange value, such as a home or other real estate, cash, savings and checking accounts, stocks and bonds, mutual funds, cash value of life insurance, automobiles, furniture, home appliances, art, antiques, jewelry, and stamp and coin collections. Many types of assets can serve as security for loans.

One widely used method of borrowing is the *home equity loan,* with which you borrow against the value of your home. However, because your home is your *collateral*—property that a creditor has the right to take from you if you fail to make payments—you run the risk of losing your house. (For a further discussion of home equity loans, see page 39.)

Borrowing against the value of a home is traditionally done by *refinancing* the original mortgage. Lending institutions are often pleased by the opportunity to take back an old low-rate mortgage and issue a new first mortgage at a higher rate. Your lender may even offer you a few percentage points less than the current rate of mortgage interest, or possibly even forgive part of your indebtedness. Another possible source of retirement income is the *second mortgage*—a loan on a home that already has an outstanding mortgage. However, the interest rate charged may be two or three percentage points higher than the current mortgage rates, and the repayment period is usually limited to between five and fifteen years. Monthly mortgage payments, therefore, can be quite high.

A *reverse mortgage* is another potential source of retirement income—one in which you borrow against the value of your home. This mortgage reverses the normal flow of money in a home loan, with the lending company making periodic payments to the homeowner based on the value of the home (see page 40). Essentially, a reverse mortgage takes advantage of the increase in the value of your home over the years.

Other possible sources of collateral when borrowing against your assets are negotiable securities such as stocks or bonds, savings in a passbook account, certificates of deposit, and credit union shares. When you use your passbook savings as collateral, the interest rate charged on the loan is generally low, usually just a point or two above the interest you collect on your account.

Most banks, credit unions, and consumer finance companies accept a car, boat, or plane as collateral for a loan. However, interest rates are at about the level charged on *installment loans,* which are loans repaid through a series of installments, and the repayment periods are short.

Individuals approaching retirement or already retired usually find that their best bet for a modest-sized loan is a *credit union*, a type of bank formed as a cooperative by a group of individuals. For a larger loan, the lowest rates are generally charged by commercial banks.

CREDIT CARDS

If financial planning for retirement is to be effective, individuals in their working years must learn the meaning of discipline in credit and money management. American society is geared to the philosophy of "buy now, pay later." Unfortunately, the dollars are not always available later, when the bills come due. In addition, personal bankruptcy law, which was liberalized in 1979, encourages people to go deeper into debt. According to this law, if you are unable to extricate yourself from your debts, you can go to a bankruptcy attorney and possibly have your debts declared null and void.

There is no denying that credit card shopping is convenient. In addition, it can be viewed as a "free loan" because there is often a thirty-day grace period during which no interest accrues. However, the wisest way to use a credit card is to pay off the full amount of the balance due every month, and, unfortunately, only about a third of credit card users pay their outstanding balances every month.

The maximum percentage of a family's take-home pay that should be used for credit payments is 10 to 15 percent. Mortgage payments should not be greater than 25 to 30 percent of take-home pay. When credit card debt begins to exceed 15 percent, it has passed the danger point, and you must begin immediately to take remedial steps. The best course of action is to cut up and discard your credit cards. The next step should be to set up a strict budget that incorporates a schedule for paying off your creditors. (If you suspect that credit card debt or other loans may not be within reasonable limits, see Self-Study 11.1, beginning on the next page.)

Credit can enable you to make an important purchase that would be impossible if you had to rely solely on available funds. It can also help you obtain vital services, such as medical attention. But credit is a double-edged sword, and can create as many problems as it solves. To make credit work for you, it is essential to develop an effective financial plan and to manage your money in accordance with that plan throughout your retirement.

Self-study 11.1
DETERMINE THE STATE OF YOUR CREDIT

Take the following test to determine whether your outstanding credit card debt and/or installment loans are within reasonable limits.

1. Determine your grand total monthly debt repayment by filling in the following table:

CREDIT CARD DEBT		
Credit cards	**Outstanding balance**	**Monthly payment**
Total monthly credit card debt repayment		

LOAN DEBT		
Loans	**Outstanding balance**	**Monthly payment**
Total monthly loan-debt repayment		
Grand total monthly debt repayment (credit card debt + loan debt)		

2. Determine the percent of your monthly income that you owe to creditors by using the following formula:

$$\frac{\text{Grand total monthly debt repayment}}{\text{Take-home pay for one month}} = \text{Percent of your monthly income owed to creditors}$$

Divide your grand total monthly debt repayment by your take-home pay for one month. For example, if your grand total monthly debt repayment is $150 and your take-home pay for one month is $1,000, you would set up the formula as follows:

$$\frac{\$150}{\$1,000} = .15 \ or \ 15\%$$

If the percent of monthly income that you owe to creditors is greater than 15 percent, you should begin immediately to take remedial steps (see page 176).

INFLATION

In economic terms, the word *inflation* refers to a persistent increase in the general level of prices for goods and services. Most people understand this very well. They know that a shopping trip to the supermarket may cost more than the previous visit. In 1942, bread cost 9¢ a pound and coffee was 28¢ a pound. Today, the price of a pound of bread ranges from $1.50 to $2.00, or even more, and a pound of coffee ranges in price from $3.00 to $4.50. In 1942, you could buy a Cadillac for $3,000; today, the price is about $40,000. Not only have the costs of these items risen, but it is more expensive to go to a movie or a play; to take a vacation; to buy heating oil; to purchase clothing, furniture, and household appliances; and to obtain medical and other services.

Increases in living costs have been especially serious since 1973, although they have shown a downward trend in the last several years, as shown in Table 12.1 on page 181. Four categories of necessities—food, shelter, energy, and medical care—make up about 60 percent of the total market basket of expenditures of the typical urban family. In 1973, the costs of goods and services in these categories began increasing sharply and at an accelerated rate, hitting retirees forcefully because they are so dependent on these necessities. High levels of inflation continued through 1982.

Inflation also affects nest egg savings accounts. Such accounts shrink in value when the rate of inflation exceeds the interest rate. This hurts both retirees and those who are approaching retirement.

THE IMPACT OF INFLATION ON RETIREES

One way to look at inflation is as a loss in real income at a percentage equivalent to the inflation rate. For example, if the inflation rate were 4.3 percent, a retiree with a $10,000 income would lose 4.3 percent—in this case, $430—of real income. Or the $10,000 would buy just $9,570 of goods and services. Continuing inflation eats away at fixed incomes, making it more and more difficult to make ends meet.

As prices rise, retirees find that they must spend more for necessities and other items and services. If you are living on a budget, the problem becomes obvious immediately, because your spending pattern is based on costs that apply to

How Do We Measure Inflation?

The most commonly used measure of inflation is the Consumer Price Index (CPI), which is prepared by the Bureau of Labor Statistics (BLS) of the United States Department of Labor. Often referred to as the "cost of living index," the CPI measures the average change in prices of a selected list of goods and services purchased by the average consumer on a regular basis.

To compute its monthly CPI, BLS collects 100,000 price quotes a month for 365 goods and services that make up the "market basket" that is studied. It then assigns a weight to each price, with larger weights assigned to goods that represent larger proportions of consumer expenditure. The index costs $26 million a year to produce, and requires 40 economists and statisticians and thousands of price collectors who visit 57,000 housing units and 19,000 establishments across the country every month.

Economists have actually devised a number of indexes to measure different aspects of inflation. For instance, the Producer Price Index (PPI) measures inflation at earlier stages of the production and marketing process, and the Employment Cost Index (ECI) measures inflation in the labor market. The CPI is the best means of determining the consumer's changing ability to purchase goods and services over time.

an earlier period. You must revise your budget to accurately reflect the new economic picture. In a noninflationary situation, you can revise your budget annually, but in an inflationary period, you should adjust it on a monthly basis. Retirees living on fixed incomes should react to price increases immediately.

Even if you are operating without a budget, you are probably aware of inflation, whether you are retired or are still in the work force. During times of inflation, your money may seem to simply evaporate. Of course, a financial situation such as this can also be caused by carefree spending and the overuse of credit cards, but inflationary conditions will alert you to such poor money management practices more quickly.

Many older workers' dreams of retirement become unaffordable during periods of inflation. These workers find it difficult to make ends meet while fully employed, and become seriously concerned about trying to live on a lower re-tirement income. Most stay at work longer and postpone retirement in the hope that economic conditions will become more stable.

It is obvious, therefore, that high rates of inflation have a detrimental financial impact on fixed-income retirees.

TAKING MEASURES AGAINST INFLATION

During times of inflation, the options available to people living on limited or fixed incomes are few. The three alternatives are to consume capital, to increase income, and to reduce expenses.

Consuming capital is hardly a long-term solution to the problem of coping with inflation—unless you are sure that your capital supply will not be consumed in your lifetime. The average person does not have a very large nest egg to begin with. But even for those who have managed to accumulate some savings and investments, consuming capital is not a recommended solution.

One of the soundest ways to keep your nest egg from melting away after you retire—and your second option—is to increase your income by adding a fresh flow of new, inflated earnings. To earn an income after you retire, you do not have to return to what you did before retirement. You can work part-time, possibly through one of the new job-sharing or flextime systems that some companies are adopting to make part-time employment more attractive. You can also set up your own business or expand a favorite hobby or pastime into a money-making proposition. (See Chapter 1, "Working in Retirement," for more detailed information.)

Your third alternative is to trim your ex-penses. This means that you must study all of your major budgetary items—including food, clothing, shelter, and health care—and then sharpen your shopping skills so that you can reduce the amount you spend on them. If you choose this third option, you must learn to time your purchases so that they coincide with sales, to use discount stores, to avoid impulse buying, to carefully examine your purchases for quality, and to make your clothing and other items last longer by following care instructions. Energy costs and medical costs—which are important in everyone's budget, but especially in those of retirees—will probably continue to exceed the inflation rate in the first decade of the twenty-first century. It is therefore crucial to adopt cost-saving energy tactics, including installing

TABLE 12.1

ANNUAL RATE OF INFLATION, 1960–2000									
Year	% Increase	Year	% Increase	Year	% Increase	Year	% Increase	Year	% Increase
1960	1.7%	1970	5.7%	1980	13.5%	1990	5.4%	2000	3.4%
1961	1.0	1971	4.4	1981	10.3	1991	4.2		
1962	1.0	1972	2.5	1982	6.2	1992	3.0		
1963	1.3	1973	6.2	1983	3.2	1993	3.0		
1964	1.3	1974	11.0	1984	4.3	1994	2.6		
1965	1.6	1975	9.1	1985	3.6	1995	2.8		
1966	2.9	1976	5.8	1986	1.9	1996	3.0		
1967	3.1	1977	6.5	1987	3.6	1997	2.3		
1968	4.2	1978	7.6	1988	4.1	1998	1.6		
1969	5.5	1979	11.3	1989	4.8	1999	2.2		
Average 1960s	2.4%	*Average 1970s*	7.0%	*Average 1980s*	5.6%	*Average 1990s*	3.0%	*Average 2000s*	3.4%

Source: U.S. Department of Labor, Bureau of Labor Statistics, as measured by the Consumer Price Index for All Urban Consumers, U.S. City Average, All Items, CPI-U, Annual Averages, Year to Year.

insulation, updating your heating system to make it more efficient, and possibly lowering the thermostat setting. Solutions to rising medical costs are not readily available. Perhaps the expansion of Medicare health care coverage can be of some assistance.

If you are unable to cope with inflation, you should not hesitate to seek professional assistance. Financial counseling is available through credit unions and some banks, among other institutions. Check with your local senior citizens center.

Inflation is a matter of concern to everyone, but is especially worrisome to retirees who live on fixed incomes. By being aware of the problem and, when necessary, taking steps to reduce expenses or increase income, you can insure a comfortable retirement despite any ups and downs of the economy.

13

TAXES *and* TAX SHELTERS

No doubt about it, taxes are a confusing subject for all taxpayers, not just for seniors. This chapter tries to take the mystery out of taxes by giving you an overview of how *personal income tax*—tax imposed on the income of individuals and families—is computed each year. It then lets you in on the different tax shelters that can help you defer or diminish your yearly tax burden.

THE HISTORY OF TAXES

In colonial America, the early settlers resented direct taxes imposed by Great Britain, particularly the Stamp Tax, which taxed tea and business documents. Ultimately, this led to revolts such as the Boston Tea Party.

When the United States was established, the Constitution required that taxes be apportioned among the states by population, so that more highly populated states would assume a greater share of the tax burden. Efforts by Congress to establish a direct income tax were struck down by the United States Supreme Court.

Finally, the Sixteenth Amendment to the Constitution was ratified in 1913, granting Congress the power to approve and collect income taxes without apportioning the tax among the states. Since 1913, the United States income tax system has grown and become highly complex. Some even refer to it as a nightmare. The explanation of the Tax Reform Act of 1986 was more than 1,300 pages long. No wonder the business of tax preparation has become so lucrative!

Like all taxes, personal income tax—the focus of this chapter—is exacted by law to raise revenue for the general support of the government and the maintenance of public services. The government has tried to create a fair system of income taxation by imposing greater taxes on individuals with higher levels of income, and by allowing deductions to people with a greater number of dependents and/or higher expenses.

THE COMPUTATION OF FEDERAL INCOME TAX

The Internal Revenue Code (IRC), enforced by the Internal Revenue Service (IRS), contains the federal rules and regulations for the income tax. Many changes have been made since 1913, but the basic formula for computing the amount of tax owed has remained the same. To calculate taxes owed, specified deductions are taken from an individual's gross income to arrive at an adjusted gross income. Additional deductions are then taken to arrive at taxable income, which is then taxed according to a rate determined by the individual's income level. The resulting amount is then compared with the amount already paid through tax withholdings from paychecks or through tax prepayment, and it is this comparison that determines whether the taxpayer is entitled to a refund or must pay additional taxes to the IRS. The following discussions provide more insight into each stage of the computation process.

Calculating Gross Income

The first step in computing your taxes is the determination of gross income. *Gross income* is all income derived from all sources, including personal services, business activities, and property (capital assets) owned for personal or business purposes. Thus, gross income includes wages; salaries; tips; bonuses; fees; commissions; interest earned on bank accounts; dividends; rent from property owned; royalties from copyrights, trademarks, and patents; annuities; gambling winnings; IRA distributions; and Social Security benefits.

Calculating Adjusted Gross Income

Once the amount of gross income is determined, you can often take deductions to arrive at your *adjusted gross income* (AGI). Examples of allowable deductions include contributions made by employees to an Individual Retirement Account (IRA) or by self-employed individuals to Keogh plans; interest paid on student loans; alimony payments made by the taxpayer; and penalties on early withdrawal from a tax-deferred annuity. Once all of the legally allowed deductions

are subtracted from gross income, the remainder is adjusted gross income.

Making Deductions and Exemptions

The government recognizes that people with the same income may have different circumstances. For instance, one household may have more children than another, and one family may have higher medical expenses than another. Thus, exemptions and deductions are provided to lighten the burden of taxpayers with larger families and/or greater expenditures.

Deductions

The law allows you to take certain deductions from your adjusted gross income. In some cases, these deductions can be itemized, meaning that you list each deduction along with the amount involved. In other cases, you can take what is called a standard deduction.

TAKING THE STANDARD DEDUCTION

The standard deduction is a single amount that should cover all the itemized deductions for an average taxpayer. This single figure is increased every year to keep up with inflation. In the preparation of 2001 income taxes, the standard deduction for people under 65 is as follows:

❏ Single: $4,550

❏ Married, Filing Jointly: $7,600

❏ Married, Filing Separately: $3,800

❏ Head of Household: $6,650

❏ Qualifying Widow or Widower With Dependent Child: $7,600

You are entitled to a higher deduction if you are age 65 or older, or if you are blind. The standard deduction for a single individual age 65 or older is $5,650. If you are blind, the standard deduction is $6,750.

In most cases, it is recommended that you take the standard deduction. However, if the total of itemized deductions is greater than the standard deduction, you will pay less taxes by itemizing the deductions.

ITEMIZING DEDUCTIONS

As explained above, it is sometimes beneficial to itemize your deductions rather than taking the appropriate standard deduction. Categories of itemized deductions include the following:

❏ Medical and dental expenses if they exceed $7\frac{1}{2}$ percent of the adjusted gross income.

❏ State and local taxes.

❏ Home mortgage interest.

❏ Charitable contributions.

❏ Casualty and theft losses.

❏ Job expenses.

❏ Miscellaneous deductions.

If your itemized deductions total more than your standard deduction, explained previously, you will want to deduct your total itemized deductions from your adjusted gross income. If not, you will want to deduct your standard deduction from your adjusted gross income.

Exemptions

Exemptions lighten your tax load by allowing you to deduct a specified amount of money—$2,900 for the 2001 tax year—for yourself and each of your dependents. Exemptions are divided into two categories: personal exemptions and exemptions for dependents.

In the category of *personal exemptions,* you are allowed one exemption for yourself and, if you are married, one exemption for your spouse. In the category of *exemptions for dependents,* you are allowed one exemption for each person you can claim as a dependent, including minor and adult children, parents, and anyone else whom you support.

If your adjusted gross income is above a certain amount, you are not allowed to deduct exemptions. The amount of adjusted gross income allowed depends on filing status, and changes every year.

Once your exemptions have been totaled, you will deduct them from your adjusted gross income to arrive at your *taxable income.* Your tax rate is applied to your taxable income rather than your AGI.

Applying the Tax Rate to Taxable Income

In an effort to create a fair system of taxation—one that imposes similar taxes on people with similar incomes—the United States government created *tax brackets.* In this system, individuals and families whose taxable incomes fall within a specific range, or tax bracket, have to pay a specific percentage of that income as a tax. Table 13.1 on page 186 defines the different tax brackets and shows the percentage of tax charged on each.

Once you have determined the tax bracket into which you fall, the next step is to calculate the appropriate percentage of your taxable income. For instance, if you are in the 28-percent bracket, you would calculate 28 percent of your taxable income. Now compare this amount with any amount that was withheld through paycheck deductions or paid in estimated income taxes during the year. If the first sum is greater than the second, you must pay the difference to the United States Treasury. If the amount withheld or prepaid is greater than the first amount, the IRS will send you a refund.

TABLE 13.1

	INCOME TAX BRACKETS—2001				
Filing Status	Range for 15% Tax Bracket[a]	Range for 27.5% Tax Bracket	Range for 30.5% Tax Bracket	Range for 35.5% Tax Bracket	39.1% Tax Bracket
Married, Filing Separately	0–$22,599	$22,600–$54,624	$54,625–$83,249	$83,250–$148,674	Above $148,675
Single	0–$27,049	$27,050–$65,549	$65,550–$136,749	$136,750–$297,349	Above $297,350
Head of Household	0–$36,249	$36,250–$93,649	$93,650–$151,649	$151,650–$297,349	Above $297,350
Married, Filing Jointly, or Qualifying Widow	0–$45,199	$45,200–$109,249	$109,250–$166,499	$166,500–$297,349	Above $297,350

[a] The 15% bracket remains for 2001 taxes, with eligible taxpayers receiving the benefit of the new 10% tax rate through a refund check. For the year 2002, the new 10% bracket will be available for regular tax computation.

Special Tax Concerns for Women

While the federal income tax applies to everyone, regardless of gender, women should take note of a few pertinent items. Divorce, for example, carries with it several financial implications, such as division of marital property, alimony, and child support. Although the property divided in a divorce is not taxable, a hidden tax consequence may arise if an asset is subsequently sold showing a capital gain. And if you receive alimony, it is included in your taxable income, but is tax-deductible in your husband's tax return. Finally, child support money is neither taxable to you nor deductible by your former husband.

A host of other tax issues arise through divorce, including treatment of legal fees related to the divorce, home mortgage interest, job-hunting expenses, and educational expenses required to maintain or improve your existing job skills. These various expenses are deductible if your miscellaneous total exceeds 2 percent of your adjusted gross income.

Both divorce and widowhood have a variety of tax implications in terms of filing status. "Single" filing status applies if you are unmarried or legally separated with no children at home. "Head of household" status applies if you maintain a home for a child, children, or another dependent.

If your spouse died in 2002, you can use "married filing jointly" when filing for 2002 if you would otherwise qualify for that status. The year of the death is the last year for which you can file jointly with your deceased spouse.

You may be eligible to use "qualifying-widow(er) with dependent child" as your filing status for two years following the year of death of your spouse. For example, if your spouse died in 2002, and you have not remarried, you can use this filing status for 2002 and 2003. This filing status will entitle you to use joint return tax rates and the higher standard deduction.

STATE INCOME TAX

Of course, federal income tax is not the only tax

for which you are responsible each year. Most people also must pay state income tax. However, income tax varies widely from state to state. In fact, nine states—Alaska, Florida, Nevada, New Hampshire, South Dakota, Tennessee, Texas, Washington, and Wyoming—collect no personal income tax at all. And six states—Colorado, Illinois, Kentucky, Michigan, New York, and Pennsylvania—either exclude retirement income from taxes or allow for generous exemptions.

INCOME TAX FILING ASSISTANCE

Many of the more than 35 million Americans who are 65 or older run into problems accomplishing the annual chore of filing an income tax return with the federal government. Some of the basic difficulties include confusion over which forms to use, how to fill them out, whether or not to itemize deductions, and whether to file separately or to file jointly with a spouse. If you wish to prepare your own tax return but you have questions, the Internal Revenue Service is available to help you. Call or visit your nearest IRS office. You may also wish to obtain a free copy of Internal Revenue Publication Number 17, *Your Federal Income Tax*, from the IRS. (See the Resources section.)

You can also obtain free tax advice from the American Association of Retired Persons (AARP), which offers IRS-trained volunteers to counsel retirees. For the location of such a counselor, write to AARP or visit their website. (See the Resources section.) If you would like to obtain the details of a particular state's laws on income taxes or other taxes, contact the Public Information Division of the Department of Revenue or Taxation in that state's capital.

If you do not wish to prepare your own tax return, you will need to find professional assistance. IRS-trained tax preparers are available in IRS offices in your area. To find the location of

the IRS office nearest you, call the IRS toll-free line (see the Resources section), or check your local phone directory under "United States Government, Internal Revenue Service."

If your return is more complex, you may wish to hire a certified public accountant (CPA) who is licensed to practice in your state. CPAs are qualified to represent you at an IRS audit. If you decide to use a professional accountant, though, you must be prepared to pay the required fee.

TAX SHELTERS FOR RETIREMENT PLANNING

A *tax shelter* is an investment that legally enables you to defer taxes or, ultimately, to diminish taxes. These goals can be accomplished by investing soundly in assets that you leave untouched for a long period of time. In conjunction with the compounding of interest, this long-term strategy steadily increases the size of your investment.

Because of the relatively small risk involved, some tax-sheltered investments are particularly suitable for small investors, a category that includes most people who are retired or are approaching retirement. Because of the high risk involved, other investments are appropriate only for larger investors.

When choosing and establishing tax shelters, it is suggested that you work with a tax attorney or CPA. A knowledgeable professional will help you choose a legal tax strategy that is appropriate for your particular circumstances.

Tax Shelters for the Average Investor

If you are an average investor, you can benefit from a tax-sheltered investment by putting your money into one or more of the following:

❏ **Individual Retirement Accounts and Keogh**

plans. The traditional Individual Retirement Account (IRA) and the Keogh plan allow money to grow while sheltering it from taxes. Taxes on individual deposits and earnings are deferred until the money is withdrawn. This feature enables your investment to grow faster than it would if invested in a nontax-deferred vehicle.

Since 1998, a new IRA, known as the Roth IRA, has enabled individuals to invest money that accumulates tax-free. However, contributions to the account are not income tax-deductible. (See Chapter 8 for a more detailed discussion of IRAs and Keogh plans.)

❏ **Home ownership.** When you own your home, your mortgage interest and property taxes are deductible. Moreover, if you sell, according to the Taxpayer Relief Act of 1997, you can enjoy a tax-free profit of $250,000 for individuals or $500,000 for couples as long as you have lived in the home for at least two of the last five years.

Further tax benefits can result from renting out your old home or buying a house as a rental property. In either case, you will be able to deduct all your expenses from the rent you receive. You can also deduct the depreciation on the house based on the cost, or on the market value at the time the house was converted to a rental property—whichever is lower.

❏ **Pensions.** The money contributed to your pension account by your employer is tax-deferred. You will not be required to pay taxes on it until you retire.

❏ **Tax-deferred annuities.** The money you invest in a tax-deferred annuity is not taxed when you put it in, and is tax-free while it is accumulating. Only when you begin to receive payments will you be required to pay the taxes due. (For an in-depth discussion of this subject, see page 000.)

❏ **Municipal bonds.** These are among the best tax shelters, particularly for people in the 28-percent-and-above tax brackets. The interest earned is not taxable by the federal government and is exempt from the state income tax of the state in which the bond was issued. (For an in-depth discussion of this subject, see page 95.)

❏ **United States government savings bonds.** Series I, EE, and HH United States savings bonds offer the advantage of tax deferral. You pay taxes on the interest you have earned only when you cash in the savings bonds. The Series I bond offers the additional advantage of keeping pace with inflation. (For an in-depth discussion of this subject, see page 91.)

Tax Shelters for the Larger Investor

Tax shelters that are not designed for the average small investor because of their high risk and the possible loss of all the invested money include oil and gas drilling, cattle raising, mineral excavation, and real estate development. The Tax Reform Act of 1986 severely restricted the tax write-offs that for a long time were the major draw for investors in these types of activities. These tax shelters are now less attractive even to investors who are willing to assume such a risk.

The Rollover as a Tax Shelter

Anyone who takes a lump-sum settlement or withdrawal from an employee retirement plan or profit-sharing plan is subject to a 20-percent withholding tax on the withdrawal. Therefore, when you request a withdrawal or distribution from a qualified retirement plan, you will receive only 80 percent of the amount you requested. If you live in a state with mandatory state tax withholding, the payer must also deduct the state income tax, so you will receive an amount that is even less than 80 percent of the withdrawal amount requested.

To retain the account as a tax shelter and to avoid the mandatory 20-percent withholding tax, you can roll over or transfer the entire account to another employee retirement plan or to an Individual Retirement Account.

Be aware, though, that some distributions are not subject to the mandatory 20-percent withholding. They include:

❑ Periodic payments made over the participant's single or joint life expectancy, or over a period of not less than ten years.

❑ Minimum distributions required when you attain age 70$\frac{1}{2}$.

❑ Loans.

❑ Rollovers to another qualified employee retirement plan or to an IRA, as noted above.

Owning Your Own Business

During retirement, many people enjoy the tax shelter provided by self-employment. The business, of course, can be anything you choose. You may decide to convert a hobby into a business by selling the crafts that you have enjoyed making for years. You can offer a service such as pet-sitting or bookkeeping. Or you can open a store or restaurant. The possibilities are limited only by your imagination.

Once you establish a business, you are eligible for a variety of tax deductions. To qualify as a tax deduction, your expenses must be considered "ordinary and necessary," meaning that they are considered a necessary part of your business; must be paid or incurred during the taxable year; and must be connected with the conduct of a trade or business. Thus, you may be able to deduct automobile expenses, home office costs, and more, all the while building a business that can provide further income during your retirement years.

Everyone knows that taxes are a fact of life. By becoming aware of the taxes that you will have to pay each year, by taking advantage of available tax shelters, and by seeking professional assistance when necessary, you can prevent taxes from eroding your income during retirement.

PART
FOUR

INSURANCE

14

LIFE INSURANCE

Many people in the early and middle years of their lives purchase life insurance policies without clearly understanding how much they need, and how the policies will meet the long-term goals of their families. As time elapses, needs and goals change, and the life insurance policies purchased earlier may no longer fulfill their family's requirements. As you begin to plan for retirement, it is appropriate to review and analyze the life insurance policies you own. Decide whether you need what you have, and whether you might be able to invest your accumulated cash values more profitably.

THE CHANGING ROLE OF LIFE INSURANCE

As your retirement time approaches, you must make certain decisions about your insurance. How much financial protection do you still need for your dependents? Do you still need insurance as a means of saving money? Is this an opportune time to cash in some of your policies and use the proceeds for other investments?

In general, life insurance serves two functions during the course of an individual's work-ing years. First, it provides financial protection for survivors in case of a breadwinner's death. Second, some types assist the insured in building a nest egg, hopefully for retirement.

The principal test of whether you need life insurance is both the number of dependents you have and the circumstances of your dependents. If your death would cause economic hardship for your spouse, children, parents, or someone else you want to protect, insurance will provide you with the ability to fulfill your obligations.

The need for life insurance is great, for example, in the case of a husband and nonworking wife who have two young children. In this situation, three people are dependent on the husband for their total support, so insurance coverage is essential. If the wife were to die, the husband would have to pay for day care for the children, which is quite expensive. It would be prudent for the wife to also have a life insurance policy.

On the other hand, a young unmarried student whose parents are financing the student's education has little or no need for insurance. From an economic point of view, the student's death would create no burdens. However, an argument can be made that the young student should buy a policy simply because younger people pay lower rates.

During our working years, advertisements and insurance agents tell us that every bread-winner with a young family should carry life insurance. As the years pass, however, children grow to adulthood, retirement becomes imminent, and finances usually improve. As a result, near-retirees are almost certainly faced with premium payments for insurance that is no longer needed or wanted. Funds available from old policies can then be converted into investments, offering lifetime income.

If your children are self-supporting, your mortgage is paid off, other income-producing investments have been made, and retirement rights under Social Security and your pension plan have been achieved, you may discover that you need only a relatively small insurance policy to cover your final medical and burial expenses.

On the other hand, even during your later years, you may be well served by a life insurance policy. If you have a physically or mentally challenged child or a spouse without adequate retirement income, for instance, a life insurance policy will provide a lump-sum payment for your beneficiary when you die. This sum, if properly invested, can yield a safe, regular monthly income. If you are in a high-income bracket, life insurance can pay any federal and state inheritance taxes for your heirs, preventing the forced uneconomical and unwanted sale of estate assets to settle these taxes. Thus, life insurance can help to preserve your estate.

TYPES OF LIFE INSURANCE

All the different policies offered by insurance companies fit into one of two major categories: those that build savings and those that do not.

Term life insurance does not include savings for the future. The insurance company pays only in the event that you die during the time the insurance is in force. Your beneficiaries will receive nothing if premium payments are discontinued.

Cash value life insurance includes a savings feature. This type of insurance is popular among individuals who wish to accumulate savings that they can collect by cancelling the policy prior to their death. Cash value insurance requires policyholders to pay higher premium charges. The factors that determine the premium rate include age, sex, health, family history, status as a smoker or nonsmoker, and the amount of the death benefit.

Term Life Insurance

As previously mentioned, *term life insurance,* also known as *pure insurance,* contains no savings component and expires at the end of a specified term. The policy can be renewed at the end of the term, but a higher premium is assessed because you are older. Term life insurance is a good buy, because the premium is significantly less than that for a cash value life insurance policy, and in the event of your death, your beneficiary receives the *face value* of the policy—the amount specified in the contract as the death benefit.

There are several different types of term life insurance policies. *Guaranteed renewable term insurance* is purchased for a period ranging from one to five years, and offers the right to renew without proof of insurability. Therefore, even if you suffer a heart attack six months before renewal, the policy can be renewed. The premium cost, related to age, is increased at each renewal. The premium remains constant, however, during each individual term of the policy.

Decreasing term insurance allows you to pay a fixed and relatively low premium, and receive coverage that decreases each year. If it is purchased to guarantee paying off a mortgage for the benefit of the surviving spouse and children, the policy is a good selection, reducing insurance as the mortgage balance is reduced.

Convertible term insurance allows—but does not require—you to convert to some form of insurance that builds cash value. A medical exam is not required for conversion. The change, of course, does result in a much higher premium compared with the premium for term coverage.

Cash Value Life Insurance

Cash value life insurance, also known as *permanent insurance*, requires premium payments for a set number of years, until a specified age, or for life, depending on the specific type of policy. This type of policy remains in effect even after you have finished paying the premium. It builds cash value because the fixed premiums exceed the insurance company's cost of providing you with coverage.

Several types of this popular form of insurance are offered by insurance companies. *Whole life insurance*, also known as *straight life insurance*, provides lifetime coverage in exchange for premiums that continue throughout your life, usually to age 100. The premium is lower for younger people, who have a longer life expectancy and will be paying premiums for a longer time. Whole life insurance offers the lowest premium for a specified amount of coverage as compared with other cash value policies. But because of the lower premiums, cash values grow more slowly. The policy pays the face value if the insured dies or lives to 100.

Single premium life insurance, also known as *single premium whole life insurance*, requires the payment of a single, relatively large premium at the time the policy is purchased. No other payment is required to keep the policy in force.

Limited payment life insurance policies include *twenty-pay life*, for which you contract to pay twenty annual premiums, and *thirty-pay life*, for which you must make thirty annual payments. When all required premiums have been paid, the policies are said to be *paid up*. Paid-up policies continue to provide insurance coverage and to accumulate cash values.

Endowment life insurance requires that premiums be paid for a specified number of years, at which time the cash value of the policy equals the face value, which is paid to the insured by the insurance company. The death benefit is equal to whatever has been paid in, plus accrued interest. This is a very expensive policy, requiring very high annual premiums that generate a rapid buildup of cash value. It is most often used to help fund a child's college education or to build a retirement nest egg.

Universal life insurance divides premium payments into life insurance and savings, promising a fixed, competitive rate of return to be paid for one year on the investment portion. At the end of the year, a new rate is set for the next twelve months, and a minimum rate is guaranteed. Premium payments are flexible, permitting increased payments, decreased payments, and even skipped payments. The amount of death benefits is also flexible. The insurance company's administrative expenses are deducted from the earnings.

Variable whole life insurance charges fixed premiums, and offers a fixed minimum death benefit regardless of the performance of the investments. A policy such as this provides a new freedom to policyholders, allowing you to choose the investments you want the insurance company to make with your premiums—money market, stocks, bonds, or real estate, for instance. You can choose more than one mutual fund, and you also have the option of switching from one fund to another. Shifts between funds are not taxed because they are made inside a tax-sheltered life insurance product.

Universal variable life insurance is a hybrid form that combines universal and variable life insurance. You can set most of the terms and conditions of the policy. Instead of paying fixed, level premiums at a specific time as with variable life, you can tell the insurance company exactly how much you would like to pay and when. You can also direct how the money will be invested, and you have the right to change the face amount of the policy.

Vanishing premium life insurance has as its goal the production of enough income to pay for premiums after a set period of time, such as ten years. Dividends, which are generally higher than traditional returns, are automatically reinvested. After a specified number of premium payments, you no longer have to pay premiums and you are fully covered by the policy's death benefit.

Survivorship whole life insurance, also known as *second-to-die life insurance,* insures two lives— usually husband and wife—under one policy. Death benefits are paid on the death of the last of the two named insured. This policy is generally less expensive than two separate policies and is useful for planning the payment of estate taxes.

Options Offered by Cash Value Life Insurance

Life insurance that builds a cash value provides you with several options that are unavailable with a term policy. These options include:

❏ **Loans.** You can borrow all or a portion of the cash value of your policy at favorable rates in the event that you have a need for cash. You will pay interest as long as the loan remains outstanding. If you die while a policy loan remains outstanding, the death benefit to beneficiaries will be reduced by the amount of the loan.

❏ **Withdrawal of cash value.** If you are willing to cancel your life insurance coverage, you can withdraw the cash value.

❏ **Conversion to a term policy.** You can convert your cash value insurance to a term insurance policy that provides the same coverage. You must simply instruct the insurance company to use the cash value to pay premiums on a term insurance policy. The greater the cash value accumulated, the longer the term policy will last.

WHAT BENEFICIARIES SHOULD KNOW

To collect the proceeds of a life insurance policy as a beneficiary, you should contact your insurance agent and advise him or her to prepare the claim form. If you no longer have an insurance agent, you can contact the company directly.

Insurance companies offer a number of options for paying the face amount of the policy. The most popular option is the *lump-sum payment.* This settlement gives you the opportunity to invest the money and to earn a good return. For prudent money managers, this is the recommended option. The other choices include *life-income,* a specified amount of income paid periodically for life; *fixed-period option,* a specified amount paid periodically over a fixed number of years; and *fixed-amount option,* a specified amount paid periodically until the insurance fund is exhausted. Among these three options, each payment will include principal and interest. The principal you receive will be tax-free, but the interest earned is subject to income taxes.

LIFE INSURANCE AND TAXATION

Life insurance payments have a variety of tax implications, depending on how and to whom they are made. In many cases, though, life insurance offers real tax advantages to policyholders and beneficiaries.

Income Tax

As a policyholder, you are not required to pay income tax on the annual buildup in cash value, unless and until the money is withdrawn and the policy is surrendered. However, you will then have to pay taxes only on the amount of cash value that exceeds the total amount of premiums you paid for the insurance policy.

Life insurance death benefits are not taxable to the beneficiary(ies). However, if the proceeds are received in yearly installments, the amount of interest included in the payment is subject to tax. The interest paid on loans from your policy is not tax-deductible.

Estate Tax

Proceeds payable to a beneficiary or to your estate on a policy you own are part of your estate, and are therefore subject to estate taxes. Estate taxes can be avoided if the policy you own is transferred to someone else—your husband, wife, or children—or to an irrevocable insurance trust, more than three years prior to your death. Transferring ownership, however, results in the loss of your right to change beneficiaries, to make a loan, or to surrender the policy for its cash value. A transfer may be subject to gift tax.

REVIEWING YOUR INSURANCE NEEDS

You have already seen that the life insurance policy you buy earlier in life may not be the best option in your later years. That's why it is wise to periodically review your policy and determine if it is still a good investment. This is particularly true of cash value life insurance, which can be cashed in so that the money can be put to other uses.

Cash value life insurance policies usually include a table in the document that indicates the amount of cash the insurance company would pay if the policy were surrendered. This amount is the *cash value*. The amount becomes larger the longer the policy is owned, but it is usually less than the face value of the policy—the amount to be paid in case of death. The amount of money you receive upon surrender is equal to the total premiums you have paid, plus the interest that has been earned by those payments over the years.

If you have been paying premiums on a cash value life insurance policy for twenty to twenty-five years, the cash value of the policy is usually about half the face value. This cash-value sum can at any time be withdrawn and invested in a way that will yield a higher interest rate than that paid by the insurance company.

An alternative is to convert the cash value of your life insurance policy into an annuity contract. Although you can buy the annuity from the company that issued the life insurance policy, you are not obligated to do so, and may be able to get a better return from another company. The company from which you intend to buy the annuity should arrange the withdrawal of the cash value and the surrender of the policy in such a way that you avoid the income tax that would be imposed for a straight withdrawal of the cash value.

For help in reviewing your life insurance policy, see Self-Study 14.1, which was designed to guide you in assessing your policy in terms of its value and your current need for life insurance.

An objective investigation of the many life insurance alternatives open to you is a major facet of retirement planning. The best time for reviewing your insurance program is when your retirement is within sight. You may wish to seek the help of a trusted financial adviser or insurance agent to review and evaluate the available alternatives—including, of course, the option of continuing your current policy.

Self-Study 14.1

YOUR LIFE INSURANCE POLICY(IES) INVENTORY

Filling out the following form will enable you to inventory your life insurance policy(ies). Organizing your information in this way will be helpful in determining whether you are overinsured, and whether the cash values are large enough to be invested in a way that will yield significantly greater returns. If you do not know the type of policy you own, call your insurance agent.

LIFE INSURANCE POLICY

Name of insured

Policy number

Company name

Company phone number

Company address

Type: term, cash value,
   endowment, specialized

Face amount

Beneficiary(ies)

Current loan, if any

Current cash value, if any

Premium amount

Premium due date(s)
_____

Name of insurance agent
_____

Address of agent
_____

Telephone number of agent
_____

Location of policy(ies)
_____

The following questions will provide information you should know regarding your insurance needs. You may wish to discuss them with your insurance agent or a financial planner.

1. What is the total amount of life insurance you currently own?

_____

2. What is the ideal amount of life insurance coverage you should have at this stage of your life? (Discuss this with a financial planner.)

_____

3. Are you over or under the ideal amount?_____

4. What steps will you take, if any, to achieve the ideal amount of life insurance coverage?

_____

_____

_____

5. What is your total accumulation of cash value at this time? _____

6. List alternative forms of investment for some portion of your total cash value. (Discuss this with a financial planner.)

_____

_____

_____

15

HEALTH INSURANCE

You buy health insurance for the same reason you buy any other type of insurance—to protect yourself and your family from financial loss if a dreaded event occurs. Illness and disability can wreak havoc at any age.

As you begin to plan for your golden years, you should investigate whether your health insurance protection can be carried over into your retirement. You should also determine whether you have correct and adequate protection. This chapter analyzes the principal and specialized types of coverage available, as well as the kinds of organizations that offer them. The chapter also discusses special situations that need to be considered when selecting coverage for your retirement years, and ends by offering basic advice on health insurance.

TYPES OF GENERAL HEALTH INSURANCE

Several types of health insurance are available today for an individual, a family, or a group. These include hospitalization insurance, basic medical/surgical insurance, comprehensive major medical insurance, catastrophic major medical insurance, and disability income insurance.

Hospitalization Insurance

Hospitalization insurance covers the expenses you incur while you are a patient in a hospital. Most plans cover daily room and board as well as regular nursing services in the hospital for varying periods of time, usually from 21 to 365 days. Some plans also pay for X-rays, laboratory tests, and medications.

Hospitalization is a basic form of health insurance that everyone should have. It is usually provided by employers and unions for their members.

Basic Medical/Surgical Insurance

Basic medical/surgical insurance covers doctors' visits in and out of the hospital, diagnostic and laboratory tests, and certain surgical procedures. Insurance plans itemize the maximum benefit they will pay for each item. Many plans have an annual deductible and coinsurance clause. In other words, they state the amount you must pay towards claims before the insurance carrier takes over (the *deductible*), and the percentage of a covered claim that you are required to pay (the *coinsurance*).

Basic medical/surgical insurance is usually provided by employers and unions, and is very often offered in conjunction with hospitalization insurance.

Comprehensive Major Medical Insurance

Comprehensive major medical insurance picks up where basic medical/surgical health insurance ends, covering the high costs of serious long-term illness. Some plans have very high deductibles and provide benefits of up to $500,000 or $1,000,000. Other plans provide first-dollar coverage of some health-care services, meaning that there is no deductible. Some employers and unions provide this insurance on a contributory basis, while other groups offer noncontributory plans. In a *contributory plan*, the employer and employee each contribute some portion of the premium cost, which varies from plan to plan. In a *noncontributory plan*, the employer covers all costs.

Comprehensive major medical insurance is an appropriate form of insurance for people of any age. It can be purchased instead of Medigap insurance (see Chapter 17) by those over 65 who are on Medicare. If comprehensive major medical is provided by your employer, find out whether it can be carried over into retirement. If it can, ask if the plan would be contributory or noncontributory. For an individual 65 or older, even the combination of Medicare Parts A and B and Medicare supplementary insurance may require the additional coverage of comprehensive major medical.

Catastrophic Major Medical Insurance

Catastrophic major medical insurance provides compensation for extraordinary medical costs not covered by hospitalization insurance, basic medical/surgical insurance, or comprehensive major medical insurance. Such extraordinary costs can be the result of an accident or of a health problem such as cancer or a stroke. Plans vary regarding deductibles and coverage. For instance, a plan might have a $10,000 deductible, after which it pays as much as $2,000,000 for three to ten years from the date an initial medical expense is incurred. Other plans might require a $25,000 deductible. You must select the deductible that you feel will best supplement your basic major medical or hospital coverage. All current reasonable and customary expenses count in full towards your chosen deductible. Even those eligible expenses paid for by your basic health insurance policy, as well as those paid out of your own pocket, count towards meeting your deductible.

After your deductible is met, a plan will pay 100 percent of all eligible expenses, including all hospital charges for a semi-private room and board or intensive care; miscellaneous hospital services and operating room charges; treatment by a currently licensed physician, surgeon, or physiotherapist whether in a hospital, at home, or in the office; private duty nursing services; dental treatment if a jaw is fractured or natural teeth are injured by accident; X-ray, physiotherapy, and laboratory services for diagnosis and treatment; anesthesia and its administration; ambulance service; prescription drugs; oxygen and rental equipment such as wheelchairs or hospital beds; and hospital treatment for mental or nervous disorders, alcoholism, and drug addiction.

Disability Income Insurance

Disability income insurance pays a percentage of your regular monthly income when you become disabled because of illness or injury, and are unable to work for an extended period of time. This type of insurance is provided by the Social Security system at no extra cost to you; by commercial insurance companies, usually at a high cost to you; and by some retirement systems. (In New York City, for instance, covered employees can retire under disability provisions when they are no longer capable of fulfilling their normal job functions.) The best disability coverage begins to pay a monthly allowance after 60 or 90 days of disability and continues until age 65 or retirement, whichever comes first. Provisions vary.

During their working years, most people tend to pay too much attention to life insurance, and too little to disability income insurance. The need for disability insurance disappears after retirement when you begin to collect a pension and Social Security.

INSURANCE FOR SPECIAL NEEDS

Most people, whether actively employed or retired, can use specialized insurance coverage, which is generally excluded from basic and major medical plans. Some popular types of special needs insurance include dental insurance, optical expense benefits, hearing aids, prescription medication plans, blood programs, and long-term care insurance.

Dental Insurance

At a time when the family budget is under severe strain, the cost of dental care is becoming less of a burden for many American households. The reason for this is the rapid growth of dental insurance financed either wholly or partially by employers as a fringe benefit. Dental insurance covers necessary dental health care, including oral examinations, X-rays, cleanings, fillings, extractions, inlays, crowns, bridgework, dentures (prosthodontics), oral surgery, treatment of gums (periodontics), root canal, and teeth alignment (orthodontics).

The National Association of Dental Plans estimates that 115,000,000 people are now covered by dental insurance. One of the reasons for this level of coverage is labor unions' support of dental protection.

The dental plans now in operation pay varying amounts for dental work. While some pay 100 percent, most pay less—25 to 50 percent. To reduce expenses, some dental insurance plans split the cost of the monthly premium between employer and employee. The coinsurance rate is usually 20 percent.

Optical Expense Benefits

An optical expense program provides eyeglasses, and often a specified sum of money toward the purchase of contact lenses, to eligible members and their dependents. In one such plan, each eligible individual may obtain a pair of eyeglasses every two years from a participating optical outlet free of charge. The glasses can be either single-vision or bifocal lenses of standard prescription within a standard frame. The group administering the program reimburses the participating optician with set fees. If the member uses a nonparticipating optician, the member can be reimbursed directly for a specified amount that is usually less than the actual cost of the eyeglasses.

Hearing Aids

It is estimated that almost 4,400,000 Americans currently use hearing aids. Of these, 2,600,000 are 65 years of age or older, and 1,800,000 are under 65. The process of aging is the most common cause of hearing loss.

Many of the people who need hearing aids find the cost prohibitive. Some employers' health insurance packages include a subsidy for the purchase of a hearing aid, and some of the programs carry this benefit into retirement. Most plans, however, do not offer this benefit at all. To help offset costs, a Federal Task Force on Hearing Aid Health Care has recommended that the government consider subsidizing the purchase of hearing aids.

Prescription Medication Plan

Some employers and unions provide a prescription medication plan that may be carried over into retirement. In some plans, the full cost of prescription medications is covered, provided the prescription is filled by a participating pharmacist. In other plans, a copayment is required. If a nonparticipating pharmacist is used, reimbursement of charges is made in accordance with a schedule of allowances.

In some plans, prescriptions may not exceed a thirty-day supply, and if the physician so specifies, one or more refills are allowed. Medications, vitamins, and diet supplements that can be purchased without a prescription usually are not covered by these plans. To reduce costs without sacrificing quality, many members are advised to ask doctors to prescribe generic medications when possible as a substitute for brand-name products. Plan members are issued identification cards, and may be required to use special prescription blanks that request identifying data from the member, the doctor, and the pharmacist.

Blood Program

Many large employers, both public and private, offer membership in a blood program. An enrolled employee or a substitute is required to donate one pint of blood annually. Some of the plans provide unlimited blood credit for the member, spouse, and unmarried children of any age; for unmarried brothers and sisters of any age who live with the member; and for the member's and spouse's parents and grandparents, regardless of residence. If you donate more than a pint of blood a year, you can build up credit for future years. Some of these programs carry over into retirement and help provide the first three pints of blood not covered by Medicare (see page 218).

Long-Term Care Insurance

The major gaps in health insurance coverage for the elderly are long-term nursing home care and custodial home health care. It has been estimated that 43 percent of Americans over age 65 will spend some time in a nursing home. With costs of nursing home care ranging from $40,000 to $100,000 a year, depending on the location, it is easy to understand how the cost of long-term care is the primary cause of financial ruin among the elderly, the middle-aged, and even the young.

During the late 1980s, long-term care insurance was introduced as a new type of coverage. However, the cost is high, and coverage is limited. See Chapter 17 for an in-depth look at long-term care coverage.

SOURCES OF HEALTH INSURANCE COVERAGE

Health insurance is available from three types of organizations—Blue Cross and Blue Shield, health maintenance organizations (HMOs), and commercial insurance companies.

Blue Cross and Blue Shield

Today, Blue Cross and Blue Shield (BC/BS)—both of which are not-for-profit associations—serve every state. Coordinated through the Blue Cross and Blue Shield Association, the Blues, as they are sometimes called, protect approximately 80,000,000 people in forty-seven private and public programs.

Blue Cross plans, initiated in 1929, offer insurance for hospital expenses, and have contracts with more than 90 percent of the nation's general, nonfederal, acute-care hospitals. Blue Shield plans, initiated in 1946, offer insurance for surgical and general physician expenses, and have a working relationship with about 80 percent of the nation's practicing medical doctors.

While commercial insurance carriers provide all forms of health-care protection, BC/BS organizations are the pioneers in this type of insurance coverage. The basic goal of these plans has always been to offer high-quality, effective, and economical health-care services. Blue Cross and Blue Shield usually return between 85 and 90 percent of premiums paid, making these plans excellent.

BC/BS sponsors both individual and group memberships. As an individual or member of a group plan, you pay a monthly premium for a broad choice of leading doctors and hospitals. Group plans are a form of health maintenance organization (HMO), which is discussed at right. Like the members of all HMOs, members of BC/BS group plans are subject to coinsurance payments and deductibles.

BC/BS is funded by the premiums paid by its members. Members carry their benefits across the United States while traveling, and since the program is internationally recognized, benefits are in effect throughout the world.

BC/BS also offers a popular BlueChoice Senior Plan, an HMO with a Medicare contract. This managed-care health plan provides comprehensive coverage with no plan premiums or deductibles. Hospitalization is completely covered for as long as medically necessary, with no limitations. Doctors' visits are only $10 each; prescription medications, $5 or $15 each; dental visits, $10; and vision exams, $10. The plan also provides skilled nursing care coverage, 100-percent emergency coverage, and no fees for lab tests. You merely pay your monthly Medicare Part B premiums.

To join BC/BS as an individual or as a group, check your local phone directory and call for an application and detailed information.

Health Maintenance Organizations (HMOs)

Excellent health-care coverage can be obtained by joining a health maintenance organization (HMO), if one is operating in your area. HMOs give you medical care and hospitalization coverage without deductibles or coinsurance. Everything is prepaid, and there are no out-of-pocket expenses.

An HMO consists of one or more hospitals and a group of doctors and other health-care personnel joined together to provide necessary health maintenance and remedial services to the organization's members. The group practice plans of HMOs offer complete office and hospital care to an optimum number of members for a fixed monthly fee. Because of reduced costs and federal subsidies, the fees are reasonable when compared with those of other forms of health-care delivery systems. HMO members receive all necessary health care, including periodic checkups, X-rays, laboratory tests, mental health treatment, and twenty-four-hour emergency services. After the monthly fee has been paid, no additional fees are charged.

The nation's first prepaid health-care plan for physicians' visits and hospitalization was established in 1929 at the Roos-Loos Clinic in Los Angeles. The second was started in 1942 by Henry J. Kaiser, who founded a program to care for the workers at his isolated western industrial sites. The first HMO-type organization in New York was established in the 1940s. Known as the Health Insurance Plan of Greater New York, or simply HIP, it was designed to provide complete medical services for employees of New York City, which paid the premiums. Currently, it is known officially as HIP/HMO.

The federal government's financial support of health maintenance organizations began in 1973 in an effort to curb the quickly rising costs of health care. As amended in 1976, the law requires that a company with twenty-five or more workers offer HMO membership as an alternative to any existing health-care program the company might have. The nation's 560 HMOs now have about 80,000,000 members.

The biggest and best known HMO is the Kaiser Foundation Health Plan, which functions in California, eight other states, and the District of Columbia. This HMO has more than 8,000,000 members, operates its own hospitals, and employs more than 3,000 physicians. The smallest HMOs have only a few staff members, most often internists, obstetricians, and pediatricians. If a member needs the services of another kind of specialist, the HMO sends him or her to one and pays the charges.

The main criticisms of HMOs are that patients have a limited choice of doctors, that the relationship between patient and doctor is impersonal, and that the organizations operate on an assembly-line basis. The principal advantage is that the cost of paying for each visit to the doctor is eliminated, thus encouraging people to seek early detection and treatment of disease. It has been estimated that HMO members are admitted to hospitals 30 to 60 percent less often than are nonmembers, helping to reduce overall costs and, presumably, reflecting better health maintenance.

Since 1973, Medicare beneficiaries have been allowed to join health maintenance organizations. Certain HMOs are eligible for Medicare reimbursement. Such eligible organizations provide physicians' services; inpatient services; laboratory, X-ray, emergency, and preventive services; and out-of-area coverage.

Commercial Insurance Companies

A large number of commercial insurance companies offer a variety of health insurance plans to fill most buyers' needs. However, as with any purchase you make, you must be a wise and careful shopper. That's why it is important to study not only the insurance plan, but also the company that's behind the plan.

Some questions you should ask about the insurance company are:

❑ What are the financial resources of this company?

❑ How does the company compare in size to other health insurance companies?

❑ Does the company enjoy a good reputation?

❑ Is the company licensed to do business in your state?

❑ Does the company pay claims promptly?

❑ What is the percentage of premiums that this company returns as benefits to its policyholders? (This is known as the company's *loss ratio*, or *rate of return*.) The higher the return, the better the company and the policy.

You can get some of these answers from your state insurance department, local Better Business Bureau, or *Best's Insurance Reports*, which is available in most public libraries.

Questions you should ask about the insurance plan itself include the following:

❑ What does the plan cover?

❑ What expenses and conditions does the plan not cover? (These are known as the plan's *exclusions*.)

❑ Is the plan a *service benefit contract*, which pays a percentage of charges and therefore keeps up with inflation, or an *indemnity benefit contract*, which pays fixed dollar amounts?

❑ What is the maximum amount that the plan will pay for each service?

❑ How does the plan handle *pre-existing conditions*—conditions that exist before the contract goes into force?

You can get some of these answers by studying the *policy*—the legal contract that sets forth the rights and obligations of both the policyholder and the insurance company. By comparing plans and the companies that provide them, you will be able to make an educated decision about the health insurance that will protect you and yours throughout your retirement years.

SPECIAL CONSIDERATIONS FOR RETIREMENT PLANNING

When planning for your retirement, you should be aware of special situations related to health insurance coverage. For example, if you are under 65, still working, and not yet covered by Medicare, you must make a special effort to obtain adequate health insurance at a reasonable price. Similarly, if you are 65 through 69 years of age, covered by Medicare, but still working, federal law requires that your employer's health insurance plan be the *primary payer*, with Medicare serving as the *secondary payer*. Finally, if you are retiring and your spouse is under 65, you must make sure that your spouse has adequate health insurance coverage, and that he or she will continue to have coverage in the event of your death. A discussion of each of these situations follows.

If You Are Under 65 and Still Working

For people under 65 who are still working and not yet covered by Medicare, essential healthcare coverage includes basic Blue Cross hospitalization insurance; basic medical/surgical insurance; a comprehensive major medical plan to supplement the basic coverage; and disability income insurance if it is offered by your employer or union, or if you can afford to pay for it on your own.

Most people are offered some degree of health insurance as an employment benefit. Those not so fortunate have a major problem in getting adequate health insurance at a reasonable price. Private coverage purchased by an individual from a commercial insurance company is very expensive. Moreover, most private plans have a deductible and a 20-percent coinsurance provision.

An individual or couple without basic health insurance coverage (hospitalization and medical/surgical protection) should join either an HMO, which will provide full coverage without deductibles or coinsurance, or Blue Cross and Blue Shield, which are nonprofit groups whose premiums reflect actual costs.

If You Are 65 Through 69 and Still Working

If you are age 65 through 69 and are still actively employed, the Tax Equity and Fiscal Responsibility Act (TEFRA) changed health insurance coverage for you in 1982. TEFRA amended the Age Discrimination in Employment Act and the Social Security Act in two ways. First, employers of twenty or more people must give 65-and-over workers the same health insurance coverage offered to younger employees. This is true even for older employees covered by Medicare. To reduce an older employee's benefits in any way is considered age discrimination and is, therefore, illegal.

Second, TEFRA stipulates that Medicare is

no longer the insurer of first resort for older employees. Instead, the employer's plan must be the primary payer, with Medicare serving as the secondary payer. An active employee of age 65 or older has the right to reject the employer's plan, and make Medicare the primary payer with no benefits paid by the employer's plan.

These changes, which became effective in 1983, have been saving the federal government hundreds of millions of dollars a year by transferring the primary insurance bill to the private sector.

If You Are Retiring and Your Spouse Is Under 65

If you are retiring and your spouse is under age 65, check your employer's health insurance coverage—if it carries over into retirement—to determine whether your spouse will still be covered as a dependent after you stop working. Most employer group health insurance plans that carry over into retirement continue coverage for the spouse and other eligible dependents. If yours does not, however, you may be able to convert from group coverage to an individual self-pay plan. If not, you may need to purchase individual hospitalization and medical/surgical insurance for your spouse from a commercial carrier. In any case, it is vital to provide your spouse with adequate health insurance.

If You Are a Surviving Spouse

A spouse whose status changes from dependent to survivor should check the deceased's health insurance coverage to determine whether protection is still in effect. If the coverage has been terminated, the survivor will have to purchase an individual hospitalization/health insurance plan on a self-pay basis.

COBRA COVERAGE

The *Consolidated Omnibus Budget Reconciliation Act*, known as COBRA (Public Law 99-272), has been in effect since 1986. Under COBRA, businesses that have more than twenty employees and offer health insurance must continue coverage at group rates for up to eighteen months for employees who retire, quit, switch from full-time to part-time status, or are laid off. These former employees must pay the full cost of the group insurance plus a 2-percent surcharge to cover administrative expenses.

In addition, companies are required to continue coverage for three years, at a premium rate of 102 percent of the employer's group rate, for an employee's spouse and dependents if the employee dies or becomes entitled to Medicare. COBRA also applies in the event of a legal separation or divorce. Moreover, an employer must offer to provide the same three years of continued coverage to a dependent who reaches the maximum age for dependent coverage. Those eligible have at least sixty days to decide if they want to continue their health insurance protection.

Before COBRA, employees and dependents usually lost their health insurance benefits upon job termination. Similarly, widows, divorcees, and spouses of retired employees who qualified for Medicare lost their health insurance coverage.

About 45,000,000 men, women, and children in the United States are currently without health insurance. This is 14,000,000 more than in 1980, and the number is growing. These people are predominantly young, poor, and in worse health than the general population. COBRA's purpose is to provide some protection for people who are eligible according to the law. Severe penalties are imposed on employers who fail to meet COBRA requirements.

than the general population. COBRA's purpose is to provide some protection for people who are eligible according to the law. Severe penalties are imposed on employers who fail to meet COBRA requirements.

BASIC ADVICE ON HEALTH INSURANCE

The following six guidelines concerning health insurance should be helpful for people of all ages and employment status:

1. If you are under 65, are still working, and have an individual or group health insurance plan, you should:

   ❏ Determine what benefits your coverage will provide when you reach 65 and whether you can carry the coverage over into retirement. (Self-Study 15.1, beginning on page 210, will help you detect gaps in your health-care coverage both now and after retirement.)

   ❏ Consider buying disability income insurance. Most people insure their home, car, and jewelry, but it is their regular income that makes these kinds of amenities possible.

2. Consider purchasing a comprehensive major medical plan that will cover both you and your spouse.

3. Obtain insurance for as many other health-care needs as you can afford, including dental care, prescription medications, optical expenses, and hearing aids. If possible, obtain catastrophic major medical insurance and long-term care insurance, as well.

4. In general, avoid mail-order health insurance plans and cancer or other dread disease insurance.

5. Protect your health insurance policies by keeping them in a safe place and letting a close relative or friend know where they are. In a separate place, keep a list of your policy numbers, the companies that issued them, and the name of your agent, in case the originals are lost.

6. Keep a record of your medical expenditures and reimbursements. This is the only way you can follow up on unresolved claims to be sure you receive what you are owed. (Self-Study 15.1 includes a form for recording medical expenditures and reimbursements.)

You can never have too much medical insurance. If you don't believe it, ask someone who has recently returned home following an extended hospital stay. Invariably, such a person will tell you about the exorbitant fees charged by the hospital and by their doctors. While it may be impossible to avoid such costs, by having adequate health insurance, you can be sure of getting the care you need when you need it—without destroying your nest egg.

Self-Study 15.1
CHECKLIST FOR YOUR HEALTH INSURANCE

1. To ascertain the gaps in your overall health care coverage, check what you have and what you lack, and note whether the coverage you have carries over into retirement.

Type of health-care insurance	Do you have the coverage indicated?		If you are covered, will it carry over into retirement?	
	Yes	No	Yes	No
Hospitalization	❏	❏	❏	❏
Basic medical/surgical	❏	❏	❏	❏
Comprehensive major medical	❏	❏	❏	❏
Disability income	❏	❏	❏	❏
Blood	❏	❏	❏	❏
Dental	❏	❏	❏	❏
Hearing aids	❏	❏	❏	❏
Long-term care	❏	❏	❏	❏
Optical expenses	❏	❏	❏	❏
Prescription medications	❏	❏	❏	❏

2. List the gaps in your present health insurance coverage.

_____

_____

_____

_____

3. List the health insurance coverage you have that will not carry over into retirement.

_____

_____

_____

_____

4. How do you plan to fill the gaps in your retirement health insurance package that you noted in questions 2 and 3, above?

_____

_____

_____

_____

_____

_____

_____

_____

5. You should maintain a record of medical expenditures and reimbursements for yourself and for your spouse and other dependents. Worksheet 15.1, on the following page, shows you what kind of details you should keep track of and provides a convenient form for doing so. If you are not reimbursed within a reasonable period of time, it will show up clearly on this type of record, and you can follow up on the claim. The worksheet provides room for keeping track of claims submitted to Medicare, if you are a member, and to one supplementary plan. If you are not covered by Medicare, change that column heading to the name of the coverage you have. If you have additional coverage, such as dental insurance, the form can be expanded by adding columns similar to the two included. You can purchase multi-column worksheet paper in a stationery store to make your own forms.

WORKSHEET 15.1	MEDICAL EXPENDITURES AND REIMBURSEMENTS

Patient _____ Year_____

Treatment Information	Payment Information	Medicare		Supplementary policy or other coverage	
		Claim submitted	Check received	Claim submitted	Check received
DATE OF VISIT OR SERVICE	DATE	DATE	DATE	DATE	DATE
NAME OF DOCTOR, HOSPITAL, LAB, OR OTHER	AMOUNT				
		AMOUNT	AMOUNT	AMOUNT	AMOUNT
NAME OF ILLNESS OR TREATMENT	CHECK NO.				
DATE OF VISIT OR SERVICE	DATE	DATE	DATE	DATE	DATE
NAME OF DOCTOR, HOSPITAL, LAB, OR OTHER	AMOUNT				
		AMOUNT	AMOUNT	AMOUNT	AMOUNT
NAME OF ILLNESS OR TREATMENT	CHECK NO.				
DATE OF VISIT OR SERVICE	DATE	DATE	DATE	DATE	DATE
NAME OF DOCTOR, HOSPITAL, LAB, OR OTHER	AMOUNT				
		AMOUNT	AMOUNT	AMOUNT	AMOUNT
NAME OF ILLNESS OR TREATMENT	CHECK NO.				
DATE OF VISIT OR SERVICE	DATE	DATE	DATE	DATE	DATE
NAME OF DOCTOR, HOSPITAL, LAB, OR OTHER	AMOUNT				
		AMOUNT	AMOUNT	AMOUNT	AMOUNT
NAME OF ILLNESS OR TREATMENT	CHECK NO.				
DATE OF VISIT OR SERVICE	DATE	DATE	DATE	DATE	DATE
NAME OF DOCTOR, HOSPITAL, LAB, OR OTHER	AMOUNT				
		AMOUNT	AMOUNT	AMOUNT	AMOUNT
NAME OF ILLNESS OR TREATMENT	CHECK NO.				
DATE OF VISIT OR SERVICE	DATE	DATE	DATE	DATE	DATE
NAME OF DOCTOR, HOSPITAL, LAB, OR OTHER	AMOUNT				
		AMOUNT	AMOUNT	AMOUNT	AMOUNT
NAME OF ILLNESS OR TREATMENT	CHECK NO.				

16

MEDICARE *and* MEDICAID

Successful retirement depends not only on a sound financial base, but also on good health. While the maintenance of good health is a life-long project, older Americans are generally more vulnerable to health problems than younger people. In the 1960s, the government enacted two programs, Medicare and Medicaid, that provide health benefits for the elderly and the poor. This chapter offers a detailed analysis of both of these programs so that you will understand the assistance that is available to you.

MEDICARE

Many Americans enjoy the comforting thought that starting at age 65, the government will pay their medical bills. While it is true that Medicare provides significant amounts of financial assistance and some peace of mind, the program was not designed to cover *all* medical expenses for the elderly. Rather, it was intended to provide fundamental hospital and medical services at the *lowest possible cost*.

The Basics

In 1965, Congress approved amendments to the Social Security law that, among other things, established the insurance program that became popularly known as Medicare. Along with Medicaid, Medicare was one of the Great Society programs enacted that year to provide health benefits for the elderly and the poor. President Lyndon Johnson signed the Medicare-Medicaid bill into law on July 30, 1965, in Independence, Missouri, with former President Harry S. Truman at his side.

Medicare is a federal health insurance program for people age 65 or older and for certain disabled people under 65. It is run by the Centers for Medicare and Medicaid Services, formerly the Health Care Financing Administration, of the United States Department of Health and Human Services. Social Security Administration offices across the country take Medicare applications and provide information about the program.

Medicare is a two-part program. *Part A* provides inpatient hospital coverage, skilled nursing facility coverage after a hospital stay, home health care coverage, and hospice care coverage. People who have reached age 65 and are eligible for Social Security benefits, whether or not they are still working, are entitled to Part A coverage without having to pay any premiums, or fees. However, they must meet certain deductibles and make coinsurance payments. A *deductible* is an annual maximum amount you must pay on claims before the insurance carrier begins to calculate benefit allowances due you. *Coinsurance* is the percentage of a covered expense that you are required to pay.

Part B of Medicare pays for doctors' services, outpatient hospital services, and specified medical items and services not covered under hospital insurance. The supplementary medical insurance provided under Part B is voluntary, requiring recipients to pay a monthly premium either directly to the Centers for Medicare and Medicaid Services or as a deduction from their monthly Social Security check, if they receive one. After a deductible and *copayments*, which are the specific coinsurance payments, Medicare Part B pays a "reasonable and customary" amount for each service covered.

Part A is financed through Social Security taxes paid by people who are still working, and by their employers. Part B is financed through premiums paid by Medicare beneficiaries and, in addition, is subsidized by the federal government.

The Costs of Sustaining Medicare

Medicare cost approximately $3.5 billion in 1967. In fiscal year 2001, it cost $241 billion—$141.6 billion for hospital care and $99.4 billion for physicians' services. Despite the cost increase, the Medicare program enjoys strong bipartisan support in Congress. The number of people enrolled in Medicare has increased from 19.5 million in 1967 to about 40 million today. It is estimated that Medicare now pays about 48.8 percent of the medical costs of the elderly. But, as you've already read, this program also helps many severely disabled people. A 1972 law

expanded Medicare to cover disabled people under 65 years of age, and people with chronic kidney disease requiring a kidney transplant or dialysis.

What Medicare does *not* cover, however, can mean financial disaster for the elderly, since they spend three times more for health care than younger people do. Present and future beneficiaries should, therefore, clearly understand who is eligible for Medicare, what Medicare does and does not provide, how you collect benefits, and what additional insurance is needed for maximum protection.

Eligibility for Medicare

More than 98 percent of the nation's elderly and disabled are covered by Medicare. People are not eligible if they have reached age 65 without becoming eligible for Social Security retirement benefits. This includes individuals who have not been credited with a sufficient number of quarters of coverage; individuals who are not members of Social Security, such as some state and local government workers; noncitizens; and people convicted of particular crimes. (For a full discussion of Social Security and its terminology, see Chapter 7.) Federal employees, originally ineligible for the Medicare program, have been eligible since January 1983. Ineligible individuals can receive Part A and Part B Medicare benefits by paying monthly premiums—$319 for Part A and $54 for Part B for the 2002 calendar year.

Enrollment in Medicare

Enrollment in Medicare Parts A and B is automatic upon application for monthly Social Security benefits. If you plan to continue working past age 65, you should apply for Medicare separately. You can do this at your nearest Social Security office about three months prior to turning 65. If you retire before age 65 and file an application for Social Security benefits, you do not have to file a separate application for Medicare.

Medicare coverage becomes effective the month you reach 65, even if you elect to begin receiving Social Security retirement benefits at age 62. When you apply for Social Security benefits or enroll in Medicare, you have the option of turning down Part B coverage. If you retire at age 65 and decline Part B coverage at that time, you will have to pay higher Part B premiums if you decide later to enroll. The penalty for late enrollment in Part B is a 10-percent increase in premiums for each twelve-month period in which you could have been enrolled but were not. If you have Medicare hospital insurance but not the medical insurance, you can sign up for the medical insurance during the general enrollment period, which is the same every year— January 1 through March 31. Your protection will begin the following July 1. For more information about obtaining the part of Medicare you do not have, contact your Social Security office.

If you continue working past age 65 and remain covered by an employer's group health-insurance plan, you may wait to enroll in Part B without penalty until either age 70 or retirement, whichever comes first.

AN OVERVIEW OF MEDICARE COVERAGE

The services and supplies covered under Medicare vary for Part A and Part B. In addition, the *benefit periods*, or periods of time during which the services and supplies are covered, vary for the different types of care facilities covered in Part A. A detailed description of the benefits, benefit periods, and deductibles begins on this page. Table 16.1 provides a quick overview.

The following alphabetical list shows most of the major services and supplies usually *not* covered by Medicare.

❑ Cosmetic surgery

❑ Custodial care

❑ Dental care

❑ Dentures

❑ Emergency care outside the United States

❑ Eyeglasses

❑ Hearing aids

❑ Orthopedic shoes

❑ Outpatient prescription drugs

❑ Routine foot care

❑ Routine physical exams

If you are in doubt about coverage for a particular service or supply, call Medicare to inquire. (See the Resources section.)

MEDICARE HOSPITAL INSURANCE

Medicare hospital insurance (Part A) provides four types of benefits—inpatient hospital coverage, skilled nursing facility coverage after a hospital stay, home health-care coverage, and hospice care coverage. In each case, Medicare pays for most but not all of the services you receive.

The unit of measure used to keep track of consumption of services under Medicare hospital insurance is the benefit period. A *benefit period* starts the day you enter a hospital and is a maximum of 90 days long. In addition to the 90-day benefit periods, you are given a lifetime allotment of 60 *reserve days* to be used for hospital confinements of more than 90 days. Once you have used up your 60 reserve days, your benefit periods are limited to the basic 90 days. There is

TABLE 16.1

MEDICARE FACT SHEET		
Medicare Coverage	**2002**	**2001**
Your Premium Payment		
Part B premium[a]	$54/month	$50/month
Part B deductible	$100/year	$100/year
Part B coinsurance	20%	20%
Hospitalization		
Day 1 in hospital	$812	$792
Days 2–60	No charge	No charge
Days 61–90	$203/day	$198/day
Days 91–150 if you use 60 lifetime reserve days	$406/day	$396/day
Beyond day 150, or after day 90 if all 60 *reserve days* have been used	All charges	All charges
Skilled Nursing Facility	100 days after a minimum of 3 days in a hospital	
Days 1–20	No charge	No charge
Days 21–100	$101.50/day	$99/day
Beyond Day 100	All charges	All charges
Home Health Care if Homebound	Unlimited number of medically necessary home health visits or physical therapy sessions, provided a doctor sets up the home health plan.	
Hospice Care	Hospice care is provided in two 90-day visits followed by an unlimited number of 60-day visits.	

[a] The Part B premium covers physician services, hospital outpatient care, durable medical equipment, and other services outside hospitals.

no limit to the number of 90-day benefit periods you can have, but in order to be eligible for a new benefit period, you must have been out of the hospital for *60 consecutive days*.

If, after a hospital confinement of more than 3 days, you need additional care, Part A provides 100 days of skilled nursing facility benefits for each benefit period. These 100 days are in addition to the 90 days of hospital benefits. When you have been out of a skilled nursing facility for *60 consecutive days*, you are eligible to begin a new benefit period.

The covered services and benefit periods as well as the deductibles vary for each type of benefit, and are explored in the following discussions. Note that the *covered services* discussed below are services and supplies for which Part A will pay. *Noncovered services* are services and supplies for which you must pay.

Inpatient Hospital Care

Medicare hospital insurance will pay for inpatient hospital care if *all four* of the following conditions are met:

1. A doctor prescribes inpatient hospital care for the treatment of your illness or injury.

2. You require the kind of care that can be provided only in a hospital.

3. The hospital is a Medicare participant—in other words, a *participating hospital*.

4. The utilization review committee of the hospital or a peer review organization does not disapprove your stay. (For a full discussion of peer review organizations, see page 220.)

Covered Services

When you are an inpatient in a Medicare-approved hospital, the following services are covered:

❏ A semiprivate room (a room with two to four beds).

❏ All your meals, including special diets.

❏ Regular nursing services.

❏ Special care units, such as intensive care and coronary care.

❏ Medications furnished by the hospital for use during your stay.

❏ Blood transfusions after the first three pints.

❏ Laboratory tests.

❏ X-rays and other radiology services, including radiation therapy.

❏ Medical supplies such as casts, surgical dressings, and splints.

❏ Appliances such as wheelchairs.

❏ Operating room and recovery room, including anesthesia services.

❏ Rehabilitation services such as physical, occupational, and speech therapy.

Noncovered Services

The following hospital services are not covered by Medicare Part A:

❏ Doctors' fees. (These fees are covered by Medicare Part B.)

❏ Private duty nurses.

❏ Personal convenience items in your room, such as a television, radio, or telephone.

❏ A private room, unless it is determined to be medically necessary.

Deductibles

You are entitled to receive up to 90 days of inpatient care in a Medicare-participating hospital during each benefit period. For the first 60 days of a benefit period, Medicare pays for all covered services after the first $812 (2002 amount). This deductible is increased annually. For days 61 through 90, Medicare pays for all covered expenses except for $203 a day (2002 amount).

Up to all 60 reserve days can be used in one benefit period. Each reserve day you use permanently reduces your total number of lifetime reserve days. For every reserve day, Medicare pays for all covered services except for $406 a day (2002 amount).

After day 90 of the benefit period, if all reserve days have been used, you must pay all charges, while Medicare pays nothing.

Psychiatric Hospitals

Medicare hospital insurance will not pay for more than 190 days of care in participating psychiatric hospitals in your lifetime. Once you have used your 190-day allotment, Part A will not pay for any further care in any psychiatric hospital.

Foreign Hospitals

Medicare generally cannot pay for hospital or medical services provided outside the United States. Along with the fifty states and the District of Columbia, the following are considered part of the United States—Puerto Rico, the United States Virgin Islands, Guam, American Samoa, and the Northern Mariana Islands. However, Medicare can help pay for care in a qualified Canadian or Mexican hospital if you are in one of the following three situations:

1. You are in the United States when an emergency occurs, and a Canadian or Mexican hospital that can provide the care you need is closer than the nearest United States hospital.

2. You live in the United States, but a Canadian or Mexican hospital is closer to your home than the nearest United States hospital and can provide the care you need, regardless of whether or not an emergency exists.

3. You are in Canada traveling by the most direct route to or from Alaska, and an emergency occurs that requires you to be admitted to a Canadian hospital.

Skilled Nursing Facility Care

A *skilled nursing facility* is a specially qualified facility that has the staff and equipment necessary to provide skilled nursing care or rehabilitation services and other related health services. To be eligible for care in a skilled nursing facility, *both* of the following conditions must be met:

1. A doctor certifies that you need skilled nursing or skilled rehabilitation services on a daily basis.

2. The Medicare intermediary or the facility's utilization review committee does not disapprove your stay.

Covered Services

When you are an inpatient in a Medicare-approved skilled nursing facility, the following services are covered:

❏ A semiprivate room (a room with two to four beds).

❏ All your meals, including special diets.

❏ Regular nursing services.

❏ Medications furnished by the facility for use during your stay.

❏ Blood transfusions after the first three pints.

❏ Medical supplies such as casts and splints.

❏ Appliances such as wheelchairs.

❏ Rehabilitation services such as physical, occupational, and speech therapy.

Noncovered Services

The following skilled nursing facility services are not covered by Medicare Part A:

❏ Doctors' fees. (These fees are covered by Medicare Part B.)

❏ Private duty nurses.

❏ Personal convenience items in your room, such as a television, radio, or telephone.

❏ A private room, unless it is determined to be medically necessary.

❏ Custodial nursing home care services for chronic, long-term illnesses or disabilities.

Deductibles

You are entitled to receive up to 100 days of care in a Medicare-participating skilled nursing facility during each benefit period. Medicare pays all covered services for the first 20 days. For days 21 through 100 of continuous confinement, you pay $101.50 a day (2002 amount) and Medicare pays the balance. After day 100, you must pay all costs, and Medicare pays nothing.

Home Health Care

A *home health agency* is a public or private agency that specializes in providing skilled nursing services and other therapeutic services in your home. To be eligible for home health care, *all four* of the following conditions must be met:

1. The care you need includes intermittent skilled nursing care, physical therapy, or speech therapy.

2. You are confined to your home except for absences to receive health care in an adult day care center or to attend religious services.

3. A doctor determines that you need home health care, and sets up a home health plan.

4. The home health agency is a Medicare participant.

Covered Services

The following services provided by an approved home health agency are covered:

❏ Part-time or intermittent skilled nursing care.

❏ Physical therapy.

❏ Speech therapy.

In addition, if any of the above services are required, Medicare will also pay for:

❏ Occupational therapy.

❏ Part-time or intermittent service by home health aides.

❏ Medical social services.

❏ Medical supplies and equipment provided by the agency.

Noncovered Services

The following services are not covered by Medicare Part A:

❏ Full-time nursing care at home.

❏ Medications and biologicals.

❏ Meals delivered to your home.

❏ Homemaker services.

❏ Blood transfusions.

Deductibles

Medicare pays the full approved cost of all covered home health-care visits. You pay nothing. However, you may be charged for noncovered services and supplies. The home health agency will submit the claim for covered items to Medicare. You are not required to send in any bills yourself.

Hospice Care

The Tax Equity and Fiscal Responsibility Act of 1982 extended Medicare coverage to hospice care services. A *hospice* is a program that provides pain relief and supportive services for terminally ill patients, usually in a patient's home. Hospice care includes nurses, medication, home helpers, counseling, and other assistance. This care emphasizes relief of pain and suffering as opposed to hospital technology and cures.

Respite care is a short-term inpatient hospital stay that may be necessary for the patient in order to give temporary relief to the *caretaker*, who is the person who takes care of the at-home patient. Each inpatient respite-care stay is limited to five consecutive days.

To be eligible for hospice or respite care, *all three* of the following conditions must be met:

1. A doctor certifies that you are terminally ill.

2. You choose to receive care from a hospice instead of taking the standard Medicare benefits for terminal illness.

3. The hospice program is a Medicare participant.

Covered Services

When you are in a Medicare-approved hospice program, the following services are covered:

❏ Doctors' services.

❏ Nursing services.

❏ Medications for pain relief and symptom management.

❏ Physical therapy, occupational therapy, and speech-language therapy.

❏ Home health aide and homemaker services.

❏ Medical social services.

❏ Medical supplies and appliances.

❏ Short-term inpatient care, including respite care.

❏ Counseling.

Deductibles

Special benefit periods apply to hospice care. Medicare hospital insurance pays for two 90-day periods followed by an unlimited number of 60-day periods. During a hospice benefit period, Medicare pays the full cost of all covered services for the terminal illness. The only deductibles and copayments are for part of the cost of outpatient medications and part of the cost of inpatient respite care. While receiving hospice care, if a patient requires treatment for a condition that is not related to the terminal illness, Medicare continues to help pay for all necessary covered services under the standard benefit program.

The Role of Peer Review Organizations

Peer review organizations (PROs) are groups of practicing doctors and other health-care professionals paid by the federal government to review the hospital care of Medicare patients. Each state has a PRO to help Medicare decide whether care is reasonable and necessary, is provided in an appropriate setting, and meets the accepted standards of the medical profession. PROs have the authority to deny payments if those conditions are not met. PROs also respond to requests for review of hospital notices of noncoverage issued to beneficiaries. In addition, they respond to hospital requests for reconsideration of PRO decisions, and they investigate individual patient complaints. If you are admitted to a Medicare-participating hospital, you will receive "An Important Message From Medicare," which explains your rights as a hospital patient and provides the name, address, and phone number of the PRO for your state.

If you feel that you have been improperly refused admission to a hospital or that you are being forced to leave the hospital too soon, ask for a written explanation of the decision. Medicare regulations require that a notice fully explain how you can appeal the decision, and give the name, address, and phone number of the PRO to which you can submit your appeal or request for review.

Your Hospital Rights Under Medicare

Whether you go to a hospital emergency room on your own or are taken there by ambulance, the hospital must do certain things for you. The hospital is required by law to:

❑ **Provide a medical screening examination** to determine whether or not an emergency medical condition exists.

❑ **Provide stabilizing treatment** prior to transferring you to another facility if you have an emergency medical condition or if you are a woman in active labor.

If you cannot be stabilized, you can be transferred to another hospital *only*:

❑ If the responsible physician certifies in writing that the benefits of the transfer outweigh the risks.

❑ If the receiving hospital has space and personnel to treat you, and has agreed to accept you as a patient.

❑ If the transferring hospital sends medical records along with you.

❑ If the transfer is made in appropriate transportation with life support equipment if necessary.

Many Medicare beneficiaries have complained that they were discharged from hospitals "too quick and too sick" because of pressures on hospitals to cut costs. Elderly patients are sometimes told by hospitals that their Medicare benefits have run out, and then are forced to leave before they are well. As a result, the Health Care Financing Administration of the United States Department of Health and Human Services has set up a "Medicare Patient Bill of Rights," which provides Medicare patients with a clear understanding of their rights when they are hospitalized. According to this bill, you have the following rights as a Medicare hospital patient:

❑ **The right to proper care.** You have a right to receive all of the hospital care that is necessary for the proper diagnosis and treatment of your illness or injury. Your discharge date should be determined solely by your medical needs, not by Medicare payments.

❑ **The right to information.** You have the right to be fully informed by the hospital about decisions affecting your Medicare coverage and the length of your stay.

❑ **The right to appeal.** If, in your opinion, the hospital wants to discharge you too soon, you have the right to appeal the decision to your local peer review organization. You cannot be dismissed before your appeal decision is made.

This "Medicare Patient Bill of Rights" is in force in hospitals throughout the country.

MEDICARE MEDICAL INSURANCE

Medicare medical insurance (Part B) helps pay for doctors' services—those of your regular doctor, as well as those you might need in a hospital, such as anesthesiology, radiology, and pathology. Medicare medical insurance can also help pay for outpatient hospital care and certain medical services and supplies not covered under hospital insurance.

Medicare medical insurance payments for covered services or supplies are based upon approved charges, not on your doctor's or supplier's actual, or current, charges. *Actual charges* are the actual fees charged by your doctor, and are most often considerably higher than approved charges. *Customary charges* are the fees that were most frequently charged by doctors and suppliers for specific services and supplies during the previous calendar year. An *approved charge* is an amount set by the Medicare carrier in your area and based primarily on the customary charge in your locale for the service or supply in question.

You must pay the full amount of all charges in excess of Medicare's approved allowance. In addition, every calendar year, you must pay as a deductible the first $100 of approved charges. After you have met the deductible, Medicare pays 80 percent of the approved charge and you pay the remaining 20 percent, which is known as the *Part B coinsurance.*

Medical Insurance Payments

There are two ways in which Medicare medical insurance payments are made.

1. **Assignment Method.** When the *assignment method* is used, the doctor or supplier agrees that his or her total charge for the covered service will not be more than the charge approved by the Medicare carrier. Medicare pays your doctor or supplier 80 percent of the approved charge, first subtracting any part of the $100 deductible you have not yet met. The doctor or supplier can charge you *only* for the part of the deductible you have not met and for the coinsurance, which is the remaining 20 percent of the approved charge. Your doctor or supplier can also charge you for any services that Medicare does not cover.

2. **Payment-to-You Method.** The *payment-to-you method* is used if your doctor does not accept Medicare assignment. Under this method, the doctor bills you for his or her actual charge, which you pay. You or the doctor then submits a claim to your Medicare carrier, which decides on the approved charge for the service or supply. The carrier pays you 80 percent of the approved charge, first subtracting whatever part of the deductible remains. The amount charged by the nonparticipating provider cannot be in excess of 15 percent above the Medicare-approved amount.

Whether or not your physician accepts assignments—and no matter what payment method is used—Medicare will send you an "Explanation of Medicare Benefits." This notice will show which services are covered, what charges are approved, how much is credited toward your $100 deductible, and how much Medicare has paid. You have the right to ask the carrier for a review of any decision.

Coverage

Medicare medical insurance covers some doctors' services, but not all. The following lists show which basic and preventive services are covered.

Basic Covered Services

Medicare medical insurance covers the following services:

❏ Medical and surgical services, including anesthesia.

❏ Diagnostic tests and procedures that are part of your treatment.

❏ Radiology and pathology services while you are a hospital inpatient or outpatient.

❏ Services that are ordinarily furnished in a doctor's office and included in his or her bill, such as:

- X-rays that you receive as part of your treatment.

- The services of the nurse in your doctor's office.

- Medications and biologicals that cannot be self-administered.

- Transfusions of blood and blood components.

- Medical supplies.

- Physical therapy, occupational therapy, and speech therapy services.

Covered Preventive Care Services

Several Medicare benefits are aimed at keeping older Americans healthier by detecting medical problems earlier. These benefits, which became effective between 1998 and 2001, include:

❏ **Breast cancer screening.** Mammograms are reimbursed once every year for female beneficiaries over age 40.

❏ **Vaginal and cervical cancer screening.** Pap smears and pelvic exams are reimbursed once every two years for women who are at low risk for these disorders, and once every year for women who are at high risk. Your doctor must decide about your level of risk.

❏ **Colorectal cancer screening.** Fecal-occult blood tests are reimbursed once every year, and flexible sigmoidoscopies are reimbursed once every four years for beneficiaries who are at average risk and age 50 and over. Colonoscopies are reimbursed every two years for those at high risk, and every ten years for those at average risk.

❏ **Prostate Cancer Screening.** Prostate cancer tests are available once a year for men age 50 and older. These tests include a digital rectal exam and a prostate-specific antigen (PSA) blood test.

❏ **Bone-density measurements.** Tests for bone density are reimbursed every two years for men and women who are at risk for losing bone mass.

❏ **Training services for outpatient diabetes self-management.** Training in diabetic self-management is available for all diabetes patients, both insulin-dependent and non-insulin-dependent, and includes coverage for home glucose monitors, testing strips, and lancets. Your doctor must refer you for training.

❏ **Vaccinations.** A flu shot is reimbursed once every year, and a hepatitis B vaccination is reimbursed as needed for those at high or intermediate risk. Pneumonia shots are reimbursed as needed.

MEDICARE PLAN OPTIONS

Medicare offers a variety of health plans. All of the plans provide all Medicare-covered services, but all may not be available in your area. Some, like the Fee-for-Service option, have been in use for many years. Other options became effective in 1999. The purpose of these different plans is to give you greater freedom of choice regarding doctors, hospitals, and other health-care providers, and to offer you extra benefits, such as prescription drugs.

Fee-for-Service (FFS) Option

This traditional plan allows you to select any doctor or hospital that you choose. You pay the monthly premium to Medicare, which covers doctors' fees under Part B. Medicare then pays 80 percent of its approved amount of the bill, and you pay the 20-percent balance.

Health Maintenance Organization (HMO)

As in the Fee-for-Service option, in the HMO option, you pay the monthly Part B premium to Medicare. Medicare, in turn, pays the HMO plan a fixed sum for your coverage, usually at a lower cost than FFS coverage. As an HMO member, you must receive your health care from the HMO's network of approved physicians and hospitals if the services are to be covered. If you choose a health-care provider from outside the network, you must pay the entire bill out-of-pocket. A primary care physician, whom you choose, must approve any referral to a specialist and/or entry into a hospital in the group's network.

Private Contracting

Private contracting permits doctors to charge Medicare beneficiaries whatever fees they wish. The doctor may not submit the reimbursement claim to Medicare, and you must pay the entire contracted fee out-of-pocket, without any reimbursement from Medicare or Medigap insurance.

Preferred Provider Organization (PPO)

A PPO combines features of fee-for-service and managed care. The PPO contracts with a network of doctors and hospitals to furnish health services to its enrollees. You pay the monthly Part B premium to Medicare, and Medicare, in turn, pays the PPO a fixed sum for your coverage. You can then use physicians or hospitals on a "preferred" list to obtain medical services, or, at some additional cost, you can use out-of-network doctors or hospitals. A percentage of the additional cost is paid for by the PPO.

Provider-Sponsored Organization (PSO)

With this option, you pay the monthly Part B premium to Medicare, which, in turn, pays a fee to the PSO. Then the PSO—a group of physicians and/or hospitals that join together—offers services directly to you without an insurance company as an intermediary. An advantage of a PSO is that medical decisions for a patient are made by doctors rather than insurance officials.

Point-of-Service (POS) Plan

Again, with this option, you pay the monthly Part B premium to Medicare, which then pays a fee to the POS. After this, you are able to choose providers from a network of physicians and hospitals. Like a PPO, a POS plan has a fee-for-service option that allows you to seek specialist care outside the network at some additional cost, a portion of which is paid by the POS. But unlike a PPO plan, a POS plan requires you to obtain permission before seeking out-of-network care. The POS plan may also set an annual expenditure limit on out-of-network benefits.

Private Fee-for-Service Plan (PFFSP)

Under a PFFSP, you first choose a private insurance plan. You then pay the Part B premium to Medicare which, in turn, pays the private plan a lump sum for your coverage. The PFFSP plan enables you to go to any doctor or hospital you choose. The insurance plan, which may charge you for deductibles and copayments, reimburses your health-care providers for the services you receive.

Choosing a Plan

If you are already using a traditional Medicare plan—a Fee-for-Service (FFS) plan—and you are happy with the way your health care is provided, you need not choose another plan. If you are not entirely satisfied with your current health care, however, you should consider how each of the Medicare plans would meet your needs. As discussed earlier, you may be limited in your choice by the options offered in your area. To learn about and compare the plans that are available to you, either check the official Medicare website or call Medicare directly. (See the Resources section.)

WHO FILLS THE GAPS?

Medicare was never designed to cover the first-dollar costs of basic health-care services. From the outset, Medicare did not cover all the charges incurred by beneficiaries, requiring the recipient of the services to pay the balance. These out-of-pocket expenses are referred to as *gaps*. Medigap plans—insurance policies designed to fill the gaps left in Medicare coverage—are discussed in detail in Chapter 17.

BASIC ADVICE FOR THE MEDICARE RECIPIENT

The following nine suggestions should guide you in your acquisition and use of Medicare.

1. Apply for Medicare coverage at your local Social Security office at least three months before your sixty-fifth birthday to make sure your benefits start on time.

2. Be sure to purchase Medicare medical insurance (Part B). It requires that you pay a monthly premium, but it is one of the best buys available.

3. Buy Medigap insurance, which pays for the gaps in Medicare coverage. A Medigap policy will reduce your out-of-pocket costs. (See Chapter 17.) If you can afford it, comprehensive major medical insurance is even better, as it provides coverage for the same types of services covered under basic health insurance plans—hospital, medical, and surgi-cal—picking up where the basic protection ends. (See Chapter 15.)

4. In addition to subscribing to Medicare and Medigap insurance, set up a health emergency fund to cover out-of-pocket expenses connected with illness.

5. When shopping for Medigap insurance, compare the benefits of at least three companies to be sure that you get the specific coverage you want. Avoid policies with confusing language.

6. Avoid exploitive salespeople seeking to sell you coverage that you do not need or cannot afford. If you are in doubt about a policy or salesperson, contact your State Insurance Commissioner.

7. When visiting a physician or surgeon, do not hesitate to ask about the fees and how they are to be paid. If you think the fees are too high, check with other physicians or surgeons.

8. If your spouse is under 65 and dependent, be sure that he or she has adequate coverage for hospitalization and medical care. (See Chapter 15.) The coverage should be at least equal to the protection of Medicare Part A and Part B.

9. Be aware that it is not uncommon for medical bills that should have been handled directly by Medicare to end up in your mail—often because the person filling out the form left out important information, such as your Medicare number. When these bills arrive, don't panic, and don't assume that you must pay the money due. Simply read the material and, if necessary, fill in the missing data and resubmit the claim. If you have both Medicare coverage and supplementary insurance, most medical costs should be covered.

MEDICAID

Medicaid is a public-assistance program that was designed to provide benefits to people who are unable to pay for health care. The official name of Medicaid is *Medical Assistance.* While it has special provisions for persons 65 and older, Medicaid helps anyone who is in need of medical services, but cannot afford them.

Medicaid is part of the Social Security law, Title 19. This portion of the law provides for the coverage of medical expenses of people who are unable to pay for such care. The program is financed primarily by the federal government. For its first full year of operation in 1967, Medicaid cost about $1.5 billion. The cost for 2001 was $129 billion for services to 33.9 million recipients, including the aged, the blind, the disabled, and the poor.

Medicaid is administered as part of state or local welfare departments. Each state designs its own program in accordance with federal guidelines. With the exception of Arizona, all states—as well as the District of Columbia, Puerto Rico, and the Virgin Islands—have a Medicaid program. A retired person who cannot afford the premium for Part B of Medicare and the additional expense of Medigap insurance should apply for Medicaid—a task that is not always easy simply because of the difficulty in finding the correct place to apply. Your best first step is to contact your local welfare office, Red Cross office, or Social Security office, all of which are listed in the phone book. Or contact your representative in the local or state legislature.

Eligibility

Your local welfare office can explain the qualifications for Medicaid in your area. Basically, people earning low incomes meet the test. While you must be age 65 to qualify for Medicare,

Medicaid covers people of all ages, including the 65-or-older group, some of whom are already receiving welfare benefits. Also eligible are the blind, the disabled, and members of low-income families, both adults and children.

Even though your income may fall within the limits prescribed by your state, the agency will check your savings account and assets. Most states permit you to keep some savings as a reserve without losing eligibility for Medicaid.

If you are eligible, the welfare department will give you an identification card that you can use to get the medical services you need. The state's administrative agency will pay the doctors, pharmacists, and others who serve you. Simply present your card in advance of receiving the service to be sure that the fees set by the state are acceptable to the supplier.

A unique aspect of the Medicaid law is that it has relieved adult children of the legal responsibility for their parents' medical expenses. Even if your grown children have provided financial assistance or are currently able to help you, it will not affect your eligibility for Medicaid. However, husbands and wives are still legally responsible for each other and must contribute to each other's support.

Covered Services

If you are eligible for both Medicare and Medicaid, Medicaid will cover all the gaps and deductible charges of Medicare. In many states, Medicaid pays for such additional services as dental care, prescription medication, eyeglasses, clinic services, intermediate care facility services, and other diagnostic, screening, and rehabilitative services.

Advice on Medicaid

If you need the financial support offered by

Medicaid, don't hesitate to apply for it. There is no shame in having inadequate resources. All levels of the government are striving to fill people's needs and are available to process your application. With the costs of health care as high as they are, and always on the rise, it is virtually impossible for an individual or family to cope with the expense of a catastrophic illness. If your income is low and you need financial support to cover the costs of an illness, be sure to apply for Medicaid as soon as the need arises.

One of the major goals of Medicare and Medicaid is the provision of medical care for all retirees who need it. By choosing the plan options that best fit your needs and circumstances, you will be taking one more step towards a healthy and financially secure retirement.

Managing the High Cost of Prescription Drugs

One of the most unexpected challenges for those who are approaching retirement age is managing the high cost of prescription drugs. It is a concern that stems from the increased need for prescribed medication among seniors. According to a report by Express Scripts, Inc.—one of the nation's largest pharmacy benefit management companies—seniors are four times more likely to require prescribed medication than those under sixty-five. And drug costs are spiraling out of control. In addition to price increases that consistently exceeded the inflation rate throughout the 1990s, during the first years of the new millennium, the cost of the fifty drugs most frequently prescribed to seniors rose, on average, more than twice the rate of inflation.

A growing number of seniors, particularly those on fixed incomes, cannot afford their medicine. Medicare does not cover the cost of prescription drugs. And although some managed heathcare plans do provide varying degrees of coverage, they do not necessarily protect the consumer from high out-of-pocket expenses, such as co-payments and deductibles. As a result, many seniors are taking their medication in smaller doses or taking it less frequently than prescribed. Most distressing is that some are simply not taking their medication at all.

If you or someone you know is experiencing difficulty in bearing the brunt of prescription drug costs, there are a number of alternatives that can help defray these expenses:

❑ **Substitute a generic drug.** Ask your doctor if you can replace the prescribed brand-name drug with a generic alternative. A generic drug has the same potency and chemical composition as a commercial brand, and generally costs much less. If a generic option is not available, ask your doctor if a different, less-expensive drug is appropriate for your particular needs.

❑ **Consider natural alternatives.** Ask your physician if there are natural alternative therapies that may be used to treat your specific condition. Natural therapies are generally less expensive than conventional drugs.

❑ **Shop for the best price.** Drugstores—even those within the same chain—can charge different prices for the same drug. Research the pharmacies in your area and shop for the best price. If you have access to the Internet, be aware that many online pharmacies offer prescription medications at discounted prices. But be cautious when shopping online. Learn as much as you can about the site before buying prescription medications.

❏ **Buy in bulk.** If you have to take a prescribed medication for an extended period, see if you can order it in bulk at a discount. On the other hand, if you must take the medicine for a short period, don't buy more than you need.

❏ **Check out pharmaceutical company drug-assistance programs.** In an effort to assist people who cannot afford prescription medication, many pharmaceutical companies have established free prescription drug programs for those who qualify. Although each company has established individual qualifications, typically, most applicants are required to have a low income. They must also have exhausted all other options for prescribed benefits. Most companies require forms to be filled out and submitted by the prescribing physician.

A number of Internet sites provide information on the drug-assistance programs offered by pharmaceutical companies. Two very helpful websites are www.medicare.gov and www.phrma.org. Both present detailed information that specifies the name and contact of each company, including telephone number, street address, and website link; the drugs that are covered by the program; eligibility requirements; the person who is required to submit the application; and other important data.

❏ **Check with your state and community for drug-assistance programs.** A number of drug-assistance programs are available through state and local communities. These programs offer discounted or free prescription medication to people in need. For more information about these programs, call your state, county, or community medical assistance office. These offices may be listed in your telephone book under Medicaid, Medical Assistance, Social Services, Human Services, or Community Services. You can also contact Medicare for the phone number for state services by calling 800-MEDICARE (800-633-4227). If you have access to the Internet, check the official Medicare site at www.medicare.gov. Here you will find all of the prescription drug-assistance programs that are offered in various states.

❏ **Have prescriptions filled by Canadian pharmacies.** Because Canada's system of socialized medicine keeps pharmaceutical costs under tight control, Canada's prescription drugs are much less expensive than those sold in the United States. For years, Americans have crossed the Canadian border to have their prescriptions filled at a substantial savings, and this trend continues to grow. Services such as the We Care Medical Mall—a California-based nonprofit group—help Americans get their prescriptions filled in Canada, and assist them in accessing other cost-saving medical services. For information about this program, call the group toll-free at 800-771-3325, or visit it online at www.WeCareMedicalMall.org. Also look for those Canadian pharmacies that have websites on the Internet. However, always exercise caution when shopping online.

A number of the suggestions above involve doing research on the Internet. If you do not have access to a computer, consider using one at your local library. If you are unfamiliar with the Internet, one of the librarians will be glad to help you.

17

MEDIGAP *and* LONG-TERM CARE COVERAGE

Medicare was not designed to cover the entire health care bill for older individuals. When Medicare was created in 1965, it left relatively small gaps in insurance coverage, and the premiums for supplemental policies were low. But as health care costs escalated, the gaps widened. Currently, Medicare supplement insurance—known as Medigap—has become a major expenditure of older Americans. About 80 percent of all Medicare beneficiaries own a supplemental policy.

One major gap in both Medicare *and* Medigap policies is long-term care, which is often referred to as custodial care. Senior citizens without long-term care insurance coverage can lose all their assets—assets accumulated over a lifetime of work, saving, and investment—if they have to enter a nursing home. Private insurance companies offer long-term care insurance to protect the elderly from such a catastrophe, but the cost for such insurance is relatively high. Thus, long-term care remains the most significant gap in America's health insurance system.

MEDICARE GAPS

Medicare provides basic coverage for hospital and medical expenses, but the huge gaps in coverage must be paid by the insured. Medicare recipients are responsible for paying the annual hospital and medical deductibles, which keep rising every year. The Part A hospital deductible has risen from $160 in 1979 to $812 in 2002. The Part B medical care deductible is $100 in 2002. And you are also responsible for the 20-percent coinsurance payment on Part B medical bills.

Medicare has other serious gaps. Hospital coverage can run out after a fixed number of days, leaving you exposed to significant financial liability in the event of a serious illness. Medicare covers 90 days of hospitalization plus 60 *lifetime reserve days*. Therefore, for a first hospitalization, Medicare covers up to 150 days. You will then have used up your 60 lifetime reserve days. For subsequent hospital stays, Medicare covers 90 days (see page 215 for more information). And if a physician charges more than the approved Medicare allowance for a particular procedure, you must pay the difference as well as the coinsurance. Moreover, Medicare does not pay for any prescription drugs for outpatients, and does not cover all preventive medical care.

MEDIGAP INSURANCE

Because of the gaps in Medicare coverage, seniors are encouraged to supplement their Medicare coverage with an additional policy that pays all or part of the additional costs. Actually a type of private commercial insurance, this coverage is referred to as a *Medigap policy.*

The Standardization of Medigap Policies

In 1990, Congress passed a law requiring states to standardize Medicare supplement policies. It delegated the National Association of Insurance Commissioners (NAIC) to develop ten standardized Medicare supplement benefit policies. The ten plans developed by NAIC became effective July 1992, and are identified by the letters A through J. Once the plans were devised, each state insurance department decided which of the ten policies—all or only a few—would be available for sale in that state.

Insurance companies in each state now offer only the standardized supplement plans, and must use the standardized designations for the ten different plans. (See Table 17.1.) The states are not allowed to change the combinations of benefits in any of the standard policies. This has eliminated the confusion that previously existed in this insurance policy market.

Individual states may limit the number of plans for sale within their borders to fewer than ten, but every state that adopts the new regulations must approve the sale of Plan A, which offers certain basic minimum benefits. Those few states whose own standardized policy regulations predated the new federal law may retain

their regulations if granted a waiver by the Secretary of Health and Human Services. However, these states must offer the same basic minimum benefits in their benefit packages.

To determine the standardized policies available in your state, contact your state insurance department. Be aware, though, that the new regulations do not apply to Medigap policies that went into force before the requirements took effect in a particular state. If you own such a policy, there is no requirement that you switch to a new standard policy, but it's probably a good idea to do so. Your insurance company can inform you of your options.

The Core Benefits

Table 17.1 specifies the different benefits of each of the ten standard Medigap plans. All Medigap policies supplement Medicare benefits, and all ten plans offer the same core benefits. These benefits pay the patient's 20-percent share of Medicare's approved amount for physician's services after the $100 annual deductible. Also covered is the patient's cost of a long hospital stay. (In 2002, a patient covered by Medicare spends $203 a day for days 61 through 90, $406 a day for days 91 through 150, and all approved costs not paid by Medicare after day 150.) Charges for the first three pints of blood, which are not covered by Medicare, are also part of the core benefits.

Additional Benefits

Most of the ten standardized policies provide not only the core benefits, but also one or more additional benefits. (See Table 17.1.) These include coverage for:

❏ **Skilled nursing care.** This benefit pays the coinsurance amount—in 2002, $101.50 per day for days 21 through 100 per benefit period—in

TABLE 17.1

THE MEDIGAP GUIDE: THE TEN STANDARD MEDICARE SUPPLEMENT BENEFIT PLANS (A–J)										
Core Benefits	Plan A	Plan B	Plan C	Plan D	Plan E	Plan F	Plan G	Plan H	Plan I	Plan J
Part A Hospital (Days 61–90)	X	X	X	X	X	X	X	X	X	X
Lifetime Reserve (Days 91–150)	X	X	X	X	X	X	X	X	X	X
365 Life Hospital Days—100%	X	X	X	X	X	X	X	X	X	X
Parts A and B Blood	X	X	X	X	X	X	X	X	X	X
Additional Benefits										
Skilled Nursing Facility Coinsurance (Days 21–100)			X	X	X	X	X	X	X	X
Part A Deductible		X	X	X	X	X	X	X	X	X
Part B Deductible			X			X				X
Part B Excess Charges						100%	80%		100%	100%
Foreign Travel Emergency			X	X	X	X	X	X	X	X
At-Home Recovery				X				X	X	X
Prescription Drug Option 1								X	X	
Prescription Drug Option 2										X
Preventive Medical Care					X					X

Source: US Department of Health and Human Services. *Guide to Health Insurance for People with Medicare.*

a skilled nursing facility. A *benefit period* starts when you enter a hospital, and has a 90-day maximum. There is no limit on the number of 90-day benefit periods, but to be eligible for each benefit period, you must have been out of the hospital for 60 consecutive days. (See page 218 for additional information on Medicare coverage for skilled nursing.)

❏ **Medicare Part A hospital deductible.** This benefit pays the Medicare Part A inpatient deductible—in 2002, $812 per benefit period.

❏ **Medicare Part B deductible.** This benefit pays the Medicare Part B deductible—in 2002, $100 per calendar year.

❏ **Percentage of Part B excess charges.** This benefit pays either 100 percent or 80 percent of Medicare Part B *excess charges*—the portion of the doctor's actual charges that are greater than Medicare's approved or reasonable charge. Without Medigap insurance, excess charges are an out-of-pocket expense for the patient.

❏ **Emergency care in a foreign country.** This benefit pays medically necessary emergency care when you are traveling in a foreign country.

❏ **At-home recovery.** For those recovering from surgery, illness, or injury, this benefit covers short-term, at-home assistance with such activities of daily living (ADLs) as bathing and dressing.

❏ **Prescription drug option 1.** After a specified annual deductible has been met, this benefit pays 50 percent of the cost of prescription drugs up to a specified annual maximum amount.

❏ **Prescription drug option 2.** After a specified annual deductible has been met, this benefit pays 50 percent of the cost of prescription drugs up to a specified annual maximum amount that is larger than the maximum benefit paid in prescription drug option 1.

❏ **Preventive medical care.** This benefit pays a specified amount per year for such preventive measures as physical checkups.

Which Medigap Policy Should You Purchase?

The cost of a Medigap policy depends on the carrier you choose, the area in which you live, and, of course, the coverage provided in that particular policy. The basic core benefits for Plan A cost a few hundred dollars a year, while Plan J, which offers the most comprehensive coverage, generally costs several thousand dollars. Like all health-care costs, policy premiums tend to increase annually. Self-Study 17.1, found on page 237, was designed to help you compare the costs of three different Medigap policies; and Self-Study 17.2, beginning on page 237, allows you to determine how three different policies will fill the "gaps" in Medicare coverage.

When choosing coverage, you should evaluate the cost of the insurance versus the risk that you are willing to take. If are able to pay for those medical services not included in core cov-

erage as the need for them arises, you may not have to pay the premium cost for the extra coverage. Generally speaking, however, if you can afford the additional insurance, you should buy it to minimize your risk. To learn more about the important topic of Medigap insurance, write for the helpful booklet *Guide to Health Insurance for People with Medicare,* available from the United States Department of Health and Human Services. (See the Resources section.)

LONG-TERM CARE

Older Americans, age 65 and over, make up the fastest growing part of the population, and this trend will continue as the baby boomers become seniors. In 1984, 12 percent of the American population was age 65 or over. By the year 2030, it is estimated that over 21 percent of the population will be in this age group. This "graying of America" has brought new concerns to the forefront. One of the most vexing of these is the issue of long-term care.

The term *long-term care* generally refers to care that is provided over a long period of time for people who have chronic health conditions and/or disabilities. This type of care becomes necessary when an individual needs assistance with life's daily tasks. Such assistance, commonly called *custodial care,* is the cornerstone of long-term care, which ranges from nursing home care to at-home help with personal hygiene and mobility.

A Common Story

A couple plans carefully for the future, saving money to put their children through college and to retire in comfort. As the couple grows older, one of them becomes seriously ill and must enter a nursing home. To the couple's surprise and dismay, they discover that neither their health insurance nor Medicare will cover the cost. Within months, their lifetime savings and other assets are completely wiped out.

Unfortunately, this story is quite common. In fact, two out of five Americans age 65 or older will enter a nursing home at some time in their lives. And the cost of nursing home care is frightening. A one-year stay in a nursing home can cost $40,000 to $100,000, depending on the geographical area in which the home is located. In fact, nursing homes are the most expensive form of long-term care facility. While we automatically equate this story with growing older, even younger people are not immune. An unexpected accident or illness can make long-term care necessary at any age.

WHO LEFT THE LONG-TERM COVERAGE GAP?

Medicare, Medigap, and Medicaid all fail to shelter you from the inroads that long-term care can make on your finances.

Medicare serves as insurance against the costs of acute care only. No provision is made for long-term care. Medicare supplement insurance—so-called Medigap policies—also provides no coverage for long-term care services.

Medicaid, the government program of social welfare that funds long-term care, does not merit the title of "insurance" in the accepted sense. Instead of protecting you from the staggering costs of long-term care, Medicaid requires you to deplete your assets before you can be eligible for its funding. In other words, you are covered only if you are poor enough to qualify for public welfare. Because spouses have a legal responsibility to support each other, in order for an ill spouse to qualify for Medicaid, the healthy spouse must first spend the assets of both partners. You may keep your home without disqualifying yourself from Medicaid, but your

home may be subject to a lien by Medicaid after the home is sold by the surviving spouse or the estate.

Some middle income families resort to financial shuffling and become eligible for Medicaid benefits by "spending down" their assets to state-required levels, meaning that they deplete their assets through spending in order to qualify for Medicaid assistance. Some families manage to qualify for Medicaid and still protect their assets by giving those assets to their children or other family members three years (thirty-six months) prior to entering a nursing home. Other families choose to transfer their assets into an irrevocable trust, specifying that the money and interest earned from it cannot be applied to nursing home costs. Some elder-care lawyers specialize in this procedure.

Under current laws and regulations, the best solution for a middle income household is to buy long-term care insurance.

Private Insurance: One Solution to Long-Term Care Coverage

To obtain long-term care coverage, you can purchase long-term care insurance, a policy that pays a specified amount every day, whether you're in your own home, a nursing home, or an assisted living facility. The policy pays benefits for all levels of care—skilled, intermediate, and custodial—and covers 100 percent of costs up to the daily benefit you select, regardless of where you receive the care. A long-term care policy pays benefits even if there is no prior hospitalization.

More than 300 insurance companies sell long-term care insurance. Most policies are sold to people over age 65 by individual agents. Long-term care policies offer asset protection for middle income people, those with over $25,000 in assets, and those with above-minimal income.

On average, a person holds a policy for ten years before filing a claim. If you are convinced that you or someone in your family should purchase insurance to cover the cost of long-term health care, you should begin to consider the types of policies available and decide whether you can afford the annual premium.

Table 17.2 shows one company's premium for individuals at various ages. This particular policy provides a $150 daily nursing home benefit or a $150 daily home care benefit, payable for a period of five years, for a total of $273,750—the lifetime maximum. ($150 x 365 days x 5 years.) There is a 90-day waiting period and an automatic inflation adjustment of 5 percent every year for the daily allowances. The premiums are higher than those for many policies, but they remain unchanged even in the event of inflation.

TABLE 17.2

ONE COMPANY'S PREMIUMS FOR A LONG-TERM HEALTH CARE POLICY	
Age	**Annual Premium**
45	$1,830
50	$1,935
55	$2,190
60	$2,595
65	$3,165
70	$4,080
75	$5,730
80	$8,385
84	$12,150

Selecting a Long-Term Care Policy

Before purchasing a long-term care policy, it is important to compare features and prices. Self-

Study 17.3, beginning on page 239, will help you record and compare information so that you can make the best choice. Space is provided for data from three insurance companies.

When researching policies, be sure to pay special attention to the following key elements:

❑ **The Company.** It is important to deal with a financially secure company that will provide good service. To be sure about your choice, you should select companies rated A++ or A+ by A.M. Best, a widely respected independent company that rates the financial stability of insurance companies. Also look for an AA rating by at least one of the other major rating services—Standard & Poor's or Moody's. You can obtain the ratings at your local library.

❑ **Daily benefits.** Most insurance companies offer a wide range of benefits, which usually pay from $100 to $250 a day. Because nursing home charges vary, it is suggested that you check actual costs in your area before choosing a policy. Be aware that a nursing home usually bills its patients monthly. Generally, to obtain the daily benefits, the insured files a claim, and the insurance company pays the agreed amount to the insured. Some insurance companies send the payment directly to the nursing home.

❑ **Maximum benefits in years.** Companies generally allow you to choose benefit periods of from one to six years, with some offering lifetime coverage. Statistics on nursing home patients indicate that the typical stay is two to three years. Based upon these figures, the coverage you purchase should be a minimum of three years.

❑ **The elimination period in days.** Most policies state an *elimination period*—the number of days between the time you enter the nursing home and the time the insurance company begins payments. This period usually ranges from

20 to 100 days. If a nursing home charges $120 per day and you buy a policy with a 20-day elimination period, you will have to pay $2,400 out-of-pocket before the insurance company begins to pay. With a 50-day elimination period, you will have to pay $6,000, an amount that would not cause an upper middle income family financial catastrophe. The longer the elimination period, the lower the insurance premium.

❏ **Gatekeeper mechanisms.** The goal of an insurance company is to minimize claims payments in order to earn a profit. To limit payments, the insurance company writes restrictions—*gatekeeper mechanisms*—into the policy contract, making it more difficult for the insured to qualify for a benefit. While these mechanisms protect the insurance company, they may be totally unacceptable to you, the buyer of the policy.

An example of a gatekeeper mechanism is the number of *activities of daily living* (ADLs) you must be unable to perform to be eligible for admission to a nursing home. ADLs include bathing, dressing, eating, transferring from a bed to a chair, maintaining bowel and bladder control (continence), and toileting. Some policies require the inability to perform three of six ADLs; others, two of six. Obtain a list of ADLs covered in the policy, and also request definitions. Make sure that the definitions are not too restrictive.

Other gatekeeper mechanisms include a requirement for prior hospitalization, a doctor's certification, and the exclusion of patients with Alzheimer's disease.

❏ **Pre-existing conditions.** Pre-existing conditions are illnesses that were diagnosed and/or treated for some specified period before you purchased your policy. Most companies do cover ailments disclosed on the application, so do not hesitate to completely and truthfully fill out the form. However, be aware that most companies do not cover these conditions until a period of time has elapsed after the purchase of the policy. This time period should not exceed six months.

❏ **Inflation protection.** Long-term care policies offer inflation protection to meet rising costs of nursing home care. Some policies include an automatic inflation adjustment for which the insured pays. The company usually offers a choice: a simple increase or a compounded increase.

In a *simple increase*, the policy may provide a 5-percent yearly increase of the original benefit. For instance, if the original benefit was $100 per day, the increase would be an additional $5 each year. The second-year coverage would be $105; the third year, $110; and so forth. In fifteen years, a simple increase would raise the coverage to $175 per day.

With a policy that provides a 5-percent *compounded increase*, the benefit of $100 per day would rise to $208 in fifteen years. Of course, the annual premium cost is higher for policies that provide a compounded increase.

Some companies offer an inflation adjustment annually for four years, indicating the amount of the increased benefit and the higher premium. If you accept the higher benefit and the higher premium, the company will offer the inflation adjustment option for four more years. If you reject the inflation adjustment for four consecutive years, it will no longer be offered to you.

The inflation adjustment provision you buy will depend on the cost you are willing to pay. Obtain figures on the coverage without inflation protection and with such protection. This information will allow you to make an informed decision.

❏ **Home care benefits.** Some policies will pay for custodial care only if you are in a nursing home. Most people, however, prefer home care. Seek a policy that provides coverage for different kinds of care facilities. Also make sure that the policy provides for skilled and custodial care, as well as homemaker services. Some good policies also offer coverage for adult day care and respite care.

❏ **Other features.** The policy should have a *waiver of premium* feature. Good policies waive the premium after an individual has been in a nursing home for a specified period of time, typically 90 days. Some policies also provide a *death benefit*. Usually payable only if the insured dies before a certain age, typically 65 or 70, this benefit refunds to the insured's estate any premiums paid, less any benefits the company paid on the policyholder's behalf.

A Final Tip

An excellent long-term care policy is one that will provide a minimum of $120 per day of coverage after a fifty-day elimination period, coverage for three to six years, and an inflation adjustment feature. You should consider broader coverage if you can afford it. A rule of thumb is that premiums for a long-term care policy should not exceed 10 percent of your gross income. Buyers should look for a policy that is renewable for life and that cannot be cancelled for any reason other than failure to pay premiums, which should remain level over the policy's life.

The prime candidate for a long-term care policy is someone 50 to 60 years old. Premiums rise sharply for older individuals. Furthermore, if you wait until after retirement to buy a policy, you may be considered unacceptable. A disorder such as a stroke, Parkinson's disease, or failing vision will further increase the chance of rejection. It is best to sign up while you are still young and healthy.

Although Medicare and Medicaid do much to insure adequate health care for retirees, unfortunately, they don't cover all of the health expenses that you are likely to encounter. Medicare supplement policies can do a great deal to fill the gaps left by Medicare. In addition, depending on your age and situation, you may want to seriously consider purchasing a long-term care insurance policy. These added policies can provide you with the peace of mind you want as well as the health care you need during your golden years.

Self-Study 17.1
COMPARATIVE COSTS OF MEDIGAP POLICIES

This self-study will enable you to compare costs of three different Medigap policies.

Private Insurance	Policy 1	Policy 2	Policy 3
Company name			
Pre-existing condition waiting period (days)			
Guaranteed renewability			
Medigap Plans	**Annual Premium**		
Plan A			
Plan B			
Plan C			
Plan D			
Plan E			
Plan F			
Plan G			
Plan H			
Plan I			
Plan J			

Self-Study 17.2
COMPARATIVE ANALYSIS OF DIFFERENT COMPANIES' MEDIGAP POLICIES

If you are considering the purchase of Medigap insurance to supplement your Medicare coverage, use the worksheet on the following page to compare the benefits and costs of each company's policy.

COMPARISON OF MEDIGAP INSURANCE POLICIES

Medicare's Major Gaps (2002 figures)		COMPANY NAME POLICY TYPE	COMPANY NAME POLICY TYPE	COMPANY NAME POLICY TYPE
Part A—Hospital insurance	**You pay**			
Hospital deductible	$812			
Days 61–90	$203/day			
Days 91–150	$406/day			
Beyond day 150	All costs			
After day 90 if 60 reserve days have been used	All costs			
Post-hospital skilled nursing care:				
Days 1–20	No charge			
Days 21–100	$101.50/day			
Beyond day 100	All costs			
Part B—Medical insurance	**You pay**			
Excess charge	All			
$100 annual deductible	All			
Medicare's approved charge	20%			
Other gaps	**You pay**			
Long-term custodial care:				
At home	All costs			
In a nursing facility	All costs			
Care outside the United States	All costs			
Total annual premium				

Benefits and Premiums

Self-Study 17.3

COMPARATIVE FEATURES
OF THREE LONG-TERM CARE POLICIES

If you are considering the purchase of Long-Term Care insurance to supplement your Medicare coverage, use this worksheet to compare the different features of each company's policy.

	Policy 1	Policy 2	Policy 3
Company Name			
Daily benefits for:			
Skilled nursing care			
Intermediate care			
Custodial care			
Home care			
Other noninstitutional care			
Maximum years for:			
Nursing home benefits			
Home care benefits			
Total lifetime benefits in dollars			
Elimination period in days			
Gatekeeper mechanisms:			
Activities of Daily Living (ADLs), number needed			
Are ADLs specifically defined?			
Is doctor certification required?			
Is Alzheimer's disease covered?			

	Policy 1	Policy 2	Policy 3
Pre-existing conditions:			
Months before coverage starts			
Inflation protection:			
Type of inflation adjustment			
Is adjustment annual or periodic?			
Home care benefits:			
Skilled care			
Intermediate care			
Custodial care			
Are homemaker services included?			
Other features:			
Waiver of premium			
Death benefit			
Annual premium with an inflation adjustment:			
Simple increase			
Compounded increase			
Annual choice option			

PART FIVE

FINAL FACTS

ESTATE PLANNING
and WILLS

Many people think that estate planning is a concern reserved for wealthy individuals. This is not true. The typical middle class family owns a home, furniture and furnishings, an automobile or two, and hobby items. It also has savings, some investments, and life insurance. When you add it all up, the total is usually surprising. This is the package to be analyzed in estate planning.

Most people cringe at the thought of planning for death, and therefore postpone the task. In fact, three out of four adults die without having finalized a will. However, the head of a household and that person's spouse should have an estate plan, including a will and other essential documents. Anyone who fails to undertake estate planning will impose upon his or her heirs a host of unnecessary costs and problems.

ESTATE PLANNING BASICS

Your *estate* consists of the assets you leave for your heirs. *Estate planning* is the process of managing your assets effectively during your lifetime, and arranging for the disposal of assets at your death so as to best serve the needs of your beneficiaries. The goal of estate planning is the establishment of an *estate plan*, the overall arrangement for the disposal of your wealth both before and after death. It takes a lifetime to create an estate, yet at death, many estates are reduced by as much as 20 to 50 percent because of taxes and settlement costs resulting from poor planning. It takes careful planning to minimize estate shrinkage and transfer as great a portion of your assets as possible to your heirs.

The Objectives of Estate Planning

Estate planning has three principal objectives:

1. To make certain that your property is distributed according to your wishes and the needs of your beneficiaries. An effective estate plan will provide for the individuals about whom you care, leaving them what you want them to have. This is your primary objective.

2. To minimize federal and state estate and inheritance taxes, which are levied on an individual's estate at death.

3. To keep settlement costs to a minimum. The goal is to lower legal fees, accounting fees, and other nontax costs associated with dying.

The Steps in Estate Planning

There are five basic steps you must take to prepare an effective estate plan—a plan that will meet the three principal objectives just discussed. These steps are detailed below. As you follow these steps, use Self-Study 18.1 to organize the data you must gather for your estate plan.

1. **Inventory Your Assets and Their Value.** The first step in estate planning is to identify each of your assets and estimate the value of each. You can take these directly from the net worth statement that you prepared in Chapter 10. (See page 163.) This inventory of your assets should be compiled in cooperation with your spouse and, if they are old enough, with your children. A full and accurate inventory is helpful to your attorney in implementing your wishes correctly.

2. **Identify Your Heirs and Their Needs.** The major concern of most married men is their wives. Children grow up, get married, and pursue their own careers. At that point, a wife who had only a short-term career may have only a modest pension, and a wife who did not pursue any career at all may be out of touch with the job market. Because of her age and lack of marketable skills, she may have a problem in obtaining paid employment. Therefore, a husband's first responsibility usually is to take care of the needs of his spouse. In most cases, the home is owned in an arrangement known as *joint tenancy with right of survivorship.* This means that the property is held jointly, with each partner owning an equal share, and with the entire property passing to the survivor in the event of the other owner's death. Property held in this way avoids probate.

   If there is any question about prudent management of the balance of your assets,

you and your spouse should discuss this important matter together. The best interests of the children, grandchildren, and other heirs must also be considered in this discussion. Together, you must decide whether these assets should be placed in a trust to be managed by a trustee. (Trusts are discussed in Chapter 20.)

3. **Estimate Your Final Cash Requirements.** The *testator,* or maker of a will, must estimate cash requirements to cover the costs of the last illness and funeral expenses. In addition, several other obligations must be paid in full before any property can be distributed to the beneficiaries. These include estate and inheritance taxes, if any; debts of the deceased, such as outstanding loans and unpaid bills; property taxes, if any; and legal fees for administering the estate.

   If sufficient cash or near-cash assets are not available to satisfy these obligations as they become due, the nonliquid assets of the estate must be sold to pay them. Funds should be available in the form of cash, highly marketable stocks or bonds, savings accounts, or life insurance.

4. **Consult With a Specialist in Estate Planning.** Theoretically, an individual can do his or her own estate planning. While this practice might initially save you money, it can also lead to costly errors. Because, ultimately, outside experts tend to save more money than they cost, it is strongly recommended that you seek professional advice. Professionals will help you plan your estate while you are living. Then, after your death, they will administer the estate to insure that your wishes are followed.

   A lawyer who is a specialist in estate planning should be called upon to handle the details of any estate plan, whether it seems simple or complex. A competent lawyer can be obtained through the recommendations of a friend or by contacting your local bar association. Good rapport between you and your lawyer is essential. It is important to discuss fees before any work is initiated, and to receive a realistic estimate of total costs in advance. If you do not feel comfortable with the lawyer you have chosen, find someone else. You have the right to look elsewhere. (For more information on finding an appropriate attorney, see "Choosing a Lawyer" in Chapter 5.)

While a lawyer who specializes in estate planning is essential, advice can also be obtained from trust departments in banks, as well as from life insurance salespeople—although their possible bias must always be kept in mind.

5. **Select Appropriate Estate Planning Tools.** The fourth step in estate planning is to decide which of the available tools you will need to achieve your objectives:

❑ A will.

❑ A supplemental letter of instructions.

❑ A durable power of attorney.

❑ Advance directives.

❑ A trust or trusts.

You and your spouse will certainly require wills. The need for the other tools varies from one situation to another. An appropriate combination of these tools will help you meet your goals concerning distribution, property management, tax planning, and any other objective you may have. The services of a lawyer are needed to select the most appropriate tools for your particular circumstances. The following pages contain information on each of these elements except for the trust, which is covered in Chapter 20.

WILLS

Preparing a will is not easy. It means making decisions—sometimes, heart-rending decisions—that will become final. It is so much easier to postpone the task. In fact, even some people in high places, who should be aware of the importance of preparing a will, have been careless. Four presidents, including Abraham Lincoln, Andrew Johnson, Ulysses S. Grant, and James A. Garfield, died without creating this vital document. But despite the fact that this is a difficult task, it is imperative—especially when contemplating retirement—to take an inventory of your wealth and possessions, and decide upon their final distribution.

What Is a Will?

A *will* is a legal document, almost always in writing and properly executed, that describes how a person wants his or her property to be distributed after death, and designates the person or institution that will carry out the terms of the will. In effect, your will is the center of your estate plan. In your will, you will designate an *executor*, who is responsible for carrying out the provisions of your will; and, hopefully, an alternate executor, who will serve if your original choice is unable or unwilling to serve. If necessary, you will also designate a *guardian* and an alternate guardian, who will have the responsibility of caring for a minor or an incompetent adult; and a *trustee*, who will be responsible for managing the assets of a trust.

Why Make a Will?

A duly executed will reflects your wishes in regard to your property and your family. A will offers the following advantages:

❑ It will guarantee that your property is distributed according to your wishes, which reflect thoughtful planning.

❏ It will minimize taxes and other expenses in the distribution of your assets.

❏ It will accomplish the transfer of your estate to your heirs with a minimum of delay.

❏ It will take care of special problems, such as provision for children or an incompetent dependent.

❏ It will minimize the possibility of costly and family-disrupting lawsuits.

❏ It can provide for continued income to your family during the period in which the estate is being settled.

❏ It can direct that particular beneficiaries receive specified assets, known as *bequests*.

❏ It is the appropriate means of setting up a trust after death.

Note that some assets *cannot* be bequeathed or disposed of through your will because the beneficiaries for these assets have already been named. These assets include life insurance, pension benefits, and jointly owned property.

Also be aware that a will allows you to make bequests as percentages of your total estate. Because of the continuing problem of inflation, experts suggest that bequests be made as percentages of your estate, rather than dollar amounts.

The Risks of Dying Without a Will

If you die leaving a valid will, you are said to have died *testate*. If you die without a will, you are said to have died *intestate*. If you die intestate, the laws of the state in which you live at the time of your death will provide for the distribution of your assets. These state laws will determine who will inherit your property; which property will be inherited, and in what proportions; when and under what conditions the property will be inherited; and what federal, state, and local taxes might be levied. The actions taken by the state may not coincide with what you wanted or planned, and may result in many inequities.

Thus, dying without a will may create serious problems for your survivors. For example:

❏ If you are a married man with three grown children, you may want your assets to go to your wife so that she will be supported for the rest of her life. Without a will, she may get only a half or a third of the assets, with the rest divided among the children. If your wife cannot live on her share, it will be necessary for the children to support her. Thus, in this case, the lack of a will would impose a real hardship on all survivors.

❏ If you are a married man and have no children, in the absence of a will, money meant for your wife may go instead to your parents or even your brothers and sisters, who may feel no obligation to support your wife.

❏ Without a will, adopted children or stepchildren may inherit nothing.

❏ Where no will exists, the court appoints an administrator to manage and distribute your estate. The fees he collects may be greater than the combined cost of your making a will and your survivors' paying for probate.

Even if you have not made a will, your state has one tucked away for you. According to its laws, it will distribute your assets *by intestacy*. And, as you've seen, the laws of your state will not take into account your own wishes or the financial needs of your survivors. Table 18.1 illustrates one state's distribution of assets by intestacy.

Types of Wills

A will can take many forms. These forms include the fill-in-the-blanks will, also known as a statutory will; the handwritten will, also known as a holographic will; the oral will; and a will drawn up by your lawyer.

The Fill-in-the-Blanks Will

How often people ask, "Why do I need an attorney to help me write a will? I know what I want." In truth, you do not need an attorney to help you write your will. In fact, in four states, you can use a standard fill-in form known as a *fill-in-the-blanks will,* or *statutory will.*

The state of California became the first state to approve a legal standard will. This option is intended for low- and middle-income people with fairly simple legal needs. The document was drawn up by the state bar of California and approved by the legislature. The bar still recommends that people see a lawyer before filling in the blanks. The terms of the California document apply only to California residents. Other versions of the fill-in-the-blanks will have been authorized in Maine, Michigan, and Wisconsin.

As discussed earlier, writing your own will certainly saves time and money, but it can also create serious problems for your heirs. These can be costly and time-consuming, and may provoke family squabbles.

The Handwritten Will

A handwritten will is known as a *holographic will.* To be valid, it must be fully written in the handwriting of the person who is making the will. In the states where it is recognized, it does not require witnesses.

The risks and hazards of a holographic will are numerous. Only a minority of the fifty states recognize this type of will. Lacking legal knowledge, you may fail to use language which can guarantee that your estate is handled in the manner you intended. You may also include an instruction which provides for an action that is not permitted by the laws of your state, thereby

TABLE 18.1

EXAMPLE OF DISTRIBUTION OF ASSETS BY INTESTACY	
Survivors	**Division of Assets**
Surviving spouse, no children	Spouse, 100 percent
Surviving spouse, one or more children	First $50,000 to surviving spouse Rest of estate: 50 percent to surviving spouse 50 percent to child/children
One or more children, no surviving spouse	Child/children get 100 percent
Surviving parents, no surviving spouse or children	Parents, 100 percent
Surviving brothers and sisters, no surviving spouse, children, or parents	Divide among brothers and sisters, or to their issue, *per stirpes* (according to the line of descendants)
No surviving relatives	100 percent to state

invalidating your will. And even a seemingly inconsequential error—such as failure to include the date or part of the date, or use of a stamped date—may make a handwritten will worthless under the law.

Other technicalities by which a handwritten will may be invalidated are listed below:

❏ Part of the will is handwritten and part is typed. This raises a question as to whether the typed part was added by you or by someone else.

❏ A sentence has been crossed out, but no initials appear next to the affected portion to show that you approved of the deletion. Anyone could have deleted the sentence—not necessarily the maker of the will.

❏ After you signed the will, an additional paragraph was added, leaving some of your property to another person. This paragraph could have been added by someone else without your knowledge.

The Oral Will

An oral will is one made within the hearing of two witnesses. Because it is valid only under special circumstances, such as when the will maker is in danger of imminent death or on active duty in the United States military, it is used primarily by soldiers or sailors in active service, and by mariners at sea. Oral wills are valid in only a few states; may be recognized only for a short time after the soldier, sailor, or mariner is discharged; and usually provide for minimum estates. Moreover, they always bear the risk that the witnesses may not accurately recall what was said.

A Will Drawn Up by Your Lawyer

Although there are several types of wills that

can be created without professional help, as you have seen, each of these wills has a number of drawbacks. That's why throughout this chapter, I emphasize the importance of finding a lawyer who specializes in estate planning. Such a lawyer is able to give you the advice and guidance you need to meet your goals, and to draw up a legally valid will that apportions your property according to your wishes. Depending on the complexity of the document, the lawyer's fee for making the will can range from $75 to $250 and up.

Where Should You Store Your Original Will?

You have several choices regarding the safekeeping of your will.

❏ **The lawyer's vault.** It is most common for the attorney who drew up the will to retain the original document in his or her vault, along with the wills of other clients.

❏ **A locked file or safe.** If you feel more comfortable keeping the original will in your possession, you can store it at home in a locked file or safe to which your heirs have access.

❏ **A safe deposit box.** A safe deposit box is not the best place to keep your will. When a bank becomes aware that the renter of a safe deposit box has passed away, the box is sealed until its contents can be officially inventoried. This enables the state to collect estate or inheritance taxes on any valuable assets that may have been stored in the safe deposit box. Unfortunately, it also delays access to the will. To avoid such delay, your will can be stored in a safe deposit box rented in your spouse's name, and your spouse's will can be kept in a box rented in your name.

❏ **Probate court.** In some localities, a will can be filed with the clerk of the probate court. Your heirs should be advised of this. After your death, your heirs can report to the court and initiate probate proceedings.

Regardless of where your will is stored, you may wish to keep a copy at home for easy reference. Remember that it is important for your heirs to know where the original will is kept. It is also important to review your will periodically—every two or three years—to make sure that the provisions conform with changing state and federal laws, as well as your own resources and wishes. Self-Study 18.2 will help you organize the data you need for the making of a will, and guide you in determining whether an existing will needs to be updated or replaced.

FIDUCIARIES

In your will, you can name one or more *fiduciaries*—people to whom you grant specific rights, duties, and powers to act in your behalf and carry out the provisions specified in your will. Other fiduciaries may be named as part of a trust document or appointed by a court after your death.

The principal fiduciaries are as follows:

❑ An *executor*—called a *personal representative* in some states—is responsible for carrying out the provisions of the will. Your executor must be named in your will.

❑ An *administrator* is a court-appointed fiduciary who is designated when someone dies intestate—in other words, without a will. An administrator is also appointed when a will does not name an executor, when a will cannot be located, or when a will is declared invalid.

❑ A *guardian* has the responsibility to care for a minor or an incompetent adult, to control his or her property, or to do both. Like an executor, a guardian should be named in your will.

❑ A *trustee* is responsible for managing the assets of a trust carefully and prudently. A trustee may be named in your will or in a separate trust document.

Before naming fiduciaries in your will, get the approval of those whom you have chosen to fill these roles. For every fiduciary you select, also choose an alternate, or successor, who will serve if your original choice is unable or unwilling to serve. These alternates should also be named in the will.

The Executor and Administrator

An *executor* (masculine) or *executrix* (feminine) is the person responsible for the management of property specified in the will until disposition of the estate is completed. Known in some states as a *personal representative*, the executor serves in a *fiduciary relationship* to the beneficiaries of the estate, meaning that the executor must comply with high standards of integrity and responsibility in managing the estate's property and carrying out the provisions of the will. The executor must make periodic reports to the probate court, and must actually make a final accounting to the court before being released from the fiduciary relationship.

The responsibilities of the executor include the following:

❑ To prepare an inventory of all estate assets.

❑ To pay all federal, state, and local taxes owed by the estate.

❑ To pay all of the estate's debts and expenses incurred during the administration of the estate.

❑ To decide on the validity of claims against the estate.

❑ To represent the estate in case of lawsuits.

❏ To fund and establish any trusts created under the will.

❏ To manage any other financial matters pertaining to the estate.

❏ To keep complete records of all transactions made on behalf of the estate or in accordance with the will.

❏ To distribute, according to the terms of the will, any estate assets that remain after all settlement obligations are met and all specific bequests are satisfied.

❏ To make a final accounting to the court and the beneficiaries.

Who should be the executor of your will? It is important to choose a competent executor who has your confidence. It is also vital to choose an alternate in case the executor is unable to serve in this capacity.

When selecting an executor, first consider the size of your estate. If the estate is relatively small, a spouse, a son, or a daughter can be the executor. If the estate is large and involves difficult tax and investment decisions, it would be best to select an estate lawyer or the trust department of a bank. In such a case, a spouse or other relative may be called upon to serve as a coexecutor.

Special qualities of an executor that should be examined include the ability to get along with your heirs; the ability to command respect; the availability and time needed to get the job done; and, finally, executive and administrative ability.

Before you select a professional fiduciary, discuss the fees, philosophy, and method of operation to be sure that the individual meets both your needs and those of your beneficiaries. You can change an executor during your lifetime, but once you die, your will is irrevocable, and only the probate court can name a replacement.

An *administrator* is appointed by a probate court at the request of a family when an individual dies without a will, when a will does not name an executor, when a will cannot be found, or when a will is declared invalid. The responsibilities of an administrator are the same as those of an executor.

The fees or commissions charged by executors vary from state to state. Your relatives would probably not accept a commission, but if your lawyer serves as your executor, he will charge a fee. The commission is computed on the gross value of the estate, including income that passes through the executor's hands. It is fixed by state law, and is payable only once during the administration of an estate. The following are examples of an executor's commissions:

5 percent on the first $100,000 ($5,000)

4 percent on the next $200,000 ($8,000)

3 percent on the next $700,000 ($21,000)

2.5 percent on the next $4,000,000

2 percent on any excess over $5,000,000

The commission on a $300,000 estate would, therefore, be $13,000—5 percent of $100,000 ($5,000) plus 4 percent of $200,000 ($8,000).

The Guardian

A *guardian* is a person who has the responsibility to care for a minor or an incompetent adult, to control the property of a minor or incompetent adult, or to do both. A will usually names the person who will serve as the guardian of minor children in the event of your death or the death of your spouse. But if the guardian or successor guardian you select is deemed incompetent by a probate court, the court has the power and authority to disregard the nomination set forth in the will, and to appoint another guardian who will serve the best interests of the individual requiring this care.

When selecting a guardian, many people gravitate toward relatives, particularly their own parents. However, estate attorneys caution against this. Your parents may make wonderful grandparents, but they may not wish or be able to assume the responsibility of child rearing. Moreover, you should not assume that a married sibling who is childless will want to act as guardian. Often, friends with children of about the same age are a fine choice. Frequently, friends make reciprocal agreements, in which each couple agrees to act as the guardian of the other's children. In any case, be sure that you check with the people you have selected before you name them in your will. Some lawyers think it wise to name guardians who reside in the same state, because legal complications may arise if you select nonresidents. It is certainly a good idea to name successor guardians in case your initial choices die or become divorced. And, of course, any guardians or successor guardians you choose should share your values and your child-rearing philosophy.

Guardianship lasts only until a child reaches the age of majority, typically age 18. At that age, the child becomes fully entitled to whatever property is in the estate. In many cases, it is wise to establish a trust that will manage the assets for a number of years. For instance, you might stipulate that the child will receive a weekly or monthly allowance at age 18, a third of the assets at age 25, half the balance at age 30, and the remainder at age 35.

The Trustee

The job of a trustee is to administer and distribute property held in a trust. (For more information on trusts, see Chapter 20.) Every trust requires that a person or institution maintains records, keeps custody of securities, and files whatever tax returns are necessary. Generally, such a job is long-term. Thus, the testator, or maker of the will, may designate one individual as the *first trustee,* and another individual or a bank as the *successor trustee.*

In the case of a living trust created during an individual's lifetime, that individual can act as trustee of his or her own trust. In such a situation, the individual does not want to give up management of his or her own affairs, but wants to be sure that if he or she becomes ill, becomes incapacitated, or dies suddenly, the terms of the trust will be carried out. Thus, a successor trustee is available to step in and carry on.

The most important job of a trustee is to manage the assets of the trust carefully and prudently for the benefit of the beneficiary or beneficiaries. Often, a trustee is given discretionary authority in deciding who should receive income from a trust or even, in some cases, whether to dip into the principal if income is insufficient to meet a beneficiary's needs. If, for example, an elderly person is in a nursing home and for a time has extremely large medical bills, the trustee may use not only the income from the trust, but also some of the principal to pay the medical bills.

Many individuals choose a relative or close friend as a trustee. If you are considering this course of action, weigh your decision carefully. An individual may not have the time or inclination to properly manage a trust fund and, even more important, may not have the background and knowledge to do so wisely.

If you do name an individual, remember to also name a successor trustee in case the first individual cannot fulfill his or her obligation. It is wise also to include a provision that, after your death, your spouse or another heir can name a successor to the original trustee.

While an individual family member or trusted friend probably will charge little or nothing to manage a trust, institutional managers do charge for this service. However, any fees paid are tax-deductible. In addition, institutional trustees provide the following advantages:

❏ The institution will most likely continue doing business in the same city and state for many years to come, while an individual may move.

❏ Trust officers devote their time to managing money, and are among the most knowledgeable people in handling trust funds.

❏ Your money is protected because banks and other financial institutions are subject to periodic state and federal audits, whereas individual trustees are not under any such scrutiny.

❏ An institution provides continuity in the management of your funds. If your trust officer is unable to continue handling your account, another trained and knowledgeable individual will be available.

THE SUPPLEMENTAL LETTER OF INSTRUCTIONS

Everyone who has a will should also have a *supplemental letter of instructions*. Designed to assist the executor as he or she carries out the provisions of the will, this letter should provide the following types of information:

❏ **Persons to be notified.** The supplemental letter of instructions should include the names, addresses, and telephone numbers of those persons who are to be notified at the time of your death—relatives, friends, and associates, for instance.

❏ **Location of the will.** The letter should include the names, addresses, and telephone numbers of your lawyer and the executor of your will, as well as the location of the will.

❏ **Location of vital documents.** The letter should specify the location of documents such as certificates of birth and marriage, veteran's discharge, and Social Security card, as well as past tax returns, paid bills, cancelled checks, and bank statements from the last several years.

❏ **Location of assets.** The letter should state the location of safe deposit boxes; stock and bond certificates; insurance policies; pension documents; bank accounts; and real property documents, such as mortgages, deeds, and titles.

❏ **Professional advisers.** The letter should include the names, addresses, and telephone numbers of your lawyer, accountant, stockbroker, insurance agent, banker or trust officer, and minister or rabbi.

❏ **Employment or business information.** The letter should state the name, address, and telephone number of your present or last employer, as well as instructions relative to any business enterprises you may own or in which you have an interest.

❏ **Personal valuables.** The letter should list your personal valuables—jewelry, collections, cameras, antiques, and home furnishings, for instance—and name the recipient of each item.

❏ **Funeral and burial instructions.** The letter should spell out instructions for the disposition of the body, the type of funeral service desired, and the charity to which any memorial donations should be made.

The form provided in Self-Study 18.3 will allow you to create a complete, well-organized supplemental letter of instructions by simply filling in the blanks. After you have completed your letter of instructions, make two copies and file the original with your will. Give one of the copies to your executor, and retain one in a place that is accessible to you and your spouse so that it may be kept up-to-date. If you are single, give one copy to your executor and one to a close friend or relative.

DURABLE POWER OF ATTORNEY

In addition to a will and a supplemental letter of instructions, you should provide for a durable power of attorney. As explained in Chapter 5, an ordinary *power of attorney* is a legal document in which you designate another person—a lawyer, relative, or friend—to act as your legal representative in financial transactions. This ordinary power of attorney will terminate immediately if you become incompetent or otherwise disabled. However, state law provides that a power of attorney can be worded so that in the event of the maker's disability, the holder of the power can continue to act on behalf of the person who granted the power. A power of attorney that contains this language is known as a *durable power of attorney*. A durable power of attorney may allow the holder of the power to:

❏ Handle banking transactions such as deposits and withdrawals.

❏ Buy, sell, or lease assets.

❏ Sue on the principal's behalf.

❏ Collect from creditors.

❏ Operate the principal's business.

After you have completed your will, ask your lawyer about drawing up a document that designates someone to assume durable power of attorney for you. When it is complete, give copies to family members, your lawyer, and the executor of your will. Just keep in mind that a durable power of attorney applies to financial affairs only. If you want to designate someone who can make health decisions for you in the event that you are unable to do so, you will need a *durable power of attorney for health care*, which is discussed on page 255. Any power of attorney can be revoked as long as its maker is competent to act.

ADVANCE DIRECTIVES

Through advance directives, your wishes about life support systems can be made known in the event that you become terminally ill or incompetent. These advance directives—which include the health care proxy, the living will, and the durable power of attorney for health care—can be drawn up by your attorney at the same time he or she draws up your will and durable power of attorney.

The Health Care Proxy

A *health care proxy* gives an individual other than you the power to decide about medical treatment on your behalf in the event that you lose the capacity to decide for yourself. Your agent will then be able to apply your wishes and instructions in the light of changing medical circumstances. A health care proxy is legally recognized in some states, but not all. Each spouse should have his or her own health care proxy. A health care proxy can be changed or revoked as long as you are competent to act.

The Living Will

A *living will* expresses *your own personal wishes* about medical treatment by requesting that your life not be prolonged by artificial means or "heroic measures" if there is no expectation of recovery. It is suggested that each individual or spouse have both a health care proxy and a living will. See Figure 18.1 for a sample living will.

FIGURE 18.1. A LIVING WILL

TO MY FAMILY, MY PHYSICIAN, MY LAWYER, MY CLERGYMAN
TO ANY MEDICAL FACILITY IN WHOSE CARE I HAPPEN TO BE
TO ANY INDIVIDUAL WHO MAY BECOME RESPONSIBLE FOR MY HEALTH, WELFARE, OR AFFAIRS

Death is as much a reality as birth, growth, maturity, and old age—it is the one certainty of life. If the time comes when I, _____ can no longer take part in
(please print)
decisions for my own future, let this statement stand as an expression of my wishes, while I am still of sound mind.

If the situation should arise in which there is no reasonable expectation of my recovery from physical or mental disability, I request that I be allowed to die and not be kept alive by artificial means or "heroic measures." I do not fear death itself as much as the indignities of deterioration, dependence, and hopeless pain. I, therefore, ask that medication be mercifully administered to me to alleviate suffering even though this may hasten the moment of death.

This request is made after careful consideration. I hope you who care for me will feel morally bound to follow its mandate. I recognize that this appears to place a heavy responsibility upon you, but it is with the intention of relieving you of such responsibility and of placing it upon myself in accordance with my strong convictions, that this statement is made.

Date_____   Signed_____

Witness_____   Witness_____
       (please print)   (signature)

Witness_____   Witness_____
       (please print)   (signature)

Copies of this request have been given to: _____

Directions for the Living Will

1. Sign and date before two witnesses. (This is to insure that you signed of your own free will and not under any pressure.)

2. If you have a doctor, give him a copy for your medical file and discuss it with him to make sure he is in agreement. Also give copies to those most likely to be concerned "if the time comes when you can no longer take part in decisions for your own future." Enter their names on the bottom lines of the living will. Keep the original nearby, easily and readily available.

3. Above all, discuss your intentions with those closest to you, now.

4. It is a good idea to look over your living will once a year, redate it, and initial the new date to make it clear that your wishes are unchanged.

5. Make a copy of the living will above for your spouse, if he or she desires. Attach the copy to this page for future reference.

Source: The *Living Will* and directions appeared in *Your Vital Papers Logbook,* 1981 edition, and are reprinted with the permission of Action for Independent Maturity, a division of the American Association of Retired Persons.

The Durable Power of Attorney for Health Care

A *durable power of attorney for health care* is a signed, dated, and witnessed document that gives someone else the power to make medical decisions for you if you are unable to make them for yourself. This document is sometimes combined with the durable power of attorney that was discussed previously. This directive offers a potentially useful legal instrument by which you can protect your right to refuse life-sustaining procedures in the event of a hopeless condition and incapacity to make decisions. Without a durable power of attorney for health care, your physician or hospital will have to search for a family member or other individual, and ask the court to approve that person's right to act in your behalf.

ANATOMICAL GIFTS

The donation of human organs can save lives and ease suffering. Through organ transplants, the life of a dying patient can be sustained. Transplant gifts include the heart, lungs, kidneys, pancreas, liver, corneas, skin, and bone. Nationwide, it has been estimated that more than 50,000 patients could benefit from transplants if gift organs were available.

If you wish to have your organs donated, you can sign and carry an organ donor card, or you can indicate your wish to donate organs by marking the appropriate spot on your driver's license. Discuss your wishes with members of your family. Although the decision to donate organs—your own or those of another family member—may be a difficult one, many families find that when faced with the loss of a loved one, donating organs for transplantation provides consolation and comfort.

Everyone should be considered a potential donor, regardless of age or medical history. The suitability of donated organs and tissues will be determined by the medical team at the time of the donation.

The following information may help you decide whether you should become a donor:

❑ Organ donation does not affect or delay customary funeral arrangements.

❑ The donation involves no cost or payment.

❑ Funeral expenses and hospital expenses incurred prior to the donation of organs remain the responsibility of the donor's family.

❑ Donation of the body to a medical school can save funeral expenses. Contact a medical school in your community.

❑ Individuals under the age of 18 may sign an organ donor card with the consent of a parent or legal guardian.

❑ It is not necessary to mention organ donation in your will.

For further information about organ donation, contact The United Network for Organ Sharing (UNOS) by mail or phone, or visit their website. (See the Resources section.)

Although estate planning can be a difficult task, and a time-consuming one as well, the results are well worth the effort. Once your will and other related documents have been prepared with care and thought, you will have the peace of mind that comes with knowing that your affairs are in order, that your personal requests will be followed in the event of illness, and that your dependents will be provided for in the manner that you wish.

Self-Study 18.1
DATA FOR YOUR ESTATE PLAN

1. Refer to your net worth statement, which you prepared in Chapter 10, Worksheet 10.1. Review this inventory to be sure that the list of assets is complete and that the values are up-to-date.

2. List your heirs, including spouse, children, grandchildren, relatives, charities, and other beneficiaries you wish to consider. Based upon individual needs, estimate the proportion of your assets each beneficiary should receive. (Set up a worksheet.)

3. Estimate the cash required to cover costs of last illness, funeral expenses, and settlement costs. Remember that costs of illness may be covered in part or in full by medical insurance.

   $_____

4. List the names, addresses, and telephone numbers of two or three lawyers in your area who specialize in estate planning. You will need a lawyer's assistance in selecting appropriate estate planning tools.

   _____   _____

   _____   _____

   _____   _____

   _____   _____

   _____   _____

   _____   _____

   _____   _____

   _____   _____

5. Working with your lawyer, select the estate planning tools you will need to reach your objectives.

Self-Study 18.2
DATA FOR YOUR WILL

1. If you have no will and wish to have a lawyer draw one up for you, contact a qualified lawyer and arrange to have an estate planning conference. In preparation for this conference, you should assemble all the facts concerning your estate and your family. Following is a list of the types of data you should assemble:

- ❏ Family information
- ❏ Beneficiary information
- ❏ Executor, guardian, trustee information
- ❏ Asset information

2. If you have a will, check your answers to the questions that appear below. You may have to amend your will by adding a codicil. A codicil must be signed with the same formality as a will. If the changes are major, it may be wiser to draw up a new will.

Are the beneficiaries you named still alive and still worthy of your bequest?	❏ Yes	❏ No
Have you moved to another state since making this will?	❏ Yes	❏ No
Are you now living in a community property state?	❏ Yes	❏ No
Do you still want to keep the same executor and alternate executor?	❏ Yes	❏ No
Do you still own the same assets mentioned in your will?	❏ Yes	❏ No
Do you wish to take advantage of, and are you taking advantage of the maximum marital deduction allowable under the Economic Recovery Tax Act of 1981? (See Chapter 19.)	❏ Yes	❏ No
Should this will be reviewed with your lawyer?	❏ Yes	❏ No

ESTATE PLANNING CONFERENCE

After setting up an appointment with the estate lawyer you have selected, you should compile the basic information that you will need for the conference.

BASIC INFORMATION FOR ESTATE PLANNING CONFERENCE

FAMILY INFORMATION	Date _____

PERSONAL

Full legal name:

_____

Home address:

_____

_____

Home phone number:

_____

Birth date:

_____

Employers (last two years):

_____

_____

Social Security number:

_____

Veteran? ❑ Yes   ❑ No   If yes, service number: _____

Disability? ❑ Yes   ❑ No   ❑ Service connected   ❑ Nonservice connected

Marital status: ❑ Single   ❑ Married   ❑ Widowed   ❑ Separated   ❑ Divorced

Do you have a will?   ❑ Yes   ❑ No   If married, does spouse have a will?   ❑ Yes   ❑ No

Full legal name of spouse:

_____

Home address (if different from above):

_____

_____

Birth date of spouse:

_____

Social Security number of spouse:

_____

Home phone: _____

Veteran? ❑ Yes   ❑ No   If yes, service number: _____

Disability? ❑ Yes   ❑ No   ❑ Service connected   ❑ Nonservice connected

CHILDREN (including those legally adopted)

First child's name:

_____

Address:

_____

_____

Phone:

_____

Date of birth:

_____

Extent of dependency:

_____

Second child's name:

_____

Address:

_____

_____

Phone:

_____

Date of birth:

_____

Extent of dependency:

_____

Third child's name:

_____

Address:

_____

_____

Phone:

_____

Date of birth:

_____

Extent of dependency:

_____

Fourth child's name:

_____

Address:

_____

_____

Phone:

_____

Date of birth:

_____

Extent of dependency:

_____

PARENTS

Father's name: *Mother's name:*

_____   _____

Address: Address (if different):

_____   _____

_____   _____

_____   _____

Phone: Phone (if different):

_____   _____

Date of birth: Date of birth:

_____   _____

Extent of dependency: Extent of dependency:

_____   _____

BROTHERS AND SISTERS

Sibling's name: *Sibling's name:*

_____   _____

Address: Address:

_____   _____

_____   _____

_____   _____

Phone: Phone:

_____   _____

Date of birth: Date of birth:

_____   _____

Extent of dependency: Extent of dependency:

_____   _____

BROTHERS AND SISTERS *(continued)*

Sibling's name:

_____

Address:

_____

_____

_____

Phone:

_____

Date of birth:

_____

Extent of dependency:

_____

Sibling's name:

_____

Address:

_____

_____

_____

Phone:

_____

Date of birth:

_____

Extent of dependency:

_____

OTHER NEXT OF KIN *(nieces, nephews, etc.)*

Name of kin:

_____

Relationship:_____
Address:

_____

Phone:

_____

Date of birth:

_____

Extent of dependency:

_____

Name of kin:

_____

Relationship:_____
Address:

_____

Phone:

_____

Date of birth:

_____

Extent of dependency:

_____

ASSET INFORMATION   As of _____

ANNUAL INCOME

Salary _____   Investment income _____

CASH AND INVESTMENT DISTRIBUTION

Checking Accounts

			Check ownership		
Name of institution	Account number	Amount	Joint	Husband	Wife
_____	_____	_____	❑	❑	❑

Branch: _____   Phone: _____

| _____ | _____ | _____ | ❑ | ❑ | ❑ |

Branch: _____   Phone: _____

Savings Accounts

			Joint	Husband	Wife
Name of institution	Account number	Amount			
_____	_____	_____	❑	❑	❑

Branch: _____   Phone: _____

| _____ | _____ | _____ | ❑ | ❑ | ❑ |

Branch: _____   Phone: _____

Stocks and Bonds

			Joint	Husband	Wife
Name of investment firm	Account number	Amount			
_____	_____	_____	❑	❑	❑

Contact: _____   Phone: _____

Location of account statements: _____

| _____ | _____ | _____ | ❑ | ❑ | ❑ |

Contact: _____   Phone: _____

Location of account statements: _____

% of Investments: ❑ Individual stocks _____%   ❑ Mutual Funds _____%   ❑ Bonds _____%

Real Property

		Check ownership		
Address of Residence/Investment Property:		Joint	Husband	Wife

Primary_____   Purchase cost: _____   ❏   ❏   ❏

_____   Current value:_____

Secondary_____   Purchase cost: _____   ❏   ❏   ❏

_____   Current value:_____

Investment_____   Purchase cost: _____   ❏   ❏   ❏

_____   Current value:_____

Investment_____   Purchase cost: _____   ❏   ❏   ❏

_____   Current value:_____

Life Insurance Policies

Company:_____   Broker:_____

Phone: _____   Broker's phone: _____

Policy number:_____   Policy type:_____

Insured:_____   Owner: _____

Face value:_____   Cash value: _____

Outstanding loans against policy? ❏ Yes   ❏ No   Amount:_____

Names of beneficiaries: _____

_____   _____

Company:_____   Broker:_____

Phone: _____   Broker's phone: _____

Policy number:_____   Policy type:_____

Insured:_____   Owner: _____

Face value:_____   Cash value: _____

Outstanding loans against policy? ❏ Yes   ❏ No   Amount:_____

Names of beneficiaries:_____

_____   _____

Privately Held Business Interests (Partnership, limited partnership, corporate)

Type of business	Original investment	Current value	Check ownership		
			Joint	Husband	Wife
_____	_____	_____	❑	❑	❑
Contact: _____ Phone:_____					
_____	_____	_____	❑	❑	❑
Contact: _____ Phone:_____					
_____	_____	_____	❑	❑	❑
Contact: _____ Phone:_____					
_____	_____	_____	❑	❑	❑
Contact: _____ Phone:_____					

Executor, Guardian, Trustee Information

The following person and/or bank trust department should be the executor of my estate:

Name:_____   Alternate:_____

Address:_____   Address:_____

_____   _____

Phone: _____   Phone: _____

The following person(s) should be the guardian(s) of my children:

Name:_____   Alternate:_____

Address:_____   Address:_____

_____   _____

Phone:_____   Phone:_____

The following person and/or bank trust department should be the trustee for any established trust:

Name:_____   Alternate:_____

Address:_____   Address:_____

_____   _____

Phone:_____   Phone:_____

Beneficiary Information

Individual or charity name	Phone number	Bequest: $ or % of estate
_____	_____	_____
_____	_____	_____
_____	_____	_____
_____	_____	_____

Personal Property (Autos, furniture, jewelry, furs, hobby items, etc.)

Check ownership

Item	Purchase cost	Current value	Joint	Husband	Wife
_____	_____	_____	❑	❑	❑
_____	_____	_____	❑	❑	❑
_____	_____	_____	❑	❑	❑
_____	_____	_____	❑	❑	❑
_____	_____	_____	❑	❑	❑
_____	_____	_____	❑	❑	❑
_____	_____	_____	❑	❑	❑
_____	_____	_____	❑	❑	❑
_____	_____	_____	❑	❑	❑

Liabilities (Loans, mortgages, consumer credit, etc.)

Check debtor

	Type of debt	Joint	Husband	Wife

Creditor: _____ Type of debt _____ ❑ ❑ ❑

Account number: _____ Amount due: _____

Interest rate: _____% Date due: _____

Contact: _____ Phone: _____

Creditor: _____ _____ ❑ ❑ ❑

Account number: _____ Amount due: _____

Interest rate: _____% Date due: _____

Contact: _____ Phone: _____

Self-Study 18.3

SUPPLEMENTAL LETTER OF INSTRUCTIONS

Prepare a separate Supplemental Letter of Instructions by filling in the required information. Data for the Supplemental Letter of Instructions can be taken from the Inventory of Personal and Financial Data, beginning on page 331.

IMPORTANT NAMES AND ADDRESSES

Husband's
Name:_____

Wife's
Name:_____

Address:_____

Address:_____

_____

_____

_____

_____

Phone:_____

Phone:_____

Persons to be notified of death

Name:_____   Phone:_____

Name:_____   Phone:_____

Name:_____   Phone:_____

Name:_____   Phone:_____

Name:_____   Phone:_____

Location of the original will

Husband's
Name:_____

Wife's
Name:_____

Address:_____

Address:_____

_____

_____

_____

_____

Phone:_____

Phone:_____

❑ Safe deposit box   ❑ Lawyer   ❑ Safe deposit box   ❑ Lawyer

❑ Bank trust department   ❑ Executor   ❑ Bank trust department   ❑ Executor

VITAL DOCUMENT INFORMATION

Birth certificate location	**Husband**	**Wife**
Birthdate		
Birthplace		
Father's name		
Mother's name		

Location of veteran's discharge certificate	**Husband**	**Wife**
Service serial number		
Date discharged		
Place discharged		

Location of Social Security card

Social Security number

Location of marriage certificate

Date married

Place married

Prior marriages

Names; dates

How terminated

Location of financial documents

Paid bills

Past tax returns

Cancelled checks

Location of assets

Safe deposit boxes

Stock and bond certificates

Insurance policies

Pension documents

Bank accounts and books

Real property documents

My Professional Advisers

Lawyer's
Name:_____

Address:_____

_____

_____

Phone:_____

Insurance Agent's
Name:_____

Address:_____

_____

_____

Phone:_____

Banker's
Name:_____

Address:_____

_____

_____

Phone:_____

Accountant's
Name:_____

Address:_____

_____

_____

Phone:_____

Broker's
Name:_____

Address:_____

_____

_____

Phone:_____

Clergyman's
Name:_____

Address:_____

_____

_____

Phone:_____

Employment or Business Data

Present
Employer:_____

Address:_____

_____

_____

Phone:_____

Last
Employer:_____

Address:_____

_____

_____

Phone:_____

Personal Valuables

List your personal valuables (e.g., jewelry, collections, cameras, antiques, home furnishings) and name the recipient for each item.

Item	Recipient
_____	_____
_____	_____
_____	_____
_____	_____
_____	_____
_____	_____
_____	_____
_____	_____
_____	_____
_____	_____
_____	_____
_____	_____
_____	_____
_____	_____
_____	_____
_____	_____
_____	_____
_____	_____

Item	**Recipient**
_____	_____
_____	_____
_____	_____
_____	_____
_____	_____
_____	_____
_____	_____
_____	_____
_____	_____
_____	_____
_____	_____
_____	_____
_____	_____
_____	_____
_____	_____
_____	_____
_____	_____

Funeral and Burial Instructions

See Self-Study 22.1: Instructions for Your Survivors, on page 300.

Signature _____ Date _____

Signature _____ Date _____

19

MINIMIZING
ESTATE *and* GIFT TAXES

The *federal estate tax* was signed into law by President Woodrow Wilson in 1916 to help finance World War I, and has been in effect ever since. The tax is paid to the federal government by the executor of the estate of the deceased. Some states also tax estates, but most states levy an *inheritance tax,* which is paid by the inheritor rather than the estate. Some wills specify that the inheritance taxes be paid out of the estate's funds in order to minimize the shrinkage of an individual's inheritance. The federal estate tax and state inheritance and estate taxes are referred to as *death taxes.*

In addition to taxing estates, the federal government levies a gift tax that applies to transfers of gifts between living individuals. Gift taxes are imposed in order to make the taxation of estates and gifts equitable. If there were no gift tax, wealthy individuals could make large gifts immediately prior to death, thus reducing their estates and the taxes on those estates. The average citizen, on the other hand, has to maintain maximum assets until death; the estate tax is, therefore, levied on all accumulated property.

Prior to 1976, the gift and estate taxes were separate. In 1976, the federal government combined the gift and estate tax schedule and created a single schedule called the Federal Unified Gift and Estate Tax System.

DEDUCTIONS AND EXCLUSIONS FROM ESTATE AND GIFT TAXES

The Economic Recovery Tax Act (ERTA) of 1981, along with the Taxpayer Relief Act of 1997, made several sweeping changes that affected estate- and gift-tax-related deductions and exclusions.

Unlimited Marital Deduction

The single most significant change in the tax structure has been the unlimited marital deduction, whereby all transfers between husband and wife became free of estate taxes. This allows estates of *any* size to be passed tax-free from spouse to spouse. This change simplifies estate planning for the initial transfer from one spouse to another, but requires very careful planning for the transfer when the surviving spouse dies.

Tax-Free Transfers to a Beneficiary Aside From Spouse

From 1987 through 1997, the amount of an estate that could pass tax-free to any beneficiary was $600,000. The Taxpayer Relief Act of 1997 increased the $600,000 exemption to $625,000 in 1998; to $650,00 in 1999; and to $675,000 in 2000 and 2001. Table 19.1 shows future increases. The new law does not change the unlimited marital deduction rule that permits a tax-free transfer of any amount to a spouse.

TABLE 19.1

CHANGES IN ESTATE TAX EXEMPTION	
Year of Death	**Tax-Free Amount**
2001–2002	$ 675,000
2002–2003	$1,000,000
2004–2005	$1,500,000
2006–2008	$2,000,000
2009	$3,500,000
2010	No limit[a]
2011	$1,000,000

[a] Anyone who dies in 2010 can leave any amount to heirs with no tax due. But unless Congress acts before 2011, the tax-exempt amount will return to the 2002 level of $1,000,000.

The Annual Gift Tax Exclusion

Since 1981, the annual gift tax exclusion has been $10,000 per donee. This means that each member of a married couple can give $10,000 per donee—for a total of $20,000 per donee per couple—every year, without the recipient paying income tax on the gift. This money can be given to either an individual, such as a child, or a charity.

ESTATE AND GIFT TAX RATES

As explained earlier, in 2002, $1 million of an estate can pass tax-free to a beneficiary after the death of an estate owner. Furthermore, during the estate owner's lifetime, on a yearly basis, he or she can give $10,000 as a gift to another individual without that person being taxed. Anything above these amounts is subject to taxes.

Understanding How Estate Taxation Works

Until ERTA 1981, the maximum tax rate on the taxable portion of estates and gifts was 70 percent. ERTA set the maximum tax rate on estates and gifts at 55 percent, effective 1985, with the tax rate starting at 37 percent.

Estate taxes are due within nine months of death, and the rate of taxation increases as the estate increases. In addition to any potential federal tax, most states impose their own gift, estate, and/or inheritance tax. These state taxes should be taken into consideration when an individual is planning his or her estate.

Table 19.2 explains how the Federal Unified Gift and Estate Tax is calculated. Columns 1 and 2 show the lower and upper limits of the net taxable value of an estate at each level of taxation. For instance, the lower and upper limits of the first level are $1,000,000 and $1,250,000.

Column 3 shows the tax due for every amount that falls between the lower and upper limits, and Column 4 shows the marginal tax rate for any amount over the lower limit of each level. To compute taxes at any level, add the taxes due on any excess over the lower limit (Column 1) to the taxes due as shown in Column 3.

Consider an estate with a net taxable value of $1,200,000. If you look again at the first level, you'll see that this amount falls between $1,000,000 (the lower limit shown in Column 1) and $1,250,000 (the upper limit shown in Column 2). The taxable value of the estate above the lower limit is $200,000 ($1,200,000 – $1,000,000 = $200,000). $200,000 multiplied by 41 percent—

the marginal tax rate at that level—equals $82,000, which is then added to the base amount of $345,800, shown in Column 3. Therefore, the total estate tax due is $427,800. ($345,800 + $82,000 = $427,800.)

Case Studies in Estate Planning

The Federal Unified Gift and Estate Tax System can be intimidating to the average person who wants to understand how his or her estate may be diminished as it is passed on to heirs. The following case histories show how the system affects small, medium-sized, and large estates.

Small Estates ($1,000,000 or less)

If an estate is valued at $1,000,000 or less, assets can be held jointly with the right of survivorship. Each will can leave all property to the surviving spouse or to children and/or grandchildren. Since up to $1,000,000 can pass tax-free, a small estate avoids estate taxes.

Medium-Sized Estates ($1,000,000 to $2,000,000)

Let's assume that an individual with a wife and two children has an estate that totals $2,000,000.

Most of the assets of that estate—home, insurance, investments—are owned jointly with the right of survivorship. If the husband were to die, leaving everything to his wife under the unlimited marital deduction, the wife would then possess assets worth $2,000,000.

Under federal law, up to $1,000,000 can pass tax-free from a decedent to beneficiaries. In this case, the wife possesses $2,000,000, and when she dies, she can pass $1,000,000 of this total to her children tax-free, but the remaining $1,000,000 is taxable.

With planning, all the taxes can be saved and the money transferred to the children. Each spouse should have a maximum of $1,000,000 of the assets held in sole ownership or tenancy in common. An attorney can set up a trust in each spouse's will to absorb $1,000,000 if the individual should die. The trust will guarantee income to the surviving spouse for life from the $1,000,000 invested by the trust, specifying that when the surviving spouse dies, the $1,000,000 should pass to the children. Since each spouse can legally pass up to $1,000,000 to the children tax-free, no taxes will be paid on this estate, and either spouse can enjoy lifetime income from the trust if the other spouse dies.

TABLE 19.2

Net Taxable Estate		Base Amount Taxes Due (3)	Marginal Tax Rate for Excess Over Lower Limit (4)
UNIFIED FEDERAL ESTATE AND GIFT TAX RATES, 2002			
Lower Limit (1)	Upper Limit (2)		
$1,000,000	$ 1,250,000	$ 345,800	41%
$1,250,000	$ 1,500,000	$ 448,300	43%
$1,500,000	$ 2,000,000	$ 555,800	45%
$2,000,000	$ 2,500,000	$ 780,500	49%
$2,500,000	—	$1,025,800	50%[a]

[a] The top marginal rate will be reduced between the years 2003 and 2009 according to the Economic Growth and Tax Relief Reconciliation Act of 2001.

Large Estates (Over $2,000,000)

If a couple's estate is valued at more than $2,000,000, it is necessary to pay an estate tax in accordance with the figures in Table 19.2. With an estate of this size or larger, it is wise to consult with an estate attorney and/or an accountant.

OPTIONS FOR MINIMIZING ESTATE TAXES

Only a small number of all estates are taxed. In fact, of all the people who died and left estates in 2001, less than 2 *percent* had estates large enough to be subject to estate taxes. Nevertheless, for some people, estate taxes can take a big chunk out of the assets left to beneficiaries. Fortunately, there are a number of ways in which people with medium-sized and large estates can help minimize estate taxes.

Give Gifts During Your Lifetime

If you have a taxable estate, consider sharing your wealth with children, grandchildren, a charity, or an institution to decrease the total estate. As explained earlier in the chapter, this involves the option of giving $10,000 as an individual gift, or $20,000 as a couple, to each child, grandchild, and/or charity per year, *tax-free*. Regular gift giving of this magnitude can reduce your estate to the $1,000,000 level that is exempt from federal estate taxes for 2002 to 2003. At the same time, you will be able to see your family enjoy your largess while you are still alive. Naturally, you must be careful to retain enough of your assets to insure your own secure retirement.

Purchase a Life Insurance Policy

Some individuals prefer to retain all their assets rather than sharing their wealth during their lives. To accommodate this choice, a new life insurance policy can be bought. The new policy should be large enough to provide money at death to pay all estate taxes. If you choose this route, you can also create a life insurance trust to receive the proceeds of the policy at your death. The money will not be part of your estate when you die. After you have purchased a new policy, you can help your intended heirs pay the policy premiums by making annual tax-free gifts to them.

Give Money to a Charity

Another route is to leave a portion of your estate to a favorite charity in the form of a charitable remainder trust. (See Chapter 20.) You can arrange to receive annual income from the trust as long as you or your spouse live, and can also benefit from an income tax deduction for a charitable gift. The amount you leave to the charity in the trust will reduce your taxable estate when you die. The income from the trust can be given as annual gifts to your heirs if you do not need the money.

Set Up Bypass or Credit-Shelter Trusts

Married couples have the option of creating his-and-her trusts, known as *bypass trusts* or *credit-shelter trusts* because they bypass estate taxes. Each spouse should have a maximum of $1,000,000 of assets held in sole ownership or tenancy in common. (See Chapter 5.) The estate attorney can then set up a trust in each spouse's will to absorb $1,000,000 if the individual should die. The trust will guarantee income to the surviving spouse for life from the $1,000,000 invested by the trustee, specifying that when the surviving spouse dies, the $1,000,000 will pass to the children or to other heirs. Since each spouse can legally pass up to $1,000,000 to the heirs tax-free, no taxes will be paid on this estate, and either spouse can enjoy lifetime income from the trust if one spouse dies.

This option is illustrated in Table 19.3. Each member of the couple represented in the table owns half of their primary residence as tenants in common, a form of joint ownership described in Chapter 5. All other assets have been divided between the spouses so that each owns 50 percent of their *total* assets. For any couple, the net tax savings of this strategy—which can be large—will depend on the size of the estate.

Set Up a Family Limited Partnership

In a family limited partnership, parents, children, and other relatives own assets together. Usually, the parents are the general partners, which gives them the power to make decisions about the assets, and the other family members are limited partners with no control over asset management. Over time, assets owned by the parents are transferred to the other family members, thus increasing asset ownership for children and/or relatives. Eventually, the estate of the parents is reduced, thus lowering or eliminating an estate tax when death occurs.

Often, family limited partnerships are used to hold business interests and real estate, although they may also be used to hold other assets, such as stocks and bonds. Family businesses get a $1.3 million estate-tax exemption.

TABLE 19.3.

		With Planning (Assets Held in Sole Ownership or Tenancy in Common)	
CASE STUDY IN ESTATE PLANNING			
Asset	Survivor's **Estate**	**Husband**	**Wife**
Cash	$ 50,000	$ 25,000	$ 25,000
Certificates of Deposit	$ 100,000	—	$ 100,000
Stocks	$ 300,000	$ 250,000	$ 50,000
Municipal Bonds	$ 200,000	$ 50,000	$ 150,000
Mutual Funds	$ 300,000	$ 200,000	$ 100,000
Primary Residence	$ 600,000	$ 300,000	$ 300,000
Vacation Home	$ 250,000	$ 125,000	$ 125,000
Individual Retirement Accounts	$ 100,000	$ 50,000	$ 50,000
Autos, Furniture, Jewelry	$ 100,000	—	$ 100,000
Total	$2,000,000	$1,000,000	$1,000,000

Disclaim Insurance, Inheritances, and Payouts

When an individual receives a life insurance settlement, inherits money, or receives a payout from a tax-deferred annuity, such as a 403(b) or 401(k) plan, the individual can *disclaim* (refuse to accept) the money, and allow it to go to the alternative beneficiary or beneficiaries. This keeps the estate from growing larger, enabling the individual to reduce potential estate taxes at the time of his or her death.

Over the last two decades, changing laws have meant that most estates escape federal estate tax. In addition, individuals with estates large enough to be taxed can minimize taxation through smart estate planning. But it is important to understand that such planning is not a do-it-yourself activity. It requires the expertise of a qualified estate planning attorney who will set up your financial affairs in a way that will best serve both your own needs and those of your heirs.

Self-study 19.1
UNDERSTANDING YOUR ESTATE TAXES

1. Assume that your estate is worth $350,000. Will the federal government levy an estate tax?

   ❑ Yes   ❑ No

   Explain:_____

   _____

   _____

   _____

   _____

   _____

   _____

   _____

2. Would your answer change if the estate were worth $1,500,000?   ❑ Yes   ❑ No

   Explain:_____

   _____

   _____

   _____

   _____

   _____

   _____

   _____

20

TRUSTS

An important tool of estate planning, a trust is a legal entity that can own, hold, and pay out assets. A trust is similar to a life insurance policy in that the trust property is ultimately distributed to beneficiaries under the terms of the trust agreement. A major benefit of a trust is that the property passes to beneficiaries outside an individual's will, and thus avoids probate. A trust can also result in tax savings.

WHAT IS A TRUST?

A *trust* is a legal entity consisting of assets that are administered by an individual or an institution for a beneficiary or beneficiaries, who may be the owner of the trust, the children or spouse of the owner, or others. Any asset you own—including cash; securities; real estate; and proceeds of life insurance, annuities, or pension funds—can be put into a trust. The *trustee*, who manages the trust, can then invest these assets according to the instructions of the creator of the trust, or *truster*.

USES OF TRUSTS

Depending on the type of trust you choose and on your own circumstances, a trust can help you achieve any one of a number of financial goals. Among the possible uses of trusts are the following:

❏ **To Provide Management of Funds Left to a Spouse.** A spouse may lack the ability or the knowledge needed to manage a large sum of money effectively. In such a case, assets can be set up in a trust to be managed by a trustee who does have this specialized knowledge and experience. Your spouse will thus be guaranteed an income for life. At the spouse's death, the assets in the trust can be distributed to your children and/or grandchildren, or to any other beneficiary you name.

❏ **To Hold Money Until a Child Reaches Maturity.** Funds can be set aside in a trust until a child reaches maturity, usually 18 years of age. If you believe that this is too tender an age for your child to assume the responsibility of money management, you can provide that the funds be paid out in a series of installments, such as the first third at age 25, the second third at age 30, and the last third at age 35. Or you can stipulate that the funds be paid out in a lump sum either at a specified age or at the discretion of the trustee.

❑ **To Provide for a Mentally or Physically Challenged Child.** In the case of a mentally or physically challenged child, you may wish to set up a trust that would provide income for the life of the child. In this way, you can insure that the individual will have spending money, clothes, and incidentals. Keep in mind that federal and state programs pay for basic residential and medical costs for mentally and physically challenged children and adults.

❑ **To Save on Estate Taxes.** The Economic Recovery Tax Act of 1981 provides for an unlimited marital deduction, which means that any assets left to a spouse are completely untaxed. However, when the spouse dies, if the amount in the estate exceeds the limits set up by law—$1,000,000 at this time—taxes are imposed. (See Chapter 19 for details.) Fortunately, the spouse's will can set up a trust for the children and/or grandchildren for the amount that exceeds the tax-free portion.

❑ **To Protect the Children of a First Marriage When a Second Marriage Takes Place.** Before marrying a second time, it is essential that you protect the children of your first marriage. This can be done by setting up a trust that will provide your children first with income, particularly during their college years, and ultimately with the principal.

❑ **To Pay for a Child's College Education or Other Needs.** Property can be placed in a trust for a minor child, either for the purpose of financing education or for other needs, such as medical emergencies. The trust can be set up so that income from trust property can be distributed to the child while he or she is a minor. Then, at age 21, the beneficiary can receive all the trust assets and accumulated trust earnings.

❑ **To Avoid Probate.** Probate, the court procedure for validating a will and disposing of an estate at death, is often a very costly and time-consuming process, as well as one that makes your estate affairs part of public proceedings. Many people place assets in a living trust so that they can transfer ownership to others while bypassing the probate system.

Any of these goals can be achieved through setting up a trust. However, this is not a do-it-yourself project. You must rely upon the guidance of an experienced lawyer who specializes in estate planning and trusts. (To help determine if a trust will be useful in your estate planning, see Self-Study 20.1.)

TYPES OF TRUSTS

The two major types of trusts are the living trust and the testamentary trust. A living trust, also known as an *inter vivos trust*, goes into effect while you are still living. (The Latin words *inter vivos* mean "among the living.") The arrangements for a testamentary trust are made in your will, and the trust comes into being after your death. Other types of trusts include the charitable remainder trust, the Totten trust, and those trusts set up under the Uniform Gifts to Minors Act and the Uniform Transfers to Minors Act.

Living Trusts

Living trusts are of two types. A *revocable living trust* is one that can be changed or cancelled during your lifetime, which is a distinct advantage. An *irrevocable living trust* is one that cannot be amended or revoked during your lifetime.

When to Use a Living Trust

Living trusts are useful if your wealth is substantial enough to warrant professional management; if you are the key person in a family business; or if you do not have a spouse or child capable of managing your affairs in the event that you become incapacitated. It is advisable to combine a durable power of attorney (see page 253) with a living trust.

How to Implement a Living Trust

You may immediately place the desired assets in your living trust. Alternatively, you may leave it empty but assign someone durable power of attorney with instructions to pour all your money into the trust if you become incompetent or die. With a revocable living trust, you control the assets while you are alive and competent. You can receive income from the trust, which is taxable to you. When you die, the assets will pass to your heirs without going through probate.

Comparing Revocable and Irrevocable Living Trusts

Each of the two types of living trusts has its own advantages and disadvantages. The *advantages* of a revocable living trust are as follows:

❑ It offers flexibility because it can be changed or cancelled during your lifetime.

❑ It avoids probate when assets are transferred into the trust before your death.

❑ It insures that your assets will be managed by someone in whom you have confidence if you become unable to manage them yourself.

❑ It enables you to see how well your trustee functions, and to make changes if necessary.

The *disadvantages* of a revocable living trust are as follows:

❑ Income earned by the trust is subject to income tax.

❑ When you die, trust assets are subject to estate tax.

❑ Setting up the trust involves a legal fee.

The *advantages* of an irrevocable living trust are as follows:

❑ It can shift income from the trust to a beneficiary in a lower tax bracket, resulting in income tax savings.

❑ Capital appreciation of trust assets is free of estate taxes when you die.

❑ It avoids probate when assets are transferred into the trust before death.

The *disadvantages* of an irrevocable living trust are as follows:

❑ You lose control of the trust assets forever.

❑ If the property is sold after your death, the profit is subject to income taxes.

❑ Setting up the trust agreement involves a legal fee as well as the annual cost of commissions charged by the trustee.

Testamentary Trusts

A *testamentary trust* is created by the terms of a will. It, therefore, takes effect some time after your death and, consequently, is irrevocable. Estate planning is usually directed toward the creation of testamentary trusts rather than living trusts.

Examples of some testamentary trusts include the following:

Qualified Terminable Interest Property Trust (or Q-Tip)

The *Q-Tip* enables you to provide income for your spouse for his or her lifetime, and allows you, the maker of the trust, to designate how the property will be distributed upon your spouse's death. The Q-Tip prevents your spouse from having access to the principal, and prevents your assets from going to someone your spouse later marries. If you are in a second marriage, the Q-tip can also insure that your assets will go to the children of your first marriage.

Standard Marital Trust

A *standard marital trust* provides trust benefits to your spouse for life. After the death of your spouse, your children and/or grandchildren will become the beneficiaries.

Sprinkling Trust

A *sprinkling trust* allows the trustee to distribute trust income to your children or other beneficiaries according to their needs, rather than according to a specific formula. If one beneficiary has a greater need than another, the trustee has the power to "sprinkle" more of the money to the needier beneficiary.

Life Insurance Trust

The *life insurance trust* is designed to accept the proceeds of a life insurance policy of the deceased.

Other Types of Trusts

Some trusts have characteristics of both the irrevocable and revocable trusts, and others are simply custodial accounts for minors. Examples of some of these are the following:

Charitable Remainder Trusts

To set up a *charitable remainder trust*, a donor places assets into an irrevocable trust and names a trustee, who invests the assets. The trust then provides an income to the beneficiaries for life, or for a set term of years. When the last beneficiary dies or the trust's term ends, the trust dissolves and the remaining assets are distributed to the specified charitable organization.

The exact manner in which the trust operates will depend upon the way you set it up. If set up as a living trust, it will give you an immediate tax deduction for your charitable contribution, and will also provide income for you and/or your family while the property is in trust. Then, at some future date—say at your death, or ten, twenty, or twenty-five years later—the charity or institution will receive the trust's assets. If you set it up as a testamentary trust, you can specify that the trust will provide income to your beneficiary for life, and that the remainder of the trust's assets will go to a specified charity or institution at the beneficiary's death.

Totten Trusts

A *Totten trust* is a bank account that is "in trust for" a named beneficiary, such as "Jack Smith in trust for Jane Smith." As long as Jack Smith lives, he maintains control over the account with the right to withdraw funds. Jane Smith has no right to the funds in the account until Jack Smith dies, at which time the funds in the account go directly to Jane Smith, avoiding probate. Certificates of deposit and other investments can be registered in this manner. The Totten trust is an alternative to putting savings in joint tenancy, as discussed in Chapter 5.

Uniform Transfers to Minors Act

The *Uniform Gifts to Minors Act* (UGMA) was in effect throughout the United States until 1983. Then the *Uniform Transfers to Minors Act*

(UTMA) was introduced as a substitute. So far, more than thirty states have adopted the UTMA. The remaining states still use the UGMA.

Both UGMA and UTMA are simply ways for a minor to own assets. It is important to understand they are trusts, like any other trusts, except that their terms are set in statutes instead of trust documents. If a trustee fails to comply with the terms of a UGMA or UTMA account, the trustee is exposed to the same actions as a trustee who fails to comply with the terms of a trust document.

There are two key differences between the UGMA and UTMA accounts. The UGMA is a custodial account that allows a minor child to own property such as cash, stocks, bonds, mutual funds, and, in some states, life insurance policies. The UTMA, a similar custodial account, allows the child to own *any* kind of property, including real estate, partnership interests, and even artwork. And UTMA does not limit donors to adults, as UGMA does. Trusts and estates can give to UTMA, too, if authorized by the governing document. With this added flexibility, you can now use a UTMA account to make gifts to a minor by will, or to provide income through a trust to the custodian.

An UGMA account is not affected if your state switches to UTMA. You can still add cash or securities to this type of account. But you should use the UTMA designation for the title to securities: (Name of donor), as custodian for (name of minor), under the (name of state) Uniform Transfers to Minors Act.

Both UGMA and UTMA accounts are subject to limitations. Gifts qualify for the annual exclusion from the gift tax. Under both acts, gifts are irrevocable—you part with the assets forever. In addition, UTMA and UGMA custodianships end as soon as your child becomes an adult—commonly, at age 18 or 21—unless your state provides otherwise.

With a UTMA account, each parent can contribute a gift maximum of $10,000 a year to each minor, and the recipient will pay no income, gift, or estate taxes. Therefore, a couple can give up to $20,000 a year to each minor without being taxed. The Tax Reform Act of 1986 added the Kiddie Tax. According to this, assuming that the child has no other income and is under age 14, the first $700 of investment income from the account is tax-free. The next $700 is taxed at 15 percent, and the rest is taxed at the parents' top bracket. When the child is age 14 or older, income from the account is taxed at the child's personal income tax rate.

It is no longer true that only wealthy people put their money and property in trusts. While people with high incomes still use trusts to pass along their wealth, more and more middle income people are now using trusts in their estate planning. These people have learned that trusts offer a variety of advantages by transferring assets to their children or other heirs without significant taxes, legal fees, or delays. Regardless of your income, a trust may prove to be an important tool in the planning of your estate.

Self-study 20.1
SHOULD YOU SET UP A TRUST?

1. Based upon your reading of this introduction to the subject of trusts, do you believe that you have need for a trust in your estate plan? ❏ Yes ❏ No

   If yes, what type of trust are you considering?_____

   Why? _____

   _____

   _____

2. Do you have a relative or close friend qualified to serve as a trustee? ❏ Yes ❏ No

   If yes, who? _____

   Address: _____

   _____ Phone:_____

   If no, you have the choice of any bank trust department.

   List your first choice. _____

   List your second choice. _____

   Present the above choices to your lawyer when you discuss your estate plan and will.

3. Are you interested in charitable bequests in order to:

   ❏ Help the causes you have always supported, the ones that will miss your help when you are gone?

   ❏ Make a charitable gift as a living memorial for a loved one?

   What charitable causes have you always supported?_____

   _____

   _____

   _____

21

PROBATE

Probate is a state's court procedure for establishing the validity of a will and supervising the distribution of an estate's assets. The laws of probate have evolved over centuries and operate in all fifty states. The probate process serves an important function—to make certain that your assets are distributed as specified in your will, thus protecting the interests of your beneficiaries. Probate also serves to insure that the property of an individual who dies without a will is distributed in accordance with the laws of the state.

Over the years, criticisms of the probate process have included high costs, a slow and cumbersome system, and corruption among probate lawyers and judges.

As a result, much has been written on how to avoid probate. The thrust of much of the writing is that the average layman can probably handle whatever probate proceedings are required without the assistance of a lawyer, and that assets can be legally transferred without going through probate.

Whether you are preparing your own will or are facing probate after the death of a loved one, it is wise to have a general understanding of the probate process. In the former case, such

an understanding can help you arrange your financial affairs so that many of your assets can bypass probate and go directly to your beneficiaries. In the latter case, you may find that by taking certain steps on your own, you can avoid some of the costs often associated with probate proceedings.

THE ROLE OF A PROBATE COURT

As already mentioned, part of the job of the probate court is to establish the validity of the will and supervise the distribution of an estate's assets. Therefore, the probate court studies the will to see if it is a valid document. If the court accepts the will as valid, the property owned solely by the *testator*—the maker of the will—is distributed.

Alternatively, for any number of reasons, the probate court may consider the will invalid. For instance, if a will is handwritten, and that state does not accept handwritten wills, the document will be considered invalid. Or the will may not have been properly witnessed; there may have been too few witnesses, or one of the witnesses may also be a beneficiary. Possibly all the heirs named in the will are deceased, or the property that was bequeathed in the will was sold prior to the death of the testator. The probate court generally tries to weed out any parts of a will that are invalid, and to honor any valid instructions as closely as possible. If this is not possible, the court may declare the entire will invalid and distribute the assets of the deceased in accordance with the state's laws of intestacy.

Whenever necessary, the probate court also serves as a referee, examining the wishes expressed in the will and resolving any questions of interpretation. A poorly worded will may raise questions among the heirs; it is the court's job to resolve these questions. The court must also consider whether undue influence was used to obtain particular benefits, whether the maker of the will was of sound mind, and whether the *executor*—the person charged in the will with the responsibility of carrying out its provisions—is handling the estate properly.

When an individual dies *intestate*—without a will—it is the job of the probate court to insure that the property of the individual is properly distributed. In these cases, the probate court has the responsibility of appointing an *administrator* who must inventory the assets of the deceased, and then have them appraised to get an accurate value. The court also must determine the number of beneficiaries related to the deceased. The court then applies the state's intestacy law to distribute the assets to the legitimate claimants.

It has been estimated that almost three-quarters of the people who die each year leave no will. These are mainly wives and single people. In these instances, no one knows what the wishes of the deceased were, nor is it possible to make allocations according to need. The law spells out what the spouse receives and what each child receives. The 8-year-old gets the same amount as the adult child; the affluent adult child gets the same amount as the mentally challenged child.

So far, we have discussed only the probate court's role in the distribution of assets. But the probate procedure also involves the payment of taxes and creditors. In fact, this takes place before any property is distributed. In settling the estate, the probate court takes off the top of the estate the following payments in the following order: the lawyer's fee, funeral expenses, and payment of any debts and taxes owed by the deceased. Only after these payments are made is the remainder of the estate made available for distribution to the beneficiaries.

WHAT ASSETS ARE SUBJECT TO PROBATE?

Assets subject to probate are those held in sole ownership that are usually included in the will, such as cash on hand, individual savings and checking accounts, certificates of deposit, government securities, mutual funds, stocks and bonds, money owed to you, life insurance, a share in a business, automobiles, household furnishings, art objects and antiques, jewelry and furs, and other valuables, including stamp and coin collections.

CAN YOU AVOID PROBATE?

Probate can be avoided by transferring property to a beneficiary *outside your will*. The following is a list of the most common methods of avoiding probate. Use Self-Study 21.1 to record those assets in your estate that will have to go through probate, and those that can bypass the probate process.

❑ **Joint Ownership.** When you die, all property held in joint tenancy with right of survivorship automatically goes to the survivor—usually your spouse—outside the probate process. Generally, this form of ownership is used only for your home, but the technique of joint ownership can also be applied to other types of property such as stocks and bonds, bank accounts, and mutual funds.

❏ **Living Trusts.** The two types of living trusts, revocable and irrevocable, can also be used for transferring property outside the will and the probate process. The trust instrument specifies who shall receive the property when death occurs. (For more information on living trusts, see Chapter 20.)

❏ **Life Insurance.** The proceeds of a life insurance policy are paid directly to the named beneficiary at the time of the policyholder's death. Because the money is transferred by contract, it is not considered part of a probate estate.

❏ **Gifts.** By giving gifts to your heirs before your death, you will reduce the size of your estate. While the gifts may be subject to the federal gift tax, they are not part of the probate estate. Gifts are usually given as cash. You can give a $10,000 annual gift to as many people or charities as you wish, and your spouse can do the same, making a $20,000 gift possible per individual or charity per year. Gifts can also include any form of property you own, thus reducing your probate estate.

Many people believe that a will can be drafted in a way that will allow survivors to *completely* avoid the probate process. Others feel that small estates do not have to go through probate. However, the fact remains that all wills in almost every state are subject to the probate process.

With that said, you should be aware that about twenty-five states have instituted simplified probate proceedings by adopting, in whole or in part, the Uniform Probate Code (UPC). The procedure for the settlement of small estates is designed to eliminate a large part of a probate court's administrative requirements. In such states, if the gross estate is $10,000 or less of per-

sonal property, the simplified proceedings are fast and inexpensive. Although there may be a filing fee involved, it will be minimal.

HANDLING PROBATE

In some jurisdictions, you, as a survivor, may be able to handle many aspects of the probate proceeding without an attorney. Details of the probate process vary greatly by locality, but in general, after a person dies, the executor of the will, or anyone who is handling matters for the deceased, must file a notification of the death with the probate court in the county where the person lived. Notification usually must be filed within nine months of the death.

For relevant material on handling the simple, routine tasks that are involved in the probate process, visit the personnel at your local probate court. These people are usually cooperative and will assist you in filling out and filing required forms.

With a little time and effort, you can most likely deal with the details of settling an estate as a do-it-yourself project. Even if you ultimately seek the assistance of a lawyer, you can probably complete most of the routine, preliminary paperwork on your own, thus reducing your lawyer's workload. This will significantly diminish the lawyer's fee, resulting in large savings.

It is usually difficult to avoid the probate process. Even when an estate is relatively small and uncomplicated, a trip to probate court is generally required. However, when doing your own estate planning, your use of a qualified lawyer and your chosen method of transferring property to your beneficiaries can help reduce both problems and costs for your survivors. Later, beneficiaries can often further reduce costs by handling much of the probate process on their own, without the help of an attorney.

self-study 21.1
LIST OF YOUR PROBATE
AND NONPROBATE ASSETS

On this worksheet, enter your probate and nonprobate assets.

Probate Assets	Nonprobate Assets

PLANNING
for the INEVITABLE

While many people prefer to ignore the subject, the fact remains that death is inevitable. Just as you make preparations for other facets of life, so, too, must you make careful preparations for the final event. It is not an easy job to tackle. But a death in the family is a deep wound, and survivors invariably react with shock and disbelief, even on those occasions when the death was anticipated. The grief and sense of loss are overwhelming, and people are not prepared to cope. That is why thoughtful people who are concerned about their families should prepare for their death in every way possible. Planning will insure that you have a voice in your own disposition. It will also save your loved ones the headaches and problems of making decisions on matters they may be too bereaved to handle effectively.

This chapter provides checklists of tasks that must be accomplished before and after a death, examines the details involved in arranging a funeral, discusses funeral ceremonies and costs, and explains how funeral expenses can be defrayed or reduced through survivors' benefits and memorial societies.

WHEN DEATH OCCURS

It is precisely during the period of suffering which follows a death that survivors are required to handle complex and often expensive business arrangements. Under normal conditions, arrangements of such complexity would require calm detachment and presence of mind. Yet when a death occurs and you become highly emotional, it is difficult to exercise sound judgment. It is often sensible at such a time to call upon a close relative, friend, clergy member, or family lawyer to make the decisions that have to be made, and to do the things that have to be done.

The following checklists of tasks that must be performed after a death and after the funeral and interment will help guide you through the days and weeks following the death of a loved one. This section also explains the importance of the death certificate.

Checklists of Tasks to Accomplish After a Death

After a death, some tasks must be accomplished

immediately. Other tasks must be performed after the funeral and interment.

Immediate Tasks

Immediately following a death, you must do the following:

❏ **Obtain a death certificate.** Get a death certificate from the physician attending at the time of death, or from the physician who examined the body after death. If a funeral home is making all the arrangements for you, it will obtain and file the death certificate, and provide you with the necessary copies. (See page 291 for more details on the death certificate.)

❏ **Obtain a copy of the will.** The will and/or supplemental letter of instructions may have directions concerning disposal of the body.

❏ **Notify a religious leader.** A member of the clergy can help you to make decisions at this time, and can offer spiritual comfort, as well.

❏ **Arrange for disposal of the body.** Determine if the deceased had any specific wishes regarding disposal of the body, including possible donation of organs or of the entire body for medical purposes. An organ donor card may have been prepared in accordance with the Uniform Anatomical Gifts Act. Check the deceased's will, driver's license, or supplemental letter of instructions, if available.

❏ **Notify any burial or memorial society.** If the deceased was a member of a burial society or a memorial society, notify an official of that group, and find out what services the society provides.

❏ **Choose a funeral home.** After comparing the costs of two or three funeral homes, engage the services of one. The first service performed by the funeral home will be to transfer the body to the home's facilities.

❏ **Get the cemetery plot location.** Determine whether the deceased owned a burial plot. If a family plot is to be the site of the burial, obtain the consent of the individual responsible for the interment. If no gravesite is available, but one is necessitated by the type of body disposal chosen, it will have to be purchased.

❏ **Make the funeral arrangements.** Make final arrangements for the funeral and interment.

❏ **Notify relatives and friends.** Advise relatives and friends of the date, time, and place of the funeral and burial.

❏ **Prepare obituary notices.** If desired, prepare an obituary or death notice and place it in appropriate newspapers and other publications.

❏ **Notify the employer of the deceased.** Notify the decedent's employer. Also notify any fraternal orders or lodges of which the decedent was a member.

Tasks After the Funeral and Interment

After the interment has occurred, you must do the following:

❏ **Contact the deceased's lawyer.** Inform the deceased's lawyer of the death. The original will may be in the lawyer's vault or in a safe deposit box. Probate proceedings should also be initiated.

❏ **Collect all official documents.** Collect the official documents left by the deceased—birth and marriage certificates, veteran's discharge papers, Social Security card, and copies of tax returns, for instance. Turn all of this information over to the lawyer and/or the executor or executrix, so that the settlement of the estate can begin. The locations of these documents may have been listed in the supplemental letter of instructions, attached to the will.

❑ **Determine any funeral and burial allowances.** Prepare a list of funeral and burial allowances to which the survivors may be entitled. Sources of such allowances include the Department of Veterans Affairs, the Social Security Administration, a labor union, a fraternal organization, an employer, burial insurance purchased from an insurance company, or other sources. Obtain and prepare the necessary applications.

❑ **Arrange for a tombstone.** Begin to make arrangements for a tombstone or grave marker.

The Death Certificate

A *death certificate* stating the date, time, place, and cause of death, is required in all states. The document is prepared by a physician, medical examiner, or coroner who examines the body.

Depending on state laws, the death certificate must be filed in the appropriate county office within a few days of death. It is important that you obtain several copies of the death certificate. These are required as proof of death in order to arrange for probate of the will and to secure Social Security benefits, life insurance payments, and pension benefits. A death certificate is also required to gain access to the deceased's safe deposit box and to obtain possession of the deceased's assets. Additional copies of the death certificate can be obtained later if they are required. The funeral home that is handling all arrangements will both file the certificate and provide you with any copies needed.

In most cases, death is due to natural causes. However, if death is due to an accident or other unnatural causes, such as murder or suicide, a medical examiner or coroner must determine the date and probable cause of death. An autopsy may be performed if the cause of death is doubtful, or to provide the medical profession with additional information about any illness from which the deceased may have suffered. Except in the case of murder or suicide, an autopsy requires the consent of surviving relatives. It is important that the cause of death be correctly entered on the death certificate since accidental death sometimes results in higher life insurance benefits for the survivors.

DISPOSAL OF THE BODY

State laws generally require that a dead body be buried or otherwise legally disposed of within a specified number of days. Generally, these laws further specify that only a licensed funeral director is authorized to move the deceased.

The law usually honors a decedent's right to donate the body or specific body organs. Every effort, of course, should be made to satisfy the decedent's wishes as specified in the will or supplemental letter of instructions.

The choices of disposal of the body for the typical family are:

❑ **Earth burial.** In the United States and Canada, earth burial is the most widely used form of disposal, involving the interment of uncremated remains in a grave.

❑ **Entombment.** In entombment, the casket with the remains is placed in a mausoleum—an above-ground tomb.

❑ **Cremation.** In cremation, the body is first reduced to ashes. The ashes are then either scattered; or placed in an urn and buried, placed in a vault known as a *columbarium,* or otherwise stored, depending on your wishes and on local ordinances. While most religious groups approve cremation, some, such as certain Protestant denominations, Islam, Eastern Orthodoxy, and Orthodox Judaism, do not.

❑ **Whole-body or organ donation.** You may

wish to consider donating a particular organ or organs of your body—eyes, kidneys, or heart, for instance—or your entire body for research or educational purposes, or to save the life of another individual. Donating a particular organ or organs of your body can help someone who is in desperate need. Such a donation is probably the most meaningful gift you can make to promote life and happiness for someone else.

The donation of organs through a properly signed and witnessed document is legally binding on the heirs of the deceased. Often, however, some of the survivors object, and medical schools, research foundations, and hospitals are reluctant to go to court to enforce such a gift because the delays of a court case make the organ useless for transplantation. If you desire to donate your entire body or any part of it, discuss your wishes with your family to obtain their agreement. Be sure that they understand the procedure to be followed after your death. To obtain a free organ donor card, contact the United Network for Organ Sharing (UNOS) by mail or phone, or visit their website. (See the Resources section.)

❏ **Direct disposition.** In direct disposition, the body is transferred from the place of death to the place of disposition, either a cemetery or a crematory. Direct disposition is less expensive than a traditional funeral because it involves no embalming, no viewing, and no need for an expensive casket.

The two least expensive options are whole-body donation and direct disposition.

ARRANGING A FUNERAL

Unless funeral arrangements are made in advance, the time available to arrange the funeral is limited. Nevertheless, crucial decisions must be made regarding the type of funeral service, selection of the casket, disposal of the body, and other details.

The Funeral Ceremony

A funeral ceremony offers an opportunity to commemorate the life of the deceased and to recognize the loss that has occurred. The type of funeral ceremony is determined by one's personal preferences and religious beliefs. If you wish to plan your own funeral, you should record your preferences in your supplemental letter of instructions. Traditional religious funerals vary among different religious groups. Whether you are planning your own funeral or the funeral of a relative or friend, you can obtain excellent guidance from your local spiritual leader, minister, priest, or rabbi, or from a funeral director.

Memorial services, at which the body is not present, are becoming increasingly popular. The memorial service is generally held after a burial or cremation and is conducted in a church, a synagogue, a funeral home, a private home, or any other meeting place. The service is very flexible and is designed to suit the preferences of the deceased or the family. Other types of services include fraternal ceremonies, such as those conducted by the Masons or Knights of Columbus. These services are supplementary to a regular funeral service.

If you are planning a funeral ceremony, consider whether you desire a religious or a nonreligious service; the type of readings and/or music to be included; the number and names of the participants; and whether the body will be present. If the body is to be present, do you want the casket open or closed?

The *Final Report* of the Federal Trade Commission (FTC) on the Funeral Industry Regulation Rule revealed that 66 percent of funerals held are open-casket services with earth burial;

20 percent are closed-casket services with earth burial; 12 percent involve cremation, either before or after a service; and 2 percent involve above-ground burial.

Funeral Costs

Funeral costs vary—not only because of the different types of funerals available, but also due to regional differences. For many consumers, however, a funeral represents one of the most expensive purchases of a lifetime.

How Much Does a Funeral Cost?

The charges now billed through a funeral home for funeral services and casket average about $5,500. The burial plot, vault, grave-opening fee, and monument cost another several thousand dollars. These figures confirm the high cost of dying. The cost of direct cremation is, of course, significantly less than that of ground burial, averaging between $1,200 and $2,700. The United States funeral industry consists of about 22,000 funeral homes, with an annual volume of $10 to $15 billion in merchandise and services.

The economics of the funeral industry requires high charges. With about 2 million people dying each year, the 22,000 funeral homes handle an average of 100 funerals each per year. At least half of the nation's funeral homes, particularly in rural areas, do fewer than 25 cases a year, while those in urban areas may average well over 1,000 a year. This volume must generate enough income to keep the facility attractive, to maintain a year-round staff, and to provide for new hearses and limousines. To meet the costs of overhead, the funeral director must generate maximum income out of every funeral.

Critics of the funeral industry state that some funeral directors take advantage of grief-stricken and ill-prepared customers who, under the pressures of bereavement, make poor deci-sions that prove to be very costly. These critics argue that more government regulation is needed to protect the public. They advise consumers to learn well in advance about the choices that are available.

The Trade Regulation Rule on Funeral Practices

In response to widespread problems in the funeral industry, the Federal Trade Commission established a rule on funeral trade practices, effective April 30, 1984. This rule requires the nation's funeral directors to:

❑ Provide purchasers with full disclosure of prices on caskets, burial vaults, and other elements of a funeral, and present an itemized list before the funeral is scheduled.

❑ Refrain from misleading advertising and deceptive practices, such as advising a prospective customer that embalming is required and that this process will preserve a body indefinitely.

❑ Provide price information over the telephone to customers who request it.

❑ Refrain from the "bundling" of services into packages that force the consumer to buy unwanted services.

In 1994, the funeral rule was renewed and toughened by the FTC. The commission expanded the funeral rule by banning casket handling fees, which some funeral directors had charged customers who bought caskets from another source.

What's Included in a Complete Funeral?

The price of a *complete funeral* includes certain standard items, extra items, and burial or cremation costs.

❑ **Standard items.** Funeral directors generally include the following standard items in the price of a complete funeral: transfer of the body to the funeral establishment; use of funeral home facilities; embalming and restoration; dressing of remains; cost of casket; use of hearse and one limousine; staff services; arranging for religious services, burial permit, death benefits, and newspaper obituary notices; provision of pallbearers; arranging and care of flowers; provision of guest register and acknowledgment cards; obtaining copies of the death certificate; and, in some cases, extension of credit.

❑ **Extra items.** Extra items that may be purchased include a vault or liner; extra limousines; music; an honorarium for clergy, which may be handled directly by a survivor; flowers; and burial clothing. The tax on these items is an added cost.

❑ **Burial costs.** Burial costs—charges for opening and closing a grave—also add to the cost of a funeral. The funeral director may be called upon to assist survivors with the purchase of a cemetery plot, and will arrange with the cemetery for preparation of the grave. These burial costs are often paid by the funeral director and then reimbursed by the survivors.

Price itemization makes it easier to reject those goods and services that are not wanted. In some instances, though, the funeral director may increase other prices to compensate for the items rejected. In one study, the FTC notes that unscrupulous funeral directors put higher price tags on caskets before prosperous-looking survivors enter the selection room. Another fraudulent tactic is the substitution of a less-expensive casket for the more-expensive one selected by the survivors.

Even when prices are itemized, however, you have no way of knowing whether you are being charged the same prices as everyone else. The FTC notes that documents obtained from a large California mortuary revealed a compensation system for salespersons that penalized them for low-priced sales and rewarded them for high-priced ones.

Prepaid and Prearranged Funerals

Prepaid funerals have increased in popularity in recent years for a variety of reasons. Some people prepay in order to "spend down" their assets and thus qualify for Medicaid. Others are forced to prepay in order to gain admittance to a nursing home. But perhaps the most common reason for prepaying is that people want to spare their family the financial and emotional stress associated with arranging a funeral after the death of a loved one.

The price quoted in a prepaid funeral arrangement is a guaranteed amount that cannot change. Sometimes the payment covers only the funeral director's charges, so that at the time of death, the family has to cover other charges, such as the cost of a gravesite. In other cases, the individual prepays all expenses, from the cost of the flowers to the clergy's charge to the casket to the gravesite.

Another option is to prearrange a funeral without actually paying for it. People do this because they want a voice in their own funeral arrangements, or because they want to spare their survivors the task of making difficult decisions during their time of grief. But because the funeral is prearranged but not prepaid, the agreement made with the funeral home is not binding. The survivors can choose to honor the wishes of the deceased, or opt for different arrangements. (If you want to make your wishes regarding your own funeral known more informally, Self-Study 22.1 will enable you to record instructions for your survivors on a fill-in form.)

Each state has legislation that spells out individual variations of prepaid funeral plans. The legislation also specifies how the money paid into the plan is handled. These rulings are known as *Pre-Need Funeral Laws*.

New York State recently revised its 1994 law so that the money advanced in planning a funeral must be placed in an escrow account. All interest earned on the deposit must be retained in the account until the time of need or until the cancellation of the plan. In some states, the money is placed in an irrevocable trust. Also, some states do not require that 100 percent of the deposit be placed in an escrow account, and often permit deductions of fees and commissions from the account.

Some states allow burial insurance that is earmarked for the costs of a funeral. Burial insurance policies are sold through a funeral home in some states, and by an insurance company in others.

The Casket

Caskets are made of a variety of materials, including wood; metals such as steel, copper, and bronze; and fiberglass. While the average price of a casket is now about $2,000, prices vary widely—from less than $500 to as much as $50,000. Price is determined by the materials used for the casket itself, the material used for the interior trim, and the manufacturing costs, which differ from one area of the country to another. And, part of the cost of the casket is the shipping charge from the factory to the ultimate destination.

Some families choose an *alternative container* rather than a casket. Made of cardboard or another inexpensive material, alternative containers are sometimes used when a family cannot afford a standard casket, or when the remains are to be cremated.

Embalming

Second to the coffin in the price of a funeral is embalming, which makes possible the viewing of the body in an open casket. If survivors reject embalming, the funeral home will add a charge for *preservation*, which is simply refrigeration.

The Vault and Liner

A *liner* is a container made of concrete that surrounds the casket when it is placed in the ground. The liner does not, however, have a full bottom, and, therefore, does not fully enclose the casket.

The liner is designed for the sole purpose of supporting the grave, so that the ground around it doesn't collapse as the casket gradually disintegrates. It is not intended to protect the casket or the body. Certain cemeteries—for instance, those in areas with a high water table, which would hasten the breakdown of the casket—demand that all gravesites include a liner.

A *vault* is similar to a liner in that it surrounds the casket. A vault, however, is sealed, with a full bottom, and usually has a liner made of plastic, stainless steel, copper, or bronze. Therefore, the vault not only supports the gravesite, but also provides protection for the casket and the remains that lie within. Although most vaults are made of concrete, some are made of other substances, such as steel.

The Monument

The manufacture and sale of a marker or monument for a gravesite is a separate industry. Markers or monuments are usually granite, marble, or bronze, and are a major expense associated with interment. The monument is selected by the survivors and must then be inscribed, moved to the cemetery, and erected on a concrete foundation on the gravesite. A considerable amount of time elapses after burial before a monument is erected.

Cemetery Plots

As indicated previously, state law requires that a human body be buried in an officially designated cemetery or graveyard, or that it be otherwise legally disposed. If you plan to continue to live where you are now living, and if you wish an earth burial, you should buy a burial plot or grave in your area. This will spare your survivors the unpleasant and painful task of having to buy a gravesite quickly after your demise.

All cemeteries are regulated and supervised by agencies of the federal, state, or local governments. Depending on their ownership, cemeteries may be classified into three categories:

1. Those owned and operated by religious, fraternal, and philanthropic groups with private funds.

2. Those owned and operated by private corporations for profit.

3. Those owned and operated by a public authority and supported by tax funds.

When buying a cemetery plot, the factors to consider are:

❑ **Location.** You must decide whether you wish to be buried where you grew up, where you spent your adult life, or where you are living in retirement. You should also find out whether you have the right to resell your plot if you decide to buy one elsewhere, or whether the cemetery will buy it back from you.

❑ **Size.** Cemetery plots are usually sold as single graves; as two gravesites (one for each spouse); or as family plots. Some cemeteries allow double-depth graves, where one casket can be buried on top of another. This is a cost-saving factor that should be considered.

❑ **Maintenance Costs.** Determine what the annual upkeep costs are as compared with the costs of perpetual care of the grave or graves.

If you buy a cemetery plot before it is necessary, you will have the opportunity to look around and compare prices. You can ascertain the reputation of a cemetery by checking with the local Better Business Bureau or a member of the local clergy.

Memorial and Burial Societies

Memorial and burial societies are nonprofit, cooperative-type organizations created by consumers and designed to help people get the kind of funeral they want at a reasonable price. Over 200 such societies have been organized in the United States, with about 1,000,000 members. They are usually affiliated with religious organizations, senior citizen centers, unions, or civic groups, and are staffed primarily by volunteers. They provide information about low-cost funerals, cremation, bequeathal of the body or organs of the body, and other information on death arrangements.

Since memorial and burial societies are operated by volunteers, they have no incentive to earn a profit or to sell any funeral merchandise or services. Instead, they serve as liaisons with funeral directors to fulfill the needs of their members. Generally, the price of a funeral arranged by these societies is lower than that arranged by a funeral home because the memorial societies are larger purchasers of funeral services. While these societies are geared specifically to assist their members, most will also assist nonmembers in obtaining low-cost funerals. Some societies may even furnish comparative cost data for your area.

To locate your nearest memorial or burial society, contact the Funeral Consumers Alliance

(FAMSA-FCA). (See the Resources section.) Besides offering information by mail and phone, this nonprofit funeral consumer group has a website that will guide you to helpful societies in your area.

Death Announcements

An *obituary* is a news article about the deceased individual that appears on the obituary page. It is printed by the newspaper at the editor's discretion, and is free of charge. (Self-Study 22.2 allows you to record basic information about yourself, so that you can aid your family in the writing of an obituary or eulogy.)

A *death announcement* is a paid announcement, and the cost varies from newspaper to newspaper. A prominent East Coast paper, for example, charges over $20 per line for papers printed from Monday through Saturday, and even more for the Sunday paper—probably the highest rates in the country.

BENEFITS THAT DEFRAY FUNERAL EXPENSES

The two most important benefits generally available to survivors are the Social Security death benefit and the Department of Veterans Affairs death benefit. Many people do not realize that they are entitled to one or both of these, and often money is lost because the time limit for application has expired.

Social Security Survivor Benefit

The Social Security survivor benefit is a lump-sum payment made to a survivor in an amount of up to $255. The application for death benefits must be submitted within two years from the date of death, using Form SSA8.

If the deceased left no surviving spouse, the death benefit may be paid to any survivor responsible for the expenses of the funeral. If the survivor wishes, Social Security will send the payment directly to the funeral home. If a body is donated to a medical facility, Social Security will reimburse the cost of transporting the body up to the maximum payment of $255.

Veterans' Survivor Benefits

The Department of Veterans Affairs will pay a $300 burial and funeral allowance for deceased veterans who had been receiving a pension or compensation at the time of death. This department will also assume responsibility for the burial of those veterans whose deaths occurred while in a hospital facility or nursing home of the department. If specified eligibility requirements are met, the department will pay an additional $150 plot or interment allowance. This benefit, however, is payable only if the veteran is interred in a private cemetery. Grave space in a national cemetery is free for any veteran who served honorably in the armed forces. All veterans are also entitled to a United States flag with which to drape the coffin.

If the veteran's death is service-related, the government will pay an allowance of up to $1,500. Veterans Form 21-530 must be filed within two years of the death, whether it is service-related or nonservice-related. The payment will be made to the individual who covered the funeral costs. Contact your local Department of Veterans Affairs office for further details.

Documents Required for Collecting Funeral Benefits

Survivors need copies of the following documents when applying for various funeral allowances:

❑ A copy of the death certificate, certified by the issuing agency.

❏ A certified copy of the birth certificate of both the surviving spouse and minor children for Social Security and Department of Veterans Affairs benefits.

❏ A certified copy of the marriage certificate.

❏ A copy of the W-2 form or the federal income tax return for the most recent year as proof of the deceased's recent employment record for the Social Security benefit.

❏ A copy of the veteran's discharge papers for Department of Veterans Affairs benefits.

❏ A copy of the receipted bill from the funeral home for Department of Veterans Affairs benefits and for Social Security benefits.

❏ The Social Security number of the deceased to claim Social Security benefits.

DEALING WITH THE LOSS OF A LOVED ONE

Most individuals prefer to avoid the topic of death and dying. The subject is ignored or spoken about only in private. Actually, it cannot be brushed aside and must be confronted honestly. Death does occur. It is a reality you must face because it is the ultimate human experience.

Discussion of death has increased significantly over the last several years. A large number of books and articles have been published on the subject, and colleges and universities around the country are offering courses about death and dying. Psychologists are helping survivors deal with the complex problems associated with adjustment after the loss of a loved one. Two of the major aspects of dealing with loss are discussed below.

The Crisis of Bereavement

The loss of a loved one creates a deep wound. It is natural to think that you cannot live without the deceased and to feel lost. You may appear to function normally— arranging the funeral, giving away the deceased's clothing and other items, and otherwise doing what needs to be done—but you are in shock. The healing process is often slow and painful. But although the wound may never heal completely, an adjustment to living will ultimately be effected.

As the shock of the event wears away, the pain will become more evident. It will be difficult to shake off, and will seem to persist over the weeks and months. During this time, you will need the support of relatives, friends, and clergy to help you come to terms with reality. Eventually, you will begin to emerge from this phase of grief, and start to take note of the world around you. The experience will help you grow, an understanding of the feelings and needs of others will emerge, and you will become wiser and warmer in your relationships. (Self-Study 22.3 will enable you to record some of your thoughts on surviving a loss.)

Living Alone

Once you are alone, the daily chores of running a household will continue. Food will have to be bought and stored; a meal for one will have to be prepared; the house will need cleaning; and you may have to report back to work. And then, every night you will come home to an empty house that is silent and dark. Living alone may, at first, be a fearful experience. You may worry about locking the door and windows at night. The slightest sound may awaken you. The reality of your aloneness may be devastating.

As a widow or widower, you must now become active in the handling of the details of the will, of probate proceedings, of distributions to children and possibly grandchildren, and of a variety of other financial matters with which you may be unfamiliar. Questions may arise, requiring solutions. A change in housing arrangements may be in order. You may wish to pursue a second career or a new one. This may require training and career counseling. Other issues may arise: dating, sexuality, and remarriage. You may wish to develop new friendships, continue your education, or enjoy new leisure activities. Certainly, you should seek to get involved in new interests and to widen your circle of friends. But it is wise to avoid making major changes—remarrying or changing your living arrangements, for instance—until one year has elapsed.

If you are having trouble coping with grief or adjusting to life alone, do not hesitate to seek the help and advice offered by your local clergy or your doctor. Private counsel or participation in a support group can help you come to terms with your loss, assume new responsibilities, and regain your interest in life.

Most of us avoid thinking about the inevitable until circumstances force us to deal with the realities of death. But it's important to remember that by preparing for death in every way possible, you will not only spare your loved ones a good deal of suffering and expense, but will also help insure that your wishes regarding the management of your own funeral are both known and followed.

Self-Study 22.1
INSTRUCTIONS FOR YOUR SURVIVORS

The following is a sample list of instructions that you should prepare for your survivors. When it is completed, make it available to your spouse, a relative, or a close friend.

INSTRUCTIONS FOR FUNERAL AND BURIAL

Name of individual _____

1. Funeral home: _____

   Address: _____

   Phone: _____

2. Type of service preferred: _____

   At funeral facility? _____

   House of worship? _____

   Name: _____

   Address: _____

   Gravesite? _____

   Name: _____

   Address: _____

   Religious or nonreligious service? _____

   Type: Private? Public? _____

   Memorial service later? _____

   Name of person to conduct service: _____

   Phone number: _____

   Names of speaker(s): _____

   Phone number(s): _____

   Music? Flowers? _____

   Casket flag for a veteran? _____

3. Casket:

Type:

Price range:

Open for viewing or closed?

4. Disposition of body:

Burial. Earth burial, or above ground in a mausoleum. Specify:

Cremation. Earth burial of urn, niche in columbarium, delivered to survivors, scattered on land or at sea. Specify:

Organ donation. Entire body, or specific parts. Specify:

Recipient organization (attach authorization):

Address:

Phone number:

5. Cemetery:

   Name: _____

   Address: _____

   _____

   Phone number: _____

   Individual grave or plot? _____

   Location of cemetery deed: _____

6. Memorial contributions or donations to charity or other organization:

   Name: _____   _____

   Address: _____   _____

   _____   _____

   Phone number: _____

7. Organizations to be notified:

   Name: _____   _____

   Address: _____   _____

   _____   _____

   Phone number: _____   _____

   Contact: _____

8. Membership in memorial society:

   Name: _____

   Address: _____

   _____

   Phone number: _____

   Contact: _____

Self-Study 22.2
BASIC INFORMATION ABOUT YOURSELF

Collect basic information for your obituary and/or eulogy. It will be very helpful for your survivors.

Full name:

Place of birth: Date of birth:

Schools and colleges attended, degrees, and honors awarded:

Your occupation: Years in occupation:

Place of work:

Armed services record (branch, years of duty, rank, awards, etc.):

Memberships in clubs and/or fraternal organizations:

Father's name:

Birthplace: Occupation:

Mother's maiden name:

Birthplace: Occupation:

Your children's names and addresses:

Names of grandchildren:

Self-Study 22.3
YOUR THOUGHTS ON SURVIVING A LOSS

1. From your personal experience, what problems have you observed in the life of an individual who has suffered a loss?

_____

_____

_____

_____

_____

_____

2. If you had the opportunity, what suggestions would you make to this grieving individual in order to alleviate the problems?

_____

_____

_____

_____

_____

3. What plans do you have for dealing with a loss if you should suffer one?

_____

_____

_____

_____

_____

CONCLUSION

Congratulations! Those of you who have read through the entire book and have reviewed the Self-Study sections, personalizing the material and applying the relevant information to your own situation, are well on the road to a future free of financial anxiety. You stand on the threshold, ready to join millions of other Americans who are enjoying a comfortable retirement.

For them and for you, a sound financial base is the heart of the golden years ahead. This base relies on three fundamental sources of income: Social Security, a pension, and savings and investments. It is important to stay alert and aware of changes that may occur in any of these three areas.

First, consider Social Security. You can be assured that Social Security—so much a part of the American social and economic fabric—will be there for you when you retire, and will continue for generations to come.

Next, consider pensions. Employers are moving more and more from the traditional, predominantly employer-paid, defined benefit pension plans to defined contribution plans that require employee contributions. Future benefits will be determined by the amount contributed over one's working years and by the success of the investments made with the funds contributed.

With the uncertainty regarding future pension benefits, you, as a retirement planner, will have to rely more heavily on your own personal savings and investments. To plan for a successful retirement today, you should take a greater responsibility for your own future by becoming a regular saver and a prudent investor. To guarantee a comfortable retirement, you must start your savings and investment program as early as possible to enable your money to grow through the magic of compounding.

By working through this book, you have learned the basics of Social Security, pensions, savings, and investments. You have taken the first important step toward a comfortable future by coming to grips with the basic considerations in financial planning. Along the way, you studied all the other components of a complete retirement plan: life and health insurance, including Medicare and Medigap; budgeting; taxes and tax shelters; estate planning, including wills and trusts; retirement housing; and work and leisure plans. Finally, you learned about coping with life's inevitable losses. You are now far better equipped than most to begin the retirement lifestyle. The time and effort you have expended will return significant dividends in the years ahead.

Having said all of this, my final advice is to be prepared for retirement's change of pace. If possible, retirement should not be a complete break with your working lifestyle. Try to ease into the transition. Before you stop working, give more time to interests you want to pursue in the future. And along the way, keep updating and revising your retirement plan as developed in the Self-Study sections of the book. Move for-ward with confidence in all you have discovered, and with a positive approach to the years ahead.

One last thought: This book will be updated and revised annually to provide you with the most current figures and information. Therefore, should you have any comments, additions, or suggestions that you would like to offer, please write to:

Att: Retiring Right Department
Square One Publishers
16 First Street
Garden City Park, NY 11040

APPENDICES

GLOSSARY

Activities of daily living (ADLs). Activities that people must perform every day, such as bathing, dressing, eating, transferring from a bed to a chair, using the toilet, and maintaining bowel and bladder control.

Actual charge. The fee billed by the doctor or supplier—usually considerably higher than the Medicare-approved charge. The actual charge is also known as the current charge. (*See also* Approved charge; Customary charge.)

Acute care. Medical care that is required for a short period of time to cure a certain illness and/or condition.

Adjustable rate mortgage. A mortgage in which at specified intervals—such as every six months, thirty months, or three years—the interest rate may be raised or lowered by the lender. (*See also* Conventional mortgage.)

Adjusted gross income (AGI). A sum derived by subtracting allowable deductions—alimony, business expenses, moving expenses, and IRA or Keogh plan contributions, for instance—from gross income. (*See also* Gross income.)

Administrator. The person appointed by a court to administer and settle the estate of a person who dies without a will, or a person whose will does not name an executor, cannot be located, or is declared invalid. (*See also* Executor.)

Adult day care. Health support and rehabilitation services provided in the community for people who are unable to care for themselves independently during the day, but are able to live at home at night.

Advance directives. Legal documents that express an individual's wishes concerning the use of life support systems if he or she becomes terminally ill or incompetent. Advance directives include the durable power of attorney for health care, health care proxy, and living will. (*See also* Durable power of attorney for health care; Health care proxy; living will.)

Age discrimination. A situation in which an employer or other person makes a decision about an individual because of age alone, overlooking individual merit and competence. (*See also* Age Discrimination in Employment Act.)

Age Discrimination in Employment Act (ADEA). A federal law, passed in 1968 and amended in 1978 and 1986, that makes it illegal for employers to refuse to hire an individual because of age. (*See also* Age discrimination.)

Aggressive growth mutual fund. A growth mutual fund that takes more risks than normal to earn higher returns.

Alternative container. An inexpensive alternative to a casket. Alternative containers—or minimal containers, as they are sometimes called—are made of cardboard or another inexpensive substance, and are usually rigid. These containers are often used in cremations.

Amortization. A method of liquidating a debt by making periodic payments of the principal and interest over a fixed period of time.

Annuitant. The buyer of an annuity.

Annuitize. To convert accumulated savings into an annuity.

Annuity. A tax-favored investment that generates a series of regular payments guaranteed to continue for a specific time, such as ten years or twenty years, or—more usually—for the recipient's lifetime, in exchange for a single payment or a series of payments.

Antenuptial agreement. *See* Premarital agreement.

Any substantial gainful work. Any significant physical or mental duties or a combination of both that is productive in nature.

Approved charge. An amount set by the Medicare carrier in your area based primarily on the customary charge in your locale for the service or supply in question. (*See also* Actual charge; Customary charge.)

Assets. All money, investments, and other property owned by an individual, a family, or a business. (*See also* Liabilities; Net worth.)

Assignment method. A method of payment in which the doctor or supplier agrees that his or her total charge for the covered service will not be more than the Medicare-approved charge. The doctor or supplier can charge the insured individual only for the part of the deductible that the individual has not yet met and for the coinsurance. (*See also* Payment-to-you method.)

Assisted living facility. A residence for people who are not completely able to live independently, and who need help with the activities of daily living. (*See also* Activities of daily living.)

Average covered monthly earnings. A basic measure of a worker's earnings derived from average indexed monthly earnings over most of a worker's lifetime. Average covered monthly earnings are used to compute an individual's Social Security retirement allowance.

Average indexed monthly earnings (AIME). The monthly income for past years adjusted and then averaged, and used to calculate Social Security benefit rates. Monthly earnings are adjusted to reflect the impact of inflation and current higher earnings levels. The adjusted earnings are then averaged to obtain a benefit rate that is more in line with today's earnings.

Balanced mutual fund. *See* Growth and income mutual fund.

Banker's acceptance. A type of loan used in international trade. A seller draws a draft that is payable by a buyer within a stipulated period of time. A bank accepts the draft, guaranteeing payment of it at maturity, and thus enabling it to be sold in the open market.

Bankruptcy. A court proceeding in which an individual declares that he or she is unable to pay his or her debts, and seeks the court's guidance in removing or reducing those debts. (*See also* Straight bankruptcy; Wage earner's plan bankruptcy.)

Basic medical/surgical insurance. A type of health insurance that provides coverage for doctors' visits in and out of the hospital, diagnostic and laboratory tests, and certain surgical procedures.

Bearer bond. A bond that does not have the owner's name registered on the books of the issuing company or governmental agency, or noted on the certificate. Interest and principal, when due, are payable to the holder. (*See also* Coupon bond; Registered bond.)

Beneficiary. A person or organization designated to receive the income from an insurance policy, will, or trust.

Benefit period. The unit of measure used to keep track of consumption of services under Medicare hospital insurance. Benefit periods vary in length for the different facilities involved.

Bequest. A gift of property made through a will. This is also known as a legacy.

Binder. A payment requested by a seller to hold a piece of property for an interested buyer until a set date.

Blood program. A type of health insurance program that provides either a specified or an unlimited amount of blood credit for members and their eligible relatives in return for a donation of one pint of blood annually. Some of these programs carry over into retirement and help provide the first three pints of blood not covered by Medicare.

Blue Book. A publication of the National Automobile Dealers Association (NADA) that lists the average prices paid for used cars at a specified time.

Blue chip stock. Stock in a company known nationally for the quality and wide acceptance of its products or services, and for its ability to earn large profits and pay regular dividends.

Blue Cross and Blue Shield. Not-for-profit insurance associations that pioneered health insurance coverage. Blue Cross provides hospitalization insurance. Blue Shield provides surgical and general physician expense insurance.

Blue-collar worker. A person whose employment requires manual labor and who wears work clothes or other specialized clothing on the job.

Bond. A written promise to repay a loan on a specified date while paying the bondholder a specified amount of interest at regular intervals, usually twice a year; basically an IOU or promissory note. (*See also* Bearer bond; Convertible; Coupon bond; Debenture bond; General mortgage bond; Registered bond.)

Break in service. A temporary leave of absence from employment.

Budget. A spending plan designed to help you efficiently manage your income.

Burial. *See* Earth burial.

Burial society. *See* Memorial society.

Bypass trust. A trust designed to bypass estate taxes. The money in the trust passes directly to beneficiaries.

Call option. The right to buy a fixed number of shares of a particular stock at a specified price within a limited period of time. The purchaser hopes that the stock's price will go up by an amount sufficient to provide a profit when the option is sold. If the stock's price remains the same or goes down, the investment in the call option is lost. (*See also* Put option.)

Capital. Money or its equivalent in property and/or securities.

Capital asset. A long-term asset, such as stocks, bonds, and real estate.

Capital gain. The profit resulting from the sale or exchange of a capital asset. (*See* Capital asset.)

Capital loss. The loss resulting from the sale or exchange of a capital asset. (*See* Capital asset.)

Care facility. A form of housing for the individual or couple beginning to encounter some health problems requiring professional help.

Caretaker. The person who takes care of an at-home patient.

Cash refund annuity. A type of annuity that pays income for life, but that, if the annuitant dies before the payments equal the amount he or she put into the annuity minus specified administrative charges, pays the balance to the designated beneficiary in a lump sum. (*See also* Installment refund annuity; Joint and survivor annuity.)

Cash value. The dollar value of a life insurance policy that has a savings component as part of the premium. The cash value—which changes over time—is equal to the amount accumulated plus the interest earned. (*See also* Face value.)

Cash value life insurance. A type of life insurance, also known as permanent life insurance, that requires premium payments for a specified number of years or for life and, over the years, builds up savings, referred to as cash value. The policy's face value is paid at the insured's death, regardless of the policy's cash value.

Casket. A coffin or rigid container that encases a body. A casket may be ornamented and lined with fabric. (*See also* Alternative container.)

Catastrophic major medical insurance. A type of health insurance that provides compensation for extraordinary medical costs not covered by hospitalization insurance, basic medical/surgical insurance, or comprehensive major medical insurance.

Cemetery. A burial ground or tract of land set aside for graves or tombs.

Cemetery plot. A burial site for one or more graves owned by an individual, family, or organization.

Central listing service. A service through which information on dwelling units for sale or rent is disseminated to all member real estate brokers in a given area. Each of the member realtors then has the right to sell or rent, splitting the commission with the broker who obtained the listing. This is also known as a multiple listing service. (*See also* Exclusive listing; Exclusive right-to-sell listing.)

Certificate of Accrual on Treasury Securities (CATS). Securities that represent ownership of interest or principal payments made on United States Treasury notes or bonds. CATS are taxable zero coupon securities that are extremely liquid. (*See also* Zero coupon bond.)

Certificate of deposit (CD). A type of savings account in which a specified sum of money is deposited for a set period of time. Each bank has its own rates, terms, and minimum deposit requirements, and most charge a penalty for the early withdrawal of funds.

Charitable remainder trust. 1. An arrangement with a charity under which a property is donated to the charity in exchange for a lifetime annuity and the right to remain in the home for life. **2.** An irrevocable trust that provides income to the trust's beneficiaries for life, or for a set term of years. When the last beneficiary dies or the trust's term ends, the specified charity receives the trust's remaining assets.

Chattel mortgage. A type of sales agreement in which the buyer acquires title to the purchased property, but pledges it as security for the balance due. The buyer's failure to meet the payments gives the lender, usually a bank or finance company, the right to foreclose the loan, repossess the item, and sue for the remaining balance plus court costs. (*See also* Conditional sales agreement.)

Cliff vesting. A type of vesting in which an employee with five years of service has a nonforfeitable right to 100 percent of the accrued benefit derived from employer contributions, with no vesting before then. (*See also* Graded vesting; Vesting upon entry.)

Closed-end mutual fund. A mutual fund that issues a fixed number of shares, which are traded at the prevailing market price and listed on one or more of the major stock exchanges. New shares are issued infrequently. (*See also* Open-end mutual fund.)

Closing costs. Costs resulting from the financing and transfer of property ownership in a real estate sale.

Codicil. An amendment to a will that must be signed and witnessed with the same formality as a will.

Coexecutor. An additional executor who works with the executor to carry out the provisions of a will.

Coinsurance. The percentage of an approved health-care charge that the insured individual is required to pay. (*See also* Copayment.)

Collectible. An item purchased by an investor for its value. The investor hopes that the value of the collectible will increase and thus yield a profit when the item is sold. Collectible items include jewelry, diamonds, rare books, paintings and other art works, stamps, antiques, and Oriental rugs.

Columbarium. A building in which cremation urns are stored.

Commercial paper. A corporate promissory note, usually issued in denominations of $100,000 or more. It is used to raise funds for a limited period of time, usually sixty days or less. Higher-risk loans pay higher interest rates.

Common law. Law based on court decisions and customs rather than on written codes.

Common stock. A security that represents an owner-

ship interest in a corporation and the right to share in profits. Owners of common stock have the potential of earning not only dividends but also capital appreciation. (*See also* Preferred Stock.)

Common stock mutual fund. *See* Growth mutual fund.

Community property. A form of concurrent ownership in which property acquired after marriage is considered to be owned equally—50 percent each—by the two spouses, no matter who contributes the money to pay for its purchase or upkeep. (*See also* Concurrent ownership; Joint tenancy with right of survivorship; Separate property; Tenancy by the entirety; Tenancy in common.)

Compounding. The process of earning interest on interest already earned on an investment. When interest is left to accumulate, compound interest is earned.

Comprehensive major medical insurance. A type of health insurance that covers the high costs of serious long-term illness, picking up where basic health insurance ends. Some plans have very high deductibles and provide benefits of $500,000 to $1,000,000. Other plans provide first-dollar coverage of some health-care services, meaning that there is no deductible. (*See also* Basic medical/surgical insurance; Catastrophic major medical insurance.)

Compressed work week. A rearrangement of work time so that more hours are worked on some days, and no hours on other days. For example, five 8-hour days may be compressed into four 10-hour days.

Concurrent ownership. Ownership and control of property by more than one person. The various types of concurrent ownership are treated differently at death. This is also known as plural ownership. (*See also* Community property; Joint tenancy with right of survivorship; Sole ownership; Tenancy by the entirety; Tenancy in common.)

Conditional sales agreement. A type of sales agreement in which the buyer agrees to pay a specified amount of money per month for a given number of months. Title remains with the seller until the final payment is made by the buyer. The buyer's failure to meet the payments gives the seller the right to repossess the item and sue for any deficiency plus court costs. (*See also* Chattel mortgage.)

Condominium. A legal plan of ownership in which the purchaser buys and owns a house or apartment, and has joint ownership of any common grounds or facilities, such as recreational areas. The purchaser of a condominium owns the space he or she occupies and has the right to dispose of this space as he or she wishes.

Conservator. An individual who is court-appointed to look after the financial affairs of a person (known as a ward) who has been judged incompetent.

Consolidated Omnibus Budget Reconciliation Act (COBRA). A law passed in 1986 that requires businesses that have more than twenty employees and offer health insurance to continue coverage at group rates for up to eighteen months for employees who retire, quit, switch from full-time to part-time status, or are laid off.

Continuing care retirement community (CCRC). A facility that combines features of standard retirement communities, assisted living facilities, and nursing homes in one complex that is appropriate for both healthy and active retirees, and retirees who require either minimal assistance or skilled nursing care. A CCRC is sometimes called a life care community.

Contract. A legally binding agreement between two or more parties.

Contributory insurance plan. A type of health insurance plan in which the employer and employee each contribute some portion of the premium cost.

Contributory pension plan. A type of pension plan in which both the employer and the employee share the cost of the contribution in some prescribed proportion. (*See also* Noncontributory pension plan.)

Conventional mortgage. A home loan available to good credit risks, with fixed monthly payments that cover interest and amortization for the life of the loan. This type of loan is usually not insured by the Federal Housing Administration or guaranteed by the Veterans Administration. It is also known as a fixed rate mortgage. (*See also* Adjustable rate mortgage.)

Convertible. A corporate bond or preferred stock that may be exchanged by the owner for common stock or another security, usually of the same company, in accordance with the terms of the issue.

Convertible term insurance. A term policy that allows you to convert the policy to some type of cash value life insurance policy without a medical examination.

Cooperative. A legal plan of ownership in which the purchaser buys shares in the corporation that owns the land and the entire structure or complex, but does not own the land or housing unit itself. The purchaser cannot get a mortgage, but may get a loan to purchase the shares. If the occupant wishes to sell his or her shares, permission must be obtained from the board of directors of the cooperative.

Copayment. The specific dollar amount of an approved health-care charge that must be paid by the insured individual. (*See also* Coinsurance.)

Corporation. A form of business organization in which the enterprise is a legal entity that is treated like a natural person. It can make contracts; own, buy, and sell property; incur debts; and engage in lawsuits in a court of law. The corporation enjoys perpetual life, and the stockholders enjoy limited liability. (*See also* Individual proprietorship; Partnership.)

Cost-escalator clause. A statement in a lease which stipulates that as maintenance costs and taxes rise, the rent can be increased.

Cost-of-living adjustment (COLA). Annual increases in Social Security benefits designed to protect retirement income against the inroads of inflation.

Coupon bond. A bond that has postdated interest coupons attached. As they become due, the coupons are clipped and presented at a bank for deposit or cash. The bank is then reimbursed by the issuing corporation or government agency. (*See also* Bearer bond; Registered bond.)

Coupon rate. The interest rate of a coupon bond.

Covered services. Services and supplies for which Medicare will pay. (*See also* Noncovered services.)

Credit-shelter trust. *See* Bypass trust.

Cremation. The act of incinerating a body. The residue of ashes includes small bone fragments.

Crematory. An establishment that incinerates a body as the means of disposal.

Crypt. A vault or underground chamber for burial of the dead.

Current charge. *See* Actual charge.

Currently insured. Having earned six quarters of coverage, or six units of Social Security credit, in the three years before death. (*See also* Quarter of coverage.)

Custodial care. Help in meeting personal needs such as walking, getting in and out of bed, bathing, dressing, eating, and taking medication. Custodial care can be provided by persons without professional skills or training.

Customary charge. The fee that was most frequently charged by doctors or other suppliers for a specific service or supply during the previous calendar year. (*See also* Actual charge; Approved charge.)

Date of maturity. The date on which a loan matures, or becomes due.

Death benefit. 1. A refund to the policyholder's estate of any premiums paid, minus any benefits the company paid on the policyholder's behalf. Usually, this benefit is payable only if the policyholder dies before a certain age, typically 65 or 70. **2.** A benefit paid to survivors to cover funeral costs. The two most important benefits generally available to survivors are the Social Security survivor benefit and the Department of Veterans Affairs' death benefit.

Death certificate. A document, signed by a physician, medical examiner, or coroner, giving pertinent information about a deceased person, such as name; age; and date, time, place, and cause of death.

Death taxes. Those taxes levied upon property that is transferred to heirs upon the death of the estate owner. Death taxes include the federal estate tax and state inheritance and estate taxes.

Debenture bond. A corporate bond that is backed by the general credit of the issuing corporation, and not by any specified piece of property.

Decreasing term insurance. A term policy whose face value is reduced in stages over a prescribed period. The reduction is often tied to the unpaid balance of a mortgage or other type of loan so as to pay off the debt at the insured's death.

Deductible. The amount that an insured individual must pay toward claims before the insurance carrier begins to calculate benefits due the individual.

Deduction. An amount that may be deducted from gross income as a means of lowering taxable income. (*See also* Gross income; Taxable income.)

Deed. A written instrument that conveys title to real property, such as a house. (*See also* Title.)

Deferred annuity. A type of annuity that begins making payments to the annuitant at a later date, which is specified in the annuity contract. (*See also* Immediate pay annuity.)

Deficit. The amount by which expenditures exceed income.

Defined benefit plan. A type of pension plan in which a formula is used to determine the pension, and the employer is responsible for contributing enough to the pension fund over the years to insure that the retirement allowance equals the amount prescribed by the formula. (*See also* Defined contribution plan.)

Defined contribution plan. A type of pension plan in which the employer and/or employee contributes a fixed amount each year to a fund that is then invested in some way by the plan's administrator to earn income. At retirement, the money credited to the employee's account is used to purchase an annuity, which provides the monthly pension. The employee receives only as much of an annuity as the accumulation in the account will buy. (*See also* Defined benefit plan.)

Delayed retirement credit (DRC). An additional cash benefit awarded for each year of work after the normal retirement age during which an eligible individual does not draw Social Security benefits. (*See also* Primary insurance amount.)

Dental expense insurance. A type of health insurance that provides coverage for necessary dental care, including oral examinations, X-rays, cleanings, fillings, extractions, inlays, crowns, bridgework, dentures, oral surgery, treatment of gums, root canal, and teeth alignment.

Dependent child. A person under 18 years of age, a full-time elementary or secondary school student up to 19 years of age, or an older child with a disability that began before age 22.

Dependent parent. A person who is receiving at least 50 percent of his or her support from an offspring.

Direct disposition. The act of burying or cremating a body without embalming, a ceremony, or a viewing.

Disability. A condition in which an individual is so severely disabled physically or mentally that he or she is unable to do "any substantial gainful work." The condition must be expected either to last at least twelve months or to result in death. (*See also* Disability insurance.)

Disability benefits. The benefits provided by some pension plans if an employee is unable to work because of illness or disability. Plans vary in their definitions of "disability," as well as in the age and service requirements that determine eligibility for the benefits.

Disability income insurance. A type of insurance that provides a percentage of your regular income when you are unable to work for an extended period of time because of illness or injury.

Disability insurance (DI). A Social Security benefit that protects an individual, his or her spouse, and his or her children during working years by providing benefits if the individual becomes unable to work because of an extended illness or other disability. The amount of the disability benefit is the primary insurance amount at the time the worker becomes disabled. (*See also* Disability; Primary insurance amount.)

Diversification. The allocation of investment funds among stocks, bonds, and instruments of the money market in order to reduce the risks associated with the volatility of the market.

Dividend. The payment that a corporation makes to the holders of its common stock or preferred stock. On common stock, the dividend varies with the fortunes of the company and may be skipped if business is bad. On preferred stock, the dividend is usually a fixed amount. (*See also* Common stock; Interest; Preferred stock.)

Domicile. A legal residence.

Donee. A person to whom a gift is made.

Donor. A person who makes a gift.

Down payment. The cash a borrower puts toward a purchase, with the remainder of the purchase cost borrowed from a creditor.

Draft. A document for transferring money.

Durable power of attorney. A legal document in which an individual designates another person to act as his or her legal representative in financial transactions. Unlike an ordinary power of attorney, a durable power of attorney remains in effect even if the individual becomes incompetent or otherwise disabled.

Durable power of attorney for health care. A legal document in which an individual designates another person to make medical decisions for him or her if the individual becomes unable to make them for him- or herself.

Early retirement. Retirement before age 65. A worker can retire as early as age 62 and receive Social Security retirement benefits if he or she is fully insured. But if the worker retires at 62, he or she will receive only 80 percent of the primary insurance amount. This reduction is permanent; the primary insurance amount will not increase to the full amount when the worker reaches normal retirement age. (*See also* Fully insured; Primary insurance amount.)

Earth burial. The act or ceremony of burying the remains of a deceased person in the ground. This is the most widely used form of disposition in the United States and Canada.

Elder-care lawyer. A lawyer who focuses on the legal needs of the elderly, and works with a variety of legal tools to meet the goals and objectives of the older client. Areas of expertise may include estate planning; probate; nursing home and other senior housing and health-care issues; Medicaid and Medicare; and other areas of importance to the elderly.

Elimination period. The period between the time a policyholder becomes disabled and the date when payments by the insurance company begin.

Embalming. The process of treating a dead body using chemicals so as to preserve it and make possible open-casket viewing. (*See also* Preservation.)

Emergency savings fund. A cash reserve that will serve as a cushion in case of an unexpected emergency. The size of the reserve should be equal to the cost of living for three to six months, depending on individual needs.

Employee Retirement Income Security Act (ERISA). A federal pension reform act, approved in 1974, that established rules for private employers engaged in interstate commerce regarding eligibility for pensions, funding, vesting, financing, survivors' benefits, and disclosure to participants.

Employment agency. An organization that helps people find jobs. The services of a public agency are free; private agencies charge a fee. Employment agencies are also known as personnel agencies.

Endowment life insurance. A cash value life insurance policy for which premiums are paid for a specified number of years. At the end of this time, the cash value of the policy equals the face value, which is paid to the insured by the insurance company. The death benefit is equal to whatever has been paid in, plus accrued interest. This type of policy is usually used to help fund a child's college education or to build a retirement nest egg.

Equity. The dollar value of a property owned by an individual or individuals beyond any mortgage on it; the difference between fair market value and current indebtedness.

Escrow. The deposit of money and documents placed in the custody of a neutral third party until the terms and conditions of an agreement or contract are fulfilled.

Estate. The assets that an individual leaves to his or her heirs.

Estate planning. The process through which an individual analyzes his or her assets and liabilities, manages them effectively during his or her lifetime, and arranges for their disposal at death so as to best serve the needs of the beneficiaries.

Estate tax. A federal tax levied upon the gross estate of a deceased person prior to its division, and paid by the executor of the estate.

Eulogy. A speech or writing in honor or praise of a deceased person.

Eurodollars. American dollars invested in banks in foreign countries, especially in Europe.

Exclusion. An expense or condition that a health insurance plan does not cover and toward which it will not pay.

Exclusive listing. A written agreement that gives one real estate agent the right to sell a property for a specified period of time, but does not restrict the right of the owner to sell the property on his or her own without payment of a commission. (*See also* Central listing service; Exclusive right-to-sell listing.)

Exclusive right-to-sell listing. A written agreement that entitles a real estate agent to a commission regardless of who sells the property during the period of the agreement. (*See also* Exclusive listing.)

Executor *(masculine)*, Executrix *(feminine).* A person designated in a will to carry out the provisions of the will. An executor is also known as a personal representative. (*See also* Administrator; Successor executor.)

Exemption. A fixed deduction allowed to every taxpayer, except those whose gross income is above a certain level, for each of the taxpayer's dependents and for the taxpayer himself.

Extensive Agreement. A care facility contract that offers housing and residential services as well as most health-related services for one monthly fee. (*See also* Fee-for-Service Agreement; Modified Agreement.)

Face value. The amount of a life insurance policy that is scheduled to be paid at the death of the insured or at the maturity of the policy. (*See also* Cash value.)

Family plot. A burial site for one or more graves owned by a family.

Fannie Mae. The nickname for a bond issued by the Federal National Mortgage Association (FNMA), a private corporation created by Congress to serve as a secondary mortgage market. Fannie Mae bonds may be purchased through a bond broker or by buying into a mutual fund that specializes in them. (*See also* Ginnie Mae.)

Federal Insurance Contributions Act (FICA). The federal law that sets the tax rate and maximum taxable amount for Social Security taxes. (*See also* Tax rate.)

Fee-for-Service Agreement. A care facility contract that offers housing and residential services, but no health care, for a monthly fee. (*See also* Extensive Agreement; Modified Agreement.)

Fee-for-service (FFS) plan. The traditional Medicare health plan that allows the insured individual to select any doctor or hospital he or she chooses. Medicare then pays 80 percent of the approved amount, and the individual pays the 20-percent balance.

Fiduciary. An individual or institution granted specific rights, duties, and powers to act for a person in his or her behalf, and carry out the provisions specified in that person's will. (*See also* Administrator; Executor; Guardian; Trustee.)

First dollar coverage. A type of health insurance that pays full coverage with no deductible.

Fixed dollar annuity. A type of annuity that pays a fixed amount every month because the funds in the annuity account are invested in a portfolio of bonds that pay a set amount of interest. (*See also* Variable annuity.)

Fixed income asset. An asset, such as a bond, that has a fixed rate of return or interest.

Fixed premium annuity. A type of annuity purchased by making a fixed payment each month or each year. (*See also* Single premium annuity; Variable premium annuity.)

Fixed rate mortgage. *See* Conventional mortgage.

Flexible location. A work arrangement under which part of the time is spent working on the company's premises, and the rest of the time is spent working at home.

Flextime. A work schedule in which the starting and stopping times are arranged to satisfy the special needs of the employee.

Freddie Mac. The nickname for a bond issued by the Federal Home Loan Mortgage Corporation.

Fully funded pension plan. A pension plan that has enough funds contributed each year to cover the obligations to pay future benefits that build up during the year. (*See also* Underfunded pension plan; Unfunded pension plan.)

Fully insured. Completely eligible for Social Security benefits. When a worker is fully insured, he or she has worked the required number of quarters of coverage (QCs) for the worker's age. Being fully insured does not mean that the worker will get the highest monthly benefit; it means that he or she will be eligible for benefits at retirement, and that survivors can get benefits when the worker dies. (*See also* Quarter of coverage.)

Funeral director. An individual who arranges burial or cremation of the dead, and assists in funeral rites. A funeral director is sometimes called a mortician or undertaker.

Funeral home. An establishment where the body of the deceased may repose before the funeral, and where those who knew the deceased may pay last respects. A funeral home is also known as a funeral chapel, funeral parlor, or mortuary.

Funeral service. A ceremony held in connection with the cremation or burial of a dead person.

Futures contract. A contract to buy or sell a given commodity on a future date for a specified price. The market that handles futures contracts is known as the futures market, and trades in agricultural products such as wheat, soybeans, and pork bellies; metals; and financial instruments. Businesses utilize futures as a hedge against price changes. Speculators buy and sell futures to profit from price changes.

Gaps. Out-of-pocket expenses for medical costs, including deductibles and copayments.

Gatekeeper mechanisms. Restrictive clauses in a policy developed by insurance companies to reduce their exposure to the policyholder's claims, and thereby increase their profits.

General mortgage bond. A corporate bond that is secured by a blanket mortgage on the borrowing company's property. (*See also* Mortgage bond.)

General obligation bond. A municipal bond whose payment of interest and repayment of principal are backed by the full faith and credit of the issuing government. (*See also* Revenue bond.)

Gift. A voluntary transfer of property from one person to another. An individual can give gifts to his or her children, grandchildren, relatives, or other people, or to charities, either while the individual is still living or after death through a charitable foundation or trust.

Gift tax. A federal tax levied upon a gift transferred between living individuals.

Ginnie Mae. The nickname for a bond issued by the Government National Mortgage Association (GNMA), a subsidiary organization of the United States Department of Housing and Urban Development, which guarantees funds invested in the mortgage market by institutional investors such as pension funds. Ginnie Mae bonds may be purchased through a bond broker or by buying into a mutual fund that specializes in them. (*See also* Fannie Mae.)

Graded vesting. A type of vesting in which an employee becomes vested in stages. Companies vest 20 percent after three years, and an additional 20 percent every year thereafter, until the employee is fully vested after seven years. (*See also* Cliff vesting; Vesting upon entry.)

Grave marker. *See* Monument; Tombstone.

Gross income. The total income received from all sources before deductions and exemptions.

Growth and income mutual fund. A mutual fund whose investment holdings are balanced among common stocks, preferred stocks, and bonds, giving the investor a balanced risk and return. This is also known as a balanced mutual fund.

Growth mutual fund. A mutual fund whose investments are primarily in common stocks. This is the most popular type of mutual fund.

Guaranteed renewable term insurance. A life insurance policy that is purchased for a term of one to five years, and offers the right to renew without proof of insurability—namely, a medical examination.

Guardian. A person who has the responsibility to care for a minor or an incompetent adult, to control the property of such an individual, or to do both. (*See also* Successor guardian.)

Health care proxy. A legal document in which an individual gives another person the power to decide his or her medical treatment in the event that the individual loses the capacity to make such decisions for him- or herself.

Health maintenance organization (HMO). An organized system of health care that provides a full range of health maintenance and treatment services to an enrolled population in return for a fixed sum of money agreed upon and paid in advance. An HMO bands doctors and hospitals into a network. Members must then choose health-care providers from the network.

Heirs. Those who inherit the property of another individual.

High-grade bond. A bond that is rated triple-A.

Holographic will. A handwritten will that is signed and dated by the person writing the will. Recognized in a minority of the fifty states, holographic wills require no witnesses.

Home equity loan. A loan that uses an individual's home as collateral, and enables that individual to borrow money as needed by writing a check or using a credit card.

Home health agency. A public or private agency that provides home care through physicians, nurses, therapists, social workers, and homemakers.

Home health care. A wide range of services, from skilled care and physical therapy to housekeeping and personal care, delivered at home or in a residential setting.

Homemaker. A home care worker who supports individuals through meal preparation and housekeeping services.

Hospice. A program through which a terminally ill patient is provided with pain relief and supportive services, either as an inpatient or at home.

Hospital insurance (HI). Part A of Medicare. Hospital Insurance pays for the costs of hospitalization.

Hospitalization insurance. A type of health insurance that provides coverage for the expenses incurred while an individual is a patient in a hospital.

Immediate disposal. *See* Direct disposition.

Immediate pay annuity. A type of annuity that begins making payments to the annuitant immediately. (*See also* Deferred annuity.)

Income mutual fund. A mutual fund that seeks to return a higher level of dividends than do other types of mutual funds by investing in high-yielding common stocks, preferred stocks, and bonds.

Incompetent. A legal term describing an individual who, because of mental or physical disabilities, is incapable of managing day-to-day affairs, such as paying bills, making bank transactions, and handling mail.

Indemnity benefit contract. A type of health insurance plan that pays fixed dollar amounts and, therefore, may not keep up with inflation. (*See also* Service benefit contract.)

Indexing. The adjusting of past earnings to account for changes in average wages since the year the earnings were received. Indexing is part of the current method of calculating Social Security retirement benefits. (*See also* Average indexed monthly earnings.)

Individual proprietorship. A form of business organization in which one individual owns and manages the enterprise, assumes all the risks, and derives all the profits. (*See also* Corporation; Partnership.)

Individual Retirement Account (IRA). A personal retirement fund that an individual can establish by making contributions of up to $2,000 per year. Depending on various factors, money contributed to a traditional IRA may be partially or totally tax-deductible the year it is contributed, but is subject to income tax the year it is withdrawn. (*See also* Roth Individual Retirement Account.)

Inflation protection. A type of protection offered by some insurance companies so that benefits paid will be adjusted to keep up with inflation.

Inheritance tax. A tax levied upon the property that individual beneficiaries receive from the estate of a deceased person.

Installment refund annuity. A type of annuity that pays income for life, but that, if the annuitant dies before the payments equal the amount he or she put into the annuity minus specified administrative charges, pays the balance to the designated beneficiary in regular payments. (*See also* Cash refund annuity; Joint and survivor annuity.)

Insurance premium. An installment payment toward the purchase of a life insurance policy. Each payment increases the cash value of the insurance policy.

Intangible personal property. *See* Personal property.

Integrated pension plan. A type of pension plan that is tied in with Social Security. A participant's monthly pension amount is reduced by a percentage of his or her monthly Social Security benefit.

Inter vivos trust. *See* Living trust.

Interest. The fee a borrower pays a lender for the use of money. A corporation pays interest on its bonds to its bondholders. Banks pay interest to depositors.

Interview. A meeting between an employer or employer representative and a job-seeker to determine suitability for a job.

Intestate. One who dies without leaving a valid will.

Irrevocable living trust. A trust that cannot be changed or cancelled during the lifetime of the person who created the trust. (*See also* Living trust; Revocable living trust.)

Itemized deduction. A deduction that gives preferential treatment to taxpayers who report certain expenditures, such as unusual medical expenses, and thereby lowers the taxes of these individuals.

Job reassignment. The shifting of an employee from one job to another job with a different set of job specifications.

Job redesign. A change in job specifications or job description.

Job sharing. The splitting of the hours and responsibilities of a single full-time job between two workers.

Job specifications. A detailed description of the functions that must be performed in a particular job.

Joint and survivor annuity. 1. A pension plan provision in which an individual designated by the covered employee, usually the spouse, receives the pension benefits if the worker dies. The annuity gives the survivor a minimum of 50 percent of the benefit that would have been payable to the retiree. However, to pay for this coverage, the retiree must accept a lower pension while alive. **2.** A type of annuity that guarantees income for life to two or more people, generally a husband and wife, so that the survivor can receive the same monthly income or some percentage of the monthly income as long as he or she lives. (*See also* Cash refund annuity; Installment refund annuity.)

Joint tenancy with right of survivorship (JTWROS). A form of concurrent ownership in which property is held jointly, with each partner owning an equal share, and with the entire property passing to the survivor in the event of the other owner's death. Property held in this way avoids probate. (*See also* Community property; Tenancy by the entirety; Tenancy in common.)

Keogh plan. A type of retirement plan for self-employed individuals.

Late retirement. Retirement after age 65. For each year an individual works beyond retirement age, but does not collect Social Security benefits, he or she earns a bonus benefit that is a percentage of the primary insurance amount. (*See also* Delayed retirement credit; Primary insurance amount.)

Lease. A contract that gives a tenant possession and use of a property under the conditions and terms stated.

Legacy. *See* Bequest.

Liabilities. All forms of indebtedness for which an individual, a family, or a business is legally liable.

Life annuity with a term certain. A type of annuity that guarantees income for life, but if the annuitant dies within the designated "term certain"—a guaranteed period, such as ten years or twenty years—provides the designated beneficiary with payments for the remainder of the term. (*See also* Straight life annuity.)

Life care community. *See* Continuing care retirement community.

Life insurance. Protection for an insured's dependents against the hardships they might suffer due to the loss of the insured's income because of death.

Life insurance trust. A trust that is designed to accept the proceeds of a life insurance policy.

Limited liability. The legal condition in which a stockholder cannot be held personally responsible for the debts of the corporation beyond the amount that he or she has already invested in the enterprise.

Limited payment life insurance. A cash value life insurance policy that is similar to a whole life insurance policy except that the premium payments are made for a specified number of years or until a specified age. The policy remains in effect after the premiums have all been paid.

Liner. An outer receptacle made of concrete that surrounds a casket on all sides but the bottom. The liner is designed to support the gravesite in the event that the casket disintegrates. (*See also* Vault.)

Liquid. Readily converted into cash. Used to describe an asset such as a savings account.

Living trust. A trust that becomes effective during the lifetime of the maker of the trust. The property is placed in the hands of a *trustee,* and is managed by the trustee for the benefit of one or more individuals. It does not pass through probate when the holder dies. (*See also* Irrevocable living trust; Revocable living trust.)

Living will. A legal document in which an individual requests that his or her life not be prolonged by artificial means when there is no expectation of recovery.

Load mutual fund. A mutual fund that maintains a sales force and charges a commission, or load, for the purchase of shares. In most cases, no commission is charged when shares are sold. About half of all mutual funds are load funds. (*See also* No-load mutual fund.)

Long term. Ten or more years.

Long-term care. Assistance provided over a long period of time to people with chronic health conditions and/or physical disabilities who require help with life's daily tasks.

Long-term care insurance. A type of health insurance, available through private insurance companies, that provides coverage for long-term nursing home care and long-term custodial home care.

Long-term growth mutual fund. A growth mutual fund that takes less risk and seeks long-term growth.

Loss ratio. The amount an insurance company pays out in benefits compared with the amount it collects in premiums. This is also known as the rate of return.

Lump-sum death benefit. A one-time lump sum of money paid by Social Security upon the death of an insured individual, either working or retired. This benefit is paid to the surviving spouse or minor children.

Margin account. A brokerage account in which an investor maintains a deposit of money. When an investor buys stock, he or she pays only part of the purchase price with cash; the investor borrows the rest of the purchase price from the broker. The investor buys on margin in the hope of a price advance, enabling him or her to repay the loan and make a profit. If the market declines, however, the investor may be asked by the broker to make an additional deposit in the margin account. If the investor cannot make the deposit, the broker can sell the stock to liquidate the loan, and the investor suffers a loss.

Mausoleum. A large tomb for burial of the dead.

Maximum family benefit. The limit on the total amount of Social Security benefits that all members of one family may receive based on the earnings record of one worker. This limit varies with the primary insurance amount. (*See also* Primary insurance amount.)

Maximum taxable amount. The maximum amount of an individual's earnings that can be taxed each year. Individuals do not have to pay any taxes on earnings over this amount.

Medicaid. A public-assistance program designed to provide benefits to people who are unable to pay for health care. The official name of this program is Medical Assistance.

Medicare. A federal health insurance program for people 65 or older, and certain disabled people under 65. It is run by the Health Care Financing Administration of the United States Department of Health and Human Services, and paid for through Social Security taxes.

Medicare supplement insurance. Private commercial insurance that covers some of the gaps in Medicare coverage. This is often referred to as Medigap insurance.

Medigap insurance. *See* Medicare supplement insurance.

Memorial service. A ceremony, usually held after a body has been buried or cremated, to honor the dead.

Memorial society. A nonprofit cooperative designed to help people arrange for the funeral services they want at a reasonable price.

Minimal container. *See* Alternative container.

Mobile home. A factory-manufactured housing unit that is transported on wheels to a site where the wheels are removed and the unit is set up on a permanent foundation of concrete blocks or poured concrete.

Modified Agreement. A care facility contract that offers housing and residential services as well as a specified amount of long-term health care for one monthly fee. (*See also* Extensive Agreement; Fee-for-Service Agreement.)

Money market. The collective name for transactions involving the borrowing or lending of money for a short term by the government, banks, large corporations, securities dealers, or individual investors. A short term is considered to be one year or less.

Money market deposit account (MMDA). A type of savings account offered by savings banks, savings and loan associations, and commercial banks, which invest the savings in money market instruments. In return, the depositor earns a relatively high rate of interest.

Money market instruments. Short-term paper traded in the money market. Examples are United States Treasury bills, certificates of deposit, commercial paper, banker's acceptances, and repurchase agreements.

Money market mutual fund. A mutual fund whose investment holdings are in high-yield money market instruments. The purpose of the fund is to make high-yield money market instruments, which are normally purchased by institutions in denominations of $100,000 or more, available to individuals of moderate means, who can buy into the fund with only a few hundred dollars.

Monument. A tombstone or other structure erected as a marker for a grave. (*See also* Tombstone.)

Moody's Investors Service. A well-known stock and bond rating service.

Mortgage bond. A corporate bond that is secured by a mortgage on a specific piece of the borrowing company's property, which is usually of a durable nature, such as land, buildings, or machinery.

Mortgagee. A borrower or owner in a mortgage transaction who pledges property as security for a debt.

Mortgagor. A lender in a transaction involving a mortgage instrument.

Mortuary. *See* Funeral Home.

Multiple listing service. *See* Central listing service.

Municipal bond. A debt security issued by a state, county, or city that pays interest, which is usually exempt from federal income taxes and from the income tax of the state that issued the bond. Bonds issued by counties or other subdivisions within a state are exempt from the income tax of the home state as well as from federal income taxes. This is also known as a municipal. (*See also* General obligation bond; Revenue bond.)

Mutual fund. A company that collects the funds of hundreds of thousands of small investors through the sale of stock, and then uses the funds for a variety of investments. Mutual funds are classified according to their investment objectives. (*See also* Growth and income mutual fund; Growth mutual fund; Income mutual fund; Specialized mutual fund.)

Nasdaq. The National Association of Securities Dealers Automated Quotation system. This computerized system provides price quotations for stocks that are traded over-the-counter, and for many stocks listed on the New York Stock Exchange. The Nasdaq Composite Index is a widely quoted benchmark for these stocks.

Negotiable interest rate. An interest rate that is negotiated between investor and institution.

Net worth. The monetary value of an individual, a family, or a business. It is equal to total assets minus total liabilities. (*See also* Assets; Liabilities.)

No-load mutual fund. A mutual fund that does not have a sales force, does not charge a commission or sales fee, and waits for investors to buy its shares. About half of all mutual funds are no-load. (*See also* Load mutual fund.)

Noncontributory insurance plan. A type of health insurance plan in which the employer pays the full premium cost.

Noncontributory pension plan. A type of pension plan financed entirely by the employer. The majority of corporate pension plans are noncontributory. (*See also* Contributory pension plan.)

Noncovered services. Services and supplies for which Medicare will not pay, and that must be paid by the insured individual. (*See also* Covered services.)

Normal retirement benefits. The benefits received when retiring at the normal age of 65. Most pension plans have designed their benefit programs for retirement at this age.

Nursing home. A facility that provides room and board and a planned, continuous medical treatment program, including twenty-four-hour-a-day skilled nursing care and custodial care, for people of all ages who are unable to care for themselves.

Obituary. A notice of the death of a person, generally printed in a newspaper, and often containing a brief biographical sketch.

Ombudsman. Someone who investigates complaints and problems, reports findings, and mediates settlements.

Open-end mutual fund. A mutual fund that continuously sells new shares of stocks, and purchases the shares of investors desiring redemption. It buys and sells shares at a fixed price, and uses whatever funds it has for investment. (*See also* Closed-end mutual fund.)

Optical expense program. An insurance benefit plan that provides eyeglasses, and often a specified sum of money toward the purchase of contact lenses, to eligible members and their dependents.

Option. The right to buy or sell a certain number of shares of a particular stock at a specified price within a limited period of time. (*See also* Call option; Put option.)

Oral will. A will that is made within the hearing of two witnesses, and is valid only if the maker of the will is in danger of imminent death or on active duty in the United States military.

Organ donor card. A card prepared in advance of death, indicating the deceased's wishes for disposal of the body, including possible donation of the body or specific organs for medical purposes.

Over-the-counter stock. Stock of companies that do not have sufficient shares, stockholders, or earnings to qualify for listing on a major exchange, and therefore is traded directly by the buyer and seller, not through a broker.

Paid-up life insurance. Cash value life insurance that remains in force even though no additional premiums are required.

Par value. The face value printed on a stock certificate or bond instrument, and assigned at the time of original issue. Many stocks are issued with no par value.

Participating supplier. A physician, facility, or other supplier that accepts Medicare insurance.

Partnership. A form of business organization created through a contractual arrangement between two or more individuals, each of whom assumes unlimited personal liability for the debts of the joint enterprise. (*See also* Corporation; Individual proprietorship.)

Part-time work. Employment of fewer than 35 hours a week.

Passbook savings account. A basic savings account, which usually pays a relatively low interest rate.

Pass-through security. A United States agency bond such as a Fannie Mae or Ginnie Mae. The homeowner's payments of interest and principal are passed through to the investors, who have bought shares in one or more of the mortgage pools.

Pay-as-you-go system. The system by which almost all of the taxes paid by workers into Social Security in a particular year were paid out to that year's Social Security beneficiaries. The Social Security Amendments of 1983 replaced this system with one that accumulates reserves for future beneficiary payments.

Payment-to-you method. A method of payment in which the doctor or supplier bills the insured individual for the actual charge. The individual pays the bill, after which either he or his doctor submits a claim to the Medicare carrier, which decides on the approved charge for the service or supply, and reimburses the individual 80 percent. (*See also* Assignment method.)

P/E. The price-to-earnings ratio calculated by dividing the price of a stock by its earnings per share. Mutual fund managers often use P/Es to determine how much they are paying for each stock's growth potential.

Peer review organization (PRO). A group of practicing doctors and other health-care professionals paid by the federal government to review the hospital care of Medicare patients.

Penny stock. An issue that sells for less than $1 a share. Such a low-priced stock is often highly speculative.

Pension. A benefit, usually monthly, paid to an individual who has retired from active work.

Pension Benefit Guarantee Corporation (PBGC). An agency established by the Employee Retirement Income Security Act (ERISA) of 1974 that guarantees benefits to private pension plan members even when a plan's assets are insufficient to fulfill its commitments.

Permanent insurance. *See* Cash value life insurance.

Personal care. Assistance with the activities of daily living, such as bathing, dressing, and eating. (*See also* Activities of daily living.)

Personal income tax. A tax based on income received, and imposed on individuals and families.

Personal property. The things that people own other than land and the buildings on it. The two types are *tangible personal property*, which is something you can touch, such as clothing, a car, and a boat; and *intangible personal property*, which is a right or an interest protected by law, such as an invention, a stock certificate, or a savings account. (*See also* Real property.)

Personal representative. *See* Executor.

Phased retirement. A program that helps older employees ease into retirement by gradually reducing their work time, but without reducing their ultimate pension benefits.

Plot. The cemetery land purchased by an individual for burial in a grave.

Plural ownership. *See* Concurrent ownership.

Point-of-service (POS) plan. A Medicare health plan much like an HMO, except that members are allowed to seek health-care services outside the network at some additional cost, a portion of which is paid by the POS. This differs from a preferred provider organization (PPO) in that the insured individual must obtain permission before seeking out-of-network care.

Policy. A legal contract that sets forth the rights and obligations of both the policyholder and the insurance company.

Policyholder. The person who owns an insurance policy.

Power of attorney. A written instrument by which one person, known as the principal, appoints another person as an agent with the authority to perform certain specified acts on his or her behalf. (*See also* Durable power of attorney.)

Pre-existing condition. A health condition that existed before the policyholder became insured.

Preferred provider organization (PPO). A Medicare health plan that combines features of fee-for-service (FFS) and managed care by allowing members to choose health care from a network of providers and, at additional cost, from outside the network.

Preferred stock. A security that entitles its holder to receive fixed and stated dividends before earnings are distributed to the common stockholders. Preferred stock represents an ownership interest in a corporation and gives its holder the right to vote when preferred dividends are in default for a specified period. In case of bankruptcy or liquidation, preferred stockholders have priority over common stockholders in the division of the company's assets. However, the claims of bondholders come first. (*See also* Common stock.)

Premarital agreement. A legal agreement that sets forth the details of property distribution in the event that one of the partners in a marriage dies or the marriage is dissolved. Also known as an antenuptial or prenuptial agreement, this contract is most commonly prepared before a second or subsequent marriage.

Premium. The amount of money paid to the insurance carrier in return for insurance protection.

Prenuptial agreement. *See* Premarital agreement.

Prescription medication plan. A type of health insurance that provides coverage for all or part of the cost of prescription medications.

Preservation. Refrigeration of a dead body to make open-casket viewing possible. (*See also* Embalming.)

Primary insurance amount (PIA). The largest Social Security benefit a worker can receive upon retiring at retirement age based on his or her earnings over a lifetime. All Social Security benefits are based on this amount.

Primary payer. The insurance company to which a medical bill is sent for payment first.

Private contracting. A health plan that permits doctors to charge Medicare beneficiaries whatever fee they choose. Beneficiaries then pay the fee out-of-pocket.

Private fee-for-service plan (PFFSP). A Medicare health plan under which the individual chooses a private insurance company that accepts Medicare beneficiaries. Medicare then pays the plan a lump sum for coverage. The private company may charge the insured individual for deductibles and copayments.

Probate. The judicial process of establishing the validity of a will and supervising the distribution of an estate's assets.

Probate court. A lower-level state court that acts as a referee and decision maker by establishing the validity of a will; resolving conflicts of interpretation of a will; and—whether the individual died with or without a will—supervising the distribution of an estate's assets, and paying any debts or taxes owed by the deceased.

Property. An individual's possessions, including, but not limited to, cash, securities, and real estate.

Provider-sponsored organization (PSO). A Medicare health plan that is run by the providers themselves— doctors and hospitals—and offers services directly to members without an insurance company as an intermediary.

Put option. The right to sell a fixed number of shares of a particular stock at a specified price within a limited period of time. The purchaser hopes that the stock's price will go down by an amount sufficient to provide a profit when the option is sold. If the stock price remains the same or goes up, the investment in the put option is lost. (*See also* Call option.)

Qualified pension plan. A type of pension plan that meets a set of criteria developed by the Internal Revenue Service. An employer with a qualified plan can deduct contributions to the plan from taxable income as a business expense.

Qualified terminable interest property trust (Q-Tip). A type of testamentary trust through which the spouse of the maker of the trust has a right to the income from the principal for life, but has no access to the principal. On the death of the surviving spouse, the property goes to such person(s) or organization(s) as determined by the spouse who was the first to die.

Quarter of coverage (QC). A designated time period during which an individual must earn a certain amount of money to receive credit toward being eligible to receive Social Security benefits. The number of QCs that must accrue depend upon the individual's age, with forty being the maximum number required. One quarter is one-fourth of a year.

Rate of return. *See* Loss ratio.

Real estate. *See* Real property.

Real Estate Investment Trust (REIT). An investment fund that is similar to a mutual fund. Small investors buy shares in a REIT, which then uses the funds collected to invest in real estate, including shopping centers and large commercial properties. The return on investments is liberal. However, because of the nature of the real estate market, a REIT is highly speculative.

Real property. Land and the buildings on it. Real property is also known as real estate. (*See also* Personal property.)

Registered bond. A bond that has the owner's name registered on the books of the issuing company or governmental agency, and noted on the bond. A registered bond can be transferred only when endorsed by the registered owner. (*See also* Bearer bond; Coupon bond.)

Renewability. A feature of an insurance policy that guarantees that the company cannot cancel your coverage as long as you pay the premium.

Rental apartment. A dwelling unit that is leased from an owner, and for which the occupant pays rent in accordance with the terms of a lease. (*See also* Lease.)

Repurchase agreement. A type of loan, also known as a repo, in which a bank in need of money for a short period of time, usually one or more days, borrows money from a money market mutual fund using United States Treasury securities as collateral. In effect, the bank sells the Treasury paper to the money market fund with the provision that it will buy the paper back within the specified period of time.

Reserve days. A lifetime allotment of 60 extra days that can be used to lengthen Medicare benefit periods for hospital confinements of more than 90 days.

Respite care. A short-term hospital stay of a hospice patient intended to give temporary relief to the person who regularly assists with home care.

Resumé. A summary of a person's work experience, education, and training. A resumé is one of the most important tools used in job hunting.

Retirement age. The age at which an individual becomes eligible to receive Social Security benefits—currently, age 62. *Full* retirement age is 65, at which time an individual can begin to collect full Social Security benefits. Full retirement age is gradually being increased to 67.

Retirement community. A facility that provides secure accommodations and services for individuals who are capable of meeting their own basic needs, while paying special attention to the social and recreational requirements of the residents.

Retirement insurance. A Social Security benefit that enables workers to retire at age 62 or over, and receive a monthly payment for life.

Revenue bond. A municipal bond designed to raise money for a specific municipal facility, such as an airport or bridge. The payment of interest and repayment of principal are backed by the income earned by the facility. (*See also* General obligation bond.)

Reverse mortgage. A monthly payment made to a homeowner by a mortgage lender, using the home equity as collateral, whereby the monthly payment amounts are accumulated as a mortgage against the house, to be repaid when the homeowner(s) dies and the house is sold. (*See also* Charitable remainder trust; Sale leaseback.)

Revocable living trust. A trust that can be changed or cancelled during the lifetime of the person who created the trust. (*See also* Irrevocable living trust; Living trust.)

Rollover. A tax-free transfer of money from one investment program to another.

Roth Individual Retirement Account (Roth IRA). A type of personal retirement fund that an individual can establish by making nontax-deductible contributions of up to $2,000 per year. Money contributed to the account is taxed the year the contribution is made, but is withdrawn tax-free. (*See also* Individual Retirement Account.)

Sale leaseback. Sale by a homeowner of his or her home in exchange for lifetime tenancy and a guaranteed monthly income. (*See also* Charitable remainder trust; Reverse mortgage.)

Sales contract. An agreement between two or more parties, containing the terms and conditions of the sale. The contract must be written, and must be signed by both parties.

Savings bond. A security sold by the United States government that offers a fixed income with minimum risk and minimum investment. The bonds are sold at a discount, and the interest accumulates over a designated time period.

Savings Incentive Match Plan for Employees (SIMPLE). A type of retirement plan that allows nongovernment employers in small businesses to set up retirement plans for their employees. Contributions are made by both the employee and the employer.

Savings rate. The percentage of an individual's disposable income that is not spent.

Secondary payer. The insurance company to which a medical bill is sent for payment after the first insurance company—the primary payer—pays a benefit. The secondary payer receives the original bill and an explanation of the payment by the primary payer, and then may pay the balance or some portion of the balance.

Second-to-die life insurance. *See* Survivorship whole life insurance.

Sector growth mutual fund. A growth mutual fund that invests in particular areas of the economy, such as energy, chemicals, or nonprecious metals.

Securities Investor Protection Corporation (SIPC). A nonprofit association created by Congress to insure the securities and cash in customer accounts of member brokerage firms against failure of the firms.

Self-Employment Contributions Act. The federal law that sets the tax rate and maximum taxable amount for the self-employed.

Separate property. Property other than real estate that is acquired after marriage but owned by the individual spouse who purchased it. (*See also* Community property.)

Service benefit contract. A type of health insurance plan that pays a percentage of charges and, therefore, keeps up with inflation. (*See also* Indemnity benefit contract.)

Short term. One year or less.

Simplified Employee Pension (SEP). A type of retirement plan that allows nongovernment employers in small businesses to contribute to IRAs set up for their workers. The employees make no contribution.

Single premium annuity. A type of annuity purchased with a single lump-sum payment. (*See also* Fixed premium annuity; Variable premium annuity.)

Single premium life insurance. A cash value life insurance policy for which the insured individual makes a single premium payment, and no further payments are required. This type of policy is also known as single premium whole life insurance.

Skilled nursing care. Nursing and rehabilitative care provided by and under the direction of skilled medical personnel.

Skilled nursing facility. A specially qualified facility that has the staff and equipment to provide skilled nursing care or rehabilitation services and other related health services. Most nursing homes in the United States are not skilled nursing facilities, and many skilled nursing facilities are not certified by Medicare.

Small Business Administration (SBA). A United States government agency created in 1953 to aid small business concerns by providing financial, technical, and managerial assistance.

Social Security. A federal program established in 1935 to provide retirement, survivors', disability, and medical benefits through a payroll tax paid by both employers and employees.

Social Security trust funds. Separate trust funds set up to hold the money allotted for old age and survivors' insurance, disability insurance, and health insurance. Employers and self-employed individuals remit their contributions to the United States Treasury, which credits them to the separate trust funds. A fourth trust fund, for Supplementary Medical Insurance (SMI), receives Medicare Part B premiums and general revenue payments, which are used to fund that program.

Sole ownership. Ownership and control of property by one person who, upon death, leaves the property to chosen heirs. (*See also* Concurrent ownership.)

Specialized mutual fund. A mutual fund whose investment holdings are concentrated in one or two fields such as gold, Eurodollars, commodities, options, or foreign stocks.

Spending down. The practice of depleting almost all of one's assets to meet the eligibility requirements for Medicaid.

Sprinkling trust. A trust that allows the trustee to distribute income to children or other beneficiaries according to need, rather than a specific formula.

Standard & Poor's Corporation. A well-known stock and bond rating service.

Standard deduction. A fixed deduction, determined by filing status, allowed to taxpayers who do not take itemized deductions. (*See also* Itemized deduction.)

Standard marital trust. A trust that provides benefits to the spouse of the maker of the trust for life.

Straight bankruptcy. A form of personal bankruptcy in which the indebted individual is ordered by a bankruptcy court to liquidate a specified amount of assets to repay as much debt as possible. (*See also* Bankruptcy; Wage earner's plan bankruptcy.)

Straight life annuity. A type of annuity that guarantees a stipulated monthly income for life, with no death benefits paid to beneficiaries and no cash surrender value. (*See also* Life annuity with a term certain.)

Straight life insurance. *See* Whole life insurance.

Successor executor. An additional executor listed in a will, who can assume the responsibilities of the initial executor if he or she dies or otherwise becomes unable to meet his or her responsibilities. (*See also* Executor.)

Successor guardian. An additional guardian listed in a will, who can assume the responsibilities of the initial guardian if he or she dies or otherwise becomes unable to meet his or her responsibilities. (*See also* Guardian.)

Summary Plan Description (SPD). A summary description of a pension plan that the Employee Retirement Income Security Act of 1974 requires be given to each employee covered by the plan. It must include information on eligibility requirements for benefits, accumulation of benefits, loss of benefits, termination insurance, and the method of filing a claim for benefits.

Supplemental letter of instructions. A memorandum of personal details that is designed to provide information needed by the executor, who will administer the will. The supplemental letter of instructions should include such information as location of vital documents, location of assets, employment or business information, disposition of personal valuables, and funeral and burial instructions.

Supplemental Security Income (SSI). A separate Social Security program that provides a basic cash income for people age 65 or older who are in financial need, and for the needy of any age who are blind or disabled.

Survivors' benefits. Benefits paid to the surviving spouse or other designated individual of a deceased pension plan participant. (*See also* Joint and survivor annuity.)

Survivors' insurance. A Social Security benefit that is a form of life insurance, providing income to a worker's dependent spouse, children, and parents, if they are qualified, in the event of the worker's death.

Survivorship whole life insurance. A type of life insurance, also known as second-to-die life insurance, that insures two lives, usually husband and wife. Death benefits are paid upon the death of the last of the two named insured.

Tangible personal property. *See* Personal property.

Tax. A contribution exacted from individuals, businesses, or organizations by the government, according to law, for the general support of the government and for the maintenance of public services.

Tax rate. The percentage of an individual's earnings that is paid by both the worker and the employer into the Social Security program each year. A self-employed individual pays a higher rate than does a non-self-employed person. The tax rates are set by Congress.

Tax shelter. An investment that legally enables an individual to defer taxes or, ultimately, to diminish taxes.

Taxable income. A sum derived by subtracting deductions and exemptions from adjusted gross income. By law, the tax rate is applied to taxable income, not to gross income. (*See also* Deduction; Exemption; Gross income.)

Tax-deferred annuity. A type of annuity purchased with pre-tax dollars, which become tax-sheltered. The annuitant pays no income tax on the amount deposited in the annuity account or on the interest earned by the principal until he or she begins to withdraw the money after retirement.

T-bill. *See* United States Treasury bill.

Tenancy by the entirety. A form of concurrent ownership of real property in which each spouse owns the entire property in his or her own right. Upon death, the property passes to the surviving spouse. Elimination of either party's right of survivorship can be accomplished only with the consent of both parties. (*See also* Community property; Joint tenancy with right of survivorship; Tenancy in common.)

Tenancy in common. A form of concurrent ownership in which each partner owns a specified percentage of the property, but not a specific piece. There is no right of survivorship and no automatic transfer at death. The portion owned by each person can be sold, given away, used as collateral, or passed through the particular owner's will. (*See also* Community property; Joint tenancy with right of survivorship; Tenancy by the entirety.)

Term certain annuity. *See* Life annuity with a term certain.

Term life insurance. A type of life insurance, also known as pure insurance, that covers the insured for a specified number of years, and pays the beneficiary the face value of the policy if the insured dies within that specified period. The premium is less than that for any cash value life insurance policy because the policy has no cash value and represents only the cost of pure insurance plus a charge for administration. The policy may be renewable at the end of each term, but not beyond age 65 or 70.

Testamentary trust. A trust that is created by the terms of a will, and that comes into being after the death of the trust's maker.

Testate. One who dies leaving a valid will.

Testator *(masculine)*, Testatrix *(feminine)*. The person who makes a will.

Title. A document indicating the legal right by the owner of record to the possession of real property, such as a house. Title can be acquired through purchase, inheritance, gift, or foreclosure of a mortgage.

Title insurance. Insurance designed to protect owners and lenders against loss from defects in the title.

Title search. The examination of all public records to disclose all facts pertinent to the title of the property.

T-note. *See* United States Treasury note.

Tomb. A chamber or vault for burial of the dead.

Tombstone. A stone marker, usually inscribed, on a grave or tomb.

Totten trust. A payable-on-death bank account that is in trust for a named beneficiary.

Trust. A legal entity created by the owner of property for the purpose of administering and distributing such property for the benefit of the owner and/or other persons, known as beneficiaries.

Trust agreement. A legal document in which the maker of the trust (trustor) names a trustee to distribute income and/or principal to a beneficiary(ies) at specified times.

Trustee. An individual or institution that holds legal title to property in order to administer it for the use and benefit of another person, who is the beneficiary. A trustee may be named in a will or in a trust document.

Truster. The maker of a trust.

Underfunded pension plan. A pension plan with inadequate reserves to meet future pension benefits.

Unfunded pension plan. A pension plan that does not have any reserves to meet future pension benefits.

Uniform Gifts to Minors Act (UGMA). A custodial account that allows a minor child to own property, such as cash, stocks, bonds, mutual funds, and life insurance policies. The assets in the account belong to the child irrevocably, meaning that the account cannot be changed or cancelled. The account is managed by a custodian until the child reaches age 18 or 21, depending on the state's law.

Uniform Transfer to Minors Act (UTMA). A custodial account that allows a minor child to own property, including not only the types of assets allowed under the Uniform Gifts to Minors Act (UGMA), but also such assets as real estate, partnership interests, and artwork. The assets in the account belong to the child irrevocably, meaning that the account cannot be changed or cancelled. The account is managed by a custodian until the child reaches age 18 or 21, depending on the state's law.

Unit investment trust. A mutual fund whose investment holdings are a diversified but fixed portfolio of securities including corporate bonds, municipal bonds, and preferred stock, which provide a steady, guaranteed income. Ownership in the trust is purchased in units.

United States Treasury bill. A short-term security, maturing in three, six, or twelve months, that is backed by the full faith and credit of the United States government. Also known as a T-bill, it pays an attractive yield, which is exempt from state and local income taxes, and subject only to federal income taxes. A T-bill is sold at a discount from its face value.

United States Treasury bond. A bond issued by the United States government that is backed by the full faith and credit of the federal government. Treasury bonds mature in ten or more years, sell at face value, and pay a fixed rate of interest twice a year throughout ownership. The interest is exempt from state and local income taxes, and subject only to federal income taxes.

United States Treasury inflation-indexed securities. Government-issued securities that are continually adjusted for inflation. Inflation-indexed securities mature in two to thirty years, and pay a fixed semiannual rate that is applied to the inflation-adjusted principal.

United States Treasury note. A security that matures in two to ten years. Also known as T-notes, Treasury notes are backed by the full faith and credit of the United States government. The interest is exempt from state and local income taxes, and subject only to federal income taxes.

Universal life insurance. A type of life insurance that allows the policyholder to vary both the amount of the premium payment and the amount of the death benefit to fit the changing needs of his or her growing family. The cash value grows at a competitive market interest rate.

Universal variable life insurance. A hybrid form of insurance, combining universal life insurance and variable life insurance, that allows the policyholder to set most of the terms and conditions of the policy.

Unlimited liability. The legal condition in which owners of individual proprietorships or partnerships are held personally responsible for the debts of the business to the full extent of their assets and personal wealth.

Urn. An ornamental container used to hold cremated remains.

Vanishing premium life insurance. A type of life insurance that has as its goal the production of enough income to pay for premiums after a set period of time. After a specified number of premium payments, the policyholder is fully covered by the policy's death benefit, and no further premiums have to be paid.

Variable annuity. A type of annuity that pays a different amount every month because the funds in the annuity account are invested in a portfolio of stocks, the prices of which fluctuate daily. (*See also* Fixed dollar annuity.)

Variable premium annuity. A type of annuity purchased by monthly or annual installment payments, the size of which may be changed at the annuitant's discretion. (*See also* Fixed premium annuity; Single premium annuity.)

Variable whole life insurance. A type of life insurance that charges the insured a fixed premium, but allows the insured to direct the investment of the cash accumulation among a variety of mutual funds or other types of investments, while providing a guaranteed minimum death benefit.

Vault. An outer receptacle—usually made of concrete and lined with another material—that completely surrounds the casket. The vault is designed to support the gravesite and protect the casket. (*See also* Liner.)

Vesting. The absolute right of an employee to receive money from a retirement plan even if he or she resigns or is fired. Employees' contributions vest immediately and can be withdrawn when the employee leaves the job. However, the rights of employees to employer contributions are generally subject to limitations, including service time requirements and amount limits. (*See also* Cliff vesting; Graded vesting; Vesting upon entry.)

Vesting upon entry. A type of vesting in which an employee is 100-percent vested upon entry to the pension plan, usually after a short waiting period such as two years. (*See also* Cliff vesting; Graded vesting.)

Viewing. A watch or vigil kept over the body of a deceased person before burial. This is also called a wake.

Wage earner's plan bankruptcy. A form of personal bankruptcy in which the indebted individual is ordered by a bankruptcy court to set up a court-approved monthly budget plan to repay as much debt as possible within a three-year period, while still retaining ownership of all real and personal property. (*See also* Bankruptcy; Straight bankruptcy.)

Waiting period. The amount of time that must pass after a person becomes insured before his or her policy begins to pay benefits.

Waiver of premium. A long-term care policy provision that allows the insured to stop paying premiums after he or she has been confined in a nursing home for a specified period of time, typically ninety days.

Wake. *See* Viewing.

Ward. A person who is judged incapable of managing his or her personal affairs, and for whom a conservator is court-appointed.

White-collar worker. A person whose job does not involve manual labor; generally a salaried or professional worker.

Whole life insurance. A type of cash value life insurance, also known as straight life insurance, that covers the insured for life, as long as the premiums are paid. Whole life insurance includes a savings feature against which the insured can borrow, paying interest on the loan. In addition, the insured can withdraw the cash value completely if he or she terminates the insurance. When the insured dies, the beneficiary collects the face value of the policy.

Will. A legal document, almost always in writing and properly executed, which describes how a person wants his or her property distributed after death; designates an executor and, when appropriate, a guardian and/or a trustee; and may include funeral and burial instructions. (*See also* Executor; Guardian; Trustee.)

Wraparound annuity. A type of annuity in which the annuitant controls the investment of the funds in the account. The funds can be invested in stocks, bonds, or a mutual fund, and can be switched from one form of investment to another form to take advantage of changing market conditions. (*See also* Fixed dollar annuity; Tax-deferred annuity; Variable annuity.)

Zero coupon bond. A bond that makes no coupon, or interest, payments. It is sold at a substantial discount and, through the buildup of accrued interest, pays its face value at maturity.

INVENTORY OF PERSONAL AND FINANCIAL DATA

Most people are careful about maintaining records and bits of information concerning their personal and financial status. Too often, however, the material is scattered in files or drawers, recorded in places that may be forgotten, or jotted down on scraps of paper that become outdated and yellowed with age. When the person or the person's family is suddenly confronted with the need for basic information that is necessary to resolve the myriad of situations that inevitably occur, the material is often difficult to locate.

The following Inventory of Personal and Financial Data will prevent delay and confusion when time is of the essence and information must be supplied. The Self-Studies found throughout this book have already allowed you

to record some of this information, always with the goal of collecting and reviewing data that is relevant to the topic of a particular chapter. The pages that follow put all the basic information together in one place. This inventory will put you in a better position to review and evaluate your own personal and financial situation, and, if you are temporarily incapacitated or unable to handle matters because of illness, will allow your family to keep things flowing smoothly.

The time that you spend filling in this inventory now will certainly be worth the effort. Remember to check the information from time to time to be sure that the inventory is current, and, finally, be sure to keep these pages with your other important papers so that the data will always be easy to find.

PERSONAL AND FAMILY INFORMATION   AS OF:_____

(Husband or individual)	(Wife or individual)

Full legal name

_____   _____

Address

_____   _____

Address

_____   _____

City, State, Zip

_____   _____

Birth date

_____   _____

Place of birth

_____   _____

	(Husband or individual)	(Wife or individual)

Father's name _____ _____

Mother's name _____ _____

Social Security
number _____ _____

Marital status _____ _____

Most recent marriage _____ _____

Date of marriage _____ _____

Place of marriage
(church, temple, etc.) _____ _____

City and state _____ _____

Date of termination _____ _____

Reason for termination
(death, divorce, etc.) _____ _____

Previous spouse
(if any) _____ _____

Date of divorce _____ _____

State of jurisdiction _____ _____

Military Service

Serial number _____ _____

Date of entry _____ _____

Date discharged _____ _____

Place discharged _____ _____

Disability (Service connected) _____ _____

Children (including those legally adopted)

First child
Name:

_____

Address:

_____

_____

Phone:

_____

Date of birth:

_____

Extent of dependency:

_____

Second child
Name:

_____

Address:

_____

_____

Phone:

_____

Date of birth:

_____

Extent of dependency:

_____

Third child
Name:

_____

Address:

_____

_____

Phone:

_____

Date of birth:

_____

Extent of dependency:

_____

Fourth child
Name:

_____

Address:

_____

_____

Phone:

_____

Date of birth:

_____

Extent of dependency:

_____

Employment or Business Data

Present
Employer:_____

Last
Employer: _____

Address:_____

Address:_____

_____

_____

_____

_____

Phone: _____

Phone: _____

Location of Personal and Family Documents

(Husband or individual)   (Wife or individual)

Birth certificate
_____   _____

Marriage certificate(s)
_____   _____

Divorce papers
_____   _____

Adoption papers
_____   _____

Naturalization papers
_____   _____

Social Security card
_____   _____

Passport
_____   _____

Military records
_____   _____

Will: Original
_____   _____

    First copy
_____   _____

    Second copy
_____   _____

Paid bills
_____   _____

(Husband or individual)	(Wife or individual)
Past tax returns	
Cancelled checks	
Stock and bond certificates	
Stock and bond certificates	
Life Insurance	
Automobile Insurance	
Residential Insurance	
Health Insurance	
Other (specify)	
Other (specify)	
Trusts	
Pension documents (IRA, Annuities, etc.)	
Pension documents (IRA, Annuities, etc.)	
Bank books	
Bank books	
Real property documents	
Real property documents	
Deed to cemetery plot	

My Professional Advisers

Lawyer
Name:_____

Address:_____

_____

_____

Phone:_____

Insurance Agent
Name:_____

Address:_____

_____

_____

Phone:_____

Banker
Name:_____

Address:_____

_____

_____

Phone:_____

Doctor
Name:_____

Specialty:_____

Address:_____

_____

_____

Phone:_____

Accountant
Name:_____

Address:_____

_____

_____

Phone:_____

Broker
Name:_____

Address:_____

_____

_____

Phone:_____

Clergyman
Name:_____

Address:_____

_____

_____

Phone:_____

Doctor
Name:_____

Specialty:_____

Address:_____

_____

_____

Phone:_____

Dentist
Name:_____

Specialty:_____

Address:_____

_____

_____

Phone:_____

Dentist
Name:_____

Specialty:_____

Address:_____

_____

_____

Phone:_____

CASH AND INVESTMENT DISTRIBUTION

Checking accounts

Name of institution	Account number	Amount	Check ownership		
			Joint	Husband	Wife
_____	_____	_____	❏	❏	❏
Branch: _____	Phone: _____				
_____	_____	_____	❏	❏	❏
Branch: _____	Phone: _____				

Primary savings accounts

Name of institution	Account number	Amount	Joint	Husband	Wife
_____	_____	_____	❏	❏	❏
Branch: _____	Phone: _____				
_____	_____	_____	❏	❏	❏
Branch: _____	Phone: _____				

Other savings accounts

Name of institution	Account number	Amount	Joint	Husband	Wife
_____	_____	_____	❏	❏	❏
Branch: _____	Phone: _____				
_____	_____	_____	❏	❏	❏
Branch: _____	Phone: _____				

Certificates of Deposit (CDs)

Check ownership

Name of institution	Account number	Amount	Joint	Husband	Wife
_____	_____	_____	❏	❏	❏

Branch: _____ Phone:_____

| _____ | _____ | _____ | ❏ | ❏ | ❏ |

Branch: _____ Phone:_____

| _____ | _____ | _____ | ❏ | ❏ | ❏ |

Branch: _____ Phone:_____

| _____ | _____ | _____ | ❏ | ❏ | ❏ |

Branch: _____ Phone:_____

Individual Retirement Accounts (IRAs)

Name of institution	Account number	Balance	Husband	Wife
_____	_____	_____	❏	❏

Branch: _____ Phone:_____

| _____ | _____ | _____ | ❏ | ❏ |

Branch: _____ Phone:_____

Annuity Accounts

Name of institution	Account number	Premium	Husband	Wife
_____	_____	_____	❏	❏

Agent: _____ Phone:_____

Monthly Income:_____ Payout Plan:_____

Beneficiary: _____ Suvivor's rights:_____

| _____ | _____ | _____ | ❏ | ❏ |

Agent: _____ Phone:_____

Monthly Income:_____ Payout Plan:_____

Beneficiary: _____ Suvivor's rights:_____

Stocks and Bonds

Name of investment firm	Account number	Amount	Check ownership
			Joint Husband Wife

_____ _____ _____ ❏   ❏   ❏

Contact: _____ Phone:_____

Location of account statements: _____

_____ _____ _____ ❏   ❏   ❏

Contact: _____ Phone:_____

Location of account statements: _____

% of Investments: ❏ Individual stocks _____% ❏ Mutual Funds _____% ❏ Bonds _____%

Portfolio Breakdown

Number of Shares	Company/Fund/Bonds	Held by
_____	_____	_____
_____	_____	_____
_____	_____	_____
_____	_____	_____
_____	_____	_____
_____	_____	_____
_____	_____	_____
_____	_____	_____
_____	_____	_____
_____	_____	_____
_____	_____	_____
_____	_____	_____
_____	_____	_____
_____	_____	_____

Real Property

Address of Residence/Investment Property:

Check ownership

	Joint	Husband	Wife

Primary_____ Purchase cost: _____ ❏   ❏   ❏

_____ Current value: _____

Secondary_____ Purchase cost: _____ ❏   ❏   ❏

_____ Current value: _____

Investment_____ Purchase cost: _____ ❏   ❏   ❏

_____ Current value: _____

Investment_____ Purchase cost: _____ ❏   ❏   ❏

_____ Current value: _____

Life Insurance Policies

Insured:_____   Owner: _____

Company:_____   Broker: _____

Phone: _____   Broker's phone: _____

Policy number: _____   Policy type: _____

Face value:_____   Cash value: _____

Outstanding loans against policy? ❏ Yes ❏ No   Amount: _____

Names of beneficiaries: _____

_____   _____

Insured:_____   Owner: _____

Company:_____   Broker: _____

Phone: _____   Broker's phone: _____

Policy number: _____   Policy type: _____

Face value:_____   Cash value: _____

Outstanding loans against policy? ❏ Yes ❏ No   Amount: _____

Names of beneficiaries: _____

_____   _____

Insured:_____   Owner: _____

Company:_____   Broker: _____

Phone: _____   Broker's phone: _____

Policy number: _____   Policy type: _____

Face value:_____   Cash value: _____

Outstanding loans against policy? ❏ Yes   ❏ No   Amount: _____

Names of beneficiaries: _____   _____

_____   _____

Retirement Plans

If you are enrolled in a retirement plan, please supply the following information.

Name of institution	Plan number	Check ownership Husband	Wife
_____	_____	❏	❏

Name of Plan:_____   Payment: _____

Address of institution: _____

Contact:_____   Phone: _____

_____	_____	❏	❏

Name of Plan:_____   Payment: _____

Address of institution: _____

Contact:_____   Phone: _____

_____	_____	❏	❏

Name of Plan:_____   Payment: _____

Address of institution: _____

Contact:_____   Phone: _____

Safe-Deposit Box

Every household should rent at least one safe-deposit box for storing important documents and valuable jewelry. Items to be kept in your safe-deposit box include certificates of birth, marriage, divorce, and death; military discharge papers; stock and bond certificates; naturalization papers; copyrights and patents; adoption papers; deeds; mortgages; and jewelry. Your will should be kept in a box rented in your spouse's name, and your spouse's will should be kept in a box rented in your name. Usually, a bank seals a box as soon as it learns that the owner has passed away. It is important to note that the contents of a safe-deposit box are not insured. If you wish to insure the contents of your box, you can purchase a separate policy or a rider to one of your other policies. Enter below the information pertaining to your safe-deposit box(es).

	Box 1	**Box 2**
Bank name		
Branch		
Address		
Box number		
Name of 1st signatory		
Address of 1st signatory		
Name of 2nd signatory		
Address of 2nd signatory		
Name of 3rd signatory		
Address of 3rd signatory		

Box 1	**Box 2**
Location of key(s)	

Inventory of contents

Capital Improvements in Your Home

Keeping a permanent record of the capital improvements you have made in your home will help to minimize the amount of capital gains subject to tax when you sell your home.

Date　　　　　**Capital Improvement**　　　　　　　　　　　　　　　**Cost**

_____　　_____　　_____

_____　　_____　　_____

_____　　_____　　_____

_____　　_____　　_____

Collectibles and Valuable Possessions

Description of item:_____

How acquired (purchase, gift, inheritance, etc.):_____

Date acquired: _____　　Original value:_____

Current location:_____　　Current value: _____

Description of item:_____

How acquired (purchase, gift, inheritance, etc.):_____

Date acquired: _____　　Original value:_____

Current location:_____　　Current value: _____

Description of item:_____

How acquired (purchase, gift, inheritance, etc.):_____

Date acquired: _____　　Original value:_____

Current location:_____　　Current value: _____

Description of item:_____

How acquired (purchase, gift, inheritance, etc.):_____

Date acquired: _____   Original value:_____

Current location:_____   Current value: _____

Description of item:_____

How acquired (purchase, gift, inheritance, etc.):_____

Date acquired: _____   Original value:_____

Current location:_____   Current value: _____

Description of item:_____

How acquired (purchase, gift, inheritance, etc.):_____

Date acquired: _____   Original value:_____

Current location:_____   Current value: _____

Description of item:_____

How acquired (purchase, gift, inheritance, etc.):_____

Date acquired: _____   Original value:_____

Current location:_____   Current value: _____

Description of item:_____

How acquired (purchase, gift, inheritance, etc.):_____

Date acquired: _____   Original value:_____

Current location:_____   Current value: _____

Health Insurance Inventory

Medicare *(if eligible)*

Policy ownership
Husband   Wife
❏   ❏

Name of insured:_____

Claim number:_____   Info phone:_____

Hospital Insurance (Part A): _____   Medical Insurance (Part B): _____
(EFFECTIVE DATE)   (EFFECTIVE DATE)

Husband   Wife
❏   ❏

Name of insured:_____

Claim number:_____   Info phone:_____

Hospital Insurance (Part A): _____   Medical Insurance (Part B): _____
(EFFECTIVE DATE)   (EFFECTIVE DATE)

Medigap Insurance *(if necessary)*

Policy ownership
Husband   Wife
❏   ❏

Name of insured:_____

Company:_____   Broker:_____

Address:_____   Address:_____

_____   _____

_____   _____

Phone: _____   Phone: _____

Policy number: _____   Coverage dates FROM:_____ TO: _____

Risk covered: _____   Max. amount per risk: _____

Risk covered: _____   Max. amount per risk: _____

Risk covered: _____   Max. amount per risk: _____

Risk covered: _____   Max. amount per risk: _____

Premium amount: _____   Premium due date(s): _____

Name of insured:_____   ❏   ❏

Company:_____   Broker:_____

Address:_____   Address:_____

_____   _____

_____   _____

Phone: _____   Phone: _____

Policy number:_____   Coverage dates FROM:_____ TO:_____

Risk covered:_____   Max. amount per risk:_____

Risk covered:_____   Max. amount per risk:_____

Risk covered:_____   Max. amount per risk:_____

Premium amount:_____   Premium due date(s):_____

Other Health-Related Insurance Coverage

There are a wide variety of health-related insurance policies available. These programs include basic hospitalization, basic medical/surgical, supplementary hospitalization, comprehensive major medical, catastrophic major medical, disability income insurance, dental insurance, optical expense benefits, hearing aids, prescription drug plans, and blood programs. Using the following forms, indicate the type of policy and fill in the appropriate data.

Policy ownership

	Joint	Husband	Wife
Name of insured:_____	❏	❏	❏

Type of insurance/program:_____

Company:_____   Broker:_____

Address: _____   Address:_____

_____   _____

_____   _____

Phone: _____   Phone: _____

Policy number:_____   Coverage dates FROM:_____ TO:_____

Excluded conditions (if any):_____

Premium amount:_____   Premium due date(s):_____

	Joint	Husband	Wife
	❏	❏	❏

Name of insured:_____

Type of insurance/program:_____

Company:_____   Broker:_____

Address: _____   Address:_____

_____   _____

_____   _____

Phone: _____   Phone: _____

Policy number:_____   Coverage dates FROM:_____ TO:_____

Excluded conditions (if any):_____

Premium amount:_____   Premium due date(s):_____

Name of insured:_____   ❏   ❏   ❏

Type of insurance/program:_____

Company:_____   Broker:_____

Address: _____   Address:_____

_____   _____

_____   _____

Phone: _____   Phone: _____

Policy number:_____   Coverage dates FROM:_____ TO:_____

Excluded conditions (if any):_____

Premium amount:_____   Premium due date(s):_____

Name of insured:_____   ❏   ❏   ❏

Type of insurance/program:_____

Company:_____   Broker:_____

Address: _____   Address:_____

_____   _____

_____   _____

Phone: _____   Phone: _____

Policy number: _____   Coverage dates FROM: _____ TO: _____

Excluded conditions (if any): _____

Premium amount: _____   Premium due date(s): _____

	Joint	Husband	Wife
	❏	❏	❏

Name of insured: _____

Type of insurance/program: _____

Company: _____   Broker: _____

Address: _____   Address: _____

_____   _____

_____   _____

Phone: _____   Phone: _____

Policy number: _____   Coverage dates FROM: _____ TO: _____

Excluded conditions (if any): _____

Premium amount: _____   Premium due date(s): _____

	Joint	Husband	Wife
	❏	❏	❏

Name of insured: _____

Type of insurance/program: _____

Company: _____   Broker: _____

Address: _____   Address: _____

_____   _____

_____   _____

Phone: _____   Phone: _____

Policy number: _____   Coverage dates FROM: _____ TO: _____

Excluded conditions (if any): _____

Premium amount: _____   Premium due date(s): _____

Vehicle Insurance

Vehicle 1

Policy ownership

Joint   Husband   Wife

Name of policy holder: _____   ❑   ❑   ❑

Vehicle insured: _____

Company:_____   Broker: _____

Address: _____   Address: _____

_____   _____

_____   _____

Phone: _____   Phone: _____

Policy number: _____   Coverage dates: FROM:_____ TO:_____

Coverage limit: _____   Deductible: _____

Excluded conditions (if any):_____

Premium amount: _____   Premium due date(s): _____

Vehicle 2

Joint   Husband   Wife

Name of policy holder: _____   ❑   ❑   ❑

Vehicle insured: _____

Company:_____   Broker: _____

Address: _____   Address: _____

_____   _____

_____   _____

Phone: _____   Phone: _____

Policy number: _____   Coverage dates: FROM:_____ TO:_____

Coverage limit: _____   Deductible: _____

Excluded conditions (if any):_____

Premium amount: _____   Premium due date(s): _____

Vehicle 3

                                                                            Joint   Husband   Wife
                                                                            ❏   ❏   ❏
Name of policy holder: _____

Vehicle insured: _____

Company:_____   Broker: _____

Address: _____   Address: _____

_____   _____

_____   _____

Phone: _____   Phone: _____

Policy number: _____   Coverage dates: FROM:_____ TO:_____

Coverage limit: _____   Deductible: _____

Excluded conditions (if any):_____

Premium amount: _____   Premium due date(s): _____

Vehicle 4

                                                                            Joint   Husband   Wife
                                                                            ❏   ❏   ❏
Name of policy holder: _____

Vehicle insured: _____

Company:_____   Broker: _____

Address: _____   Address: _____

_____   _____

_____   _____

Phone: _____   Phone: _____

Policy number: _____   Coverage dates: FROM:_____ TO:_____

Coverage limit: _____   Deductible: _____

Excluded conditions (if any):_____

Premium amount: _____   Premium due date(s): _____

Residential Insurance

Primary Residence

Policy ownership

| Joint | Husband | Wife |

Name of policy holder: _____   ❏   ❏   ❏

Company:_____   Broker: _____

Address: _____   Address: _____

_____   _____

_____   _____

Phone:_____   Phone:_____

Policy number: _____   Coverage dates FROM_____ TO:_____

Premium amount: _____   Premium due date(s): _____

Personal liability:_____   Medical expenses:_____

Dwelling coverage:_____   Deductible:_____

Other structures:_____

Personal belongings:

Item: _____   Cost: _____

Item: _____   Cost: _____

Item: _____   Cost: _____

Item: _____   Cost: _____

Item: _____   Cost: _____

Item: _____   Cost: _____

Valuable items floater:

Item: _____   Cost: _____

Item: _____   Cost: _____

Item: _____   Cost: _____

Item: _____   Cost: _____

Item: _____   Cost: _____

Secondary Residence

Policy ownership
Joint   Husband   Wife

Name of policy holder: _____ ❏   ❏   ❏

Company:_____   Broker: _____

Address: _____   Address: _____

_____   _____

_____   _____

Phone:_____   Phone:_____

Policy number: _____   Coverage dates   FROM_____ TO:_____

Premium amount: _____   Premium due date(s): _____

Personal liability:_____   Medical expenses:_____

Dwelling coverage:_____   Deductible:_____

Other structures:_____

Personal belongings:

Item: _____   Cost: _____

Item: _____   Cost: _____

Item: _____   Cost: _____

Item: _____   Cost: _____

Item: _____   Cost: _____

Item: _____   Cost: _____

Item: _____   Cost: _____

Valuable items floater:

Item: _____   Cost: _____

Item: _____   Cost: _____

Item: _____   Cost: _____

Item: _____   Cost: _____

Item: _____   Cost: _____

Credit Cards

	Issuer	Account type		
		Joint	Husband	Wife
Card Type: _____	_____	❏	❏	❏

Cardholder: _____   Account number: _____

Interest rate:_____%   Date due:_____

Average Balance: _____   Phone:_____

	Issuer	Joint	Husband	Wife
Card Type: _____	_____	❏	❏	❏

Cardholder: _____   Account number: _____

Interest rate:_____%   Date due:_____

Average Balance: _____   Phone:_____

	Issuer	Joint	Husband	Wife
Card Type: _____	_____	❏	❏	❏

Cardholder: _____   Account number: _____

Interest rate:_____%   Date due:_____

Average Balance: _____   Phone:_____

	Issuer	Joint	Husband	Wife
Card Type: _____	_____	❏	❏	❏

Cardholder: _____   Account number: _____

Interest rate:_____%   Date due:_____

Average Balance: _____   Phone:_____

	Issuer	Joint	Husband	Wife
Card Type: _____	_____	❏	❏	❏

Cardholder: _____   Account number: _____

Interest rate:_____%   Date due:_____

Average Balance: _____   Phone:_____

INVENTORY OF THE CONTENTS OF YOUR HOME

An updated inventory of the contents of your home should be maintained for insurance purposes as well as for estate planning. Using the form below, prepare a detailed listing for each room of your house. You should also include the basement, attic, and garage. It is recommended that photographs be available showing the contents of each area. In addition, prepare a separate list for each of the following items: jewelry, furs, silverware, dishes, stemware, table and bed linens, personal belongings, and any other valuable possessions, such as art, antiques, and cameras.

Item	Date acquired	Cost	Current value

Item	Date acquired	Cost	Current value

Item	Date acquired	Cost	Current value

(If necessary, continue on a separate sheet of paper.)

YOUR WILLS

(Husband or individual)	(Wife or individual)

Have you
made a will?
_____   _____

If yes,
date of will?
_____   _____

Executor's name
_____   _____

Executor's address
_____   _____

_____   _____

Executor's phone
_____   _____

**Alternate
executor's name**
_____   _____

Address
_____   _____

_____   _____

Phone
_____   _____

**Alternate
executor's name**
_____   _____

Address
_____   _____

_____   _____

Phone
_____   _____

Have you prepared a supplemental
letter of instructions?
_____   _____

If yes, note location of
the supplemental letter*:
_____   _____

Original
_____   _____

First copy
_____   _____

Second copy
_____   _____

*The supplemental letter should be attached to original, first copy, and second copy of your wills. Another copy should be kept in your home for reference and updating.

YOUR TRUSTS

	(Husband or individual)	(Wife or individual)
Have you made a trust?		
If yes, what type? (living, testamentary)		
Date created		
Name of attorney		
Attorney's address		
Attorney's phone		
Trustee's name		
Trustee's address		
Trustee's phone		
Alternate trustee's name		
Trustee's address		
Trustee's phone		
I am beneficiary of the following trust(s):		
Name of attorney		
Attorney's address		
Attorney's phone		

LOCAL OFFICES: SOCIAL SECURITY AND INTERNAL REVENUE SERVICE
Social Security Office*

Enter here the address and phone number of your local Social Security office. If you are in doubt, check your phone book under *Social Security Administration*.

Address:_____

City: _____ State: _____ Zip Code: _____

Phone number:_____

*It is suggested that you phone the Social Security office before you go there. You may be helped on the phone. Even if you must appear in person, your individual circumstances may require specific information that you will then be prepared to provide. Always have your Social Security number available.

Internal Revenue Service Office

Enter here the address and phone number of your local Internal Revenue Service office. If you are in doubt, check your phone book under *U.S. Government, Internal Revenue Service.*

Address:_____

City: _____ State: _____ Zip Code: _____

Phone number:_____

RESOURCES

Now that you have considered all the elements of a retirement plan, you may wish to utilize the many resources that are available. For example, you might join a membership organization, such as the American Association of Retired Persons (AARP); or you might want to contact Elderhostel for information on affordable travel options. These and other helpful groups, associations, and Internet services are listed below with their addresses, phone numbers, and websites, when available. Use these resources to learn about health, legal services, paid employment, travel, volunteer work, and more.

EDUCATION

Distance and Education Training Council (DETC)
1601 18th Street, NW
Washington, DC 20009–2529
Phone: (202) 234–5100
Website: www.detc.org

A nonprofit educational association, the DETC provides information about the distance study/correspondence field, through which students can take academic, vocational, and avocational courses by mail or by telecommutation.

U.S. Department of Education
400 Maryland Avenue, SW
Washington, DC 20202–0498
Phone: (800) USA–LEARN
Website: www.ed.gov

This department establishes policy for, administers, and coordinates almost all federal assistance to education.

EMPLOYMENT

Alliance for Retired Americans
8403 Colesville Road, Suite 1200
Silver Spring, MD 20910–3314

Phone: (301) 578–8800
Fax: (301) 578–8999
Website: www.ncsinc.org

This organizations offers part-time work in community service agencies involved in activities ranging from child care and adult education, to home health and homemaker services.

Green Thumb, Inc.
National Headquarters
2000 N. 14th Street, Suite 800
Arlington, VA 22201
Phone: (703) 522–7272
Fax: (703) 522–0141
Website: www.greenthumb.org

Green Thumb provides mature- and disadvantaged-worker training and employment. Training programs allow seniors to compete in many high-demand occupations, including computer technology and health care.

National Council on the Aging (NCOA)
409 Third Street, SW
Washington, DC 20024
Phone: (202) 479–1200
Fax: (202) 479–0735
Website: www.ncoa.org

NCOA provides part-time and full-time work in Social Security and state employment service offices, public housing, libraries, hospitals, schools, food and nutrition programs, and more.

U.S. Small Business Administration (SBA)
409 Third Street, SW
Washington, DC 20416
Phone: (800) U–ASK–SBA
Website: www.sbaonline.sba.gov

The Small Business Administration provides financial, technical, and management assistance to people who wish to start or grow their businesses. SBA is the nation's single largest financial backer of small businesses.

FINANCIAL ADVISERS

Financial Planning Association
Phone: (800) 282–PLAN
Website: www.fpanet.org

This association provides a list of certified financial planners in your area, plus free information on financial planning.

National Association of Personal Financial Advisors (NAPFA)
355 W. Dundee Road, Suite 200
Buffalo Grove, IL 60089
Phone: (888) FEE–ONLY
Website: www.napfa.org/planner.htm

NAPFA offers referrals to fee-only (noncommission) financial planners in your area. All planners that belong to NAPFA have at least two years' experience and at least one professional designation.

Society of Financial Service Professionals
Phone: (888) 243–2258
Website: www.financialpro.org

This society will send you the names of up to five members in your area.

FUNERALS

Funeral Consumers Alliance (FAMSA-FCA)
PO Box 10
Hinesburg, VT 05461
Phone: (802) 482–3437
Website: www.funerals.org/famsa

In addition to offering information by mail and phone, FAMSA-FCA has set up a website that will guide you to local memorial societies, which can help you get the funeral you want at a reasonable price.

GOVERNMENT SECURITIES

Bureau of the Public Debt
Website: www.publicdebt.treas.gov
    (to buy securities online)

The Bureau of the Public Debt issues, services, and redeems Treasury securities. The Bureau sells securities through the mail, via the telephone, and online.

U.S. Department of the Treasury
U.S. Savings Bond Marketing Office
Washington, DC 20226
Phone: (808) 487–2663
Website: www.treas.gov

The Department of the Treasury provides current information on government bonds through its website and via the telephone. It also offers a free guide, *The Savings Bond Question and Answer Book*.

HEALTH

Alzheimer's Association, Inc.
919 N. Michigan Ave, Suite 1100
Chicago, IL 60611–1676
Phone: (800) 272–3900
Fax: (312) 335–8700
E-mail: info@alz.org
Website: www.alz.org

A national network of chapters, the Alzheimer's Association funds Alzheimer's research. It also provides education and a wealth of programs and services for people who are diagnosed with the condition, as well as their families and friends. Some chapters offer special programs, such as assistance to people with Alzheimer's who live alone.

American Association of Homes and Services for the Aging (AAHSA)

901 E Street NW, Suite 500
Washington, DC 20004–2037
Phone: (202) 783–2242
Fax: (202) 783–2255
Website: www.aahsa.org

The AAHSA provides information and publications on nursing homes, housing, retirement communities, health-related facilities, and services for the elderly.

American Cancer Society, Inc.

1599 Clifton Road, NE
Atlanta, GA 30329
Phone: (800) ACS–2345
Website: www.cancer.org

The American Cancer Society provides up-to-date information on cancer, its causes, and its risk factors; and on the latest diagnosis and treatment options, including alternative and complementary approaches.

American Dental Association (ADA)

211 E. Chicago Avenue
Chicago, IL 60611
Phone: (312) 440–2500
Fax: (312) 440–2800
Website: www.ada.org

The ADA provides information on a variety of oral health topics, and guides consumers to ADA-member dentists.

American Foundation for the Blind (AFB)

11 Penn Plaza, Suite 300
New York, NY 10001
Phone: (212) 502–7600
E-mail: afbinfo@afb.org
Website: www.afb.org

A nonprofit organization, the AFB collects and disseminates information to people who are visually impaired; publishes books about blindness; and produces talking books and other audio materials.

American Health Care Association

1201 L Street, NW
Washington, DC 20005
Phone: (202) 842–4444 or (800) 321–0343
Fax: (202) 842–3860
Website: www.ahca.org

A federation of organizations representing long-term care providers, the American Health Care Association guides consumers in selecting the proper level of care for their needs, and provides information on long-term care insurance and other topics related to long-term health care.

American Heart Association

7272 Greenville Avenue
Dallas, TX 75231
Phone: (214) 373–6300 or (800) 242–1793
Website: www.americanheart.org

This organization provides information about the prevention and treatment of heart disorders. It also offers an online health management program that presents information tailored to your health and lifestyle needs.

American Optometric Association (AOA)

243 North Lindbergh Boulevard
St. Louis, MO 63141
Phone: (314) 991–4100
Fax: (314) 991–4101
Website: www.aoanet.org

The AOA provides a wealth of information on common vision conditions, low vision, available surgeries for improving vision, and more.

American Podiatric Medical Association (APMA)
9312 Old Georgetown Road
Bethesda, MD 20814
Phone: (301) 571–9200
Website: www.apma.org

The APMA provides information on foot disorders, as well as a service that allows you to find member podiatrists in your area.

American Speech-Language-Hearing Association (ASHA)
10801 Rockville Pike
Rockville, MD 20852
Phone: (301) 897–5700
Website: www.asha.org

A professional association, ASHA publishes a wide variety of materials on communication disorders, provides a list of certified audiologists and speech-language pathologists, and offers a list of self-help groups.

Arthritis Foundation (AF)
1330 West Peachtree Street
Atlanta, GA 30309
Phone: (404) 872–7100
Website: www.arthritis.org

The AF seeks to improve the quality of life for those affected with arthritis. Its services include self-help courses, exercise classes, support groups, instructional videotapes, and a wide variety of free educational brochures and booklets.

Hospice Foundation of America (HFA)
777 17th Street, No. 401
Miami Beach, FL 33139
Phone: (800) 854–3402
Website: www.hospicefoundation.org

A not-for-profit group, HFA assists those who cope personally or professionally with terminal illness, death, and the process of grief. It offers a variety of educational materials, and provides a service that allows you to locate a hospice in your area.

National Association for Home Care (NAHC)
228 Seventh Street, SE
Washington, DC 20003
Phone: (202) 547–7424
Fax: (202) 547–3540
Website: www.nahc.org

A trade association, NAHC can guide you to member home care providers in your area.

HEALTH INSURANCE INFORMATION

Medicare
Phone: (800) 633–4227
Website: www.medicare.gov

Medicare offers a wealth of information about Medicare hospital and medical coverage.

United States Department of Health and Human Services
Centers for Medicare and Medicaid Services
7500 Security Boulevard
Baltimore, MD 21244–1850
Website: www.os.dhhs.gov

The Department of Health and Human Services will provide you with a booklet entitled *Guide to Health Insurance for People With Medicare*, which can help you fill in the gaps left by Medicare.

LEGAL SERVICES

American Bar Association
750 N. Lake Shore Drive
Chicago, IL 60611
Phone: (312) 988–5000
Website: www.abanet.org

The largest voluntary professional association in the world, the American Bar Association offers a variety of consumer services, including directories of lawyer referral programs, pro bono programs, and state and local legal service programs.

Attorney Locate

Website: www.attorneylocate.com

This free online service allows you to find an attorney who works in the area of your choice and has the desired expertise.

National Academy of Elder Law Attorneys, Inc. (NAELA)

1604 North Country Club Road
Tucson, AZ 85716
Phone: (520) 881–4005
Website: www.naela.com

NAELA's online service allows you to find an elder-care attorney in your area. NAELA can also be contacted by phone and mail.

National Senior Citizens Law Center (NSCLC)

1101 14th Street, NW, Suite 400
Washington, DC 20005
Phone: (202) 289–6976
Fax: (202) 289–7224
Website: www.nsclc.org

Dedicated to promoting the independence and well-being of low-income elderly individuals, the NSCLC will refer you to the website or association that can provide the legal information or counsel that you seek.

MEMBERSHIP ORGANIZATIONS

Action for Independent Maturity (AIM)

1909 K Street, NW
Washington, DC 20049
Phone: (202) 872–4850

AIM offers actively employed people between the ages of 50 and 65 a wealth of useful information about money management, health matters, leisure possibilities, and other issues, the successful management of which can make life more enjoyable and satisfying. AIM is a division of AARP.

Alliance for Retired Americans

888 16th Street, NW, Suite 520
Washington, DC 20006
Phone: (888) 373–6497
Fax: (301) 578–8911
Website: www.retiredamericans.org

An advocacy group dedicated to fighting for the interests and concerns of its members, the alliance supports increased Social Security benefits, better housing for older Americans, improved education and health programs, and Medicare. It offers advice and assistance to help members resolve specific problems, and sponsors rallies and educational workshops. All members automatically receive *Senior Citizen News*; nonmembers may request a free sample copy.

American Association of Retired Persons (AARP)

601 E Street, NW
Washington, DC 20049
Phone: (800) 424–3410
Website: www.aarp.org

AARP is the nation's largest and most experienced organization of older persons. More than 2,400 chapters work for local community welfare, and provide educational and social programs for members. Anyone who is 50 years of age or older, and is actively employed, semi-retired, or retired, is eligible to join AARP.

American Society on Aging (ASA)

833 Market Street, Suite 511
San Francisco, CA 94103
Phone: (415) 543–2617
Website: www.asaging.org

ASA is a nonprofit organization that strives to improve the well-being of senior citizens and to promote unity among those working with and for older Americans. The society monitors legislation affecting the elderly, and issues recommendations for consideration at all levels of government. The ASA newsletter, *ASA Connection,* is distributed free to members and is available to nonmembers by subscription. There are no local chapters.

Gray Panthers

733 15th Street, NW, Suite 437
Washington, DC 20005
Phone: (800) 280–5362 or (202) 737–6637
Fax: (202) 737–1160
E-mail: info@graypanthers.org
Website: www.graypanthers.org

Founded for the purpose of fighting "ageism"—discrimination against people on the basis of their age—the Gray Panthers advises and organizes approximately 70,000 members of all ages in more than eighty local chapters nationwide. Members advocate for better housing, the rights of the disabled, and the expansion of health-care programs. The group also conducts seminars and research on issues affecting older Americans. Its publications include *Health Watch* and a newspaper, *Gray Panther Network.*

Institute for Puerto Rican/Hispanic Elderly

105 East 22nd Street, Room 615
New York, NY 10010
Phone: (212) 677–4181
Fax: (212) 777–5106
Website: www.network-democracy.org/social
   security/bb/whc/iprhe.html

Founded in 1979, this institute is a nonprofit organization whose mission is the improvement of the quality of life for Puerto Rican and Hispanic elderly. The institute provides services and referral through its bilingual staff. It also offers access to government entitlements and benefits, and provides advocacy, training, and information.

National Caucus and Center on the Black Aged, Inc.

1424 K Street, NW, Suite 500
Washington, DC 20005
Phone: (202) 637–8400
Fax: (202) 347–0895
Website: www.aoa.dhhs.gov/aoa/dir/140.html

This group seeks to improve the standard of living for all older Americans, and especially for blacks. It supports changes to raise the economic, health, and social status of lower-income senior citizens; provides consultation to members; sponsors employment programs in eleven states; and publishes *Golden Pages,* available to members only.

National Retired Teachers Association (NRTA)

601 E Street, NW
Washington, DC 20049
Phone: (800) 424–3410
Website: www.aarp.org/nrta

A division of AARP, NRTA is open to all retired (and active) educators. Services include group hospital insurance, tax assistance, consumer and health education, consultation/ information services, and pre-retirement planning. Members are also eligible for discounts at certain hotel and motel chains, and from rental car companies. The NRTA distributes the same publications as AARP.

Older Women's League (OWL)

666 11th Street, NW, Suite 700
Washington, DC 20001
Phone: (202) 783–6686
Fax: (202) 638–2356
Website: www.owl-national.org

OWL educates the public on issues affecting middle-aged and older women. Nationally, and through its local chapters, OWL seeks to influence public policy on issues of health care, social security reform, pension rights for women, caregiving, job discrimination, and housing. Local and national activities are directed at improving the economic situation of older women, and alleviating economic inequalities built into public policy. Membership consists of middle-aged and older women, plus those who share the league's concerns.

ORGAN DONATION

The United Network for Organ Sharing (UNOS)
1100 Boulders Parkway, Suite 500
PO Box 13770
Richmond, VA 23225–8770
Phone: (888) TXINFO1
Website: www.unos.org

A private nonprofit membership organization, UNOS has an Organ Center that matches donors to waiting recipients. Among other services, UNOS provides donor cards and a free brochure on organ and tissue donation.

PENSIONS

Pension and Welfare Benefits Administration (PWBA)
Department of Labor
200 Constitution Avenue, NW
Washington, DC 20210
Phone: (800) 998–7542
   (for free brochure on pension rights)
Website: www.dol.gov/dol/pwba

The PWBA protects the integrity of pensions, health plans, and other employee benefits. One of its missions is to assist workers in getting the information they need to protect their benefit rights.

Pension Rights Center
918 16th Street, NW, Suite 704
Washington, DC 20006
Phone: (202) 296–3776
Fax: (202) 833–2472
Website: www.aoa.dhhs.gov/aoa/DIR/210. html

The Pension Rights Center works to protect the pension rights of workers, retirees, and their families. The center also offers a pension attorney referral service, a private bar-sponsored Case Consultation Panel, and a pleadings bank to assist attorneys who represent pension participants. A number of helpful publications are also available through the center.

RECREATION

American Radio Relay League (ARRL)
225 Main Street
Newington, CT 06111
Phone: (860) 594–0200
Website: www.arrl.org

AARL offers information about amateur radio operation, including information on getting a license.

National Recreation and Park Association (NRPA)
Information Resources Division
22377 Belmont Ridge Road
Ashburn, VA 20148–4501
Phone: (703) 858–0784
Fax: (703) 858–0794
Website: www.activeparks.org

NRPA is a public interest organization dedicated to improving the human environment through improved park, recreation, and leisure opportunities. Activities include programs for the development and upgrading of professional and citizen leadership in the park, recreation, and leisure field; dissemination of innovations and research results; and technical assistance to affiliated organizations, local communities, and members. Among its services is an online search feature that enables you to find a recreational facility in your area.

U.S. Department of the Interior
1849 C Street, NW
Washington, DC 20240
Phone: (202) 208–3100
Website: www.doi.gov

Anyone age 62 or over can obtain a *Golden Age Passport*—a free lifetime entrance pass to national parks, monuments, historic sites, and recreation areas administered by the federal government. The pass also provides for a 50-percent discount on fees charged for use of facilities and services (parking, boating, and camping). It does not cover fees levied by private concessionaires. The passport can be obtained from the office above, or from most federally operated recreation areas and National Park Service Regional Offices. Applicants must appear in person with proof of age (driver's license, birth certificate, or Medicare card). Contact the Information Office at the Washington location for the address of the office nearest you.

Anyone who has been medically determined to be blind or permanently disabled and is eligible to receive federal benefits can obtain a *Golden Access Passport*. This is a free lifetime entrance pass that provides the same privileges as the Golden Age Passport. Applicants must apply in person and provide proof of disability.

RETIREMENT COMMUNITIES AND CARE FACILITIES

American Association of Homes and Services for the Aging
2519 Connecticut Avenue, NW
Washington, DC 20008–1520
Phone: (202) 783–2242
Website: www.aahsa.com

With a membership of over 5,000 not-for-profit nursing homes and other care facilities, this association can help you locate an appropriate facility and assess the quality of the facility, as well.

New Life-Styles
Phone: (800) 820–3013
Website: www.newlifestyles.com

Once you specify the type of housing facility you desire and the preferred location, New Life-Styles, which is available online and by telephone, matches you with suitable housing facilities.

Retirement Living Information Center
19 Ledgewood Road
Redding, CT 06896
Phone: (203) 938–0417
Website: www.retirementliving.com

Established to assist seniors in finding housing that matches their needs, this center helps you find the type of facility you want in the state of your choice.

SOCIAL SECURITY

Social Security Administration
Phone: (800) 772–1213
TTY number: (800) 325–0778
Website: www.ssa.gov.

The Social Security Administration helps individuals understand the benefits of the Social Security program so that they can make informed choices about their retirement. Among other services, Social Security provides an estimate of your benefits, and offers help in understanding your Social Security Statement. A good deal of information can be found online.

TAX INFORMATION

Internal Revenue Service (IRS)
Phone: (800) 829–3676 (to order publications)
(800) 829–1040 (tax questions)
Website: www.irs.ustreas.gov

The IRS offers a number of services, including the computation of taxes. Through its website, the IRS provides a wealth of information, along with downloadable forms. It also answers tax questions both online and over the telephone, and provides a variety of booklets on tax-related subjects.

TRAVEL

Elderhostel
75 Federal Street
Boston, MA 02110–1941
Phone: (877) 426–8056
Website: www.elderhostel.org

Elderhostel is a not-for-profit organization that provides high-quality, affordable educational adventures for adults age 55 and over.

VOLUNTEER WORK

Corporation for National Service
1201 New York Avenue, NW
Washington, DC 20525
Phone: (202) 606–5000
Website: www.cns.gov

This organization works with community groups to provide opportunities for Americans of all ages to serve. The Corporation for National Service provides information about Senior Corps, which puts the experience and talents of seniors to work within communities across the country. Senior Corps programs include the Foster Grandparents Program, which offers part-time volunteer opportunities for seniors who wish to work with children with special needs; AmeriCorps VISTA, which enables individuals to supplement efforts of community organizations that work to eliminate poverty; and Senior Companion Program, which enables seniors to help adults with special needs.

Experience Corps
Civic Ventures
425 Second Street, Suite 601
San Francisco, CA 94107
Phone: (415) 430–0141
Website: www.experiencecorps. org

Experience Corps provides schools and youth-serving organizations with caring older adults who work to improve academic performance and enhance youth development. The organization also strives to promote the continued learning and growth of volunteers through training and lectures.

Habitat for Humanity
121 Habitat Street
Americus, GA 31709–3498
Phone: (912) 924–6935
Website: www.habitat.org

A nonprofit housing organization, Habitat uses volunteer labor to help build simple, affordable housing in partnership with families in need.

Literacy Volunteers of America (LVA)
635 James Street
Syracuse, NY 13203–2241
Phone: (315) 472–0001
Fax: (315) 472–0002
Website: www.literacyvolunteers.org/home

LVA is a national network of over 350 locally based programs and more than 50,000 volunteers, dedicated to changing lives through literacy. Volunteer tutors are provided with the professional training, materials, and support they need to teach either Basic Literacy or English for Speakers of Other Languages.

Service Corps of Retired Executives (SCORE)
SCORE Association
409 3rd Street, SW, 6th Floor
Washington, DC 20024
Phone: (800) 634–0245
Website: www.score.org

SCORE provides advisory and counseling services for the benefit of new and existing small businesses, as well as nonprofit community organizations, by utilizing the management experience of retired and semi-retired and active business executives. Nationwide, thousands of men and women donate their time and talent to assist American entrepreneurs.

SUGGESTED READINGS

A number of books are available on each of the many aspects of retirement planning, from recreation to housing to savings and investments. This list presents several suggested readings relevant to each chapter of the book so that, if desired, you can further explore any area that is of interest to you. Both your local library and your local bookstore are sure to have additional readings that can help you learn more about retirement planning.

First Facts

Arnold, Suzanne, et al. *Ready or Not: Your Retirement Planning Guide.* Bronx: Manpower Education Institute, 2000.

Arnone, William J. and Frieda Kavouras, et al. *Ernst and Young's Retirement Planning Guide.* New York: John Wiley & Sons, Inc., 2001.

Reed, Terence L. *The 8 Biggest Mistakes People Make With Their Finances Before and After Retirement.* Chicago: Dearborn Trade, A. Kaplan Professional Company, 2001.

Staff of Kiplinger's Personal Finance Magazine. *Retire Worry-Free.* 4th Edition. Washington, DC: Kiplinger Books, 2001.

Chapter 1

Working in Retirement

Bennett, Charles A. *Volunteering: The Selfish Benefits.* Oak View: Committee Communications, Inc., 2001.

Driskill, J. Lawrence. *Adventures in Senior Living: Learning How to Make Retirement Meaningful and Enjoyable.* Binghamton, NY: Haworth Press, 1997.

Kleiman, Carol. *The 100 Best Jobs for the 1990s and Beyond.* New York: Berkley Publishing Group, 1994.

Powers, Michael D. *How to Start a Retirement Business.* New York: Avon, 1996.

Chapter 2

Playing in Retirement

Allison, Maria. *Play, Leisure and Quality of Life.* Dubuque, IA: Kendall Hunt, 1992.

Edginton, Christopher R. *Leisure and Life Satisfaction: Foundational Perspectives.* New York: McGraw-Hill Higher Education, 2001.

McCants, Louise Spears and Robert Cavett. *Retire to Fun and Freedom.* Boston: Warner Books, 1990.

Williams, C., et al. *Service Quality in Leisure and Tourism.* New York: CABI Publishing, 2001.

Chapter 3

Retirement Housing

Cleveland, Joan. *Everything You Need to Know About Retirement Housing: Finding the Right Place at the Right Time.* New York: Penguin, 1996.

Howells, John and Don Merwin. *Choose Mexico for Retirement: Discoveries for Every Budget.* 6th Edition. Guilford, CT: Globe Pequot Press, 1999.

Lubow, Joseph. *Choose a College Town for Retirement.* Guilford, CT: Globe Pequot Press, 1999.

Valerio, Christy. *Elderly Americans: Where They Choose to Retire.* Rev. Edition. New York: Garland, 1996.

Williams, Gwyndaf. *The Experience of Housing in Retirement: Elderly Lifestyles and Private Initiative.* Avebury, 1990.

Chapter 4

Retirement Communities and Care Facilities

Cleveland, Joan. *Everything You Need to Know About Retirement Housing: Finding the Right Place at the Right Time.* New York: Penguin, 1996.

Driskill, J. Lawrence. *Adventures in Senior Living: Learning How to Make Retirement Meaningful and Enjoyable.* Binghamton, NY: Haworth Press, 1997.

Eliopoulos, Charlotte K. *Legal Risks in the Long-Term Care Facility.* 2nd Edition. Glen Arm: Health Education Network, 2001.

Chapter 5

Legal Affairs

American Bar Association. *The American Lawyer: When and How to Use One.* Chicago: American Bar Association, 1993.

Comiskey, Stephen W. *A Good Lawyer: Secrets Good Lawyers Already Know.* McLean, VA: Chaos Limited, 1997.

Curry, Haden, ed. *Legal Guide for Lesbian and Gay Couples.* 10th Edition. Berkeley, CA: Nolo Press, 1999.

Josephson-Millman, Linda and Sallie C. Birket. *Legal Issues and Older Adults.* Santa Barbara, CA: ABC-Clio, Inc., 1992.

Lesko, Matthew. *Free Legal Help.* Kensington, MD: Information USA, 1999.

Very, Donald and Eugene F. Keefe. *Legal Guide for the Family.* Chicago: Ferguson, 1993.

Chapter 6

Savings and Investments

Carlson, Charles. *Eight Steps to Seven Figures.* New York: Doubleday, 2000.

Case, Samuel. *The First Book of Investing: The Absolute Beginner's Guide to Building Wealth Safely.* Rocklin, CA: Prima Publishing, 1994.

Chatzky, Jean. *Talking Money: Everything You Need to Know About Your Finances and Your Future.* New York: Warner Books, Inc., 2001.

Cohn, Alan, et al. *The Sage Guide to Mutual Funds.* New York: Harperbusiness, 2000.

Conover, C. Todd. *The Art of Astute Investing: Building Wealth With No-Load Mutual Funds.* New York: AMACOM, 1998.

Gitman, Lawrence J. and Michael D. Joehnk. *Fundamentals of Investing.* 6th Edition. Reading, MA: Addison-Wesley, 1998.

Kapoor, Jack H., Les R. Dlabay, and Robert J. Hughes. *Personal Finance.* New York: McGraw-Hill, 2000.

Orman, Suze. *The Road to Wealth: A Comprehensive Guide to Your Money.* New York: Riverhead Books, 2001.

Time-Life Staff. *Money: Your Top Investing Moves for Retirement.* Alexandria, VA: Time-Life, 1997.

Tucker, James F. *Buying Treasury Securities at Federal Reserve Banks.* Federal Reserve Bank of Richmond, P.O. Box 27622, Richmond, VA 23261. Free.

Westbrook, Paul. *J.K. Lasser's New Rules for Retirement and Tax: Supercharge Your Retirement Savings With the New Tax Law.* New York: John Wiley & Sons, Inc., 2001.

Chapter 7

Social Security

Aaron, Henry J. and Robert D. Reischaur. *Countdown to Reform: The Great Social Security Debate.* New York: Century Foundation, 2001.

Baker, Dean and Mark Weisbrot. *Social Security: The Phony Crisis.* Chicago: The University of Chicago Press, 1999.

Ball, Robert M. *Insuring the Essentials: Bob Ball on Social Security.* New York: Century Foundation, 2001.

Matthews, Joseph and Dorothy M. Berman. *Social Security, Medicare and Pensions.* 8th Edition. Berkeley, CA: Nolo Press, 2001.

U.S. Department of Health and Human Services, Social Security Administration, Washington, DC. *Your Social Security*. Periodical.

Chapter 8

Pensions

Drucker, Peter F. *The Pension Fund Revolution*. Somerset, NJ: Transaction Publishers, 1995.

Gale, William G.; John B. Shoven; and Mark J. Warshawsky. *Private Pensions and Public Policies*. Washington, DC: Brookings Institute, 2001.

Hebeler, Henry K. *J.K. Lasser's Your Winning Retirement Plan*. New York: John Wiley & Sons, Inc., 2001.

Internal Revenue Service. *Pension and Annuity Income*. Publication #575. Washington, DC: Internal Revenue Service, updated annually.

Kass, Stephen J. *The Pension Answer Book*. 11th Edition. New York: Panel Publishers, 1995.

Mitchell, Olivia S. *Pensions in the Public Sector*. Philadelphia: University of Pennsylvania Press, 2000.

Sass, Stephen A. *The Promise of Private Pensions: The First Hundred Years*. Cambridge, MA: Harvard University Press, 1996.

Schieber, Sylvester and John Shoven, eds. *Public Policy Toward Pensions*. Cambridge, MA: MIT Press, 1997.

Chapter 9

Annuities

Donner, Eric. *Planning for Retirement Distributions: Tax, Financial, and Personal Aspects*. Gaithersburg, MD: Aspen Publishers, Inc., 2001.

Falk, Kristen L. *Introduction to Annuities*. Atlanta, GA: Life Office Management Association, 2000.

Internal Revenue Service. *Pension and Annuity Income*. Publication #575. Washington, DC: Internal Revenue Service, updated annually.

Shapiro, David and Thomas Streiff. *Annuities*. 2nd Edition. Chicago: Dearborn Financial Publishing, 1997.

Slesnick, Twila and John C. Suttle. *Creating Your Own Retirement Plan: A Guide to Keoghs and IRAs for the Self-Employed*. Berkeley, CA: Nolo Press, 2001.

Williamson, Gordon. *Getting Started in Annuities*. New York: John Wiley & Sons, Inc., 1998.

Chapter 10

Budgeting

Edwards, Carolina. *Rookie's Guide to Money Management: How to Keep Score*. New York: Random House, 1997.

Gabriel, Gwendolyn D. *Become Totally Debt-Free in Five Years or Less*. Dallas: Brown Bag Press, 2000.

Lawrence, Judy. *The Budget Kit*. Chicago: Dearborn Financial Publishing, 1993.

McVey Associates Staff. *Budgeting*. Englewood Cliffs, NJ: Cambridge, 1988.

Rubin, Rose M. and Michael Nieswiadomy. *Expenditures of Older Americans*. Westport, CT: Greenwood Publishing Group, 1997.

Chapter 11

Credit

Board of Governors, Federal Reserve System. *Consumer Handbook on Credit Protection Laws*. Washington, DC: 1992.

Leonard, Robin. *Credit Repair: Quick and Easy*. 3rd Edition. Berkeley, CA: Nolo Communications, 1999.

Strong, Howard. *What Every Credit Card Holder Needs to Know: Protect Yourself From the Outrageous Practices of Credit Card Companies*. New York: Henry Holt & Company, 1999.

Williams, D.J. *The Secrets to Good Credit and Debt Reduction: A Consumer Self-Help Guide*. Saint Louis, MO: Premier Educational Services, 2001.

Chapter 12

Inflation

Batra, Ravi. *The Crash of the Millennium: Surviving the Coming Inflationary Depression.* New York: Crown Publishers, 1999.

Froehlich, Robert J. *The Three Bears Are Dead!: Inflation, Interest Rates, Government Spending.* New York: Forbes, Inc., 1998.

Sargent, Thomas J. *The Conquest of American Inflation.* Princeton, NJ: Princeton University Press, 1999.

Chapter 13

Taxes and Tax Shelters

Internal Revenue Service. *Investment Income and Expenses.* Publication #558. Washington, DC: Internal Revenue Service, updated annually.

Internal Revenue Service. *Tax Information for Older Americans.* Publication #554. Washington, DC: Internal Revenue Service, updated annually.

Leventhal, Steven. *Working With Tax-Sheltered Annuities: 403(b) Plans Explained.* Riverwoods, IL: CCH Inc, 1997.

Starchild, Adam. *Swiss Money Secrets: How You Can Legally Hide Your Money in Switzerland.* Boulder, CO: Paladin Press, 1996.

Chapter 14

Life Insurance

Baldwin, Ben G. *New Life Insurance Investment Advisor.* 2nd Edition. New York: McGraw-Hill Professional Publishing, 2001.

Carson, James M. and Mark D. Forster. *Life Insurance Analysis: Policy and Company Performance.* Normal, IL: Iona Publishers, 1996.

Easton, Albert E. and Timothy F. Harris. *Actuarial Aspects of Individual Life Insurance & Annuity Contracts.* Winsted, CT: Actex Publications, 1999.

Graves, Edward E., ed. *McGill's Life Insurance.* 2nd Edition. Bryn Mawr, PA: American College, 1998.

Liner, John, ed. *Insurance Buyer's Handbook.* Saint Paul, MN: Standard Publishing, 1992.

Wilson, Reg. *How to Insure Your Life: A Step by Step Guide to Buying the Coverage You Need at Prices You Can Afford.* Los Angeles: Merritt Publishers, 1996.

Chapter 15

Health Insurance

Beam, Burton T. *Group Health Insurance.* 2nd Edition. Bryn Mawr, PA: American College, 1997.

Churchill, Larry. *Self-Interest and Universal Health Care: Why Well-Insured Americans Should Support Coverage for Everyone.* Cambridge, MA: Harvard University Press, 1994.

D'Amico, Raymond A., et al. *Health Insurance Primer: Werbel's Sickness and Accident.* Revised Edition. Dix Hills, NY: Werbel Publishing Company, 1997.

Hoffman, Beatrix. *The Wages of Sickness: The Politics of Health Insurance in Progressive America.* Chapel Hill, NC: University of North Carolina Press, 2001.

Orin, Rhonda. *Making Them Pay: How to Get the Most From Health Insurance and Managed Care.* New York: Griffin, 2001.

Chapter 16

Medicare and Medicaid

Moon, Marilyn. *Women and Medicare Reform.* Washington, DC: Brookings Institute, 2001.

Scanlon, William J. *Medicare and Choice.* Upland, PA: Diane Publishing Company, 2001.

White, Joseph. *False Alarm: Why the Greatest Threat to Social Security and Medicare Is the Campaign to "Save" Them.* New York: Century Foundation, 2001.

Chapter 17

Medigap and Long-Term Care Coverage

Feldman, Samuel Larry. *When Caring Isn't Enough: Meeting the Need for Long-Term Care With Long-Term Care Insurance.* Park Ridge: Million Dollar Round Table Center for Productivity, 2000.

Getting the Most Out of Medicare and Medicare Supplement Insurance. Appleton: AAL QualityLife Resources, 2000.

Goetze, Jason G. *Long-Term Care.* 3rd Edition. Chicago: Dearborn Financial, 1999.

Martin, Ernest L. *Introduction to Long-Term Care Insurance.* Atlanta, GA: Life Office Management Association, 1999.

Schroeder, Robin and Loranelle Schroeder. *And Now What Do We Do? A Guide for the Selection of the Right Care Facility for You or Your Loved One.* Northfield, MN: EMMPS, 1997.

Stein, Jane J., ed *Supplemental Health Insurance.* Washington, DC: Health Insurance Association of America, 1999.

Chapter 18

Estate Planning and Wills

Choate, Natalie B. *Life and Death Planning for Retirement Benefits: The Essential Handbook for Estate Planners.* 3rd Edition. Boston: Ataxplan, 1999.

Clifford, Denis. *Nolo's Simple Will Book.* 4th Edition. Berkeley, CA: Nolo Press, 2001.

Condon, Gerald M. and Jeffrey L. Condon. *Beyond the Grave: The Right Way and the Wrong Way of Leaving Money to Your Children (and Others).* New York: Harperbusiness, 2001.

Gentry, F. Bruce. *The Complete Will Kit.* 3rd Edition. New York: John Wiley & Sons, Inc., 2001.

Chapter 19

Minimizing Estate and Gift Taxes

Blackman, Irving L. and Brian T. Whitlock. *Tax Secrets of the Wealthy: A New System to Pass All Your Wealth, Intact and Tax-Free, To Your Family.* 2nd Edition. Chicago: Blackman Kallick Bartelstein, 1995.

CCH Editorial Staff. *Federal Estate and Gift Taxes, Code and Regulations.* Riverwoods, IL: CCH Inc., 1997.

Dunlap, Susan. *Death and Taxes.* New York: Delacorte, 1992.

Internal Revenue Service. *Federal Estate and Gift Taxes.* Publication #448. Washington, DC: Internal Revenue Service, updated annually.

Randolph, Mary and Denis Clifford. *9 Ways to Avoid Estate Taxes.* Berkeley, CA: Nolo Press, 2002.

Chapter 20

Trusts

Crouch, Holmes F. *Family Trusts and Trustors.* Saratoga, NY: All Year Tax Guides, 2001.

Crumbley, D. Larry and Edward E. Milan. *Keys to Estate Planning and Trusts.* Hauppauge, NY: Barron, 1999.

Fairfax, Sally K. and Darla Guenzler. *Conservation Trusts.* Lawrence, KS: University Press of Kansas, 2001.

Hoyt, Christopher R. *Retirement Assets and Charitable Gifts: A Guide for Planned Giving.* New York: John Wiley & Sons, Inc., 1999.

Monji, Michael A. *Does It Pay to Die? A Living Trust Workbook.* 4th Edition. Bakersfield: Michael Monji and Associates, 2001.

Chapter 21

Probate

Christianson, Stephen G. *How to Administer an Estate: A Step-by-Step Guide for Families and Friends.* Secaucus, NJ: Citadel Press, 1995.

Jurinski, James, J. *Probate and Settling an Estate Step-by-Step.* Hauppauge, NY: Barron, 1997.

Randolph, Mary. *8 Ways to Avoid Probate.* 3rd Edition. Berkeley, CA: Nolo Press, 2001.

Chapter 22

Preparing for the Inevitable

Choate, Natalie B. *Life and Death Planning.* Boston: Ataxplan, 1998.

Dass, Ram. *Still Here: Embracing Aging, Changing, and Dying.* New York: Riverhead Books, 2001.

Kubler-Ross, Elizabeth. *On Death and Dying.* Los Angeles: Simon & Schuster Trade Publishers, 1997.

Kubler-Ross, Elizabeth and David Kessler. *Life Lessons: Two Experts on Death and Dying Teach Us About the Mysteries of Life and Living.* New York: Scribner, 2000.

Scott, Milton B. *What to Do When Someone Dies: A Legal, Financial, and Practical Guide.* Alamo, CA: Pere Bruin, 1997.

INDEX